Albert Henry Newman

A History of Anti-Pedobaptism from the Rise of Pedobaptism to

A.D. 1609

Albert Henry Newman

A History of Anti-Pedobaptism from the Rise of Pedobaptism to A.D. 1609

ISBN/EAN: 9783743335783

Manufactured in Europe, USA, Canada, Australia, Japa

Cover: Foto ©ninafisch / pixelio.de

Manufactured and distributed by brebook publishing software
(www.brebook.com)

Albert Henry Newman

A History of Anti-Pedobaptism from the Rise of Pedobaptism to

A.D. 1609

Presented to the
LIBRARY *of the*
UNIVERSITY OF TORONTO
by

A HISTORY OF ANTI-PEDOBAPTISM

A
HISTORY OF ANTI-PEDOBAPTISM

FROM THE
RISE OF PEDOBAPTISM TO A. D. 1609

BY

ALBERT HENRY NEWMAN, D. D., LL. D.
Professor of Church History in McMaster University, Toronto, Canada

PHILADELPHIA
AMERICAN BAPTIST PUBLICATION SOCIETY
1897

Copyright 1896 by the
AMERICAN BAPTIST PUBLICATION SOCIETY

From the Society's own Press

To

THEODORE HARDING RAND, D. C. L.
Ex-Chancellor of McMaster University

AUGUSTUS HOPKINS STRONG, D. D., LL. D.
President of Rochester Theological Seminary

ALVAH HOVEY, D. D., LL. D.
President of Newton Theological Institution

AND

HENRY GRIGGS WESTON, D. D., LL. D.
President of Crozer Theological Seminary

BEFORE THE STUDENTS OF WHOSE INSTITUTIONS MUCH OF THE MATERIAL HERE PRESENTED WAS DELIVERED IN THE FORM OF LECTURES, AND TO WHOM IN MANY WAYS THE AUTHOR IS DEEPLY INDEBTED, THIS VOLUME IS AFFECTIONATELY AND RESPECTFULLY DEDICATED

TABLE OF CONTENTS

CHAPTER I
EARLY PERVERSIONS OF DOCTRINE AND PRACTICE IN RELATION TO BAPTISM, ... 1
   Corrupting ideas. Baptismal regeneration. Sacerdotalism. Gnostic and Ebionitic views. Rise of infant baptism. Superstition and idolatry.

CHAPTER II
ANCIENT SECTS IN THEIR RELATION TO BAPTIST PRINCIPLES, ... 15
   Montanism and Novatianism. Donatism. Jovinian and Vigilantius. Early British churches. The Paulicians. General observations.

CHAPTER III
MEDIÆVAL ANTI-PEDOBAPTISM; THE PETROBRUSIANS AND THE ARNOLDISTS, ... 30
   Peter and Henry. Anti-pedobaptists at Cologne. Arnold of Brescia.

CHAPTER IV
THE WALDENSES AND RELATED PARTIES, ... 40
   Poor Men of Lombardy. Waldensian principles. Waldensian organization. Waldensians in 1260.

CHAPTER V
THE TABORITES AND THE BOHEMIAN BRETHREN, . . . 49
   Peter Chelcicky. The Bohemian Brethren. Lollards not Anti-pedobaptists. Bohemian influence in Germany. Mysticism and millenarianism. Remarks.

CHAPTER VI
THE ZWICKAU PROPHETS, ... 62
   Social and religious agitation. Luther proves disappoint-

ing. Münzer at Zwickau. Münzer at Prague and Alstedt. The prophets at Wittenberg. Luther's triumph. Storch's later career.

CHAPTER VII

THOMAS MÜNZER AND THE PEASANTS' WAR, ... 77
  Pfeiffer and Mühlhausen. Return to Mühlhausen. The sword of Gideon. Chiliasm and mysticism. Remarks.

CHAPTER VIII

RADICAL AGITATION IN ZÜRICH AND IN WALDSHUT (1523-24), ... 88
  Agitation in Zürich, etc. Balthasar Hubmaier. Proceedings against Hubmaier. Hubmaier at Schaffhausen. Hubmaier on liberty of conscience. Hubmaier's return to Waldshut. Parties at Zürich. Zwingli's opposition.

CHAPTER IX

ZÜRICH, SCHAFFHAUSEN, AND ST. GALL (1524-25), . . . 105
  Pedobaptism enforced. Increasing severity. Hofmeister's position. Hofmeister's banishment. Agitation at St. Gall. Uolimann and Grebel. Zwingli and Vadian.

CHAPTER X

BASEL, BERNE, GRÜNINGEN, AND WALDSHUT (1524-25), . 120
  Disputation at Basel. Berne and Grüningen. Practice at Waldshut. Hubmaier and Zwingli. Conrad Grebel. Blaurock and Reublin. Denck, Sattler, and Hetzer.

CHAPTER XI

PERSECUTION AND DISPERSION, ... 134
  Motives of Persecutors. Disputation and imprisonment. Hubmaier's suffering at Zürich. Hubmaier's recantation. Hubmaier's departure. Churches organized. Conference of the cantons. Execution of Falk and Reimann. Extension of Swiss influence.

CHAPTER XII

SILESIA, ... 153
  Caspar Schwenckfeldt. Gabriel Ascherham.

TABLE OF CONTENTS

CHAPTER XIII
THE AUGSBURG CENTER, ... 159
    Ludwig Hetzer. Hans Denck. Denck's teachings. Hans Hut. Eitelhans Langenmantel. Anti-pedobaptist convention.

CHAPTER XIV
HUBMAIER'S MORAVIAN LABORS (1526–27), ... 173
    Hubmaier at Nikolsburg. Literary activity. Hubmaier on baptism and the Supper. Free will and magistracy. Hubmaier opposed to communism. Hubmaier's extradition demanded. Hubmaier's martyrdom.

CHAPTER XV
THE TYROL, ... , ... 188
    Early evangelical teaching. Sixteen hundred martyrs. Increasing severity. Jacob Huter. Persecution and failure. The Wolkensteins. Amon and Greisinger. Lanzenstiel and Lochmayer.

CHAPTER XVI
AUSTRIA, ... 205
    Anti-pedobaptists at Steyer. Hut's Austrian labors. Hut's evangelists. Anti-pedobaptists at Linz. Ambrose Spitalmaier. Spitalmaier's views. Georg Schoferl. Moravian influence.

CHAPTER XVII
MORAVIA AND BOHEMIA (1528 ONWARD), ... 222
    Blawermel and Schärding. Wilhelm Reublin. Reckless church discipline. Persecution in Moravia. Industry and prosperity. A surviving remnant. Doctrine and polity. Georg Zobel.

CHAPTER XVIII
THE STRASBURG CENTER, ... 238
    Capito on infant baptism. Carlstadt, Echsel, and Gross. Michael Sattler. Reublin and Kautz. Persecution. Marbeck and Bucer. Marbeck's teachings.

CHAPTER XIX
MELCHIOR HOFMANN AND STRASBURG, ... 254

Hofmann at Dorpat. The Supper and magistracy. Plundered and banished. Hofmann at Strasburg. Hofmann and the Münster Kingdom.

CHAPTER XX
HOFMANN AND THE NETHERLANDS. 264
  Lutheran and Zwinglian views. Hofmann's position. The end of the age, 1533. The incarnation.

CHAPTER XXI
HESSE, JÜLICH-CLEVE, AND WESTPHALIA, ... 273
  Melchior Rinck. Münster and Rothmann. Expulsion of the bishop. Roll and Rothmann.

CHAPTER XXII
THE MÜNSTER KINGDOM, ... 284
  Jan Matthys. John of Leyden. Fanaticism rampant. The fall of Münster. Rationale of the movement.

CHAPTER XXIII
MENNO SIMONS AND THE QUIET ANTI-PEDOBAPTISTS, . . 295
  Menno's conversion. Character of Menno's teaching. Philips and Bouwens. Menno in Cologne. Excessive discipline. Controversy with Micronius. Strasburg conference. Controversy on discipline. Menno's death.

CHAPTER XXIV
THE LATER MENNONITES, ... 314
  Mennonite Parties. The Bintgens controversy. Persecuted by the Reformed. The Rhynsburgers.

CHAPTER XXV
ITALY AND POLAND, ... 323
  Camillo Renato. Convention at Venice Manelfi's treachery. Letter from Moravia. Gherlandi and Saga. Polish Anti-pedobaptism. Racovian Catechism. Influence on English Baptists.

CHAPTER XXVI
ENGLAND (TO 1558), ... 340

Lollards and Waldenses. The Lollards of Kyle. Dutch immigration. Radical evangelicalism. Persecution of Anabaptists. Cranmer and foreign theologians. Cooke and Turner. Joan Boucher.

CHAPTER XXVII.

ENGLAND (1558-1602), ... 357

Enforcement of uniformity. Persecution. Foxe's petition. Dutch influence. Robert Browne. Browne in Zeeland. Separatists and Anabaptists.

CHAPTER XXVIII

ENGLAND (1602-1609), ... 376

Gainsborough and Scrooby. Smyth's separation. Smyth an Anti-pedobaptist. Smyth's defense. Se-baptism. Immersion or affusion. Smyth and the Mennonites. Helwys and Murton.

A HISTORY OF ANTI-PEDOBAPTISM

CHAPTER I

EARLY PERVERSIONS OF DOCTRINE AND PRACTICE IN RELATION TO BAPTISM

THE claim of Baptists that in doctrine and in polity they are in substantial accord with the precept and the example of Christ and his apostles would seem to make it incumbent upon them to account for the early departure of the great mass of Christians from the apostolic norm.

That the churches of the post-apostolic age did not long remain faithful to apostolic precept and example in all respects would be generally admitted. Christianity arose in an age of religious ferment. The philosophies and theosophies of the East had never been more active and aggressive than they were during the first three Christian centuries. In Alexandria, long before the beginning of the Christian era, Greek, Jewish, Egyptian, Persian, Old-Babylonian, and Indian thought had met, and eclectic systems were a characteristic feature of the intellectual life of the time. The same is true in a less degree of Rome, Antioch, and Ephesus, and indeed of the Empire in general. These elements were lying in wait, as it were, for nascent Christianity. Before the close of the apostolic age Gnosticism in some of its most dangerous forms had made its appearance and was beginning seriously to threaten the life of the churches. Is it to be wondered at that the succeeding age should have been marked by still graver and more widespread perversions?

Among the universal features of paganism was belief in the efficacy of external rites. That the ordinances of baptism and the Lord's Supper should have been allowed to remain symbolical and memorial rites to be celebrated in simple obedience to the Master's command was more than could have been reasonably expected. Similar rites existed in paganism and were regarded as possessing magical virtue. The sacrificial system of Judaism and the Jewish purificatory rites would themselves furnish a point of departure for the perversion of the Christian ordinances.

Sacerdotalism was a common characteristic of pagan and current Jewish religion. That the Christian minister should soon cease to be a brother among brethren, owing common obedience to a common Lord, and as one chosen and set apart for Christian leadership presiding over the administration of discipline, of charity, and of the ordinances, and that he should come to be regarded as a mediator between God and men, possessed of magical power by virtue of his office, was something that could have been avoided only by constant miraculous Divine interposition. Such interposition, history attests, was withheld. Christianity was a leaven. The life and personal labors of the Christ and of his apostles and the inspired body of doctrine contained in the New Testament were given to the world. Churches were planted and organized under inspired guidance. Henceforth the leaven was to be allowed to do its work, not certainly without Divine help and direction, but without such violent interposition as would interfere with development along natural lines. Pure Christianity was sure in the end to triumph; but not until it had to a great extent absorbed, or been absorbed by, paganism. By becoming assimilated to paganism Christianity was to secure the nominal allegiance of the peoples of Western Asia, Northern Africa, and Europe. Its vitality was never to be entirely destroyed, nor was there to be a time when Christ should be without faithful witnesses; but organized Christianity was to become so corrupt and so perverse that the notes of the apostolic church could scarcely be discovered.

The time would come when vital Christianity, with the Bible as its watchword and its guide, would powerfully reassert itself and would throw off the accretions of centuries; but so thoroughly entrenched did these corruptions become that the process must needs be a slow one. When we consider the obstacles to the restoration of apostolic Christianity that have presented themselves, the natural conservatism that shrinks from departure from traditional positions, the tremendous influence of State-churchism, and the preference of multitudes of people for a religion of forms and ceremonies, with its priestly absolutions and consolations, the wonder is that so much progress has been made.

If the apostolic churches were Baptist churches, the churches of the second century were not. Still less were those of the third and the following centuries.

Early in the second century, possibly during the last decade of the first, the idea came into vogue that while instruction in Christian truth and morals, repentance, faith, fasting, and prayer must precede baptism, the remission of sins takes place only in connection with the baptismal act. That certain New Testament representations, when taken alone, can easily be so interpreted as to seem to favor this view of the relation of baptism to salvation may be freely admitted. That such an interpretation is wholly inconsistent with the trend of New Testament teaching—Baptists have always uncompromisingly maintained.

In lapsing so speedily from the apostolic view of justification by faith and regeneration by the Holy Spirit and in adopting the belief that regeneration is completed only in connection with an external rite, the post-apostolic church shows that it has already begun to yield to the all-pervasive pagan idea of the magical efficacy of water baptism. "The Pastor of Hermas," an allegorical writing highly esteemed in the ancient church and probably written as early as A. D. 139, exhibits this doctrine in a transitional stage. In one passage it is said: "Whosoever with his whole heart changes his mind (repents) and purifies himself from all iniquity, and adds no more to his sin, will receive from the Lord a cure from all his former sins." Again: "The elect of God will be saved through faith." Yet (in Commandment IV., 3) it is said: "When we went down into the water and received remission from our former sins." Again (Similitude IX., 15, 16): "Into the water, therefore, they descend dead and arise living." The account of the tower (Vision III., 7) built up of stones that have passed through the water seems to imply the saving efficacy of baptism. The thought of the author appears to be, that while repentance, faith, and reformation of life must precede baptism, it is only in connection with the baptismal act that the remission of sins actually takes place.

Similar is the teaching of Justin Martyr in his "First Apology," written at about the same date as the "Pastor":

> As many as are persuaded and believe to be true these things that are taught and spoken by us, and give assurance that they are able to live accordingly, are taught to pray and fasting to implore from God the forgiveness of sins previously committed, we ourselves praying and fasting with them. Then they are led by us where there is water and are regenerated in the same manner in which we ourselves were regenerated (*chap. 61*).

His subsequent explanation makes it clear that he regarded water baptism as absolutely essential.

The so-called "Teaching of the Twelve Apostles," which may possibly belong to the second half of the second century but which in its present form is probably much later, does not so explicitly teach baptismal regeneration; but this view seems to be implied in the requirement, in case of absolute lack of a sufficiency of water of any kind for baptism proper, that pouring water on the head three times be resorted to as a substitute. Catechetical instruction, repentance, fasting, and prayer must precede the baptismal rite.

We may say in general, that during the greater part of the second century the idea prevailed that mere baptism without repentance and faith would be of no value and that the remission of sins takes place only in connection with the baptismal act. By the close of the second century the pagan view that water baptism possesses in itself magical efficacy begins to find expression.

The most striking presentation of this conception, if not the earliest, is that of Tertullian. "Is it not wonderful too," he writes, "that death should be washed away by bathing?" To justify such ascription of efficacy to water baptism he expatiates on the age and the dignity of water. "Water is one of those things that, before all the furnishing of the world, were quiescent with God in a yet unshapen state." It is venerable, therefore. It has dignity also as having been "the seat of the Divine Spirit, more pleasing to him, no doubt, than all the other then existing elements." "Water alone—always a perfect, gladsome, simple, material substance, pure in itself . . . supplied a worthy vehicle for God." "Water was the first to produce that which had life, that it might be no wonder in baptism if water know how to give life." He speaks of water as "the primary principle of baptism." "The Spirit of God who hovered over the waters from the beginning would," he maintained, "continue to linger over the waters of the baptized." "Thus," he continues, "the nature of the waters, sanctified by the Holy One, itself conceived withal the power of sanctifying." "All waters, therefore, in virtue of the pristine privilege of their origin, do, after invocation of God, attain the sacramental power of sanctification; for the Spirit immediately supervenes from the heavens and rests over the waters, sanctifying them from himself; and being thus sanctified they imbibe at the same time the power of sanctifying."

It would serve no useful purpose to multiply quotations from subsequent Christian literature. The conceptions of Tertullian speedily became the conceptions of the church. We are not aware that any contemporary writer called in question his view of the saving efficacy of water baptism. Yet Cyprian (about 253) denied that water alone, apart from the operation of the Holy Spirit, could cleanse from sin and sanctify.[1]

It is highly probable that the disposition to attach magical significance to baptism and to surround its administration with mystery and ceremonial came into the church through the channel of Gnosticism; although, as is well known, Gnostic mysteries were themselves derived from those that had long prevailed in pagan systems. We need only mention the elaborate initiatory rites of the Eleusinian, Pythagorean, Orphic, and Delphian mysteries, of the old Egyptian priesthood, and of the Mithras worship. The fact is, there was a great fund of current thought and practice on this matter that was sure sooner or later to make its influence profoundly felt by Christianity. That advanced ideas on the efficacy of baptism were prominent features of early Gnosticism the follow-

[1] Epistle LXXIV.

ing extract from the remarkable Gnostic writing "Pistis Sophia" makes clear: "Then came forth Mary and said: Lord, under what form do baptisms remit sins?" After further elaboration of the question on the part of Mary and a somewhat extended answer, Christ is represented as replying:

> Now, therefore, if any one hath received the mysteries of baptism, those mysteries become a great fire, exceeding strong and wise, so as to burn up all the sins: and the fire entereth into the soul secretly, so that it may consume within it all the sins which the counterfeit of the spirit [conscience] hath printed there. Likewise it entereth into the body secretly, that it may pursue all its pursuers and divide them into parts... The fire separates the counterfeit of the spirit, fate, and the body into one portion, and the soul and the power [spirit] into another portion. The mystery of baptism remaineth in the middle of them, so that it may perpetually separate them, so that it may purge and cleanse them in order that they may not be polluted by matter.

To show that baptismal regeneration early appeared among the speculative Ebionites, the following passages will suffice:

> If, therefore, any one be found smeared with sins and lusts as with pitch, the fire easily gets the mastery of him. But if the tow be not steeped in the pitch of sin, but in the water of purification and regeneration, the fire of the demons shall not be able to be kindled in it (*Clementine* "*Recognitions*," *IX., 10*).
>
> And this is the service he has appointed: To worship him only, and trust only in the Prophet of truth and to be baptized for the remission of sins, and thus by this pure baptism to be born again unto God by saving water (*Clementine* "*Homilies*," *VII., 8*).

With the passages from the heretical writers just quoted may be compared the following sentence from Cyprian (Ep. LXXVI.): "For as scorpions and serpents, which prevail on the dry ground, when cast into water cannot prevail nor retain their venom; so also the wicked spirits

... cannot remain any longer in the body of a man in whom, baptized and sanctified, the Holy Spirit is beginning to dwell."

Side by side with the idea of the efficacy of water baptism had grown up the conviction that apart from baptism there is no salvation. The human race being intrinsically corrupt, the guilt of race-sin attaches to unconscious infants no less than to such as have reached moral consciousness. The only avenue of escape from the guilt of race-sin was baptism. Exception was made in the case of believers who suffered martyrdom before they had had an opportunity to wash away their sins in baptism; but these were said to have had a baptism of blood. The necessity of baptism to salvation is implied in the passages above quoted, and this idea was developed in its most extreme form among the Gnostics and the Ebionites. It is set forth in a striking way in the following passages from the Clementine "Recognitions," VI., 8, 9, where Peter is represented as saying:

> And do you suppose that you can have hope toward God, even if you cultivate all piety and all righteousness, but do not receive baptism? . . When you are regenerated and born again of water and of God, the frailty of your former birth which you have through men is cut off, and so at length you shall be able to attain salvation; but otherwise it is impossible. . . Betake yourselves therefore to these waters, for they alone can quench the violence of the future fire; and he who delays to approach to them, it is evident that the idol of unbelief remains in him, and by it he is prevented from hastening to the waters that confer salvation. For whether you be righteous or unrighteous, baptism is necessary for you in every respect: for the righteous, that perfection may be accomplished in him and he may be born again to God; for the unrighteous, that pardon may be vouchsafed him for the sins which he has committed in ignorance.

When Christians had come to believe that water baptism possessed magical efficacy, and that all mankind were so involved in sin that no salvation was possible apart from baptism, it was inevitable that infant baptism should be introduced. The widespread prevalence of infant lustrations among pagans made the introduction of infant baptism easy and natural. At first it would be confined to infants in danger of death; but when the idea had taken firm hold on the Christian consciousness that it was a necessary means of securing cleansing from hereditary sin its progress could not fail to be rapid.

The universal prevalence of infant baptism was long prevented, however, by another error, for whose elevation to the position of a dogma Tertullian was chiefly responsible, but which had no doubt been more or less current since the middle of the second century. This error was, in effect, that mortal sins committed after baptism are irremissible. It was chiefly on this ground that Tertullian so earnestly insisted on the postponement of baptism until such a degree of maturity and stability should have been reached as to warrant the expectation that the candidate would be able to guard himself from the commission of mortal sins. He had no doubt whatever as to the efficacy of baptism to cleanse the unconscious infant of hereditary sin; but, on prudential grounds, he considered it important that this cleansing rite should be reserved until such time as he could have reasonable assurance that its efficacy would be permanent. From this time onward the choice between infant baptism and adult baptism was determined largely by the views of individuals as to whether the former or the latter would probably be the more advantageous. The baptized infant might on the one hand grow up and become involved in sin and so lose the opportunity that adult baptism would confer of starting out on his personal Christian life with a clean score; on the other hand the unbaptized infant might die by violence or so unexpectedly as to be out of reach of the saving bath. The rigorous view of Tertullian as regards the unpardonableness of post-baptismal mortal sin gradually gave place to a more benignant view and from the middle of the third century the church made so ample provision for the restoration of the lapsed, that infant baptism came to be generally regarded as the safer thing.

The departure of the church of the second and third centuries from the apostolic standard was by no means confined to the matter of baptism. The same influences soon caused the Lord's Supper to be looked upon no longer as a memorial feast in which believers partook in a purely symbolical way of the broken body and the poured-out blood of their crucified, risen, and glorified Lord, but rather as a mystic ceremony to be celebrated with elaborate ritual. This change was likewise due to pagan influences brought to bear chiefly through the Gnostic sects.

Other perversions of Christianity during the early centuries are so universally recognized by historians and so familiar to all readers of church history, that they need only be barely mentioned here. Sacerdotalism, a constant factor in pagan religious systems, soon intruded itself into the Christian church. The ordinances having become mysteries must be administered by a ceremonially qualified priesthood; and as the services became elaborate and each function must be performed by a properly qualified functionary, clerical gradations came to be multiplied and accurately differentiated. Out of the simple polity of the apostolic time, in accordance with which each congregation chose its own bishops or presbyters and deacons for the direction of the spiritual work of the body, the administration of discipline and the collection and distribution of charities, there was developed, under the influences of the time, a system of presidential administration in which the chief elder (or bishop) directed the affairs of the local church with the assistance and advice of a Board of presbyters. As the responsible head of the church he soon came to have chief control of the finances and such control tended to increase his relative importance. As Christian work spread from older centers the newly established congregations were kept in relations of dependence on the mother church, or rather, as integral parts thereof. Thus the pastor of the central church would have the supervision of a greater or smaller number of outside congregations over each of which a presbyter of the central church came to preside. Thus arose diocesan episcopacy. At first this arrangement was adopted without any ambitious intentions on the part of the pastors as seemingly the most effective way of conducting Christian work. But as the dependent congregations became conscious of strength and their presbyter-pastors became restless under episcopal control, which in some cases was no doubt arbitrarily exercised, friction arose between bishops and presbyters. By this time (about the middle of the third century—the case of Cyprian and the Carthaginian presbyters is in point) the sacerdotal idea was pretty fully developed. Cyprian and those who were like-minded believed that ecclesiastical unity was absolutely essential and that schism was one of the greatest of evils. They went so far as to maintain that outside of the one ecclesiastical organization, whose center of unity was found in the episcopate, there is no salvation. By the strong opposition that the presbyters made to the assumption of authority on the part of the bishops the latter were led to assert the divine right and the irresponsibility of bishops. The same sense of the necessity of organic union and unity of administration afterward led to the centralization of authority in metropolitans and finally in the papacy.

No less destructive of the spirit of primitive Christianity was the early intrusion of the doctrine of the meritoriousness of external works. Jews and pagans alike attached great merit to almsgiving, fasting, and the frequent utterance of fixed forms of prayer. By the middle of the third century leading churchmen like Cyprian did not hesitate to teach that almsgiving is a means of securing the remission of sins and of purchasing an eternal inheritance.

Asceticism also was imported into early Christianity from paganism. The disposition to regard the body as intrinsically evil and all natural impulses as worthy only of being trampled upon is a common feature of pagan religions. Fanatical seeking for martyrdom, excessive fasting, and the exaltation of virginity, were the earliest forms of Christian asceticism. It culminated in the brutalities of hermit life. It was chiefly through Gnosticism and Manichæism that ascetic ideas found entrance into the church, but these ideas were part and parcel of the spirit of the age and could not easily have been escaped. That Christianity was sadly corrupted by the intrusion of this element all evangelical Christians maintain.

Superstition and idolatry were universally prevalent in ancient paganism as they are in modern. They pervaded and corrupted every department of life and occupied a most prominent place in the popular consciousness. That these elements are not eradicated once for all by conversion, but persist and sadly interfere with the full development of Christian character, the New Testament record illustrates and ancient history as well as modern experience fully confirms. In proportion as Christianity increased in popular influence and enjoyed immunity from persecution was the accession to the church of un-Christianized or imperfectly Christianized life. Not only did the ordinances assume a pagan hue and sacerdotal and ascetic ideas become prevalent, but idolatrous practices corresponding in almost every detail with those of the surrounding heathenism came to be openly indulged in and regarded as Christian. The exaltation of saints and martyrs, the worship of images of Christ and the saints, the veneration of bones and other relics of the worthies of the past, pilgrimages to shrines and other holy places, vigils at the tombs of saints, the invocation of Mary the mother of Jesus as "the mother of God," the invocation of saints, belief in the efficacy of relics and shrines to cure diseases—these and many like superstitious practices were countenanced by some of the ablest and holiest of the Christian leaders of the fourth and following centuries, and by the fifth century had become well-nigh universal.

The church that rejoiced in the patronage of Constantine and his successors, and that so readily assumed the position of an established religion, receiving its support from public taxation and persecuting paganism and heresy, was evidently not the church of the apostles. It has been maintained that the influence of pagan thought and life on Christianity was in general wholesome, inasmuch as it gave philosophical form to Christian doctrine and freed the church from the narrowness and exclusiveness that belonged to the apostolic age. It has been urged with considerable plausibility that the complete Christianization of Europe and the establishment of a Christian civilization was greatly hastened by the readiness with which Christianity absorbed pagan modes of thought and adapted itself to pagan ideas of life and of worship. Each of these positions certainly contains a modicum of truth. Circumstances being as they were we can scarcely conceive of Christianity as holding rigidly aloof from the influences of Jewish and pagan thought and life; if such an attitude had been assumed the progress of Christianity must during the first few centuries have been slow indeed. As a matter of historical fact great masses of men do not abandon at once the religious conceptions that constitute the inheritance of centuries. Departure from apostolic doctrine and practice was gradual and unconscious, but none the less real and disastrous.

Literature: Ante-Nicene Fathers (orig. or transl.); Pistis Sophia (Ethiopic with Lat. tr. by Petermann, extracts in Eng. in King, The Gnostics); The Teaching of the Twelve Apostles (ed. by Schaff, Harnack, Hilgenfeld, etc.): Harnack, Dogmengeschichte, I.; Works on Baptism and Infant Baptism by Wall, Gale, Caspari, Hoffmann, Höfling, and Ingham; Stanley, Chr. Institutions; Hatch, Hibbert and Bampton Lectures; articles and sections on Baptism, the Supper, etc., in Smith's Dict. of Chr. Antiq., the Encyclopædias of Herzog-Plitt, Schaff-Herzog, Lichtenberger, and McClintock and Strong, and the Church Histories of Neander, Gieseler, Schaff, Möller, Müller, etc.

CHAPTER II

ANCIENT SECTS IN THEIR RELATION TO BAPTIST PRINCIPLES

BUT, it may be asked, did the church as a whole succumb to the corrupting influences to which it was subjected during the early centuries? Were there none that remained loyal to primitive Christianity among the tempted multitudes? Many Baptist writers have sought to find in the Montanists, Novatians, Donatists, Jovinianists, Vigilantians, Paulicians, Bogomiles, etc., who successively revolted from the dominant types of Christianity, faithful adherents to apostolic doctrine and practice and links in the chain of Baptist apostolic succession. Let us test the claim of these parties to this honorable distinction.

How stands the case with the Montanists? They protested most vigorously, it is true, against many of the paganizing corruptions into which the church of the latter part of the second century had fallen. They insisted most earnestly upon the rigid application of church discipline and upon the exclusion of all members whose lives fell short of a high moral and spiritual standard. They showed themselves willing to suffer all manner of persecution on behalf of the truth as they understood it. They spent much time in fasting and prayer and were zealous in good works. But was their zeal according to knowledge? Was the spirit of Montanism the spirit of apostolic Christianity? Far from it. Judaistic and pagan legalism had made their influence felt even more powerfully upon this enthusiastic sect than upon the general church of the time. Their religious enthusiasm was grounded in the erroneous belief that the end of the age was at hand. Supposing themselves to be the organs of a new revelation, which Christ had promised through the Paraclete, they felt themselves justified in disparaging the ethical teachings of the New Testament as having been accommodated to the ignorance and weakness of the apostolic times and in setting up in the name of the Paraclete a new and stricter code. The revelations that were supposed to come through their prophets were almost wholly directions for the establishment of a more rigorous morality than that of the New Testament. They claimed the authority of the Paraclete for making second marriages equivalent to adultery and hence mortal sin ; for rejecting entirely the use of wine and insisting on frequent and long-continued fasts ; for making flight in persecution or denial of the faith under any circumstances mortal sin ; and for expecting the speedy end of the present dispensation. This rigid system was emphasized by their maintenance of the theory that mortal sins are unpardonable, absolutely so as far as the church is concerned.

Montanistic prophecy, as far as appears, differed little from pagan manticism. By violent physical exertion, excessive fasting, and intense application of the mind to ethical and eschatological problems, these prophets wrought themselves up into an abnormal psychological state and gave utterance, in a more or less incoherent manner, to the thoughts that had been foremost in their minds. These morbid utterances were regarded by the Montanists as God's latest and highest revelation. Their legalistic asceticism was radically opposed to the New Testament idea of the Christian life. Their arbitrary extension of the list of mortal sins and their unwarranted insistence that all mortal sins are unpardonable tended to drive to despair those who had fallen into sin and to cultivate in themselves a spirit of self-righteousness. Tertullian, the greatest of the Montanists, was, as we have seen, among the most earnest maintainers of the saving efficacy of water baptism. Montanism, therefore, so far from being a return to primitive Christianity or an anticipation of the Baptist position, contained the germs of many of the worst errors of later Roman Catholicism.

Equally remote from the spirit of primitive Christianity were the Novatians (A. D. 251 onward). Novatianism represents an earnest protest against the relaxation of discipline in the general church of the time ; but this protest was based upon the Montanistic view that mortal sins committed after baptism are absolutely unpardonable so far as the church is concerned and on the Montanistic extension of the list of mortal sins. A person who in the stress of persecution, even under torture, had momentarily yielded to the demands of his tormentors that he should deny the faith, or had been guilty of flight in persecution, or had in any other way compromised himself in relation to the faith, had forfeited, from the Novatian point of view, once for all the right to a place and a name among God's people. He might repent in sackcloth and ashes, but so far as church privileges were concerned it was of no avail. He was encouraged to hope that after a lifetime of penance he might finally be a recipient of divine grace ; but on earth he could never expect to regain his church-membership and privileges. There was need of a vigorous protest against the extreme laxity with which many churches were dealing with the lapsed. But the Novatians erred yet more grievously in refusing, on arbitrary and non-scriptural grounds, to restore to church fellowship the truly penitent. Novatians, like Montanists, were extreme believers in the magical efficacy of water baptism and in the necessity of baptism to the remission of sins. So great was the stress laid upon the ordinance by Novatian himself, that when he was lying ill and was not expected to recover he submitted to what was afterward called clinic baptism, that is to say, he had water poured upon him while lying on his bed. This was one of the charges made against him by his Catholic opponents, who doubted the validity of such baptism and maintained that after his recovery he should have been properly baptized. It is not easy to detect in Novatianism the notes of the apostolic church, or any very close relationship to the Baptist position.

Almost identical with the position of the Novatians was that of the Donatists (A. D. 311 onward). As the Novatian schism grew out of the lapses that occurred in connection with the Decian persecution, so the Donatist schism grew out of the lapses occasioned by the Diocletian persecution. The immediate occasion of the Donatist schism was a supposed departure from Christian fidelity on the part of Mensurius, bishop of the Carthaginian church, and one of his deacons, Cæcilian. The destruction of the Christian Scriptures was one of the chief aims of the persecutors. Mensurius and Cæcilian were accused of having secreted the Scriptures belonging to the church and placing certain worthless heretical manuscripts in their place. The officers of the law were allowed, it was said, to take these worthless writings on the supposition that they were the Scriptures. Thus the bishop was enabled to save the Scriptures and his own life as well. The position of the strict party, that afterward received the name Donatist from its most prominent leader, was, that such deceit was mortal sin and disqualified those guilty of it for the Christian ministry and even for church-membership. What they should have done, in the circumstances supposed, was to hide the Scriptures and to suffer martyrdom rather than betray their place of concealment. The specific charge against Mensurius and Cæcilian was persistently denied, and although an imperial commission was appointed to visit Carthage and to gather evidence on the question of fact no sure result was ever reached. On the death of Mensurius (A. D. 311), Cæcilian, knowing that he would be strongly opposed by the strict party, got himself hurriedly and irregularly ordained by a like-minded bishop. The opponents of Cæcilian set up a rival bishop and the schism rapidly spread throughout Northern Africa and elsewhere.

The Donatists added to the disciplinary code of the Montanists and Novatians the dogma that the validity of the ordinances, especially baptism, depends on the character of the administrator. Nay, the validity of the baptism of any individual was logically conditioned not merely on the uprightness of the person who baptized him, but upon an unbroken line of ceremonially and morally unblemished administrators of the ordinance back to the apostles. To have fellowship with Mensurius and Cæcilian and their successors constituted one a *traditor*, and disqualified him for membership and ministry in a Donatist church. The only way in which admission could be secured was by renouncing the church that had made the cause of Mensurius and Cæcilian its own and by being baptized anew into the Donatist fellowship. The Donatists seem to have laid even greater stress than did the Catholics of the time on infant baptism; and so intense was their belief in the necessity of baptism to salvation that in their view Christ himself needed to be baptized in order to secure the remission of hereditary sin. Their demand for an unbroken line of worthy administrators of the ordinance was as unwarranted as it was impracticable, and tended to throw doubt on the validity of any individual case of baptism. As regards episcopacy, their practice seems to have been identical with that of their Catholic opponents. They may properly be called the high churchmen of the fourth and fifth centuries. That they were either apostolic or Baptist does not appear.

The protest of Aërius (A. D. 355) in Pontus seems to have had a more evangelical basis. He claimed that the church had substituted the yoke of Jewish bondage for the liberty of the gospel. He insisted on Scriptural grounds upon the equality of presbyters and bishops. He protested against prayers for the dead, the celebration of the Lord's Supper as an offering for the dead, and ecclesiastical fasts. There is no evidence that he rejected infant baptism or baptismal regeneration, as from his general position he might have been expected to do.

Somewhat similar in spirit was the protest of Jovinian (A. D. 385 onward), a Milanese monk, who came to see the evils of monasticism and who vigorously assailed various errors and abuses connected with current ascetic modes of thought. He denied the superiority of celibacy to married life; maintained the equality in merit of virgins, widows, and married persons who have been once washed in Christ; denied that those who with full faith have been born again in baptism can be subverted by the devil; insisted upon the equality in point of merit of those who abstain from foods and those who partake of them with thanksgiving; and maintained that for all truly regenerate persons there is one remuneration in the kingdom of heaven, all alike being saved by divine grace and not by merit, and all works of supererogation being thus impossible. He was strongly opposed to the veneration and intercession of the saints. He seems to have held, with the Christian writers of the second century, that the remission of sins takes place in connection with the baptismal act, faith and repentance having preceded. There is no evidence that he rejected infant baptism. He secured a large following, but was condemned by synods at Rome and Milan, and banished by the emperor Honorius. His persecuted followers seem to have taken refuge in the Alps, where they may have persisted until the Middle Ages.

Equally evangelical was the protest of Vigilantius, a native of Southern Gaul and a *protégé* of the celebrated Sulpicius Severus. About 394 he was sent by his patron on a visit to Paulinus of Nola, a highly educated and wealthy patrician, who had been led by the ascetic spirit of the time to devote his entire fortune to the relief of the poor and the maintenance of a monastery and church. These he had filled with relics and images and had adorned with the utmost splendor. Vigilantius was shocked by the introduction of so much of paganism into Christian worship. He afterward visited Jerome in his hermit cell at Bethlehem. The excesses of asceticism witnessed here called forth his earnest opposition. His antagonism to asceticism was intensified by a visit to Egypt where he came in contact with the swarms of monks and hermits that inhabited the Nitrian desert. He returned to Gaul and gained many adherents. Vigilantius condemned the undue exaltation of celibacy and virginity, the worship of images and relics, the invocation of saints, vigils at the tombs of martyrs, etc., and insisted on a return to the simplicity of the gospel. The movement was lost in the invasion of the Alans and Vandals, but it is probable that the followers of Vigilantius, like those of Jovinian, took refuge in the Alpine valleys. There is no evidence that this reformer rejected infant baptism or baptismal regeneration.

The best example of the persistence of a somewhat primitive type of Christianity is probably that of the ancient British church. During the fourth and fifth centuries British Christians seem to have held aloof in a measure from the paganizing influences in which the continental church became involved. Diocesan episcopacy seems not to have existed. The study of the Scriptures was pursued with zeal in the numerous semi-monastic colleges for the training of pastors and missionaries. An extensive and successful missionary work was carried on in Ireland, Scotland, France, and Germany. Human authority in matters of religion was indignantly repudiated. Humility and simplicity in Christian life were insisted upon and the pomp and worldliness of the Roman missionaries who sought (A. D. 598) to convert them proved highly offensive. British Christians were not only of a radically different spirit from the Romanists of the time, but were at variance with them as regards the time of celebrating Easter, the mode of baptism, tonsure, etc. An example of their missionary activity is the work of Patrick (432 onward), who evangelized more or less thoroughly the whole of Ireland and left a reputation for sanctity of life and spiritual power that entitles him to be considered one of the greatest of missionaries. Equally noteworthy are the labors of Columba, an Irishman by birth and education, who, under circumstances of great difficulty, succeeded (latter part of the sixth century) in planting evangelical churches throughout Scotland. Columbanus, another Irishman, is worthy of being placed by the side of Patrick and Columba. About 585, with thirteen companions, he made his way to Burgundy where he founded one after another three great mission stations that formed the centers of extensive evangelistic activity. His John-the-Baptist-like denunciation of the immoralities of the court and his resolute refusal to abandon the peculiarities of the Irish church resulted in his banishment. With a body of faithful companions he made his way up the Rhine to Switzerland where also he founded a number of mission stations. Driven hence by the malignity of his enemies he proceeded to Northern Italy where in his old age he formed yet another center of mission work.

Notwithstanding the terrible persecutions to which they were subjected during the seventh and following centuries by the Saxon kings, at the instigation of the Roman Catholic Church, Christians of the ancient British type are known to have maintained their existence in considerable numbers, especially in Wales and Scotland, until the eleventh century. It is probable that they were never completely destroyed and that they reappeared in the Lollards of the fourteenth century.

The mission work inaugurated by Columbanus was carried forward with great perseverance and success during the seventh and eighth centuries. By the middle of the eighth century the Iro-Scottish church was predominant throughout the Rhine valley, in Thuringia, and in Bavaria. In the entire South and West of Germany, before the coming of Boniface, the so-called apostle of the Germans, there existed (to quote the language of Ebrard) "a flourishing, well-organized, Rome-free church, whose only supreme authority was the Holy Scriptures, whose preaching was the word of the free redeeming grace of God." The same writer says: "A simple but well-organized church existed from the Pyrenees to the Scheldt, from Chur to Utrecht, whose only crime was that it did not recognize the Roman church as its supreme head; hence also knew no new invocation of saints, no mass, no auricular confession and the like, and did not do homage to gross Pelagianism, but preached justification through faith." Förster, another learned German writer, characterizes the Iro-Scottish Christianity of the Continent as of "apostolic simplicity," as having "simple ceremonies" and earnest moral life, and as "recognizing the Scriptures as its completely sufficient norm."

This party was crushed, but probably never utterly destroyed, by the united efforts of the hierarchy and the Frankish rulers ; yet its evangelical spirit doubtless survived in the dissenting parties that appeared in the same regions during the mediæval time. There is no sufficient evidence that the Iro-Scottish church rejected baptismal regeneration or infant baptism.

The only reason for even mentioning the Paulicians in this connection is the fact that some Baptist writers have sought to represent them as essentially apostolic in doctrine and practice. While recent investigations by Armenian scholars have seriously discredited the Greek accounts of this party, on which we have been almost wholly dependent, and have proved that such writers as Photius, Peter the Sicilian, and Zygadenus, have carelessly or maliciously confounded the Paulicians with such disreputable parties as the Manichæans and the Messalians, the positive information that has thus far been brought to light is wholly inadequate to enable us to speak definitely about their evangelical character. The date of their rise in Armenia (about 660, according to the ordinary chronology) is itself a matter of uncertainty. That they were radically opposed to the dominant church, that they were violently iconoclastic, that they were ready to co-operate with Mohammedan invaders against their persecutors, that in the ninth century large numbers of them were encouraged by the Eastern empire to settle in Bulgaria, where they served as a sort of borderguard between the empire and its northwestern enemies, that from this vantage-ground their principles extended throughout Europe, seem to be well-established facts. Whether they were originally dualistic and rejected the

Old Testament as the work of the Demiurge (worldframer), and rejected the ordinances of the New Testament, or whether these features were limited to other parties with which they came into close contact and with which they might easily have been confounded, must remain undetermined for the present. That among the Oriental Christians who settled in Bulgaria and whose teachings spread over Western Europe there were many shades of opinion and practice from crass dualism and the practice of gross immorality to comparative purity in teaching and life seems highly probable, and the same degree of probability attaches to the supposition that the more evangelical as well as the less evangelical of the mediæval European sects were due in some measure to these Oriental influences.[1]

What then are the results of this cursory survey of the first eight Christian centuries?

1. We have seen that error grappled with the infant religion in its very cradle and while it did not succeed in utterly strangling it Christianity did not escape the ordeal unscathed. This is generally acknowledged so far as Ebionitic (or Jewish-speculative) Christianity and Gnostic (or pagan-theosophical) Christianity is concerned. But some will no doubt question the assertion

---

[1] See Karapet Ter-Mkrttschian's "Die Paulikianer im Byzantinischen Kaiserreiche und verwandte ketzerische Erscheinungen in Armenien," Leipzig, 1893. Karapet is an Armenian scholar, who has studied in the German universities and has had the advantage of access to Armenian literature, printed and manuscript, as well as to the Greek sources and modern German discussions. Unfortunately his results are chiefly negative; but it is to be hoped that himself or some other will follow the lines of research marked out to more assured positive results. In the "Zeitschrift für Kirchengeschichte" (October, 1895), Karapet has given an account of a modern Anti-pedobaptist party. He imparts in German an important catechetical work that was put forth by a leader of this party in 1782. This party Karapet insists on deriving from the Thondrakians, who seem to have perpetuated in Armenia the old evangelical teaching that may have been represented in the earlier time by the Paulicians. This writing sets forth views as regards baptism, etc., almost identical with those of the Anti-pedobaptists of the sixteenth century. See summary of its contents in an article by the present writer in the Chicago "Standard" for May 16, 1896.

that error invaded the very bosom of the church early in the second century. The error is often committed of regarding the Gnostic and Ebionitic tendencies on the one hand and Catholic orthodoxy on the other as sharply defined and separate. The fact is, on the contrary, that the modes of thought that had their extreme development in Gnosticism and Ebionism were widely current during the early Christian centuries and the extent to which they were able to impress themselves upon this or that Christian individual or community depended on the degree to which Christian truth had been apprehended. Those who had been instructed by the apostles themselves and those who had been brought up under strong Christian influences were in a position to resist Judaizing and paganizing influences to an extent impossible for others. Least of all could it be expected that men educated in non-Christian philosophy and theosophy and to whom Christianity came as new wine into old bottles should at once become free from the domination of pagan thought. Many of the Christian teachers of the second and following centuries brought such non-Christian culture with them and unconsciously were instrumental in working important changes in Christian modes of thought and life. Those whose training had been in the purer systems such as Stoicism and Platonism, or in eclectic systems in which the highest elements of pagan thought were embodied, influenced Christianity in a less objectionable way; those who had been schooled in Oriental, Egyptian, and Pythagorean theosophy, could not fail to degrade Christianity almost to the level of the modes of thought that had mastered them.[1]

2. While we admire the zeal for pure membership, the fidelity to conviction, and the heroic self-denial of the

---
[1] See Hatch's Hibbert Lectures on "The Influence of Greek Ideas and Usages upon the Christian Church."

schismatic parties of the early Christian centuries, we cannot fail to see in the church of Justin Martyr, of Irenæus, of Cyprian, of Origen, of Eusebius, of Athanasius, of Chrysostom, and of Augustine, with all its errors and corruptions, more of the spirit of Christ and a nearer approach to apostolic doctrine and practice than in Montanism, Novatianism, or Donatism.

3. The case is different with the movements led by Aërius, Jovinian, and Vigilantius. Here we encounter for the first time radical opposition to the rapidly progressive paganization of Christianity, based on a tolerably correct apprehension of New Testament principles. These reformers seem to have distinctly rejected sacerdotalism and asceticism, with the doctrine of the meritoriousness of good works, and to have held fast to the doctrine of justification by faith. It is probable that if we knew more about them we should find their position even more completely in accord with New Testament Christianity than the meagre and hostile accounts that we have of them warrant us in asserting. But the current of paganizing influence was far too strong to be stayed by the protests of a few exceptionally enlightened spirits, and they seem to have made little impression on their time.

4. So also in the ancient British church we have a distinctly purer and more primitive type of Christianity than that which prevailed during the fourth and following centuries in Southern and Eastern Europe and in Asia. This was no doubt due in part to the isolation of the British church from the corrupting influences of Greece and Rome, and in part to the prominence that was given to the study of the Bible and to the remarkable activity in mission work that for generations prevailed.

5. Was there then a failure of the assurance of Christ that the gates of hades should not prevail against his

church? Far be it. We do not, it is true, find a succession of organized churches in which Christian doctrines were maintained incorrupt. We are not able to prove that from the middle of the second century onward a single congregation could anywhere be found true in every particular to the apostolic norm. Nay, it is not possible to point to an individual Christian during the millennium that succeeded the apostolic age who apprehended Christianity in a purely apostolic manner. But that there were hosts of true believers during the darkest ages of Christian history can by no means be doubted. It is comforting to know that men may be involved in grievous errors as regards doctrine and practice and yet attain to a high standard of Christian living.

That a church also may make grave departures in doctrine and practice from the apostolic standard without ceasing to be a church of Christ, must be admitted, or else it must be maintained that during many centuries no church is known to have existed. In this admission there is no implication that an individual or a church may knowingly live in disobedience to Christ's precepts without grievous sin, or can ignorantly disobey without serious spiritual loss. On the contrary, every departure, conscious or unconscious, from New Testament precept or example, not only involves loss as regards the particular defection, but brings in its train other evils, which in turn bring others, until doctrine and practice become thoroughly corrupted. For example, Baptists have always regarded infant baptism not simply as an unauthorized and useless innovation, but as involving a radical departure from the purpose of Christ in instituting the ordinance: supplanting believers' baptism, making the symbol antedate the thing symbolized, striking at the root of regenerate church-membership, tending to bring the entire population of a Christianized community into

GENERAL OBSERVATIONS

church fellowship, and making possible and fostering State-churchism. And so the consequences of any other radical departure from New Testament precept and example may be shown to be far-reaching and destructive.

Literature: On Montanism: Bonwetsch, De Soyres, Neander (Antignosticus), Ritschl (D. Altkath. Kirche), Baur, Pressensé. On Novatianism: Works of Cyprian, Novatian, Eusebius, and Socrates, O. Ritschl, Cyprian. On Donatism: Works of Augustine and Optatus, and the monographs of Völter, Seeck, and Deutsch. On Jovinianism and Vigilantianism: Jerome, Gilly, and Lindner. On Paulicianism: Photius, Peter Siculus, Zygadenus, Gieseler, Schmidt (Hist. Paul. Orientalium), Lombard (Les Paulic.), Döllinger (Sectengesch, I.), and Karapet. On all the parties treated, the pertinent articles and sections in Smith's Dict. of Chr. Biog. and in the Encyclopædias and Histories referred to in chapter I.

CHAPTER III

MEDIÆVAL ANTI-PEDOBAPTISM : THE PETROBRUSIANS AND THE ARNOLDISTS

NOT until we reach the twelfth century do we encounter Christian doctrine and practice that we can with confidence recognize as measurably conformable to the apostolic standard. During the eleventh century the dualistic heresies of the East made rapid progress in Western Europe, especially in Northern Italy and in Southern France. Like their prototypes in the East, the Cathari, as they were commonly called, were radical separatists and made uncompromising war on the corruptions and perversions of the dominant church. They not only repudiated with decision all the non-scriptural and anti-scriptural practices of the Catholics of the time, including the baptism of infants, but they rejected water baptism in general, substituting therefor a ceremony of their own called the Consolamentum. They were all dualists, some of them going to the Manichæan extreme. Like the Manichæans they rejected marriage and all intercourse of the sexes, abstained from animal food, and in general practised a rigorous asceticism.

In Peter de Bruys (1104–1124) and Henry of Lausanne (1116–1148) we have what seems to be an almost complete return to New Testament doctrine and practice. Our information about these reformers is derived wholly from their enemies, yet it is of such a nature that its authenticity can scarcely be called in question. Under what influence Peter, the French priest, came to his evangelical views we have no means of knowing. Being well educated and having access to the Scriptures, he may have been led by the zealous protests of the Cathari, who at this time abounded in Southern France, to examine the scriptural foundation of the doctrines and practices that were the special object of their attack: infant baptism, sacred buildings and shrines, the veneration of crosses, transubstantiation, sacrifices, prayers and almsgiving for the dead, liturgical services, etc. Peter the Venerable gives us a highly prejudiced but probably in the main correct account of the teaching and work of Peter de Bruys. Referring to the state of things that had resulted from Peter's activity in the regions to which his confutation was addressed, he says: "In your parts the people are rebaptized, the churches profaned, the altars overthrown, crosses burned, on the very day of our Lord's passion flesh is publicly eaten, priests are scourged, monks imprisoned and compelled by terrors and tortures to marry." He bears witness to the widespread acceptance of the views of Peter and the utter helplessness of priests and monks in the presence of his fiery zeal. "O miserable men, whoever you are," he writes, "who have yielded not to many nations but to two wretched little men only, Peter de Bruys and Henry, his pseudo-apostle." In his preface, written after Peter's death, he states somewhat fully five errors which, as he says, for twenty years have increased and multiplied. That we may be still further assured of the thoroughgoing evangelical position of Peter and Henry, we may quote from his statement:

The first article of the heretics denies that children who have not reached the age of intelligence can be saved by baptism, nor (sic) that another person's faith can profit those who cannot use their own,' since the Lord says: "Whosoever shall have believed and shall have been baptized shall be saved." . . The second article says that the building of temples or churches ought not to take place, that those already made, moreover, ought to be overthrown, nor that sacred places for prayer are necessary to Christians, since God when invoked hears as well in a tavern as in a church, in a market as in a temple, before an altar as before a manger, and hearkens to those who deserve it. The third article teaches that sacred crosses ought to be broken to pieces and burned up, because that kind of thing or instrument by which Christ was so frightfully tortured, so cruelly slain, is not worthy of adoration or veneration or any sort of supplication, but, by way of revenge for his torments and death, ought to be dishonored in every possible way, cut to pieces with swords and burned by fire. The fourth article denies not only the truth, that the body and blood of the Lord are daily and continuously through the sacrament offered in the church, but maintains that the sacrament is nothing at all, nor ought to be offered to God. The fifth article ridicules sacrifices, prayers, alms, and other good works done for dead believers by the living, and denies that these things can aid any one of the dead or in any manner.

He further mentions that these heretics hold that God is mocked by ecclesiastical chanting because he who is delighted solely by pious affections cannot be called to one's aid by high-pitched sounds nor soothed by musical modulations.

Peter's evangelistic activity extended from 1104 to 1124, when he was seized and burned on a pile of crosses that he was about to destroy. That he should have been able during so long a period to carry forward work so revolutionary is sufficient evidence that he had an immense following among the people, and that the nobility were sympathetic. It is probable that many of the Cathari were led by his intelligent zeal to abandon their dualism and to accept his scriptural position.

Henry of Lausanne, a Clugniac monk and deacon, began a similar career, probably under Peter's influence, about 1116, and continued it until 1147. He was one of the most eloquent preachers of the Middle Ages. Public testimony was borne that " never had a man been known of so great strictness of life, so great humanity and bravery"; that "by his speech he could easily provoke even a heart of stone to compunction." Having been left in charge of the spiritual work of his diocese by the bishop of Mans, during a visit to Rome, he made a wonderful commotion in the community. We learn from the records of the diocese, that while he held services for the people, the clergy likewise sitting and weeping at his feet, he resounded in such an oracular manner as if legions of demons with one howl sounded forth a murmur from his mouth. Nevertheless in a wonderful manner he was eloquent. His speech infused through the ears, adhered to the people's minds like fresh poison. By which heresy the people were roused to fury against the clergy, so that their servants threatened them with tortures, nor were they willing to sell them anything or buy anything of them, nay, they held them as heathens and publicans.

He induced immoral women publicly to burn their meretricious attire. He facilitated marriages by abolishing the requirement of a dowry; so that many young men under his direction married those with whom they had been living unchastely. When the bishop returned from Rome the people cried out: "We wish none of your ways, none of your blessing... We have a father, we have a pontiff, we have an advocate who surpasses you in authority, honesty, and knowledge." Hildebert succeeded in banishing him, but not in withdrawing from him the affections of the people. From this time onward Henry seems to have co-operated fully with Peter de Bruys in the evangelistic work that had been inaugurated by the latter twelve years before. In 1134 we find him laboring with great success in Provence, where he was seized by the Archbishop of Arles, and being sent for trial to the pope was convicted of heresy. Having been released, through what influence we are not informed, he continued his zealous labors. The passionate denunciations of the great Bernard furnish abundant evidence of his wonderful popularity and success. He was again thrown into prison through the influence of Bernard (1147), where he seems to have died about 1148.

That Peter and Henry were not Cathari, as Döllinger has recently attempted to prove, is manifest: 1. From the zeal with which they promoted marriage, which was radically contrary to the principles of the Cathari. 2. From the fact that they not only rejected infant baptism, but rebaptized on a profession of faith those who came into their fellowship. 3. From the absence of any indication that they practised themselves, or urged upon others, abstinence from animal food.

The difficulty felt by Döllinger in accounting for their rise and for the sudden disappearance of their followers as a distinct sect, apart from the supposition that Peter and Henry were themselves Cathari and that their influence persisted in the extensive Catharistic movement of the later time, is more imaginary than real. It is by no means certain that no evangelical life existed in Southern France before the appearance of Peter, and evidence of the persistence of evangelical life after the death of Henry abounds.

Contemporary with Peter and Henry were two religious enthusiasts, Tanchelm, who labored in the Netherlands with great success from 1115 to 1124, and Eudo de Stella, who closed a remarkable career in Breton in 1148. Both of these reformers denounced the Roman Catholic churches as dens of iniquity, and exhorted the people to abstain from receiving the sacrament at the hands of the corrupt priesthood. They are charged by their enemies with making extravagant statements as to their own sanctity and authority. Hugo, Archbishop of Rouen, writing in 1145 against the heretics of his locality, and probably having in mind Eudo and his followers, thus sets forth their views:

> The sacraments profit only the intelligent, not the ignorant; they profit adults, they bestow nothing upon little children. These [heretics] condemn the baptism of little children and infants and say, "In the gospel we read, Whosoever shall have believed and shall have been baptized shall be saved, but little children do not believe, therefore baptisms do not profit little children." Again: "If justification is of faith and salvation is of baptism, what does confirmation, made by the hand of a pontiff, add to those who believe and have been baptized, to those who are justified and saved?"

Contemporaneously (1115 to 1146), a similar evangelical movement was carried forward in the Rhenish provinces. In the former year several heretics, among them two presbyters, were apprehended in the neighborhood of Treves, who according to the records, denied "that the substance of the bread and the wine which is blessed at the altar through the priests is truly transmuted into the body and blood of Christ, nor did they say that the sacrament of baptism profits little children unto salvation, and very many erroneous things they professed, which I have thought it wrong to record." So numerous and aggressive had heretics become in these parts by 1146 that Evervin, provost at Steinfeld, sent for Bernard, the great heresy-hunter of the Middle Ages, to aid him in suppressing them. Having described, in his letter to Bernard, the Cathari who abounded in the neighborhood of Cologne, Evervin proceeds to write of "certain other heretics in our land, absolutely discordant from these, through whose mutual discord and contention both have been detected by us. These latter deny that the body of Christ is made at the altar. . . Concerning the baptism of little children they have no faith, because of that passage in the gospel: Whosoever shall have believed and shall have been baptized shall be saved." He further represents them as rejecting all marriages except those in which both the contracting parties are virgins, as having no confidence in the suffrages of saints, as denying that fasts and other bodily afflictions are profitable as regards the remission of sins either for the righteous or for sinners, as calling other ecclesiastical observances not founded by Christ or the apostles superstitions, as rejecting the doctrine of purgatory, and maintaining that souls immediately after going forth from the body pass either into eternal rest or eternal punishment, and as repudiating prayers or offerings for the dead. Several clergymen and monks are said to have joined themselves to this party.

Contemporary with these evangelical movements in France, Germany, and the Netherlands, was the remarkable career of Arnold of Brescia in Italy. Of noble lineage and great intellectual and moral powers, he studied under the famous French teacher and freethinker Peter Abelard. It is highly probable that, while in France, he came in contact with the widespread evangelical work of Peter and Henry. On his return to Italy, full of zeal for the reformation of Church and State, he was admitted into one of the lower grades of the clergy. He had come to see in the secularization of the church and in the devotion of clergy and monks to the accumulation of wealth as means of luxury and oppression, the root of the corruptions of the time, and he was able to give all the greater emphasis to his scathing denunciations by reason of his own austerity and sanctity of life. He demanded the complete renunciation, on the part of the church as a whole and of individual clergy and monks, of all property and entire withdrawal from all secular affairs. He insisted that the clergy should be supported entirely by the freewill offerings of the people. His views met with great favor throughout all

Northern Italy, but having been accused of heresy by his bishop in a Lateran synod he was obliged to leave Italy in 1139. He returned to France, where he defended Abelard against Bernard and others, and soon had this fierce and unrelenting heresy-hunter dogging his footsteps. He next went to Switzerland where he labored with acceptance under the protection of the Bishop of Constance until the zeal of Bernard, who warned the bishop not to harbor this "roaring lion," wrought his expulsion. He found protection with a papal legate who afterward became Pope Celestin II., and in Rome during a decade he was at the head of a popular movement that aimed at the restoration of the ancient form of government and that gained such power as to be able to expel the pope and to establish a new régime. In the treaty between Frederick Barbarossa and Alexander III. (1155), he was basely sacrificed by the former to the latter. He was hanged, his body was burned and his ashes were cast into the Tiber, lest his followers should gather his remains for relics.

The foregoing are well-established facts. The questions about which there has been difference of opinion are the following: Was Arnold a religious schismatic as well as a social and political reformer? We should attach very little importance to Bernard's railings if we had no better evidence to rely upon. Otto, of Freising, one of the best informed and most judicial of the contemporary authorities, remarks that, "Besides these things, he is said to have been astray with reference to the sacrament of the altar and the baptism of infants." The former part of this statement is confirmed by several writers. The latter part has commonly been supposed to be unconfirmed. It has recently been claimed by Breyer, a learned German writer, who has studied the career of Arnold with great care, that Durandus confirms

Otto's report as to Arnold's unsatisfactory views on infant baptism. The passage from Durandus refers not to Arnold personally but rather to his followers and is not a direct assertion that these rejected infant baptism. It is as follows: "The Arnoldists assert that never through water baptism do men receive the Holy Spirit, nor did the baptized Samaritans receive it, until they received the imposition of hands." This passage can be fairly taken to prove no more than that the Arnoldists denied that the Holy Spirit is received in baptism.

Did Arnold found a sect? We have abundant evidence that he did. It is related by Johannes Saresberensis in his "Historia Pontificalis," that during his stay in Rome Arnold "founded a sect of men which is still (about 1164) called the heresy of the Lombards," and that its adherents on account of the uprightness, rigor, and piety of their lives have found most enthusiastic popular support. Johannes was resident in Rome during Arnold's time and must have known whereof he affirmed.

The next question to be settled is, Whether he was founder of the sect known during the succeeding century as Arnoldists? Those who accept the evidence that Arnold founded a sect, can hardly fail to regard it as highly probable that the Arnoldists of history derived from him alike their impulse and their name. The fact that the Arnoldists centered in Lombardy, where Arnold's influence is known to have been greatest, is, moreover, strongly favorable to this identification.

They were at one with the Petrobrusians in their uncompromising hostility to the Roman Catholic Church, whose sacraments they repudiated. They denied the efficacy of water baptism to procure the remission of sins and the gift of the Holy Spirit, and laid considerable stress upon the imposition of hands as a complementary rite.

During the latter part of the century they seem to have united with a party of the Humiliati, a semi-monastic religious and industrial community. By 1184 some sort of union had been established in Lombardy between these Arnoldistic Humiliati and the Poor Men of Lyons, or followers of Peter Waldo; for Pope Lucius III. (1184), in a bull against the heresies prevailing in Lombardy, mentioned the Humiliati and the Poor Men of Lyons as if they were one and the same party.

Literature: On the Cathari: Döllinger (Sectengesch.) and Schmidt (Hist. d. Cathares). On Peter de Bruys and Henry of Lausanne: Peter the Venerable, Bernard, and Döllinger. On Arnold of Brescia: Otto Frising, Durandus, Bernard, Giesebrecht, Breyer, and Hausrath. On all the topics of the chapter the pertinent articles and sections in the Encyclopædias and Histories referred to in chapter I.

CHAPTER IV

THE WALDENSES AND RELATED PARTIES

THE simple and familiar story of Peter Waldo, the prosperous Lyonese merchant who about 1173 gave up property and home in order to devote himself to evangelistic work, need not be here recounted. The idea of founding a sect seems to have been as remote as possible from his thoughts. He simply claimed for himself and his followers the right to evangelize as laymen. The denial of this right by the ecclesiastical authorities drew forth an expression of the determination of the evangelists to obey God rather than men. This placed them in the position of schismatics. Persecution only served to heighten their zeal and to extend the sphere of their labors. Early in his career Waldo secured the translation into the vernacular of portions of the Scriptures. These were mastered by himself and a body of faithful followers and formed the basis of their enthusiastic proclamation of the gospel and of their denunciation of prevailing corruptions in the dominant church.

Two errors have widely prevailed regarding Waldo's relation to earlier evangelical life : that of the Waldenses themselves, followed by many Mennonites and some Baptists, in accordance with which Waldo was in no proper sense the founder of the party that bears his name but simply attained to the leadership of an evangelical party that had continuously existed from apostolic times ; the other, represented by such modern scholars as Karl Müller, which denies any sort of historical connection between Waldo and earlier evangelical life and which minimizes the evangelical character of the party.

The theory of Waldensian apostolic succession cannot be sustained by historical facts; but that Waldo had been influenced directly or indirectly by the Petrobrusian movement, which a few years before had profoundly stirred the religious life of Southern France and which must have persisted in some measure to his own time, seems highly probable. That the vigorous and aggressive party led by Waldo soon absorbed much of the evangelical life of the earlier types and was thereby itself made more evangelical can scarcely be doubted.

It must be admitted that Waldo and his early followers had more in common with modern Methodists than with modern Baptists and more in common with Roman Catholicism than with any evangelical party. His views of religious life and doctrine were scarcely in advance of those of many earnest Catholics of the time. He deprecated schism, but his evangelical zeal did not permit him to regulate his work by the will of his ecclesiastical superiors. Refused permission to carry on his work as a Catholic he must at all events carry it on.

An alliance was formed, as early as 1184, between the Poor Men of Lyons, as Waldo's followers were called, and the Poor Men of Lombardy, who were probably identical with the Arnoldistic Humiliati. The union was dissolved as early as 1205, owing, it would seem, to pronounced differences of opinion between the parties and Waldo's uncompromising attitude. In 1218, shortly after Waldo's death, a conference was held at Bergamo in Northern Italy, where the points at issue were fully discussed, but no harmonization was effected. After further correspondence the Poor Men of Lombardy (about 1230) wrote what may be called an ultimatum, in which the difficulties and the negotiations of the past are fully reviewed and the points still at issue sharply set forth.

This recently discovered Rescript is the oldest Waldensian document known and must be regarded as containing an authentic account of the views of the two parties. They were agreed as regards the necessity of water baptism to salvation even in the case of infants, and in holding to the doctrine of transubstantiation; but they differed as to whether the transmutation of the elements is due to the utterance of the divine words of consecration, so that a Jew or a harlot can effect it, or whether the power to transmute depends on the personal character of the ministrant. The Italians insisted on the latter view, the Ultramontanes on the former. Both maintained that baptism could be validly administered in an emergency by a harlot, and the Ultramontanes insisted on applying the same principle to the Supper. The Ultramontanes felt perfectly free to receive the Supper at the hands of the corrupt priests and to have their infants baptized by them. Waldo had persistently refused to consent to the appointment during his own lifetime or afterward of bishops or general superintendents, just as Wesley strenuously opposed the introduction of the episcopate into his society. The Italians preferred, it appears, to appoint superintendents for life, the Ultramontanes for a limited period They had differed also as to whether ministers should be ordained for life or for a limited period, the Italians preferring the former arrangement, the Ultramontanes the latter. In this also they were able to reach a satisfactory adjustment. Waldo had resolutely opposed the Italian "congregations of workmen," probably a perpetuation of the semi-monastic working societies of the Arnoldistic Humiliati mentioned above. The grounds of his opposition were no doubt the incongruity of this mode of life with devotion to evangelistic work, on which he laid great stress, and the grave abuses that usually grew up in organizations of this kind. The Italians were willing as far as possible to reform abuses, but did not see their way clear to the abolition of the congregations. On this matter also conciliation had been reached.

The most obstinate point of difference with which they had to deal was that with regard to the post-mortem condition of Waldo and of Vivetus, one of his chief co-laborers. The Ultramontanes made it an indispensable condition of the restoration of fellowship, that the Italians should acknowledge without qualification that these worthies "are in God's paradise." The Italians would go no further than to say, that "If before their death Waldo and Vivetus satisfied God for all their faults and offenses, they could be saved." These faults and offenses doubtless indicate the Italians' view of the procedures of Waldo and Vivetus that led to the schism. The probability is, that the Italians had used strong language reflecting on the Christian character of these leaders, implying doubt as to their saved condition. Loyalty to the founder of their society and to his honored associate required that such language should be withdrawn before communion could be re-established.

It is probable that Waldo and his immediate followers held to the set of views that soon became characteristic of the Waldenses, and were communicated by them to the Bohemian Brethren, and by both these parties to the Anabaptists of the sixteenth century. They were certainly held by the Waldenses in 1235.[1] These views were common, for the most part, to the Cathari and to the evangelical parties of the Middle Ages and their persistence in the Anabaptists is one of the most convincing proofs of the historical connection of the latter with mediæval evangelical life. On this account, and not because these views are distinctively Baptist, it seems important to give some account of them here.

While the Waldenses laid little stress on dogmatic

---
[1] See the "Supra Stella" of Salve Burce, in Döllinger, Vol. II., p. 52., *seq.*

statements, their theology was evidently strongly anti-Augustinian. They emphasized the imitation of Christ. The Sermon on the Mount was their favorite portion of Scripture. They might fairly be charged with over-emphasizing good works as compared with faith. From their literalistic interpretation of the words of Christ, they unconditionally rejected oaths, capital punishment, magistracy, and warfare. On the ground of Christ's words, they taught and practised non-resistance; yet in dire emergencies human nature sometimes reasserted itself and they repelled persecution with the utmost vigor and determination.

The Waldenses soon extended their work throughout Europe. Especially active and successful were they in Southern Germany and in the southwestern provinces of Austria. The perpetual conflict between popes and emperors from the middle of the twelfth to the middle of the fourteenth century and the degradation and schism of the papacy during the latter part of the fourteenth and the first half of the fifteenth centuries was highly favorable to their spread. Not that they had immunity from persecution. On the contrary most of the information as to the extent and character of their work we owe to the careful records of inquisitors. But they found such acceptance with the masses of the people, had effected an organization for secret work so complete, and had attained to such skill in evading persecution, that they were often able to carry forward their work with considerable vigor and success in the very face of the Inquisition. They had a three-fold ministry: "majors," ordained when practicable by another "major," otherwise by a presbyter or presbyters; "presbyters," who devoted themselves exclusively to evangelistic and pastoral work under the direction of the major; and "deacons," whose chief duty it was to provide for the support of majors and presbyters, but who also engaged largely in spiritual work. All three of these orders of ministry belonged to the inner circle of the society, to which admission could be secured only after a long period of training and testing. The outer circle were called "friends" or "believers," and from these were derived the funds for the support of the work. Hospices, presided over by elderly women, were maintained in the various communities in which they labored, where the itinerant ministers were entertained, and where devotional and educational work was conducted. Delegates from the inner circle met annually in convention, usually in Lombardy, where they brought together the funds collected for the maintenance of the work, appointed majors and presbyters when vacancies existed, planned the work of the ensuing year, and apportioned to the workers funds for their support.

It is gratifying to know that the Waldenses did not long remain in the semi-Romanist position in which we left them about 1230. From the "Supra Stella" of Salve Burce, an Italian writing of the year 1235, we get a far more favorable view of the evangelical character of the Poor Men of Lyons and the Poor Men of Lombardy than from the Rescript. They are represented as denouncing the Roman Church as a "foul harlot" and "beast," as a "serpent's nest," and yet as receiving from it "baptism and the imposition of hands."[1]

The next detailed accounts we have of them were written about thirty years later by their enemies. These inquisitorial documents show that by 1260 the Waldenses had emerged from the condition in which they saw men as trees walking into the light and liberty of the gospel.

For the purpose of exhibiting the Waldenses in this more favorable light we select the accounts of David of

---
[1] Döllinger, Vol. II., pp. 62-64.

Augsburg and of the so-called "Passau Anonymous." According to the former writer, "their first heresy" was contempt of ecclesiastical power. . . Having been cast out from the Catholic Church they affirm that they alone are the church of Christ and disciples of Christ. They say that they are successors of the apostles and have apostolic authority and the keys of binding and loosing. They say that the Roman Church is the Babylonish harlot, and that all who obey her are damned. They say that all the saints and the faithful since the time of Pope Sylvester have been damned. They say that no miracles that take place in the church are true. . . They say that no statutes of the church after the ascension of Christ are to be observed, or are of any value. The festivals, fast-days, orders, benedictions, and offices of the church they absolutely repudiate. They say that then for the first time is a man truly baptized when he has been inducted into their heresy. But some say that baptism does not avail for little children because they cannot yet actually believe. The sacrament of confirmation they repudiate, but their own masters lay their hands upon their disciples in place of that sacrament. They say that the bishops and clergy and monks of the church are scribes and Pharisees, persecutors of the apostles. They do not believe that the body and blood of Christ are truly present [in the Supper], but only bread that has been blessed, which by a certain figure of speech is called the body of Christ. . . But some say that the ordinance is validly administered only by good men, but others, by all who know the words of consecration. . . They say also, that a priest who is a sinner cannot bind and loose any one, since he himself has been bound by sin, and that any good and intelligent layman can absolve another and impose penance. . . They repudiate all clerical orders, saying that they would be rather a curse than a sacrament. . . They say that every oath is unlawful and mortal sin even if it be concerning what is true. . . They say that it is not lawful to put to death malefactors through secular judgment. . . They say that there is no purgatory, but that all on dying pass immediately into heaven or hell; therefore they assert that suffrages for the dead made by the church are of no profit, since in heaven they do not need them and in hell they are in no way aided by them. . . They say also that the saints in heaven do not hear the prayers of the faithful. . . On festal days where they cautiously can they labor, arguing that since it is good to labor it is not evil to do good things on a festal day. In Lent and on other fast-days of the church they do not fast, but eat flesh where they dare, saying that God takes no delight in the afflictions of his friends.

Elsewhere David of Augsburg bears testimony to their great devotion to the study of the Scriptures, by freely quoting which they were able to impress the people and to put the clergy at a disadvantage. The outward sanctity of their lives he freely acknowledges and accounts thereby for their strong popular influence. Their zealous and effective efforts for the salvation of men are described by the author in a way that reflects credit on the Waldenses.

The "Passau Anonymous," describing the Austrian Waldenses, of whom forty-two distinct communities are mentioned, conveys substantially the same impression as to their thoroughgoing evangelical character and their zeal in Christian work: "In relation to baptism some err in that they maintain that little children are not saved through baptism, since the Lord says: Whosoever believeth and is baptized shall be saved." He adds: "Some baptize anew, others practise laying on of hands instead of baptism." This writer accounts for the rapid spread of heresy by candid admission of the corruptions in doctrine and practice that prevailed in the church and rendered it almost defenseless in the face of such attacks.

Rainerius Sacco, writing of the Poor Men of Lombardy (about 1260), after some remarks on the strong anti-Romanist attitude of the party, says: "Likewise they say that infants are saved without baptism."

In the "Summa de Heresibus" (Döllinger, Vol. II., p. 297) it is said of the Runcarians, a sect of the Waldenses: "Concerning baptism they say that a wicked priest does not baptize but rather pollutes. . . Whence they teach that all their own ought to be baptized, and that they had not been baptized but rather polluted" in the Roman Church.

Literature: Monographs of Preger, Haupt, Keller, Comba, K. Müller, Wattenbach, Herzog, and Dieckhoff, as in the Bibliography. Döllinger, Sectengesch., II., gives most of the important documents. Gieseler, Ch. Hist., II., 531 *seq.*, gives a large amount of carefully selected extracts from mediæval works. Bern. Guidonis, Practica Inquisitionis contains much important matter.

CHAPTER V

THE TABORITES AND THE BOHEMIAN BRETHREN

THE Taborites appeared as the radical evangelicals in connection with the Hussite movement in Bohemia—first half of the fifteenth century—and were a product in part of Wycliffite and in part of Waldensian influence. Preger, Haupt, Goll, and a number of other high authorities on mediæval religious history, lay chief stress on the Waldensian element and find in the records of the Bohemian Inquisition of the fourteenth century abundant evidence of the presence and aggressive activity of a radical type of Waldensianism in regions where Taborism afterward abounded. Loserth and others, having established the fact that Huss and Jerome of Prague were deeply indebted to Wycliffe and that through their influence Wycliffe's teachings were widely diffused throughout Bohemia, feel that there is no need to suppose that Waldensianism exerted any important influence on the movement. The fact would seem to be that Bohemian religious life had been profoundly affected by the old-evangelical teaching in its various forms long before the time of Wycliffe; but that the clear and profuse utterances of the great English reformer were brought powerfully to bear through Huss and the University of Prague and gave a mighty impulse to evangelical thought and life.

The Taborites were if possible more pronounced than the most evangelical of the Waldenses in their insistence on the absoluteness and the exclusiveness of scriptural authority and in applying the Scripture touchstone to every doctrine and practice. They said:

Christ Jesus is our only truly good and perfect lawgiver. . . . The law of Jesus Christ, *i. e.*, the gospel law, which surpasses the Old Testament as all other laws in brevity, simplicity, and ease of fulfillment, is of itself alone sufficient for the government of the church militant and man needs no new law for his pilgrimage to the home above. . . . Only those truths are to be believed and accepted that are designated in the canonical Scriptures and can be derived from these directly and without the employment of far-fetched methods of interpretation. . . . Only such ceremonies and external forms in worship are to be employed as Christ himself has approved.

Baptismal regeneration and the real presence in the Supper were explicitly denied. No mediæval party came nearer to the Baptist position than the Taborites in their conception of the relation of Scripture to doctrine and practice. But they failed to see the inconsistency of infant baptism with the position they had taken and perpetuated this non-scriptural practice. Aroused to fanatical zeal by persecution, many of them took refuge in chiliastic views, as did some of the Anabaptists of the Reformation time. There is a historical connection between the chiliasm of the Taborites and that of the fanatical Anabaptists.

In Peter Chelcicky of Bohemia, the spiritual father of the Bohemian Brethren and one of the ablest Christian thinkers of the fifteenth century, we have a near approach to the position of the Anti-pedobaptists of the sixteenth century. Like the Waldenses and the Taborites he rejected transubstantiation and baptismal regeneration, and sought to make the New Testament the only standard of faith and practice. According to Chelcicky, the only source of faith is the will of God, which is set forth authoritatively and exhaustively once for all through the apostles in their writings and in the church founded by them. He regarded the apostolic church as the model. Any deviation from this model is apostasy, whether it be by way of addition or diminution. God's law is perfectly sufficient in every particular. Apostasy began when the relation of Church and State changed. If the whole population of a State were Christian, there would be no need of civil government. An insoluble contradiction is involved in the expression "the Christian State," since to the essence of the State belongs compulsion by way of protecting and rewarding the good and punishing the evil. The true Christian needs not to be compelled to the good and dares not compel others, since God desires purely voluntary good. The punishment of evil-doers that the State administers is vengeance, which Christians are forbidden to practice. Referring to Augustine's efforts to reconcile Christianity and the State, he says that he sucked blood instead of milk from the Scriptures. In the Christian State and in Christian society, as they have existed since the time of Constantine, there is no place for the true Christian except in the lowest ranks, which only obey without commanding, which serve without dominating. All dominion, all class distinctions, are radically opposed to Christ's requirement of brotherly equality. No one can be at the same time a king and a true Christian. For similar reasons Christians cannot safely or consistently occupy any civil office. So also Christians should avoid trade, because of the deceit involved in seeking advantages. He regarded cities where trade is carried on as vessels of poison in which true Christians cannot possibly escape the contamination of the world. Agriculture and handicraft seemed to him the only safe occupations for Christians. He lays great stress on the imitation of Christ, whom he regards as not only teacher and exemplar but also as Saviour and the only mediator between Creator and creature. The human will has remained free even after the fall. Good and evil stand before man, let him choose. Only the freely chosen good is truly good and valuable. Yet man does not attain to this choice without God's help. Inner regeneration cannot take place without God's grace. Such regeneration gives to man a new heart, a new understanding, new thoughts, new works. Right faith leads man to activity and works that assure him of the eternal reward. Like the Waldenses he rejected oaths and capital punishment with great decision. As regards baptism, after quoting the Great Commission, he proceeds:

> Open and clear is the word of the Son of God: first he speaks of faith, then of baptism . . . and since we find this doctrine in the gospel we should now also hold fast to it. But the priests err grievously in baptizing the great mass, and no one is found whether old or young who knows God and believes his Scripture, and this is evident in their works . . . nevertheless all without discrimination are baptized and receive the body and blood of Christ. . . But we should rather hold fast to the view that baptism belongs to those who know God and believe his Scripture.

If he had stopped here Baptists would have little fault to find with him. Unfortunately and inconsistently he adds:

> If such have children baptism should be bestowed upon their children in their conscience. But why is baptism bestowed before the other sacraments? Because the transgression which rests upon all men is hereditary sin; and this is of such kind that it robs the soul of the life of grace and of the truth of all virtues and inclines it to all sorts of sins. . . Baptism is the second birth in the Holy Spirit.

While he rejects transubstantiation, he falls short of the Taborite view of the purely symbolical character of the Supper. His position may be characterized, with reference to the later Reformation systems, as Calvinistic rather than Zwinglian or Lutheran.

The Bohemian Brethren (*Unitas Fratrum*), who arose shortly after the Hussite wars and rapidly absorbed the more evangelical elements of the Hussite movement, carried into practice to a considerable extent the views of Peter Chelcicky and were also considerably influenced by the Waldenses. Their first act after the completion of their organization (1467) was the rebaptism of all who were present. It is difficult to determine the extent to which infant baptism was rejected and adult baptism required, as the accounts that have come down to us are more or less contradictory. But as the society became widespread it is reasonable to suppose that their practice became diversified in response to the varying influences by which they were surrounded. In 1503 and 1504, with a view to warding off impending persecution, the Bohemian Brethren—they now call themselves Waldenses—addressed an "Apology" and two "Confessions of Faith" to King Wladislaus, in which they seek to minimize the extent of their departure from the Catholic Church. While admitting that in times past some of their society have rejected infant baptism they are now prepared to affirm that "Baptism is to be administered to children also, in order that guided by their sponsors they may be incited and accustomed to a life of faith." They still practised rebaptism in the case of those coming to them from the Roman Church.

That they continued this latter practice until 1519 is attested by Kostelechius, a Bohemian correspondent of Erasmus,[1] who in describing to Erasmus the religious condition of Bohemia mentions the Brethren (whom he calls Pickards) as the third sect. Having set forth in a clear but unfriendly light the decidedly evangelical character of these Christians he proceeds: "Those who come to their heresy are each compelled to be rebaptized."

In a comparative account of the Bohemian and Moravian Pickards, written in 1535,[2] we find the following concise description:

---

[1] "Erasmi Ep." Lib. XIV., Ep. 20. [2] Döllinger, Vol. II., p. 635.

The Bohemian Pickards rebaptize all those who come anew to themselves and their sect, before they are admitted; but those who have given their profession to his royal Majesty, being, as far as can be conjectured, from Moravia, say, that this custom of rebaptizing formerly prevailed among them, but now they have learned that that mode of rebaptizing ought neither to be held to nor practised. . . The Bohemian Pickards say that the priests of the Roman Church err exceedingly concerning the baptism of children.

From another document on the errors of the Pickards we learn: "Some baptize children, but many do not." After giving in some detail their views on a number of points, the writer draws this conclusion: "To sum up, almost all the articles of the Anabaptists have place in the synagogue of the Waldenses."[1]

That the Bohemian Brethren and the Waldenses abandoned their opposition to infant baptism and their practice of rebaptism was due in part to the fact that large numbers of their more radical members were being absorbed by the aggressive Anabaptists, and in part to the greatly increased danger and odium that attached to the Anabaptist name. Decisive action in this direction resulted from the rigorous decree of the Bohemian Diet (1534) for the arrest and execution, in case of refusal to recant, of every Anabaptist. A synod of the Brethren was called at Jung-Buntzlau for deciding whether rebaptism should be abolished and immunity from the danger of being confounded with the proscribed Anabaptists be secured, or they should adhere to their old practice and subject themselves to the terrible persecution that was imminent. A majority favored the former course.[2]

Nothing has been said about the old-evangelical life of Britain during the mediæval period. Unfortunately the information available is by no means satisfactory or complete. This dearth of materials may, however, be due

---

[1] Döllinger, Vol. II., p. 661.
[2] Gindely, "Gesch. der böhm. Brüder," Bd. I., p. 223 seq.

to the fortunate circumstance that the inquisition of heresy was imperfectly organized and inefficiently worked in Britain, and that heretics of the humbler type enjoyed during long periods comparative immunity from persecution. It is highly probable that the old British type of Christianity survived throughout the Middle Ages. It is also probable that the old-evangelical Christianity of the Continent made its way into Britain in the early part of the thirteenth century, if not before the close of the twelfth. The encouragement given by Wycliffe, supported by the nobility, with his "poor priests," evangelical tracts, English Bible, etc., doubtless drew out into publicity much of old-evangelical life that had been latent and caused it to glow with fresh enthusiasm.

In Lollardism we meet with the same set of views that have become familiar to us in our examination of continental sect-life, and a clearness in the apprehension of the great fundamental truths of Christianity that we encounter only here and there among the continental sectaries. Lollardism was the forerunner of all that was best in English Puritanism, from which, in an important sense, modern Baptists have derived their origin. But we have searched in vain for any satisfactory proof that it embodied distinctively Baptist principles or practices. We find views of truth that would seem logically to involve the Baptist position, but alas! men are not always logical. It is possible, nay, probable, that some of the mediæval British evangelicals rejected infant baptism and insisted on believers' baptism, but adequate proof has not yet been presented. Thomas Walden's charge against Wycliffe, that he denied infant baptism and his seeming insinuation that the Lollards, whose leader Wycliffe was, participated in this heresy, is apparently without foundation in fact. Nothing appears in Wycliffe's published writings—and Lechler claims to have read through all his extant manuscript works without finding anything—that would warrant the inference that he rejected infant baptism. The nearest approach to the Baptist position is his expression of the opinion that unbaptized infants may possibly be saved. But he did not even venture so far as to express a decided conviction that they would be. His rigid predestinarianism inclined him to the opinion that elect infants would be saved whether baptized or not; but he was not quite sure whether elect infants ever fail to receive baptism. The Lollards took a far more decided stand than Wycliffe in favor of the salvation of unbaptized infants; but no one of them so far as we are aware denied the propriety or the utility of infant baptism.

The extent and importance of the old-evangelical movement on the Continent of Europe have been for the most part greatly underestimated. In fact until recent years the materials necessary for forming a correct judgment were not available. Much documentary matter of the most valuable kind has been brought to light during the last twenty years and there is every reason to believe that important finds will yet be made. The labors of Preger, Haupt, Wattenbach, Loserth, and Karl Muller, happily still in progress, have already accomplished much and will no doubt continue to be fruitful.

The activity and success of the Waldenses and related parties during the fourteenth century were such as to cause widespread alarm on the part of the standing order. In Southern Germany and throughout the Rhine region a great part of the population became identified with the Waldenses. In Thuringia, Brandenburg, Bohemia, Moravia, Silesia, Pomerania, Prussia, and Poland, large numbers of Waldensian communities are known to have existed. In Austria they became so numerous and aggressive, that the Inquisition feared an armed uprising. From Styria they spread throughout Hungary, even to the remoter provinces, Siebenbürgen and Galicia. From 1390 onward the Inquisition was applied with considerable vigor but with small effect. Especially influential did the Waldenses become in the great commercial cities of Southern Germany and throughout the surrounding regions. In Würtzburg, Bamberg, Nürnberg, Augsburg, and Strasburg they had a large number of adherents, including a considerable number from the wealthier classes. So strong was the popular sympathy for the evangelicals, that the officers of the Inquisition found great difficulty in securing such co-operation of the local authorities as was necessary for success. Even the bishops often showed themselves reluctant to allow the introduction of the Inquisition into their dioceses.

Nowhere did the Waldensian preachers find greater acceptance than in Bohemia. The Inquisitorial procedures in 1395 tended to increase rather than to diminish their influence, which was undoubtedly one of the prime factors in the Bohemian religious revolution of the fifteenth century. The Taborites so modified Waldensianism as better to adapt it to aggressive work. During the first half of the fifteenth century large numbers of Bohemian evangelists labored in Southern Germany, confirming the old-evangelical party and gaining many new adherents. So lively was the intercourse between Bamberg and Nürnberg and the evangelical party in Bohemia, that the loyalty of these cities to the church and the empire was seriously called into question. "The Bambergers are neighbors of the Bohemians," we find written in a contemporary document. It is highly probable that the artisans' guilds, which prevailed widely during the Middle Ages and which had their lodges in all the principal cities, were largely under the control of the old-evangelical party and were utilized by them in the prosecution of their work. That such was the case to a considerable extent is beyond question. The art of printing arose out of a circle known to have been closely related to the old-evangelical party and was early utilized for the dissemination of the Bible and old-evangelical literature.

Zeal for Bible study led to the translation of the New Testament and portions of the Old Testament into the vernacular languages. A careful comparison of a fourteenth century manuscript German version of the New Testament, discovered a few years ago in the monastery of Tepl in Bohemia, with other Waldensian versions, and the fact that the manuscript contains a number of other documents of a Waldensian character, has rendered it highly probable that the version is of Waldensian origin. A comparison of the manuscript with the earliest printed German Bible reveals identity of text. The later editions of the mediæval German Bible were modified little by little toward conformity with the Latin Vulgate and with Roman Catholic dogma. The widespread circulation of vernacular versions of the Bible from 1456 to 1518 was undoubtedly due in large measure to Waldensian influence. During this period at least fourteen complete editions of the German Bible and four of the Dutch Bible, besides large numbers of Gospels, Psalters, and other Scripture portions, were printed. This fact, along with the fact that at least ninety-eight complete editions of the Latin Bible, with a correspondingly large number of Scripture portions, were in circulation by the close of the fifteenth century, shows that the Bible was anything but a neglected book at the beginning of the Protestant Revolution.

It has been estimated that by 1500 the Bohemian Brethren had from three hundred to four hundred congregations, about equally divided between Bohemia and Moravia, with a constituency of perhaps two hundred thousand.[1] They had the support in each country of a number of powerful noblemen, who were able to protect them to a great extent from the persecuting measures of popes, emperors, and kings. In the Alpine valleys of Piedmont, Dauphiny, Languedoc, and Provence, the Vaudois had maintained themselves from the rise of the party, having been frequently persecuted, but never to the extent of extermination. It is probable that at the close of the fifteenth century they had as many as one hundred congregations, with a constituency of possibly fifty thousand.

It would, we should think, be quite within the bounds, in view of what we know of the wide diffusion of old-evangelical principles during the thirteenth, fourteenth, and fifteenth centuries, if we should place the number of Waldensian adherents outside of Bohemia, Moravia, and the Alpine valleys at one hundred thousand.

We have said nothing of evangelical mysticism, with its stirring preaching, its widely circulated and highly influential literature, its schools for the promotion of evangelical learning, and its intimate relations to the Waldensian movement. The enthusiastic millenarianism of the heretical Franciscans and others exerted a profound influence over vast numbers during this period and explains some of the unhappy doctrinal developments of the sixteenth century. The combination of millenarianism with ideas of social revolution, as seen in the Geisslers of the thirteenth and fourteenth centuries, was repeated in the sixteenth century with disastrous results. Dualistic heresy greatly declined before the close of the mediæval period; but an attentive study may reveal some of its features surviving in the sect life of the sixteenth cen-

---
[1] Krummel, "Utraquisten und Taboriten," p. 247.

tury. Pantheistic mysticism, which wrought out in some of the Beghards of the fourteenth and fifteenth centuries the logical consequences of self-identification with God on the part of its adherents and denial of all moral distinctions and obligations, reappeared in the Libertines of the sixteenth century and in a less extreme form in such sect leaders as David Joris and Henry Niclaes. The influence of the Italian Renaissance, with its revival of freedom of thought and the grammatico-historical study of the Scriptures in their original languages, producing as it did such Christian scholars as Reuchlin, Erasmus, and Colet, cannot be left out of consideration in any careful study of the history of the radical evangelical movement of the sixteenth century.

1. In the above brief sketch of extra-Catholic mediæval religious life the aim has been to put the reader in a position to form right judgments of the radical movements of the sixteenth century and to understand the peculiar features of the parties that rigidly held aloof from the State-Church systems of the time and were without much discrimination lumped together and stigmatized by their opponents as "Anabaptists."

2. We have seen that the strivings of mediæval Christianity to shake off the incubus of sacerdotalism and ceremonialism and the fearful moral evils that had come everywhere to prevail in the dominant church, were far more earnest and persistent than were those of the early centuries. It seems to have required some generations for the fundamental principles of Christianity fully to reassert themselves. It required long experience of the ruinous outworking of pagan principles that had intruded themselves into the church of the time, so to stir the Christian consciousness as to compel the better life of the church to protest effectively against the prevailing evils. In fact it was only when the Roman hierarchy had be-

come thoroughly organized and was taking vigorous measures for bringing all the churches into entire subjection to itself and so into uniformity of doctrine and practice, that organized dissent began to appear, and it increased and spread as the machinery of the church for enforcing uniformity became gradually more perfect.

3. Even in the Middle Ages we do not find much of Christian life that Baptists can recognize as in every respect conformable to the apostolic standard. The Petrobrusians and Henricians seem to approach nearer to this standard than any other party. They rejected infant baptism and practised believer's baptism; they rejected the doctrine of the real presence and probably celebrated the Supper as a simple memorial, but of this last we have no direct evidence. Whether they laid stress on immersion as the only allowable form of baptism we do not know. The probability is that on this point they did not differ from the Romanists of their time, who while fully acknowledging that normal baptism was immersion had long since admitted other forms as more convenient and as answering the purpose equally well. The early Waldenses, we have seen, had scarcely anything in common with Baptists. Of the later Waldenses some, probably not a large proportion, came to reject infant baptism. But even these seem to have fallen far short of the Baptist position in other respects. The same may be said of the Taborites and the Bohemian Brethren. Even those who rejected infant baptism and practised rebaptism had much in their doctrine and practice that present-day Baptists would not fellowship.

Literature: Pertinent works of Goll, Loserth, Gindely, Palacky, Zezschwitz, Baum, De Schweinitz, Höfler, Krummel, Preger, Keller, and Lea, as in the Bibliography.

CHAPTER VI

THE ZWICKAU PROPHETS

THE so-called Anabaptist movement of the sixteenth century had its roots in the evangelical life and thought of the Middle Ages. Even the non-evangelical and corrupting elements that appeared in connection with the sect life of the sixteenth century had their antecedents in the earlier time. The term "Anabaptist" was applied indiscriminately to all who would be neither Protestants nor Catholics and who insisted on setting up separate churches for the embodiment of their peculiar views. To the dominant parties Thomas Münzer, the mystical fanatic, who neither submitted to nor practised rebaptism, who to the last practised infant baptism and who advocated the setting up of the kingdom of Christ by carnal warfare, the scholarly and soundly scriptural Hubmaier, the mystical Denck, and the chiliastic fanatics of Münster, were all alike "Anabaptists"; and even the most Christlike of these were treated as criminals of the deepest dye. There was some excuse for this confusion in the fact that most of the separatists of the time agreed in denying the scriptural authorization of infant baptism.

Difficulty has been felt by some in connecting the Anabaptist movement with mediæval parties on the ground of supposed lack of evidence of the passing over of the adherents of the older parties to the new. But are we not confronted with even graver difficulties if we deny such connection? During the thirteenth, fourteenth, and fifteenth centuries multitudes of evangelical Christians are known to have quietly yet persistently carried on their work in some of the very regions where the Anabaptist movement attained to its greatest popularity and power. How shall we account for the disappearance of this organized evangelical life that had patiently endured and survived three centuries of terrible persecution? The last years of the fifteenth century and the early years of the sixteenth were highly favorable for the development of evangelical life. The impetus given to evangelical study by Humanism, the wide circulation of the Scriptures and of evangelical literature through the newly discovered art of printing, the spirit of toleration that was fostered by Humanism and that resulted in comparative immunity for quiet dissenters—these considerations make preposterous the supposition that there had been a decline in evangelical life shortly before the beginning of Luther's reformatory work. There had doubtless been a marked increase of spiritual life in the dominant church, but as the anti-Catholic evangelical movement persisted with great vigor in Bohemia, Moravia, and the Alpine valleys, so we must believe that it persisted in Germany, Switzerland, Upper Austria, and the Netherlands, although few inquisitorial processes are recorded during the years immediately preceding the Protestant Revolution.

The beginning of the sixteenth century was a time of unrest and expectancy. A spirit of revolution was abroad. Enough of evangelical light and enough of the spirit of freedom had been diffused among the masses to insure an enthusiastic reception for any movement that should give fair promise of relief from priestcraft and of social amelioration. The clergy and monks of the dominant religion were not only as a rule ignorant, immoral, and negligent, but the extortionate methods of raising money, made necessary by the luxury and extravagance of the hierarchy, aggravated the popular discontent. They were no longer looked upon as the friends and protectors of the people, but as a privileged class whose interest lay in keeping them in bondage. The burdens of serfdom had not only become intrinsically heavier, owing to peculiar circumstances, but by reason of the growing democratic spirit of the time infinitely harder to be borne. The peasant uprisings before as well as after the inauguration of the Protestant movement show how general and profound was the popular unrest.

When Luther denounced indulgences and afterward went on assailing one after another of the corruptions and errors of the Roman Church, those who had come under old-evangelical influence, whether as members of a sect or as disaffected members of the dominant church, felt that now at last the day of deliverance had come. The bold reformer, taking his stand on Scripture and insisting on bringing every doctrine and practice to the Scripture touchstone, defying emperor and pope and boldly standing forth as the champion of evangelical truth and of the rights of man, must have made a wonderful impression on those who were listening for such a voice.

Evangelical mystics, churchly and non-churchly, hailed with delight Luther's advent as a reformer, for was he not the devoted disciple of Staupitz? Had he not published with highest commendation the "Theologia Germanica," the text-book of evangelical mysticism? And had he not commended in the highest terms the works of Tauler?

Humanists too gloried in his utter repudiation of authority and in his insistence on freedom of thought. They trusted that his influence would be strongly favorable to the advancement of the new learning and would contribute much toward the dethronement of bigotry and intolerance.

He had the ear of the nobility of Germany, for they were weary of the extortions of Rome, and eager to secure a larger share of the control and emoluments of ecclesiastical property and patronage. Moreover the spirit of revolution had made itself felt in them no less than among the people.

Thus Luther's proclamation of emancipation from Rome and restoration of a scriptural religion and morality met with very general acceptance.

The Bohemian Brethren of Bohemia and Moravia, and the Vaudois of the Alpine valleys heard thereof and were glad, and both parties sought to harmonize their views with those of the great reformer. That the old-evangelicals of Germany (Waldenses, etc.) should have promptly accepted Luther as their leader, without making public proclamation of the fact that they had belonged to a proscribed party, is what might have been expected.

The old-evangelicals, no less than the mystics, the Humanists, and the discontented masses, were destined to be sorely disappointed. That such was the case was not wholly Luther's fault. Each party no doubt expected too much. The impetuous reformer did not always weigh well his words. He spoke with enthusiasm and with power in view of the actual civil and ecclesiastical condition, and naturally did not stop to consider the bearing of his words on a different state of things, or their effect on minds differently constituted from his own and with different antecedents. He early set for himself the task of leading the German people as a body out of Roman bondage into evangelical freedom. To do this he must have the hearty co-operation of the rulers and no place must be given to internal schism. When he would arouse the German people to a sense of their dignity as Christian men and of the degradation involved in bondage to Romish priestcraft, he could proclaim with enthusiasm the universal priesthood of believers and the right of every Christian man to interpret the Scriptures for himself. He could repudiate with indignation the use of force in repressing error or in constraining men to the acceptance of truth. He could assert with utmost emphasis the sufficiency and authority of Scripture as a norm of faith and practice. In his tract on vows, written at the Wartburg (1521–2), he had condemned unconditionally "whatever falls short of, is apart from, or goes beyond Christ,"[1] and had repudiated the papal proposition, "that all things have not been declared and instituted by Christ and the apostles, but that very many things were left to the church to be declared and instituted." Even after his reactionary attitude had been assumed, we find him asserting with reference to Roman Catholic usages "that whatever is without the word of God is by that very fact against God."[2]

It was utterly impossible that, circumstances being as they were, Luther should have been able to satisfy the heterogeneous aspirations of all who centered their hopes in him. It was equally inevitable that, constituted as he was, he should modify his views materially when events seemed to him to demonstrate their unsoundness or impracticability. To demand of a popular religious leader in a revolutionary time a fully matured and enunciated programme, which should provide against emergencies that no human wisdom could foresee, would be unreasonable. Emergencies of the gravest character were not slow in arising, and as a practical man he must decide, as it seemed to him, between a complete reversal of policy as regards liberty of conscience, the rights of man, and the requirement of direct scriptural authority for every doctrine and practice, and the utter wrecking of the Protestant movement.

---
[1] "*Vel citra, vel præter, vel ultra Christum incedit.*"
[2] "*Eo ipso contra Deum, quod sine verbo Dei.*"

While Luther was still at the Wartburg, biding his time for actively proceeding with his work of reformation, revolutionary procedures at Zwickau and at Wittenberg clearly revealed to him the fact that half-way measures of reform would no longer satisfy the radical evangelicals and caused him not only to antagonize the radical party, but also to abandon completely his toleration principles.

Thomas Münzer, born 1490 or later, well educated (he was a Master of Arts and seems to have studied in more than one university), a profound student like Luther of mystic literature, having filled a number of ecclesiastical positions without dishonor was called to Zwickau in 1520. He seems to have been active in reform before Luther broke with the papacy, but he lacked the stability that was requisite for effective leadership. He was on excellent terms with Luther and went to Zwickau with his full approval. Here he at once aroused the hostility of the monks and some of the clergy by the vigor with which he denounced the avarice, hypocrisy, and unevangelical features of monastic and priestly life. He still regarded Luther (July, 1520) as "the example and light of the friends of God."

Still more bitter was his controversy with Egranus, pastor of the principal church, who resented the prominence assumed by Münzer and his aggressiveness in promulgating his ultra-evangelical views. Egranus' character, unfortunately, was not altogether above reproach, and his doctrine whether from a Protestant or from a Catholic point of view was not free from suspicion. We have no reason to suppose that up to this time Münzer had enunciated any of the fanatical teachings for which he afterward became famous. His intemperate attacks on Egranus displeased Luther and turned against him many of the more moderate men of Zwickau.

We soon find at Münzer's side, in his conflict with monks and clergy and in his strivings for radical religious and social reform, a certain weaver, Nicholas Storch by name. The accounts that have come down to us of this remarkable man are defective and somewhat conflicting. He is spoken of as a former citizen of Zwickau and may have been born there, but the authorities agree in representing him as deriving his religious views from Bohemia. As a journeyman weaver he probably spent a number of years in Bohemia where he came under the influence of a party of the Bohemian Brethren. From the peculiar type of his teaching, it may be inferred that his religious associates in Bohemia belonged to that section of the Brethren that had perpetuated the chiliastic teachings of the Taborites. After the manner of the Brethren, he had acquired a remarkable familiarity with the Scriptures, so that although a layman and illiterate he could quote at pleasure from the Old and New Testaments, giving chapter and verse in a way that astonished his contemporaries, some regarding him as divinely inspired and others as in collusion with Satan. In fact he is said to have encouraged the idea that his knowledge of Scripture, no less than his own prophetic utterances, was due to direct divine inspiration. He had doubtless been quietly propagating his socialistic and millenarian views in Zwickau for some time before the advent of Münzer. That he should have come forward boldly in support of Münzer's radical views when the latter became involved in controversy was natural enough. Münzer in turn gave him high commendation, declaring that he understood the Bible better than all the priests and that he had the Spirit of God.

Encouraged by Münzer, Storch organized a separate church on the model of the Bohemian churches with which he had been connected. He is said to have secured the appointment of twelve apostles and seventy-two disciples, after the example of our Lord, and to have considered himself divinely commissioned to lead in setting up the millennial kingdom of Christ on earth.

We have no thoroughly trustworthy account of the doctrinal system that Storch sought to embody in his new organization. It seems certain that he rejected infant baptism, though there is no evidence that he rebaptized while in Zwickau, and according to one account he regarded the protest against infant baptism as a wholly subordinate matter. Luther, however, understood him to lay more stress on this point than did some of his associates. He seems to have insisted on the separation of a believing husband or wife from an unbelieving partner. The rejection of oaths, magistracy, and warfare, and insistence on community of goods among Christians, are the other charges made against him, and as these were features common to the mediæval evangelical parties and to many of the later Anabaptists, we have no reason to call in question the correctness of the representation.

Münzer felt it advisable, if not necessary, to leave Zwickau about the end of April, 1521, on account of certain riotous demonstrations in which his followers had figured a few months before. Toward the end of the year we find him at Prague, whither he had gone to secure the co-operation of the Bohemians in a great movement for the abolition of social inequalities and the setting up of a kingdom of righteousness. By this time he seems to have been thoroughly in accord with Storch as regards millenarian expectations, and to have believed himself to be the recipient of divine communications that he exalted above the written word. "The letter killeth, the Spirit maketh alive."

In Prague he appeared as a prophet and issued a proclamation in the name of God, promising a marvelous manifestation of God's power in the setting up of a new and holy church in their own land if they would hearken to the divine message, and threatening the vengeance of God through a Turkish invasion in case they refused to hearken. He returned to Germany early in 1522 and spent the year chiefly at Nordhausen. There is little record of his activity during this year; but he could not have refrained from bringing his views to bear upon as many as he could reach.

About Easter, 1523, he accepted a pastorate in Alstedt, in Thuringia, and soon afterward married an ex-nun. He was still on friendly terms with Luther, who, as we shall see hereafter, was aware of his erratic disposition, but did not yet suspect the lengths to which he was prepared to go. Here he took a leading part in preparing and introducing an elaborate church service, wholly in German, which, together with his eloquent preaching, attracted vast audiences from all the surrounding region. It is remarkable that, although Münzer had earlier expressed himself against infant baptism, he makes provision for it in his liturgy. He afterward sought to excuse the inconsistency by saying that he baptized only once in two or three months and then sought strongly to impress the responsibility of parents and sponsors for the right training of the children. The fact is, Münzer cared little for water baptism; true baptism was baptism of the Spirit.

But we must return to Zwickau, where Münzer left Storch and his conventicle about Easter, 1521. Münzer's successor, Nicolas Hausmann, was unfriendly to the movement and began at once to take steps for its suppression. Storch and his followers were arraigned before the municipal authorities, December 16, 1521, on the charge of repudiating infant baptism. All except Storch himself and one of his disciples named Forster were brought to admit that infant baptism is of use by reason of the faith of the sponsors. Storch was required to appear at a later date for a still further examination "on some erroneous Bohemian articles." He did not respond to the summons, but confident of the correctness and the importance of his views, in company with Marcus Stübner, a former student of Wittenberg, and another weaver who had been won to his views, he set out for Wittenberg with the purpose of winning the professors of the university and thus gaining a strong support for his cause. It was a bold venture; but it showed the sincerity of the faith of these men and their eagerness to propagate their views.

Nor was their faith wholly disappointed. Carlstadt, rector of the university, and like Luther a great student of the Bible, Augustine, and the German mystics, was carried away by the enthusiasm of Storch and Stübner. He attempted to carry out in practice these radical views by removing from the church all objects of idolatry and simplifying the service so as to make a complete breach with the past. The time had come, he thought, to put an end to all temporizing and to restore the church to primitive simplicity and purity. He cast aside his scholastic attire, renounced his doctor's degree, and practised in his own life the simplicity that he thought the gospel required.

Cellarius, one of the most learned Hebrew and Aramaic scholars of the time, set himself to oppose the Zwickau prophets. The result of his efforts was his own conversion to their position. Melancthon too was greatly impressed for a time, but was able at last to throw off the spell and to join with Luther in condemning the prophets. Writing to the Elector Frederick (December 17) he says: "Wonderful are the things that they assert concerning themselves: that they have been sent to teach by the clear voice of God; that they hold familiar conversations with God; that they see the future; in short, that they are prophets and apostles. I can scarcely tell how I am moved by these things. Certainly I have weighty reasons for not being willing to treat them with contempt." He feels sure that there are in them "certain spirits." Whether they be good spirits or evil can, he thinks, be determined only by Luther. A fortnight later he has ceased to be greatly disturbed by their prophetic claims, but what they have advanced against infant baptism continues to trouble him. He finds no scriptural warrant for the practice and he is at a loss to know how to justify its retention.

Luther's letter of January 13 doubtless had the effect of restoring his equanimity. He assures Philip that he has more intellect and more learning than himself, and insists that he should have tried the spirits. These prophets had little to commend them and much to awaken mistrust. If they have the special divine commission they claim they should be in a position to furnish some sign by which they could be unmistakably recognized as prophets of God. As it regards the question of infant baptism, his arguments may have satisfied Melancthon, anxious to be reassured, but few would now consider them other than sophistical. Referring to the scripture on which the prophets based their contention: "Whosoever shall have believed and shall have been baptized shall be saved," he asks, "How will they prove that they (infants) do not believe? Because, forsooth, they do not speak and show forth faith? Very well. By this reasoning, how many hours will we ourselves not be Christians, while we sleep and do other things? Cannot God therefore in the same manner throughout the whole period of infancy, as in a continuous sleep, preserve faith in them?"

No doubt this argument first came to Luther as an *argumentum ad hominem*. These prophets were making great claims for themselves without giving proof. Why not throw on them the responsibility of proving that unconscious infants do not exercise saving faith? He proceeds to justify infant baptism on the ground of the united testimony of the church, which it is most impious to reject. Forgetting for the time being the strong statements against non-scriptural ceremonies and institutions which, by the way, he would still employ when it served his turn to do so, he formulates a new canon in the following words: "What therefore is not against Scripture is for Scripture, and Scripture for it."[1]

The disturbances at Wittenberg occasioned by the visit of the prophets, and especially Carlstadt's somewhat iconoclastic procedures, determined Luther to leave his retreat at the Wartburg, even without the full approval of the Elector. At this period he was extremely sensitive with reference to anything that might cause scandal. Any further schism than that which he had accomplished he deprecated, and he thought it highly undesirable to offend the weak by violating ecclesiastical fasts or by making radical changes in the church services. He returned to Wittenberg early in March, 1522, and was soon master of the situation. He showed little disposition to give a fair and patient hearing to such of the prophets as sought to convert him, ridiculing their extravagant claims and demanding miraculous attestations of their divine commission.

Carlstadt was completely humiliated and ultimately felt obliged to withdraw from Wittenberg. Although he denied the scriptural authorization of infant baptism, he does not seem to have gone the length of introducing believers' baptism. He took strong ground against Luther's

[1] "*Quod ergo non est contra Scripturam, pro Scriptura est, et Scriptura pro eo.*"

doctrine of the real presence and from 1530 onward allied himself with the Zwinglians. His iconoclastic precedures at Orlamünde, whither he had gone after leaving Wittenberg in 1523, resulted in his expulsion and banishment, for which Luther was largely responsible. For years he was in circumstances of the utmost hardship. He seems soon to have escaped from the prophetic infatuation and endeavored without success to restrain the extravagances of Münzer. Some years later (1534) he secured a professorship in the University of Basel, which he held until his death in 1541.

Cellarius also while persisting in denying the propriety of infant baptism and in advocating millenarian views, made little effort to put his views in practice. He also found refuge with the Swiss, gained the friendship of Œcolampadius and Capito, profoundly impressed both with his ability and sincerity, and almost won them, especially the latter, to his views. Like Carlstadt he finally secured (1546) a professorship at Basel, which he long filled in a highly honorable way.

There is no evidence that Storch returned to Zwickau after the interview of the prophets with Luther. His movements for some time are very obscure. As regards the radical movement at Zwickau, it seems to have rapidly declined after the removal of Storch and Münzer. Luther visited the city during the latter part of April and delivered to immense audiences (variously estimated at from fourteen thousand to twenty-five thousand persons) four powerful discourses against religious radicalism and fanaticism.

Storch seems to have remained in Thuringia until the autumn, for Luther writes in September of an interview with him as if it had been recent. According to Luther, he " dressed and wore his beard like a lance-knight, and was in all points in contradiction with Marcus and

Thomas "(Stübner and Münzer). We infer from another notice of Luther's, that from his point of view Storch was at this time far more pronounced in his radicalism than Münzer. He seems to have been for some time at Orlamünde after Carlstadt's settlement there in 1523, and doubtless continued to sustain intimate relations with Münzer as well.

In 1524 we find him at Hof in the employ of the burgomaster Simon Klinger, who was converted to his views and became the chief supporter of a radical movement like that at Zwickau. Here also he set forth claims to special divine illumination. The medium of the divine communications was the angel Gabriel. Even those who distrusted his claim to be a prophet of God were willing to grant that there was something supernatural in connection with his utterances, and he was accused of practising the "black art" in league with Satan. Here also he is said to have appointed twelve apostles to go forth and proclaim the setting up of the kingdom of Christ. After raising considerable commotion he felt obliged to flee from the city. After a somewhat similar experience at Glogau in Silesia, he seems to have returned to Saxony and to have spent the early months of 1525 in league with Münzer, traveling from place to place in the interest of the politico-religious revolution that culminated in the Peasants' War. Whether he was with the peasants during the struggle is uncertain. He is said to have prophesied that within four years he himself, as being divinely commissioned thereunto, would assume dominion and that the saints should everywhere reign in righteousness. According to Widemann, he died in a hospital at Munich in 1525.

Literature: On Münzer: Merx, Strobel, Seidemann, Streif, Arnold (Kirch-u.-Ketzerhistorie), Hast (Wiedertäufer), Erbkam (Prot. Sekten), Förstemann (Neues Urkundenbuch), and works on the Peasants' War (as in chap. VII). On Storch: Bachmann, Erbkam, Hast. Meyer (Zeitschr. f. Kirchegesch., Bd. XVI., p. 117, *seq.*). On Carlstadt: Jäger, Füsslin, Erbkam. The correspondence of the leading reformers (Luther, Melancthon, etc.), contains many important notices.

CHAPTER VII

THOMAS MÜNZER AND THE PEASANTS' WAR.

WE left Münzer about the middle of 1523 in Alstedt, with a new church service prepared and adopted, highly popular, and happily married withal. From this time onward his preaching grew more and more recklessly denunciatory. The lives of priests, monks, and nuns were doubtless open to criticism. He indulged in the most intemperate vilification of these classes, who were he thought, living in idleness, luxury, and vice at the expense of the workingman. He did not hesitate to advise the withholding of all tithes and rents. Under the impulse of his denunciations a nunnery was plundered, holy objects were profaned, and the inmates maltreated. The effort to punish the guilty parties led to riotous procedures which had Münzer's approval. He did not spare such high civil dignitaries as Count Ernst of Mansfeld and Duke George of Saxony, who attempted to meddle with Alstedt affairs. The Lutheran preachers also came in for a share of his denunciation so far as they fell short of the standard he had set up. Obedience to civil rulers was obligatory on Christians only so far as they ruled righteously. "God gave lords and princes in his anger and he will do away with them in his sore displeasure." The very title "prince" displeased him. It ought to be reserved for Christ, to whom alone it rightly belongs. "If princes act not only against the gospel, but also against the natural rights of the people, they should be strangled like dogs." According to his view, as set forth just before his execution, Christians should all be equal. His aim was to bring about a religio-social state in which private property should be utterly abolished, and in which each individual should have enough and no more than enough of the common product and in which each should contribute according to his ability to the work of production. He was a thorough-going socialist of the modern type; but his socialism was grounded not merely on natural right—it was the requirement of the gospel. He believed, moreover, that he was especially commissioned by God to proclaim the inauguration of this new social state, and to use every means for arousing the people to a sense of their rights. He predicted that in a short time the power would be in the hands of the people. "Whoever will be a stone of the new church, let him risk his neck, otherwise he will be rejected by the builders." "If you have not the pure fear of God," he said in a sermon, "you can stand your ground in no conflict. If you have it, you will stand victorious before all tyrants, and they shall be so miserably put to shame, that they will have nothing to say."

Münzer's influence was by no means confined to Alstedt. Eisleben, Mansfeld, Sangerhausen, Frankenhausen, Querfurt, Halle, Aschersleben, Nordhausen, Mühlhausen, and some of the Swiss communities, are known to have been more or less agitated by his teachings. He encouraged the people to form secret societies for the propagation of these views and to make ready for action when the time should come. More than thirty of these societies had been formed by the middle of July, 1524.[1]

The violent controversy into which he fell with Luther during his stay at Alstedt is of subordinate importance in the present discussion. He attacked in the most intem-

---

[1] See Münzer's letter to his Sangerhausen co-religionists, in "Förstemann," p. 237, seq.

perate way Luther's teachings on faith, Scripture, and baptism. Luther was not to be outdone when it came to the matter of invective and he did his full share of the hard hitting.

Luther's influence with Duke John and the Elector of Saxony proved sufficient to secure their active intervention. Although Münzer had a large majority of the people of Alstedt on his side, including a number of the leading officials, he was compelled to quit the city and seek another basis of operations. This occurred early in August, 1524. He betook himself at once to Mühlhausen, where he already had many who favored him, and where the eloquent and enthusiastic Heinrich Pfeiffer had already for some months been conducting a religio-socialistic agitation in Münzer's own spirit. Pfeiffer had come to Mühlhausen as a preacher about the beginning of 1523 and by his vigorous denunciations of the clergy and religious orders and the zealous promulgation of his own scheme of reform had set the city in a commotion. The monks and nuns (he was an ex-monk himself) he declared to be "servants of the devil," and their possessions "the sweat and blood of the poor."

A strong revolutionary party was soon organized, which issued a programme of reform containing fifty-three articles, only two of which are distinctively religious. Of these latter the first demanded that the parish churches and chapels be provided with evangelical preachers; the second, that there should be no interference with the preaching of the gospel. The rest of the articles were of politico-social bearing, and aimed at the abolition of abuses and the securing of a larger measure of civil liberty. The refusal of the council to accede to these demands was followed by a riot of which the sacking of the monasteries constituted the chief feature. The revolutionary party succeeded in compelling the council to accept the articles, and both parties undertook to live thenceforth in peace and unity and not to seek the intervention of emperor, kings, princes, or any other outside parties.

A reaction soon set in and the council, supported by the conservative elements, was able to banish Pfeiffer and his chief co-laborer, August 24, 1523. In December Pfeiffer was able to resume his work in Mühlhausen. During his absence, whether through personal intercourse with Münzer or in some indirect way, he had become imbued with the whole circle of Münzer's ideas. Like Münzer he now magnified the Jewish law and insisted on its being put into practice. The example of Old Testament heroes in taking up the sword against the enemies of God and meting out summary punishment to those who refused to submit to the setting up of a righteous government, he considered worthy of imitation. There was nothing good in the clergy from sole to scalp; they were worthy only of being strangled as perverters of the people. Uproar soon followed, churches were plundered, and images, relics, and other instruments of superstition destroyed.

Münzer's arrival about the middle of August could have had no other effect than to intensify the revolutionary spirit. With two such arch-agitators as Münzer and Pfeiffer in one small city a crisis must soon be reached. The flight of about ten members of the council and of the two burgomasters left that body in a crippled condition. So timid had the remaining members become, that they thought it prudent to ask the citizens for advice. Pfeiffer and Münzer were in a position to speak for the majority. Under their direction eleven articles were formulated for the guidance of the council. These provided for the constitution of a new council, that should rule according to the Bible and God's word and execute justice and judgment by the same standard. The council should be chosen in perpetuity and death should be the penalty of failure to do justice or to avoid injustice. No one should be compelled to accept a position on the council, and members of the council should be suitably supported. In case the present council should refuse to accept the proposed arrangement their acts of unrighteousness for the past twenty years would be published and the citizens would have no further communion with them. It is emphatically insisted that all works and transactions are to be carried out according to the commands of God and of righteousness, without any reference to men. Evidently a theocracy of a very rigid type was in the minds of Münzer and Pfeiffer. Supported by the neighboring villagers, who had not yet been won to the revolutionary cause, the council was able to resist the demands of the citizens and to expel Pfeiffer and Münzer from the city (September 27). They now directed their steps to Nürnberg.

Their reputation as dangerous religio-socialistic agitators followed them and after a brief sojourn they were obliged to leave the city. Pfeiffer returned to Mühlhausen in December, and with the support of the villagers, now zealous for social reform, was able to withstand his enemies in the council. It is probable that he spent the time between his expulsion from Nürnberg and his return to Mühlhausen in winning the allegiance of the villagers. Before leaving Mühlhausen Münzer had secretly printed a strong polemic against Luther and other opponents of the gospel. As Luther had dedicated his writing against Münzer to the "princes of Saxony," this rejoinder was dedicated to "the most august first-born Prince and Almighty Lord Jesus Christ, the gracious King of all kings, and to his afflicted bride, poor Christendom." In this document he set forth his social-theocratic system without reserve. He maintained, "that a community as a whole has the power of the sword, and that the princes are not lords but servants of the sword; therefore also they have unrighteously appropriated the fish in the water, the birds in the air, the products of the soil." He says in conclusion: "The people shall become free, and God will be the only Lord over them." According to his own account, he could easily have made trouble in Nürnberg, but his principal object had been not to arouse the people but to publish the writing referred to. He spent the next few months in Swabia, Switzerland, and Waldshut. Preparations for a peasant uprising in Swabia were already far advanced. Münzer undoubtedly gave all the encouragement he could to the aspirations of the people for political freedom and for the redress of social grievances. He had several interviews with Œcolampadius at Basel, who treated him more hospitably than his friends thought prudent. At Waldshut he was undoubtedly in conference with Balthasar Hubmaier, at this time the highly popular chief pastor of the city, who also was something of a religious democrat, but whose ideas of human rights were free from chiliastic fanaticism.

Münzer returned to Mühlhausen about January, 1525, and was soon made pastor of the principal church. Along with Pfeiffer he became the chief director of ecclesiastical affairs. Already before Münzer's return the churches and monasteries had been stripped of all idolatrous objects and the inmates of the latter with few exceptions had been driven away. Münzer was now in a position to put his theories in practice as never before. So great was the preponderance of influence on the radical side that the old council was compelled to allow the appointment of a new one in hearty sympathy with Pfeiffer and Münzer. The churches and their services were reduced to plainness and simplicity; the valuable articles from the churches and monasteries were sold and the proceeds applied to public uses, while the crucifixes, pictures of saints, relics, etc., were destroyed.

It is probable that during this period Pfeiffer was even more aggressive than Münzer himself. The peasants' revolt, that had for months been moving northward, after its early successes in Swabia and Alsace, reached the neighborhood of Mühlhausen early in May, 1525. Preparations had been made to join in the movement when the right time should come. Münzer had long preached revolution and had prophesied the success of the cause of the workingman. He had led the people to believe that supernatural aid would be vouchsafed to them in this righteous cause, as in the Old Testament times. He adopted as his signature "Thomas Münzer with the hammer," and "Thomas Münzer with the sword of Gideon." He had come to believe that it was the will of God that all the unrighteous should be destroyed by the righteous from the face of the earth, as the Canaanites were by divine direction destroyed by the children of Israel. "On! on! on!" he shrieked; "never mind the wail of the godless. Though they beg in friendly tones, though they cry and whimper like children, pity not. On! on! while the fire is hot. Down with the castles and their inmates. God is with you. On! on!" By this time the nobility had been able to rally their forces and to secure concerted action. Münzer and his hosts were unused to warfare and poorly equipped. They were trusting more to supernatural aid than to the use of the arts of war. They were miserably overwhelmed by their enemies. About one hundred thousand peasants are supposed to have been massacred in this misguided struggle for civil and religious liberty. Münzer was arrested and shortly afterward put to death.

What is the significance of the events that have been thus outlined?

1. We must distinguish between the aspirations and strivings of the peasants in Swabia and Alsace, and the fanatical procedures of Münzer and Pfeiffer. The cause of the peasants was a righteous cause. If ever an oppressed class was justified in rebelling against constituted authority, the peasants of Germany were surely justified in organizing themselves as they did and in venturing their lives for civil and religious liberty. The oppression under which they groaned had become intolerable, and the enthusiastic utterances of Luther and others had given them a clear consciousness of the rights of man and of the unjustifiableness of tyranny. This is not the place to give in detail the grievances of the peasants. The twelve articles in which they set forth their demands, as has been justly said, are worthy of a Solon. There is not one trace of fanaticism in the document. It is in the spirit of the best mediæval evangelical thought. It is in accord with the best that was contained in Luther's earlier utterances. It is in accord with Baptist views of civil and religious liberty. It is in accord with modern democratic principles. There is no demand for community of goods. There is no suggestion of theocratic government. The people claim the right to appoint and remove pastors and to insist upon the preaching of the gospel in its purity and simplicity. They demand the abolition of oppressive laws as regards wages, rents, tithes, the "heriot" or death gift, hunting, fishing, the use of the forests for fuel and timber, etc. The demands are all most reasonable and Christian. Moreover the authors of the demands express a willingness to abandon any one of them that shall be shown to be out of accord with Scripture. So thoroughly sound are these articles that they have by some been attributed

to Hubmaier, who probably came nearer to the modern Baptist position than any man in the sixteenth century. There is nothing in them that he might not have written, and as he was certainly in thorough sympathy with the just demands of the peasantry, it is not improbable that he had at least something to do with the drafting of the document.

2. The influence of Storch, Münzer, and Pfeiffer on the peasant movement was evil and only evil. They were in no sense the originators of it, and so far as their influence went it was in the direction of intensifying hatred and preparing the people for deeds of cruel vengeance in the name of religion. The most revolting scenes of Old Testament history were held up to the people as models of what God would approve in the setting up of a modern Christian theocracy. The corrupting elements in the teachings of this party are easy to discern. Chiliasm in time of revolution is almost sure to lead certain classes of minds into fanaticism. The man who so interprets the prophetical Scriptures as to be perfectly sure that their fulfillment is to take place at a particular time and in a particular way, and who is filled with earnest desire for social and religious reform, very easily passes over into a state in which he believes himself to be the recipient of revelations as to the practical carrying out of the Divine purposes. The more one indulges in such prophetic exercises the more fanatical is he likely to become, especially if he finds a large number of people with like aspirations who are ready to receive his utterances as the revelation of God. Chiliasm of this fanatical type is likely to occur at any time when great revolutions are in progress; but in the case before us it is possible to find a historical connection with the past. Through Nicholas Storch the chiliasm of Münzer is historically connected with that of the Taborites of the preceding century, and

this in turn doubtless had its antecedents in the earlier time, as in the chiliastic teaching of Militz of Kremsier and Matthias of Janow, in the fourteenth century, and in that of the heretical Franciscans of the thirteenth. Chiliasm is in its very nature fanatical, and if in particular individuals or in particular times we find it existing in comparatively quiet and innocent form, this in no way invalidates the principle here set forth.

So also we see in Münzer's career a natural outcome of mysticism. The tendency of mysticism is toward the depreciation of the Scriptures and the exaltation of the authority of inner illumination. Sometimes it degenerates into pantheistic self-identification of the subject with deity and the complete obliteration of moral distinctions; at other times it generates the delusion that its subject is possessed of prophetic powers, is the organ of divine revelation. Assuming this latter form in Storch and Münzer, it produced, in connection with chiliasm, the disastrous results that have been noted.

3. As has been made evident in the above discussion, neither Münzer nor Pfeiffer was a Baptist, or even an Anabaptist. Their denial of infant baptism as a scriptural ordinance was a wholly subordinate element in their teaching, and they continued to the last to practise it. There is no evidence, so far as we are aware, that either of those men either submitted to rebaptism or administered it to others. The identification of these fanatics with the Anabaptist cause in the minds of the leaders of the dominant parties of the time, was most damaging to the biblical Anti-pedobaptists, and caused them to be looked upon as capable of all the atrocities of the fanatics. The Storch-Münzer movement had its natural development in the Münster Kingdom of 1535, and not in the evangelical movement that beginning at Zürich spread rapidly throughout Europe and that before the outbreak

of the Peasants' War as well as afterward repudiated the sanguinary utterances of Münzer.

4. A most unfortunate result of the fanatical strivings of Storch and Münzer was the complete reversal of Luther's programme of reform, and through Luther of that of the leading Protestant parties. Luther would no doubt have strenuously opposed a purely Baptist attempt to restore primitive Christianity; but the effect of the movement we have considered was to embitter him against any type of reform that aimed to set up churches of the regenerate and that involved rupture with the State Church. From his point of view, the impracticability of the ideas of freedom of conscience and freedom of speech set forth with enthusiasm in his earlier writings had been fully demonstrated. He counseled the most atrocious treatment of those who rebelled against constituted authority and could see nothing but disaster in any dissenting movement. Protestants and Catholics vied with each other in their efforts to destroy from the face of the earth those who were stigmatized as Anabaptists and were supposed to be capable, whatever might be their professions and however quiet and holy might be their lives, of committing any sort of atrocity; and whose presence in a State was looked upon as a menace to constituted authority. This feeling was intensified by the horrors of Münster (1535), ten years after the Peasants' War.

Literature: Works on the Peasants' War by Stern, Seidemann, Fries, Falkenheiner, Schreiber, Zimmermann, Jörg; works on Münzer, as in chap. V.; histories of Germany in the Reformation time by Ranke and Janssen.

CHAPTER VIII

RADICAL AGITATION IN ZÜRICH AND IN WALDSHUT
(1523-24)

A RADICAL movement of a widely different type we meet in Switzerland from 1523 onward. A spirit of independence had been developed in Switzerland long before the outbreak of the Protestant Revolution. In place of the feudal system, with its serfs and petty lords, and the somewhat ill-defined subordination of the nobility to the imperial government, which in Germany obstructed efforts at reform, a republican form of government prevailed with entire independence of all foreign authority. The extraordinary valor that had won their independence and enabled them to maintain it, caused the Swiss to be in great demand as mercenary soldiers. The pope, the emperor, and the king of France were the chief employers of Swiss troops. The mercenary system was not morally elevating either to the soldiers themselves or to the influential citizens who were pensioned by the foreign powers in consideration of their good offices. But it undoubtedly had the effect of destroying superstitious veneration for the church whose carnal battles they were hired to wage and of fostering freedom of thought. When in 1518 the pope asked for twelve thousand Swiss troops to fight against the Turks, they somewhat reluctantly promised ten thousand, adding that if he liked he might take in addition the two thousand priests. The new learning had made its influence profoundly felt, especially in connection with the University of Basel. The mass of the people almost from the beginning of the Protestant movement showed a remarkable readiness to abandon the papal cause. There was no violent wrench in passing from nominal adherence to the papacy to a far more radical type of Protestantism than Luther ever thought it wise to introduce in Germany.

Zwingli, the chief leader of the politico-ecclesiastical reforming movement in Switzerland, was a thoroughgoing Humanist, free from superstition and undue enthusiasm, cool-headed, clear-headed, a good scholar, a good theologian, a skillful debater, an able administrative head. He aimed at political reform almost as much as at religious, and the practical statesman was in him quite as prominent as the theologian and the religious leader. While still living an immoral life he was led by his studies and by surrounding influences to reject the Roman Catholic system and to seek to base his teachings on the New Testament, which he studied with enthusiasm in Greek. By no sudden conversion, but by a quiet process, the truth so mastered him as to make him a comparatively worthy religious leader.

From 1518 he labored so successfully in Zürich that by the beginning of 1523 the people were prepared to adopt radically anti-Catholic measures. This took place formally after a disputation called by the council. On this occasion Zwingli set forth and defended his views in sixty-seven articles, which the representative of the bishop of Constance was unable to refute. These articles were published with full explanatory notes shortly afterward and may be regarded as the Swiss programme of reform. In the interpretation of the eighteenth article he calls attention to the fact that in the early church the baptism of infants was not so common as at present, catechetical instruction having preceded and baptism having been administered only after the catechumens had firm faith in the heart and had confessed with the mouth.

He persistently denied that infants are saved by baptism or dying without baptism are lost. Still later he confessed: "The error also misled me some years ago, so that I thought it would be much more suitable to baptize children after they had arrived at a good age." He made the impression on those who afterward came out in open hostility to infant baptism, that he favored the abolition of this practice, which he acknowledged to have no scriptural authorization.

Various practical reforms followed the first disputation. The sentiment against idolatrous objects in the churches and against the mass was intensified by the publication of a treatise on images and pictures by Ludwig Hetzer (a learned Hebraist, afterward associated with the Anabaptists) and a treatise on the mass by Zwingli. To avoid lawless iconoclasm the council arranged a second disputation for October, 1523, in which Zwingli, Leo Judae, Hetzer, Conrad Grebel, and Balthasar Hubmaier (the last two to become eminent Anabaptist leaders), took part. The sentiment was unanimous in favor of thorough-going reform, and provision was made for preparing the people, especially in the rural districts, for the abolition of images and the mass. The people of Zürich grew so impatient that the council thought it advisable to order the destruction of images in June, 1524. It was not until April, 1525, that the mass was supplanted by a simple German service with communion under both kinds.

Similar reforms, largely under Zwingli's counsel, were introduced in Basel, Berne, St. Gall, and other Swiss centers. At Basel, Œcolampadius, one of the most learned and liberal of the reformers, was at the head of the evangelical movement. Wilhelm Reublin, afterward a zealous Anabaptist leader, had preached to large audiences in Basel until 1522, when he was expelled for abetting the violation of an ecclesiastical fast on Palm Sunday. As preacher at St. Alban's Church he is said by a contemporary to have "interpreted the Scriptures so well that the like had never been heard before." At Berne John Haller and Berthold Haller were the evangelical leaders. They were less able than Zwingli and Œcolampadius, but were enlightened and tolerant and conducted the work with discretion and success. The evangelical leader at St. Gall was also the leading citizen, Dr. Joachim von Watt (Vadian), a learned layman of excellent spirit.

Outside of Switzerland, but in close affiliation with the Swiss evangelical movement, reform was carried forward in Strasburg under the leadership of Capito and Bucer, and at Waldshut, in the Austrian Breisgau, Dr. Balthasar Hubmaier labored with zeal and success. Of the Strasburg reformers, Capito was like-minded with Œcolampadius, liberal, tolerant, and hospitable toward the persecuted and oppressed; while Bucer was an ecclesiastical opportunist, ready to compromise or persecute as policy seemed to dictate.

The reforming labors of Hubmaier at Waldshut are of special interest to us by reason of his remarkable abilities as scholar, thinker, pulpit orator, disputant, and organizer and leader of men; and especially by reason of the fact that he devoted all these powers and life itself to the restoration of primitive Christianity. Born near Augsburg, about 1480, he was educated in the University of Freiburg (1503 onward), where he enjoyed the friendship of the famous dialectician, Dr. John Eck, from whom he received the most distinguished praise. He is said to have become second only to Eck in dialectics. Having already attained to great distinction in the university he received his bachelor's degree in 1512, and was probably ordained to the priesthood soon after his graduation.

Later, in the same year, he followed Eck to Ingolstadt, where the latter had accepted a professorship.

Here Hubmaier was made pastor of a church belonging to the university and instructor in the theological faculty. Through Eck's influence the doctor's degree was conferred upon him by the university shortly after his arrival. His extraordinary eloquence caused him to be sought for as preacher by the cathedral church of Regensburg. This position he accepted much to the regret of his Ingolstadt admirers. In the spirit of his time he joined in a movement for the expulsion of the Jews already in progress, and assumed the care of the chapel erected on the site of a destroyed synagogue. Pretended miracles in connection with a shrine in this chapel attracted throngs of pilgrims. He encouraged the superstition for a time, but afterward recognized the evil involved and sought to abate it. His efforts to curb certain superstitious practices somewhat strained his relations with the Regensburg authorities and he was glad in 1521 to accept a pastorate in Waldshut. Here, in his "little nest," he at once became exceedingly popular, being still scrupulously exact in conforming to the church ceremonial. He now began to study and expound the Pauline epistles and by 1522 he was reading Luther's writings with the utmost interest.

In June, 1522, he visited Basel where he met a number of leading Humanists, including Busch, Glarean, and Erasmus. He noticed that at Basel the monasteries were being emptied and their inmates were marrying. In November he returned to Regensburg at the urgent entreaty of his friends and was well received by clergy and people. By this time he had adopted evangelical views, and he soon began to realize that he was out of sympathy with his surroundings.

After a few months' stay he returned to Waldshut,

where the principal pastorate had been kept open for him. In May, 1523, he had a conference on infant baptism with Zwingli who "conceded to him that children should not be baptized before they are instructed in the faith." He also visited Vadian at St. Gall, with whom he entered into the most cordial relations. Returning to Waldshut he at once began to agitate for the abolition of the mass and of the idolatrous use of images. On the basis of Deut. 27, " Cursed be the man who makes a graven or molten image," he insisted upon the removal of all idolatrous objects from the churches. The mass he declared to be no sacrifice but the proclamation of the last will of Christ in which his bitter suffering and self-sacrifice are commemorated. It should be celebrated without unscriptural ceremonies in the vernacular and under both kinds.[1] These opinions he claimed to have drawn directly from Scripture. If he errs he is open to correction, but a heretic he will not be.

The Waldshut clergy and aristocracy were unsympathetic and his proposed innovations were promptly reported to the Austrian authorities who soon began proceedings for the expulsion of Hubmaier. The mayor and council repudiated the charge that Hubmaier had introduced false teaching or had been guilty of any act of disloyalty to the Austrian government, and refused either to expel or deliver up their favorite preacher. The people could scarcely be restrained from doing violence to the imperial commissaries who had come to demand his removal.

Having been given a fortnight for the consideration of the matter, the council sent an apology to the Austrian authorities, probably drafted by Hubmaier himself. It was claimed that Hubmaier had repeatedly preached of the obedience due to the civil magistracy; that he had

---

[1] *I. e.*, both bread and wine should be distributed to communicants.

only preached the pure gospel and that his expulsion could not be accomplished without uproar and division. They begged that the doctor be left in his place and that in any case he be not removed without a thorough investigation of his doctrine before the proper authorities. By this time Hubmaier's position in Waldshut was almost as strong as that of Zwingli in Zürich. The council refused to send him to Constance for examination before the bishop, and the people were ready to defend him with their lives.

As a basis for the reformation of the Waldshut churches Hubmaier set forth (June, 1524) eighteen propositions for the consideration of the clergy. In these he repudiates the whole ceremonial system of the Roman Church, including the use of candles, palms, and consecrated water, fasts, monastic vows, masses for the dead, the veneration of images, pilgrimages, Latin services, canonical hours for prayer, etc. All doctrines that God himself has not planted must be rooted out. Only he is a priest who proclaims the word of God and only true priests should be supported by the people. Purgatory has been fabricated by those whose God is their belly. Who seeks it seeks the grave of Moses: he will never find it. He rejects the celibacy of the clergy and denounces idlers of all kinds, whoever they may be.

The bishop of Constance and the Austrian authorities continued to insist on the suppression of "Lutheran" heresy, but so strongly had Hubmaier become entrenched in the affections of the people that in April he declined a recall to his old charge in Regensburg. He informed his Regensburg friends of the great change he had experienced in the past two years. He now curses all teaching and preaching that he formerly did in Regensburg and elsewhere, so far as it had not its foundation in the word of God. He warns them not to be misled into trusting in the authority of councils. A single pious Christian woman knows more of the divine word than such redcappers (cardinals) have any conception of.

Harassed by the charges that the bishop of Constance continued to make and the necessity put upon the Waldshut authorities to repel them, and encouraged by reformatory measures that were being introduced at Zürich, in June, 1524, Hubmaier proposed to the assembled congregation the introduction of the desired changes in worship. Some of his best friends strongly objected to this course as inopportune and as sure to involve the city in the gravest difficulties. He promptly resigned his office, but the popular demand for his re-election was irresistible. Many believed that he had been especially ordained and sent of God to reform Waldshut and were ready to defend him with property and blood. The Catholic priests had come into such disfavor that they found it advisable to leave the city. The images were destroyed, a simple German service was introduced in place of the mass, and the Supper was celebrated under both kinds as a simple memorial act. He discouraged abstinence from flesh on Fridays and Saturdays and soon afterward showed his disapproval of sacerdotal celibacy by marrying Elsbeth Hugeline, who proved worthy of his love and who died a martyr's death.

As might have been expected, the Austrian authorities now became still more peremptory in their demand for the extradition of Hubmaier and the restoration of the old *régime*. They hesitated for a long time to resort to extreme measures lest the Swiss should take the part of Waldshut and lest other expensive and troublesome complications should arise. The Waldshut officials insisted that Hubmaier was preaching the pure gospel and nothing but the gospel and could be induced by no threats to deliver him up for punishment. The Austrian authorities resolved not only to get possession of the person of Hubmaier, but also to put him out of the way of causing further trouble. At last, when resistance was no longer possible and Hubmaier was in imminent danger of being seized, he escaped by night to Schaffhausen, September 1, 1524.

The Schaffhausen authorities, though well disposed, were put thereby in a most trying position. The Austrian authorities were strenuous in their demands for his extradition, and most of the cantons of the Swiss confederacy had expressed the opinion that, according to the treaties then in force between the confederacy and Austria, extradition could not properly be refused. Hubmaier knew full well that extradition meant certain death, and he plead with the Schaffhausen authorities for protection for at least a short time, until the question at issue between the Austrian authorities and Waldshut should have been settled.

It was during his sojourn in Schaffhausen that he wrote the most remarkable plea for liberty of conscience that the sixteenth century produced, " On Heretics and their Burners." Those are heretics who perversely strive against Scripture. The devil was the first of these when he said to Eve, " Thou shalt not surely die." Those also are heretics who obscure Scripture and interpret it otherwise than the Spirit requires and seek to compel others to believe such nonsense. Heretics are to be overcome by means of holy instruction, given not contentiously but gently, although it is true Scripture contains indignation also. But this indignation of Scripture is truly a spiritual fire. If heretics will not yield to words of power or evangelical considerations they are to be left to their own condemnation. To God alone judgment belongs and he will either convert them or harden them so that the blind leading the blind both the perverted and the perverters shall be led to ruin. So Christ intended when he said, "Let both grow together until the harvest." This does not mean, however, that we should be idle, but rather that we should strive against godless doctrines instead of seeking to destroy those who teach them. Unfaithful bishops are the cause of the incoming of false teaching, for while men slept the enemy came and sowed the tares. He who watches before the bridegroom's door neither slumbers nor sits in the seat of the scornful. The greatest arch-heretics are those who against Christ's teaching and example condemn heretics to the flames and before the time of the harvest destroy wheat and tares together; for Christ did not come to butcher, to murder, to burn, but that men might have life and that more abundantly. So long as a man lives we should pray and hope for his repentance. A Turk or a heretic is to be overcome not with sword or fire but by patience and weeping. We are therefore to wait patiently for the judgment of God. As thus violating the spirit and the teaching of the gospel, the preaching orders, who were the leaders of the Inquisition, are declared to be the producers of arch-heretics. If such knew of what spirit they should be they would not so shamelessly pervert God's word nor so often cry out, "To the fire!" It is no excuse that they deliver their victims for execution to the godless secular power. Nay, in this they sin still more grievously. Every Christian has a sword against the godless, that is, the word of God; but not a sword against evil-doers. The civil power has a right to execute evil-doers, but the godless God alone should punish; for such can injure neither body nor soul, but are useful rather; for God knows how to bring good out of evil. For true faith thrives by conflict; the more it is opposed the greater it becomes. To burn heretics is to confess Christ in appearance but to deny him in reality, and is more abominable than Joachim king of Judah. If it be a great abomination to destroy those who are really heretics how much greater to burn to ashes the true preachers of God's word before they have been confuted with the truth. Those who would attempt to improve upon God's commands are like Uzzah and Peter. When Jehoiakim destroyed the book of Jeremiah, Baruch wrote a better one. He concludes, " Now it is manifest to every one, even to the blind, that the law for the burning of heretics was devised by the devil. The truth is immortal."

His presence in Schaffhausen became more and more embarrassing to the authorities and insecure for himself. Besides, circumstances had somewhat changed at Waldshut. His withdrawal had in no way appeased the Austrian authorities, who despite the earnest pleadings of the people for mercy, their protestations of loyalty, and their expressed willingness to make any reasonable reparation for their past offenses, continued to threaten them with the direst punishment and refused to accept any terms short of absolute surrender.

It is noteworthy that even with the terrible wrath of Austria before their eyes the Waldshut authorities were loyal to Hubmaier and could not be led to admit that he had preached anything but the pure gospel. Their insistence on the purity of Hubmaier's teaching constituted in fact the gravamen of their offense. Waldshut had become thoroughly evangelical, and it would not do for the Catholic Austrian government to give any quarter to heresy. Other towns and provinces would soon follow this evil example if Waldshut should go unpunished. Yet grave difficulties stood in the way of the immediate execution of the vengeance meditated and threatened. The growth of evangelical sentiment in the neighboring Swiss cantons and the peasant uprising in Swabia and upper Alsace made it probable that any attempt to punish Waldshut would be resented and strongly resisted. The intercession of the Zürich Council, while it no doubt had the effect of causing the Austrian authorities to hesitate to execute the threatened punishment, confirmed the suspicion of heresy.

Preparations had been made for the assembling of an army of twelve thousand troops for the occupation of Waldshut about October 15. The timely intervention of Zürich, which decided to send a small contingent of well-armed troops to the succor of Waldshut, caused a postponement of the invasion. The Swiss succor was not confined to the troops sent and paid by the Zürich authorities, but a number of earnest Christians seeing their Waldshut brethren in extreme danger, without commission and without pay, came to the rescue. The Zürich authorities wavered after permitting the troops to depart and sent couriers to recall them. They answered that they would die sooner than return. The succor reluctantly and waveringly afforded by Zürich had a far greater moral influence on the Austrian authorities than it was really entitled to exert; for it was reported to them that the Zürich Council had promised six thousand troops, and six thousand Swiss troops were by no means to be despised. Basel and Schaffhausen also had shown a disposition to intervene in case the Austrian authorities should proceed to extremities.

Hubmaier returned to Waldshut, apparently with the approval of the authorities, on October 28, and was received with the beating of drums and the blowing of fifes and horns "just as if he had been an emperor." On November 2 representatives of Zürich, Schaffhausen, and Basel, through special invitation of the Austrian authorities, appeared with representatives of Waldshut at a diet of the regency, to seek for an amicable adjustment of the Waldshut difficulties. The Waldshut delegates, encouraged by the interest taken in their cause by their Swiss friends, now somewhat insolently demanded not only immunity from punishment and entire religious freedom, but indemnity for the losses sustained in preparing for defense.

The Austrians would make no further concession than to leave the fixing of the civil penalty to four neighboring Austrian cities. They required the immediate removal of the evangelical preachers and of the Swiss contingent of troops. No result was reached, but it was arranged to continue the negotiations at a diet in Rheinsfelden on November 15. The Waldshut representatives now expressed a willingness to make amends for their past offenses by paying a reasonable fine, but insisted to the last on religious freedom. This the Austrians refused to accord and threatened to carry out the forcible measures that had long been purposed. Yet nothing was attempted for some time. The Swiss yielded to the Austrian demand and withdrew their contingent of troops from Waldshut, December 4, 1524.

There was general rejoicing in evangelical circles that Waldshut had been saved without making any compromise in fidelity to the truth. Bucer wrote to Zwingli, October 31, "I confidently expect that the example of the Waldshuters will encourage very many. To me the affair is like a miracle. Truly the Lord has lifted up the humble." Hubmaier soon resumed his office as chief pastor, and he did not hesitate when danger threatened to lay aside his clerical habit and to take his place in battle array among the soldiers. Such willingness to take his full share of the work of defending the city no doubt added to his already great popularity.

In the meantime, however, the question of infant baptism had come to the front in Zürich and the surrounding regions. Apart from those who continued loyal to the Roman Church, three parties, or at least three attitudes toward reform, may be distinguished in this city. The magistracy as a body were exceedingly conservative, and while they early came to feel the need of a certain amount of reform sought to reduce innovation to a minimum. Only after they had become convinced that it was impolitic longer to delay any particular item of reform could they be induced to give their sanction to it. So politic had been their proceedings that as late as 1526 they were still on friendly terms with the pope, who was heavily indebted to the council for troops furnished some years before and who in response to persistent solicitations made repeated promises to pay. He could still address the council as "beloved sons," and while he mildly remonstrated with them for tolerating heresy had not yet thought it expedient to excommunicate even such leaders as Zwingli.

Zwingli represented the middle party, that wished to carry forward reform as fast as it could be done with safety. It was with great difficulty that Zwingli could secure and maintain the co-operation of the council in such reforms as he thought desirable. In his dealings with the council he displayed political capacity of a high order. His lack of consuming zeal and of excessive scrupulosity stood him well in hand in his semi-political career.

Almost from the beginning of the evangelical movement in Zürich we notice a number of radicals who always went ahead of what Zwingli and the council thought it prudent to allow, breaking fasts before they had been authoritatively abolished, destroying images before their removal had been ordered, refusing to participate in the mass and speaking of it contemptuously while its celebration was still required by the authorities.

Zwingli had denied that under the gospel dispensation tithes are binding, and was of the opinion that rents should be so adjusted as to be less oppressive to the workingman. The radicals did not hesitate to declare the enforced payment of tithes tyrannical, and to make their protest practical by refusing to pay them and by holding meetings for the free discussion of agrarian grievances. When there was talk of sending Zwingli to Constance for examination before the ecclesiastical authorities the radicals arranged for a monster meeting to protest and if necessary to take active measures against such interference with freedom of evangelical teaching.

Among the earliest and most aggressive of these radicals were Simon Stumpf, pastor at Höngg, Froschauer, a printer, afterward to become widely known as Hubmaier's publisher at Nikolsburg, Claus and Jacob Hottinger, Heine Aberli, Andreas Castelberg (usually called Andreas-on-the-Crutches), among the less educated; and among the educated Conrad Grebel, Felix Manz, Wilhelm Reublin, Ludwig Hetzer, Georg Blaurock, and Hans Brötli.

In June, 1523, we find the Hottingers raising a commotion at Zollikon by insisting on communion under both kinds. In September we find Claus Hottinger, Hochrütiner, and others, arraigned before the council for lawless iconoclasm and sentenced to banishment.[1]

Zwingli's refusal to insist upon the immediate abolition of images and the mass was highly offensive to the radicals. Grebel, Manz, Stumpf, and others, had repeated conferences with him and demanded the setting up of a pure church, whose members should all be true children

---

[1] Hottinger went to Baden, where he was arrested for heresy and delivered over to the Swiss deputies at Lucerne, who sentenced him to death for heresy. He died heroically. See Bullinger, "Reformationgeschichte," Bd. I., p. 145, seq.

of God, having the spirit of God and ruled and led by him. They pointed out the unseemliness of making the reformation of the church dependent upon the will of an ungodly magistracy, and of allowing the ungodly to enjoy the privileges of church-fellowship. Zwingli urged them to be patient with "the feeble sick lambs," and sought scriptural support for his position in the account of the ark which contained both clean and unclean beasts, and in the parable of the wheat and the tares. The magistrates, while they may not all be true believers, are yet friendly to the gospel and should not be violently opposed. He warned them earnestly of the disastrous consequences of separation and schism. The warning was without avail, and Stumpf, whose revolutionary preaching reminds one of that of Münzer, was banished about the end of 1523.

After Zwingli had declared himself definitely against the establishment of churches of the regenerate and the immediate abolition of all unscriptural elements, the radicals lost confidence in him as a reformer and began to plan for the independent organization of New Testament churches. They met together frequently at Manz' home, where they read Hebrew together and discussed the ways and means of putting into practice their ideas of reform. In fact it appears that as early as 1522 Castelberg had held private meetings for the expounding of the Epistle to the Romans, and the free discussion of the religious questions of the time. Castelberg's views were largely socialistic. He did not hesitate to denounce usury as theft, and the oppression of the poor by the rich as murder. Warfare also he did not hesitate to denounce as equivalent to murder. From the early date at which Castelberg began his religio-socialistic agitation and the similarity of his views to those of mediæval evangelical parties it is not improbable that we have in his activity a point of contact between the earlier and the later radical movements.

Literature: Pertinent works (as in Bibliography) of Egli, Strickler, Heberle, Strasser, Nitsche, Burrage, Schaff, Baur, Keller, Usteri, Stähelin, E. Müller, Loserth, Kessler, Gast, Bullinger, Füsslin, Beck, Cornelius, Hosek, Schreiber, Zwingli, and Hubmaier.

CHAPTER IX

ZÜRICH, SCHAFFHAUSEN, AND ST. GALL (1524-25)

The question of infant baptism was first brought prominently forward by Wilhelm Reublin in the spring of 1524. As pastor at Wytikon, while not refusing to baptize such infants as were presented, he had expressed himself against infant baptism. If he had a child he would not baptize it until it should come to its days and could personally choose godfather and godmother. As a result of such teaching many withheld their children from baptism. A number of such were arraigned before the council and commanded to have their children baptized without delay. Reublin was thrown into prison and a fine was imposed upon parents who should refuse to obey the mandate. Largely through Reublin's influence the sentiment against infant baptism had extended to Zollikon, where many violated the order of the council for conscience' sake. Hans Brötli, pastor at Zollikon, Andreas Castelberg, Georg Blaurock, Conrad Grebel, and Felix Manz now declared themselves against infant baptism. After a number of private conferences between Zwingli and the opponents of infant baptism, in which the latter complained of unfair treatment at the hands of the former, the council arranged for a public disputation to be held January 17, 1525. The chief disputants on the Anti-pedobaptist side were Grebel, Manz, and Reublin. The usual arguments for and against infant baptism were ably stated. Zwingli had by this time come to feel the importance of pedobaptism as a necessary concomitant of a State church. It had not occurred to him at first that the abolition of infant baptism would involve the setting up of churches composed exclusively of baptized believers and the unchurching of the great mass of the population in each community. Such separatism, he was sure, could never secure the approval of the magistracy. Persecution would ensue and evangelical Christianity would have to give way to more politic Romanism. When these consequences had once dawned upon him he devoted all the energies of his being to the maintenance of the existing order.

The Anti-pedobaptist leaders, as was natural, bitterly charged Zwingli with inconsistency and with insincerity. Inconsistent he surely was, but it is entirely conceivable that his change of opinion was real. His opposition to infant baptism had never been based on profound conviction of its pernicious character. He had never gone much beyond the feeling that it was non-scriptural and useless. He was of a wholly different spirit from the Anti-pedobaptist leaders and was completely out of harmony with their plans and purposes. It is not improbable that he actually succeeded in convincing himself of the defensibility of a practice so essential to civil and ecclesiastical order. His chief argument was based upon the practical identity of baptism with circumcision. He did not fail to call attention to the possibility that among the households baptized in the apostolic times there may have been infants, nor to the fact that the children of believers are spoken of by the apostle as holy. "Children are with their parents in God's covenant, they belong as their parents to God's church, and hence are also God's children. Should water baptism be denied to those who are God's children?"

The council, as might have been expected, declared Zwingli victorious, commanded that all unbaptized children be baptized within eight days on pain of the banishment of the responsible parties, required the abandonment of all special meetings for the discussion of baptism and like questions, and banished such foreigners as had become prominent in the Anti-pedobaptist movement. This last ordinance involved Reublin, Brötli, Hetzer, and Castelberg.

From this time onward the radicals became more and more aggressive. They at once proceeded to introduce believers' baptism (about the middle of December, 1524).[1] In this Grebel led, baptizing first of all Blaurock, who in turn baptized large numbers. On February 7 fourteen Anti-pedobaptists from Zollikon were arraigned before the council, among them two members of the Hottinger family, who confessed that they had been baptized and expressed their resolution to act henceforth according to the directions of God's Spirit and to be deterred therefrom by no worldly power.

Rüedi Thomann gave an account of a meeting in his own house in which Brötli, Reublin, and Blaurock took part. After much conversation and reading, Hans Bruggbach stood up weeping and crying out that he was a great sinner and asking that they pray God for him. Then Blaurock asked him whether he desired the grace of God. He said he did. Then Manz rose and said "Who will forbid that I should baptize him?" Blaurock answered, "No one." Then Manz took a dipper with water and baptized him in the name of the Father, Son, and Holy Spirit. Then stood up Jacob Hottinger. Him also Manz baptized. Then the others all went away and Manz and Blaurock remained with him over night. They rose early the next morning. Then Blaurock said to his son-in-law: "Marx, you have hitherto been a gay young man. You must make a change. You must put away

---

[1] So Nitsche, " Schw. Wiedertäufer." p. 20, seq.; and Egli, "St. Galler Taufer." p. 22. Usteri, "Huldreich Zwingli." Bd. I., p. 478, thinks the latter part of January, 1525, the more probable date. Absolute certainty in this matter is at present unattainable.

the old Adam and put on a new." Marx answered "that he would do his best." Then Blaurock asked whether he desired the grace of God, and when he said that he did, Blaurock said: "Come hither and I will baptize you also." Then Marx went to him and was baptized. Then Blaurock said to him (Rüedi Thomann), that he was an old man and near to death and that he should amend his life, and said that if he desired the grace of God he would baptize him too. And when he said that he did, Blaurock baptized him. After this Blaurock would have no rest until he had baptized the whole household. He related further, how they had a loaf upon the table and Blaurock said: "Whoever believes that God has redeemed him with his death and his rose-colored blood, let him come and eat with me of the bread and drink with me of this wine." Then they ate and drank. This is a fair sample of the methods employed by these zealous men in propagating their principles. Considering the universal discontent of the working classes it is not wonderful that within a few weeks thousands had accepted the simple gospel thus earnestly proclaimed and were baptized on profession of their faith.

After the prisoners mentioned above had been detained for a time and Zwingli and his associates had striven to convince them of their errors, they were heavily fined and dismissed, a special injunction having been put upon the leaders not to engage further in holding unlawful meetings, baptizing, or celebrating the Lord's Supper. As might have been expected they went forward with their work more zealously than before. Their opinion of Zwingli was not improved by his efforts to convert them. Blaurock, Manz, and Hans Hottinger were obstinate in their heresy, and seem to have been held for further discipline. At any rate we find them in prison a short time afterward.

In a letter to the council (written shortly before February 18), Blaurock sets forth his views and aims in a simple, earnest way. Christ in sending forth his disciples commanded them to go forth and teach all peoples and promised remission of sins through the power given by God his Father to all who should call upon his name, and for an external sign commanded them to baptize. As he has taught, some have come to him weeping and begging to be baptized. Such he has not felt at liberty to refuse, but after instructing them further as regards love, unity, and community of all things, as did the apostles (according to Acts 2), he has baptized them, and that they might always keep in remembrance the death of Christ and his poured-out blood he has instructed them how Christ instituted the Supper, and they have together broken the bread and drunk the wine, in commemoration of the fact that they were all redeemed by the one body of Christ and washed by the one blood of Christ, and that all might be brothers and sisters of each other in Christ their Lord. In all this he feels assured that he has done the will of God. He beseeches the council not to come in conflict with the corner-stone, Christ.

Blaurock and Manz were firm in the position they had taken. Their teaching and practice they held to be in accord with God's will, and they demanded scriptural proof for infant baptism. Manz desired that Zwingli should express his views in writing, and promised written answers to his arguments. Blaurock expressed the opinion that Zwingli perverted the Scriptures more violently than the old pope. Further conference with Zwingli tended in no way to bring him and the Anti-pedobaptists to a better understanding. Their conceptions and aims had diverged so widely that reconciliation was utterly hopeless. We soon find Blaurock in Zollikon, preaching to a large congregation and baptizing. Here he baptized Heine Aberli, whom we have already encountered among the earlier radicals.

Finding milder measures unavailing and alarmed at the increasing aggressiveness of the Anti-pedobaptists, the council decided to examine Aberli and others, imposed a fine upon all who had submitted to rebaptism since February 7, and decreed the immediate banishment, with wife and child, of all who should henceforth do so. A thorough investigation of the Anti-pedobaptist disturbances at Zollikon was ordered. It was decided on March 16 to imprison all the suspects and to examine them on the eighteenth. A large number were arraigned and full records of the examination have been preserved. Hans Hottinger refused to receive instruction from any one but Christ. He knows not whether he was baptized in childhood, therefore he has had himself baptized. Many relate the circumstances under which they were brought to feel their need of baptism and were baptized. The brethren at Zollikon pleaded earnestly for liberty to follow God's word. No opinions or thoughts that are not based upon Scripture will move them in the slightest degree. They ask for a public disputation on baptism.

A disputation was arranged between Zwingli, Leo Judae, and Myconius, on the one side, and Blaurock and Manz on the other, before members of the council (March 20). The result was as usual. The council exhorted the Anti-pedobaptists to desist, assuring them that their separation and schism could be no longer endured. Foreigners were banished and natives were to be imprisoned on a bread and water diet, in the hope that they would be led by their sufferings and the prospect of starvation to abandon their errors. The starvation argument proved more effective by far than Zwingli's logic and exegesis. On March 25 a number promised to abandon their Anabaptist teachings and practices and were released. Zwingli was too shrewd to be misled by this temporary compliance on the part of the weaker brethren. "We have accomplished nothing," he writes, "although some have desisted, not because they have changed their mind, but because they have changed their nerve."[1]

Blaurock and his companions continued in prison. Whether by accident or by friendly human intervention, the prisoners discovered (about April 5) that one of the windows was unfastened. After some hesitation they decided that the opportunity to escape was providential and let themselves down by a rope. Among those who escaped were Grebel, Manz, and Blaurock. The precise date of Grebel's imprisonment cannot be determined. No mention of him is made in connection with the disputation of March 20, or the recantation of part of the prisoners and the refusal of others on March 25. He was probably arrested shortly before April 5.[2]

When Reublin and Brötli were banished from the canton of Zürich, they seem to have directed their steps at once to the canton of Schaffhausen. Grebel soon followed and labored faithfully in that field. We have seen that this canton was the sanctuary of Hubmaier when he was being hotly pursued by the Austrian authorities. The principal ecclesiastical personage in Schaffhausen was Dr. Sebastian Hofmeister. He received the banished Anabaptists with Christian hospitality, and listened patiently and sympathetically to their Anti-pedobaptist

---

[1] "Opera," Lib. VII., p. 398.
[2] There is considerable difficulty about fixing the dates of Grebel's movements at this time. According to Kessler ("Sabbata," Bd. I., pp. 266, 268) Grebel reached St. Gall March 26, and remained there until after Palm Sunday (April 9). This is of course inconsistent with the supposition that he escaped from prison at Zürich on April 5. That he was among the prisoners who escaped there can be no doubt. In a letter to Vadian, March 31, Zwingli mentions the fact that Grebel is at Zürich, but does not refer to his imprisonment ("Opera," Lib. VII., p. 387). It would seem that Kessler's dates are incorrect.

arguments. Brötli wrote to his friends at Zollikon: "Dr. Sebastian agrees with us as regards baptism. God grant that he may come to a better understanding in all things." Hubmaier quotes a letter from Hofmeister which leaves no doubt that for a time at least he rejected infant baptism not only in theory but in practice as well. Having apologized to Hubmaier for not communicating to him earlier his opinion on baptism and having expressed his anxiety lest disunion should grow out of the controversy that has arisen, he continues:

> However, it pleased the Heavenly Father that without me the matter came into dispute, so that it spread as far as to us, and therefore for the sake of the truth we have not been ashamed to publicly confess it before the council in Schaffhausen, that our brother Zwingli is erring from the right way and is not proceeding according to the gospel, if he determines that little children should be baptized. I have certainly not allowed myself to be compelled to baptize my children, and therefore you do what is exactly Christian when you introduce again now the true baptism of Christ, that had so long been neglected.

It is probable that Hofmeister had been brought to this position by the arguments of Hubmaier during the sojourn of the latter in Schaffhausen. But he lacked the courage of his convictions, as will hereafter more fully appear.

Brötli after visiting a number of places in the canton of Schaffhausen settled at Hallau, where his preaching met with marked acceptance. Reublin spent part of the time with him and baptized many in Hallau, but his work was rather that of an evangelist. With untiring zeal he traveled from place to place winning multitudes. Of Grebel's activity in Schaffhausen at this time we have no particulars, except as regards his intercourse with Dr. Hofmeister and other leaders. Hofmeister some months later gave to Zwingli and the Zürich Council an account of his intercourse with Grebel that is conceived in an unfriendly spirit and seems out of keeping with his earlier attitude. He states that he did not agree with Grebel as to infant baptism. Grebel had insisted that in no other way could the papacy be more effectively brought low than by the abolition of infant baptism. He had also insisted that beneficed clergymen could not rightly proclaim the truth. He had denounced Zwingli as an adulterer and had charged him with desiring to put him and his associates to death. A certain French knight had been present as a guest of Hofmeister's and had conceived a highly unfavorable opinion of Zwingli as portrayed by Grebel; but he resolved to visit Zwingli and to ascertain the truth. The result was that his ill impression was removed. Grebel had said, moreover, that Leo Judae and Caspar Grossmann were likewise of his opinion, but were overawed by Zwingli. Felix Manz had also been to Schaffhausen to seek to gain adherents to his party. He had taken strong ground not only against infant baptism, but also against the right of a Christian to exercise magistracy or to engage in warfare. The visits of Grebel and Manz to Schaffhausen referred to by Hofmeister must have occurred after the escape from the tower on April 5, as Grebel is represented as referring to the escape as due to a special divine interposition, and Manz had been for some time in prison previous to the deliverance.

The explanation of Hoffmeister's changed attitude toward Anabaptist principles is to be found in the following facts, recorded in the Schaffhausen "Chronicle." The Schaffhausen authorities became greatly alarmed on account of certain riotous outbreaks in sympathy with the peasant uprising in the neighboring countries, and Dr. Hofmeister paid dearly for the sympathy he had manifested for Anti-pedobaptist views. He was accused by his opponents of having spoken of the mass as idols' bread, idolatry, the work of the devil, etc., and of having publicly taught that the baptism of young children is useless and should be abandoned. So sensitive and timid had the council become, that instead of arranging for an examination of the honored pastor at home and giving him an opportunity to defend or explain his teachings, as he earnestly requested, they peremptorily ordered him to leave the city and not to approach within three miles of it until he could present a certificate of orthodoxy from some university. Hofmeister was not a man of heroic cast and this requirement was to the last degree humiliating to him. Whither he should direct his way he knew not. He finally decided to solicit the good offices of the University of Basel, as being near at hand and friendly to evangelical teaching; but he found that owing to the same circumstances that had led to his banishment from Schaffhausen the Basel authorities were in a supersensitive state and would have nothing to do with him. Greatly cast down, he resolved to return to Schaffhausen and to seek to satisfy the authorities as to his orthodoxy. But the council was inexorable. This decree of banishment affected also his chief colleague, Dr. Sebastian Meier. He now made his way to Zürich, determined it would seem to purge himself of all suspicion of sympathy with the Anabaptists.

One of the most important events in Grebel's Schaffhausen ministry was the baptism of Wolfgang Uolimann, a well-educated and zealous evangelical teacher from St. Gall. Uolimann, like Blaurock, had been a Præmonstratensian monk. After leaving his monastery at Chur he entered zealously upon evangelical work at St. Gall. He had reached the conviction that New Testament baptism was the immersion of the believer, and he was not content to have water poured or sprinkled upon him from a dish, but insisted upon being immersed in the river, a practice which Grebel seems afterward to have followed at St. Gall.

St. Gall now became the chief Swiss center of the Anabaptist movement. In this important manufacturing town the trades-unions were powerful and used their influence for the promotion of evangelical teaching. Vadian, a graduate and former rector of the University of Vienna, a scholar of high rank and a doctor of medicine, was the most influential citizen of St. Gall. He early declared himself in favor of evangelical reform and sustained the most cordial relations with Zwingli. Chiefly through the influence of his brother-in-law, Conrad Grebel, he was led to give attention to the baptismal question and to sympathize with those who denied the scriptural authority of infant baptism; but he urged that nothing be done rashly. In its own good time the doctrine and practice of baptism would be made right. Grebel earnestly besought him to take a decided stand, but his conservative instincts and the influence of Zwingli determined him to oppose the radicals. His strong disinclination to the use of compulsion in matters of religion and the prevailing popular sentiment in favor of radical reform gave opportunity for the Anabaptist movement to gain a momentum here that was not possible at Zürich or elsewhere in Switzerland.

Laurence Hochrütiner, when banished from Zürich in 1523, returned to his native St. Gall. Here he became a leader of the radical party among the working people. He soon declared himself against infant baptism and gained many adherents. John Kessler returned from a course of study in Basel and Wittenberg in November, 1523, and instead of seeking ordination worked at the saddler's trade and held meetings for the expounding of the Scriptures, at first in a private house but afterward in the hall of one of the guilds. When Kessler was expounding the sixth chapter of Romans, Hochrütiner objected to his interpretation of the passage about baptism, and insisted upon the Baptist view of the apostle's teaching. A long letter from Grebel on the subject was industriously used by Hochrütiner. The conservative element secured the prohibition of Kessler's meetings in September, 1524. He yielded for the time in the interest of peace; but the more radical evangelicals insisted that the word of God is not bound and that we must obey God rather then men. On Uolimann's arrival he was invited by the radicals to take up the work. He preached out of doors to large congregations, who as winter approached grew indignant that the churches were closed against the evangelical preacher.

Agitation resulted in compromise. Only priests could officiate in the churches; lay meetings must remain private, the council neither permitting nor forbidding; yet permission was granted to Kessler to expound the Scriptures in one of the churches, while Uolimann being suspected of extreme radicalism was refused the use of another and held his meetings in the weavers' hall. Having been baptized by Grebel (as already stated) in the spring of 1525, he returned to St. Gall. The breach in the evangelical ranks, long imminent, was now consummated. Uolimann began at once to baptize on a profession of faith. As Kessler observed, "The St. Gall people ran after baptism as the Galatians after circumcision."

Grebel came to the support of Uolimann and Hochrütiner in April and his popular power was nowhere more manifest than here. He seems to have brought with him two other enthusiastic Anabaptist workers, Anthony Roggenacher and Hippolytus Eberle. The latter especially proved himself a man of high character and of great popular power. Crowd after crowd went out of the city for baptism in the flowing water. In some cases tubs or vats were used.

The Anti-pedobaptist excitement spread into the surrounding villages in the abbot's domains and in the Appenzell territory. Within a few weeks one thousand two hundred were baptized. The Anti-pedobaptists had strong supporters in the council and their opponents were not in a position to deal summarily with them. Three churches were formed in Appenzell. At Teufen the pastor of the church was supplanted by an Anti-pedobaptist.

The highest praise is bestowed on the purity and simplicity of the lives of these people by contemporary writers who abhorred their schismatic principles. Considering the intense excitement that must have accompanied changes so rapid and radical, it is remarkable that so little occurred that could in any sense be regarded as fanatical. Eberle left St. Gall at the request of the burgomaster in the interest of peace. He soon afterward suffered martyrdom at Schwyz, whither information had been sent by his opponents, who did not dare lay hands on him in St. Gall.

Uolimann again came to the front as the leader of the Anti-pedobaptists of the canton. He was brought before the council on April 25, and gave an intelligent account of his position, showing a creditable acquaintance with the history of the doctrine of baptism. It was agreed that the council should in the near future arrange for a disputation in which both sides should be fully stated and argued. "For the sake of brotherly love," Uolimann agreed to discontinue baptism and the celebration of the Supper until after the proposed disputation. The Anti-pedobaptists might in the meantime continue their preaching and teaching. It seems to have been a grave error in judgment on the part of Uolimann to agree to a temporary suspension of the administration of the ordinances. It destroyed the enthusiasm of the movement and gave to its opponents the desired opportunity to mature their arrangements for its suppression.

Zwingli was urging upon the St. Gall authorities the necessity of taking decisive measures, and he wrought night and day in preparing his great work on "Baptism, Anabaptism, and Infant Baptism," with special reference to the needs of St. Gall. It was published May 27. Grebel wrote a most passionate appeal to Vadian, his brother-in-law, beseeching him not to allow himself to be influenced by worldly considerations to attempt anything against the gospel, but rather to withdraw from the bloodthirsty party of Zwingli. If he will not put himself on the side of the brethren, he is entreated at least not to persecute them. This letter (or a similar one) was read before the council and strongly disapproved by the majority. It was ordered that Zwingli's recently issued book be publicly read in one of the churches. Uolimann was present when the reading began and interrupted with the remark: "You may have Zwingli's word; we will have God's word." Others of the Anti-pedobaptists expressed strongly their dissatisfaction and the members of the party left the church. They resolved to enter anew upon aggressive work, being convinced that they could expect nothing but violence from the council swayed by Zwingli, whom they did not hesitate to declare the enemy of God.

Vadian's book on baptism was ready by June 5 and the Anti-pedobaptists were required to answer it. They presented a comprehensive answer, and a disputation followed. They were, as a matter of course, vanquished in the opinion of the party in power, and an ordinance followed prohibiting not only the administration of the ordinances but all separate assemblies for religious purposes, except a service at the St. Lawrence church. The penalty for administering the ordinances was banishment with wife and child ; for submitting to baptism a heavy fine, with banishment in case of refusal to pay.

Literature : Pertinent works (as in Bibliography) of Egli, Strickler, Heberle, Strasser, Nitsche, Burrage, Schaff, Baur, Keller, Usteri, Stähelin, E. Müller, Loserth, Kessler, Gast, Bullinger, Füsslin, Beck, Cornelius, Hosek, Schreiber, Zwingli, and Hubmaier.

CHAPTER X

BASEL, BERNE, GRÜNINGEN, AND WALDSHUT (1524-25)

BASEL was a center of evangelical free thought before and after the beginning of the Protestant revolution. It is probable that anti-pedobaptism appeared there not much later than in Zürich. When Blaurock escaped from prison in Zürich (April 5, 1525) he betook himself to Basel, where he soon succeeded in arousing to activity the Anti-pedobaptist forces already present and in adding greatly to the numbers of the party. Zwingli was ever on the alert and was ready with his earnest warnings against the growing interest that was manifest in the Anti-pedobaptist cause. Spurred on by Zwingli, Œcolampadius, tolerant at heart, opposed them as he might. But still they grew, large numbers coming to their support from without. Œcolampadius petitioned the council to prohibit their ingress into the city; but the council was not disposed to undertake such a task as the violent exclusion and suppression of a party already strong and influential and rapidly growing in power.

A disputation on baptism was appointed by the council for June 5. Blaurock and Œcolampadius were the chief disputants. As usual the Anti-pedobaptists insisted on direct scriptural proof for infant baptism, while the Pedobaptists were content to quote Origen, Cyprian, Augustine, etc. "What have we to do," said the former, "with your doctors, the church Fathers, and the councils? They were men as we are, and as subject to blindness as we are." They were not at all impressed by Œcolampadius' insistence that their view involved the condemnation of the great multitude of Christians of the past and the present, many of them men of the most exalted piety and the most profound intellects. Geierfalk, one of Œcolampadius' colleagues, thought it a fair rebuttal of their demand for scriptural proof of infant baptism, to ask them for a scriptural prohibition of the same. They were at no loss to show that infant baptism is not only not authorized by Scripture, but that it is contradictory of the entire teaching of Scripture with reference to baptism and completely perverts an ordinance of Christ.

Œcolampadius considered himself victorious. Blaurock very naturally took a wholly different view of the matter, and his followers are said to have been so imprudent as to march in procession through the city proclaiming the triumph of their cause. The council, following the advice of Œcolampadius, now took measures for the suppression of the movement. Considerable commotion followed. Many fled, while a considerable number were thrown into prison. A minority of the council urged the execution of the prisoners, as being guilty of heresy and sedition.

Hubmaier, who was still at Waldshut, wrote soon afterward a work on baptism in the form of a dialogue between himself and Œcolampadius, the utterances of the latter being taken apparently from Œcolampadius' published account of the disputation. Hubmaier's exegesis and logic are from the Baptist point of view unexceptionable. His irony is masterly, but perhaps severer than good policy would have dictated. Hubmaier can scarcely be censured for pointing out the inconsistency of his evangelical antagonists in opposing believers' baptism on the ground that rejection of infant baptism involved the condemnation of the great majority of Christians for the last fifteen hundred years, while they themselves were in open rebellion against the Roman

Church, many of whose tenets were centuries old. The objection that insistence on believers' baptism tends to separation and faction, Hubmaier meets by showing that Christ himself was spoken against as a seditious person and that he came not to send peace but a sword. If the truth produces trouble, wickedness and not truth is responsible. He charges Œcolampadius with blasphemy when he maintains that those who in striving to be obedient to Christ form a new sect, are joining themselves to the devil.

The attempt of Œcolampadius to show that infant baptism takes the place of circumcision fared no better. "Baptism," says Hubmaier, "is a ceremony of the New Testament; therefore I demand a plain text with which you support infant baptism out of the New Testament. The word, the *word*, the WORD! Why will you like the night owl hate the light and refuse to come to the sun? You prove infant baptism from Exodus, as Zwingli proves 'to be' means 'to signify' from Genesis."[1] To the contention of Œcolampadius that inward baptism is the principal thing and that it is a matter of small importance whether outward baptism be received in infancy or afterward, or indeed whether it be received at all, Hubmaier replies: "Those who are baptized inwardly will surely be baptized outwardly, and not annul the commandment of Christ by baptizing in any other way." But we must forbear to quote further from this masterly piece of polemics. No man since Hubmaier has more completely apprehended or more lucidly and logically set forth the Baptist position as regards the nature and the subjects of baptism; but he seems never to have realized the importance of immersion as the form of apostolic baptism.

This treatise of Hubmaier's was circulated secretly in

---

[1] Referring to the controversy on the real presence in the Supper.

Basel for some time before Œcolampadius succeeded in securing a copy (October, 1525). Irritated by the somewhat severe handling he had received from the Waldshut pastor, he sent a copy to Zwingli urging him to prepare a refutation.

In Berne also Anti-pedobaptist views had made a strong impression on many minds. Berthold Haller, the leader of the evangelical party, was for a time greatly disturbed by questionings as to the scriptural authority of infant baptism, but Zwingli's influence prevailed to overcome his scruples. Hubmaier's tract against Œcolampadius had circulated in Berne also, and in November Haller wrote to Zwingli: "Balthasar's plain allegation of the Scriptures seduces many." He doubts not that Zwingli will be able so to answer Hubmaier as to change the minds of those that have been affected, and he reassures Zwingli by informing him that the authorities have proscribed the new procedures.

Grüningen, a Zürich dependency, early became a stronghold of the Anti-pedobaptists. Many fugitives from the neighborhood of Zürich during the first half of 1525 took refuge there. Grebel, Manz, Blaurock, now a companion of Grebel, seem to have spent most of the summer and autumn in that neighborhood. A number of Anti-pedobaptist organizations resulted.

The mandates of the council, the imprisonment, fining, and banishment of the opponents of infant baptism, had by no means availed to suppress the movement in the immediate neighborhood of Zürich. Inquisitorial processes occurred from time to time, but few cases of baptism could be proved.

We left Waldshut at the end of 1524, when Hubmaier had just returned from his sojourn in Schaffhausen and when the impending suppression of evangelical religion by the Austrian authorities had been for the time averted.

Before leaving Schaffhausen Hubmaier had challenged his old friend, Dr. Eck, to a disputation on twenty-six evangelical propositions. He facetiously represents himself as a fly challenging Eck the elephant. In these propositions he does not, however, state distinctly his Anti-pedobaptist views.

Almost immediately after his resumption of leadership in Waldshut, Hubmaier's relations to Zwingli and his associates underwent a marked change, and he put himself definitely on the side of the Zürich radicals, who were soon to carry into effect their ideas of Christian life and church order by introducing believers' baptism as the initiatory rite into churches of the regenerate. From this time forward Hubmaier must be regarded as the great literary defender and promoter of the Anti-pedobaptist position. He had previously argued the question of baptism with Zwingli, Judae, Hofmeister, Œcolampadius, and others, but had not hitherto felt that the time had come for resolutely and without regard to consequences putting away a practice that he had long held to be unauthorized by Scripture and subversive of the purpose of Christ in instituting the ordinance. On January 16 he wrote to Œcolampadius: " Now the hour is come in which I should proclaim publicly and upon the housetops what hitherto I have kept pent up within. The great God be praised who has vouchsafed to me and equally to my hearers this spirit of liberty."

In answer to a supposed question of Œcolampadius, who was of the opinion that a mere outward sign and ceremony like baptism should not be made a matter of contention and schism, Hubmaier proceeds:

Why then do we trouble ourselves so much about a sign? A sign at least it is and a symbol instituted by Christ with the most momentous and solemn words, namely, in the name of the Father, Son, and Holy Spirit. But whosoever weakens or abuses this sign does violence to the words of Christ. The significance of this sign and symbol, the obligation of fidelity even unto death in hope of a resurrection to a future life, is moreover of greater moment than the sign itself. But these significant things can have no applicability to infants. Therefore the baptism of infants is foliage without vintage."

He lays much stress upon the fact that an obligation is assumed in baptism which an infant is incapable of assuming and which no one can assume for another.

"Dearest brother," he proceeds, "you have here my opinion. If I err recall me, for I desire nothing so much as to recant, to do everything, yea, to decline nothing, so far as I am taught by you and yours out of God's word. Otherwise I persist in my opinion, for thereto am I compelled by the institution of Christ, the word, faith, truth, judgment, conscience. . . I am a man and can fall—which is human; but in that case I desire from my heart to recover my footing."

He then asks Œcolampadius whether he thinks that Matt. 19 : 14, "For of such is the kingdom of heaven," refers especially to children, calling attention to the fact that "such" and not "theirs" is the term used.

He gives an account of the practice that he has introduced at Waldshut :

Instead of baptism, I have the church assembled, bring in the child, pronounce, in German, the gospel passage, "They brought a little child," then its name is bestowed upon it, then the whole church prays on bended knees for the child, commending it to Christ that he may be gracious to it. Are the parents still weak and determined that the child shall be baptized, I baptize it and for the time being am weak with the weak until they shall be better instructed. But in the word I do not yield in the minutest particular.

He states that he has written to Zwingli, presumably in the same tenor. He has written twenty-two propositions with sixty-four notes that Œcolampadius shall soon see.

The disputation at Zürich between Zwingli and his associates on infant baptism occurred, as we have already seen, about this time (January 17). The results also we have noticed. Some of the banished leaders made their way to Waldshut and no doubt confirmed Hubmaier in his purpose to proceed with as little delay as possible to carry his views fully into practice. On February 2 he set forth a " Public Challenge to all Christian Men " to show that baptism should be administered to infants, and that it should be celebrated with any other words than those of Scripture in the vernacular. He asks that a Bible fifty or a hundred years old (the age is mentioned no doubt to avoid suspicion of the influence of contemporary partisanship in the editing) be placed between the two articles (the positive and negative propositions he has formulated), that it be opened, that it be read with prayerful, humble spirit, and then that this controversy be decided according to God's word. " So am I well content, for I will ever give God the honor and let his word alone be umpire; to him will I subject and yield myself as well as my doctrines. *The truth is immortal.*"

Reublin visited Waldshut early in the spring, and was for some weeks closely associated with Hubmaier in evangelical work. It was doubtless his influence in part that led Hubmaier to advance from the rejection of infant baptism to the adoption of believers' baptism. Along with sixty others he accompanied Reublin (about Easter, 1525) to a neighboring village and they were baptized by the latter on a profession of their faith. Afterward Hubmaier himself publicly baptized out of a milk pail over three hundred more believers.[1] He had for a long while refrained from taking this decisive step in view of the

---
[1] The term "baptize" is used by the author in this connection to designate an act which he does not regard as apostolic baptism.

embarrassed position of the city and his fear of bringing it into still graver danger; but he had now reached the conviction that further delay would involve disloyalty to Christ and that come what might the New Testament order must be restored.

As might have been expected this radical procedure was not satisfactory to all. A large majority of the people were so devoted to Hubmaier that they were ready to sustain him in the carrying out of his convictions; but an influential minority felt that the city had been thereby seriously compromised and that the effect would prove disastrous. From a merely human and political point of view the position of Waldshut was undoubtedly made far more critical by the introduction of believers' baptism. One effect of it was to intensify the distrust of the Austrian government, which, however, was only awaiting a favorable opportunity for administering the chastisement so long threatened.

But the loss of the confidence of the ruling classes in the evangelical Swiss cantons was a more serious matter and made it easier for Austria to wreak her vengeance on the heroic little city, already weakened by internal dissension. Hubmaier knew full well that he was the occasion of the impending disaster; but truth required him to act as he had done, and "the truth," he never wearied of saying, "is immortal."

Zwingli's treatise on "Baptism, Infant Baptism, and Anabaptism" was published on May twenty-eighth. The disputation in Basel between Œcolampadius and the Antipedobaptists, in which, as we have seen, Hubmaier took a deep interest, occurred on June fifth. Five days later Hubmaier wrote the Zürich Council that he had read Zwingli's book and had nearly completed an answer. He besought the council for God's sake and in view of the future judgment to give him a safe conduct to Zürich in order that privately or publicly, before the whole council or delegated individuals, he might discuss the question of infant baptism with Zwingli. He would be glad to have Dr. Sebastian Hofmeister present. If he should be found in error he would gladly recant; should Zwingli be found in error he ought not to be ashamed to desist from the error, for the truth will be finally victorious.

Hubmaier's work on baptism (already referred to), directed nominally against Œcolampadius but having constant reference to Zwingli's work, was published July 11. Most impartial readers of Zwingli's and Hubmaier's books on baptism will agree with Usteri, a modern Swiss Reformed writer, when he says: " The reading of the writing on the Christian baptism of believers teaches clearly that a direct Scripture proof for infant baptism cannot be brought into the field. Over against Zwingli's sophistry it affords a peculiar satisfaction to see how clearly, transparently, and harmoniously with Hubmaier the richly collected biblical proof-texts group themselves around his idea of baptism. According to this [Hubmaier's view] the right scriptural order is no other than this: 1, Word; 2, Hearing; 3, Faith; 4, Baptism; 5, Work. And Hubmaier adds: ' I hold accordingly that Scripture is also a Hercules,' which is quite in accord with his device and the motto of his writings: ' the truth is immortal.' " Usteri further remarks that Hubmaier's exegesis is substantially in accord with modern scientific methods.

The profound impression produced by this writing in Basel, Berne, and elsewhere, we have already noticed. Urged by Œcolampadius, Haller, and others, who felt themselves unequal to the task, Zwingli promptly set about preparing an elaborate reply, that appeared about November. Hubmaier thought it advisable " to smite down clear out of the way this perverse booklet with the staff of Jacob, *i. e.*, with evangelical knowledge," for he regarded it as likely to prove a stone of stumbling to many pious souls. His rejoinder was completed by November 30, but was not printed until after his settlement in Moravia in 1526.

The names of the leaders of the early Swiss Antipedobaptists have become familiar through the foregoing narrative and their leading characteristics and relative importance have appeared. A few further details with reference to the more prominent characters may not be out of place.

Conrad Grebel, whom Zwingli called the "Coryphæus of the Anabaptists," and who was regarded by all the opponents of the movement as by far the most influential of its leaders, was the son of a Zürich patrician and councilor. Born some time after 1490, he spent about three years (1515-1518) in the University of Vienna, where he was in receipt of a handsome pension from the Emperor Ferdinand and where under the guidance of Vadian, then prominently connected with the university, he made great progress in classical and other studies. He proceeded next to the University of Paris, where he enjoyed an annual allowance of three hundred crowns and the friendship of the famous Swiss scholar, Glarean. Here he fell into evil ways and thereby impaired his health. He quarreled with his father, who drew his pension and partly on account of his reckless manner of life withheld it, thus bringing him into sore embarrassment. Grebel's father, by the way, was beheaded in October, 1526, for illegally receiving money from foreign princes in his son's name.

Conrad returned to his home in 1520 and soon began to take a profound interest in the evangelical movement. He was one of Zwingli's most zealous supporters up to 1523, when we find him among the radicals who insisted on the immediate abolition of tithes and readjustment of rents.

It has commonly been represented that Grebel and his associates were greatly influenced by Thomas Münzer. It is not impossible that some of Münzer's published utterances may have had an awakening influence upon them; but that they had gone far beyond him in their apprehension of Baptist principles and that they abhorred the chiliastic fanaticism which led him to seek to establish a reign of righteousness by the sword, is evident from a letter written by Grebel and others to Münzer in September, 1524, before the outbreak of the Peasants' War. They state that they have received his writing against false faith and baptism, and rejoice wonderfully to have found one who is of common Christian understanding with themselves and can point out their defects to the evangelical preachers. They hear that he has translated the mass into German and that he uses liturgical forms unauthorized by Scripture. They earnestly remonstrate with him on this matter and urge him to do away with all papal, antichristian forms and ceremonies. They understand that although he has written against infant baptism he continues to practise it. They urge him to bring his practice as well as his teaching into complete accord with God's word. They have heard that he has preached against the princes and has counseled armed resistance. If this be true, they entreat him for the sake of the cause of Christ to desist. They assure him that with the Bible he can stand before Luther and the princes. In Zürich there are not twenty who really believe the word of God. They fully expect to be called upon to suffer for their faith. Grebel expresses an intention to write against infant baptism.[1]

It is evident that Grebel, Castelberg, Manz, Aberli,

---

[1] See the letter printed in full in Cornelius, Vol II., p. 240 *seq.*

Brötli, Oggenfüss, and Huiuf, who signed this important document, were not disciples of Münzer, but would-be teachers.

We shall follow Grebel's brief career to its close in the next chapter. He died of the pestilence soon after March, 1526, having suffered much for the faith.

Felix Manz, son of a canon of the Minster Church, was closely associated with Grebel from the beginning. He was highly educated and was an accomplished Hebraist. He was unsurpassed by any of his Swiss contemporaries in his evangelistic gifts, unless it were Blaurock, and his enthusiasm in the Anti-pedobaptist cause was unbounded. He was instrumental in the conversion of hundreds, if not thousands, and when he suffered martyrdom by drowning, January 5, 1527, though still a young man he had done a noble lifework. His name will continue to figure prominently in the events to be narrated in the next chapter.

Georg Blaurock, of Chur, left his monastery to take up the cause of evangelical reform and was one of the earliest and most zealous of the radical leaders. He was the first to take the momentous step of administering a new baptism. From this time onward he seems never to have wavered, but was instant in season and out of season. His principles were identical, as far as we can see, with those of Grebel and Manz. Multitudes thronged his ministry as he journeyed from place to place, and large numbers were led to repent of their sins and to confess their Saviour in baptism. He followed the apostolic example of baptizing immediately on a confession of faith and an expression of desire for baptism. This was no doubt true in a measure of all the early Anti-pedobaptists, but few of them seem to have been so eager to baptize as he. Of his earliest labors in the Anti-pedobaptist cause we have already had some account. We shall have occasion to become better acquainted with him hereafter. His ministry extended to nearly all parts of Protestant Switzerland from 1525 to May, 1529, when he entered upon what proved to be a brief but fruitful ministry in the Tyrol, where he died heroically at the stake August 26, 1529. It is probable that he baptized a thousand or more during the four years and a half of his evangelistic career. He was known by his brethren as "Strong Georg" and was sometimes designated a "Second Paul." He seems to have been entirely free from fanaticism and to have attained to a remarkably high standard of Christian consecration.[1]

Wilhelm Reublin, whom we know as one of the earliest impugners of infant baptism and as one of the most eloquent and zealous of the Anti-pedobaptist evangelists, was born at Rottenburg on the Neckar. He was among the first of the Swiss priests to take a radically evangelical position. In 1522 we find him in Basel, where in a religious procession instead of relics he bore a large Bible, saying that this was the truly sacred thing, the others were merely dead bones. Though the most popular evangelical preacher in Basel he was driven away because he abetted the breaking of ecclesiastical fasts. He was the first pastor in the canton of Zürich to break a fast and the first to marry. He was perhaps too violently denunciatory and somewhat inconsiderate in his treatment of opponents; but he was soundly evangelical in his views and, next to Blaurock, had probably the most fruitful career of any of the early Anti-pedobaptist leaders. It was his unspeakable privilege to convince Hubmaier that the time had come for action and to baptize him who was to become the greatest and soundest of

---

[1] The most exhaustive account of Blaurock is that by F. Jecklin in the twenty-first "Jahresbericht der historisch-antiquarischen Gesellschaft von Graubünden," 1891, pp. 1-20. Blaurock's original name was Cajacob.

all the Anti-pedobaptists of the sixteenth century. After laboring in many places throughout Switzerland and Southern Germany he removed to Moravia, where his experience was for a time most unhappy.

Of Hans Denck, Michael Sattler, Ludwig Hetzer, Jacob Gross, and other leaders, whose activity as Antipedobaptists was chiefly outside of Switzerland and after the middle of 1525, we shall have occasion to treat hereafter.

Literature: Pertinent works (as in Bibliography) of Egli, Strickler, Heberle, Strasser, Nitsche, Burrage, Schaff, Baur, Keller, Usteri, Stähelin, E. Müller, Loserth, Kessler, Gast, Bullinger, Füsslin, Beck, Cornelius, Hosek, Schreiber, Zwingli, and Hubmaier.

CHAPTER XI

PERSECUTION AND DISPERSION

WE have traced the rise of the Swiss Anti-pedobaptist movement in the canton of Zürich and its rapid spread throughout the other evangelical cantons during the first half of 1525. For a time the movement threatened to sweep everything before it. Not only were the masses of the people enthusiastic in their acceptance of the new doctrine and practice, but most of the leading evangelical scholars were profoundly moved by the earnestness and zeal of the leaders of the party, and by the absence of clear scriptural warrant for the baptizing of infants.

The time was most opportune for the rapid spread of Anti-pedobaptist views. The violent breaking away from the old order of things by the politico-ecclesiastical reformers prepared men's minds for still more radical changes. The insistence of Luther and Zwingli on scriptural authority for every point of faith and practice was sure to lead to a demand for the scriptural authentication of infant baptism. The socialistic aims that found expression in the Peasants' War were based upon the people's understanding of apostolic Christianity. The leading reformers had admitted the injustice of the feudal system and had declaimed against the extortionate practices of the hierarchy. The radical party made social reform one of the chief planks in its platform. This latter consideration undoubtedly predisposed the masses to give heed to the preaching of the simple gospel in which brotherly love figured very prominently. For the permanence of the movement the time was most inopportune. The Peasants' War was already in progress when the Anti-pedobaptist movement in Switzerland became aggressive. The universal alarm and consternation caused by this determined effort of the peasantry to throw off their bondage and by the fanatical procedures of Münzer and Pfeiffer, with which the name "Anabaptist" was closely associated in the popular mind, caused the Anti-pedobaptist movement to be regarded with the utmost disfavor by all who were interested in the maintenance of existing social and religious institutions.

We shall misjudge the good men who urged the extirpation of Anti-pedobaptism, if we fail to take into consideration their view of the magnitude of the danger that threatened everything they valued in Church and State. It was not wanton cruelty but a sense of sheer necessity that made Zwingli the fierce persecutor he became. Once convinced that disaster was involved in the movement his animosity against its leaders became unbounded and he showed himself incapable of doing justice to their arguments or of seeing anything good in their lives. We abhor intolerance, but we must temper our disapproval of the intolerant by taking into careful consideration the circumstances of time and place.

The earlier stages of persecution have already been recorded. Fines and imprisonment had greatly interfered with the progress of Anti-pedobaptist principles since January, 1525. But these principles were far too popular and accorded too completely with a deep-seated and profoundly felt need to be so readily suppressed as the authorities hoped. As in the apostolic age, persecution intensified the zeal and spread abroad the principles of the persecuted. Such enthusiastic radicals as Grebel, Manz, Blaurock, Reublin, and Brötli, might have been content to labor quietly in their own communities and to carry forward the work of propagandism in an orderly and deliberate manner had they not been driven by the earlier persecuting measures to extend the sphere of their activity, and had they not been aroused by the violent treatment they suffered to do everything in their power for the overthrow of the standing order.

We have traced the progress of these radical reformers and the oral and literary controversies of which they were the occasion and in which they were participants to about December, 1525. We have seen the center of interest in the movement shift from the immediate neighborhood of Zürich first to St. Gall, from March onward, and afterward to Grüningen. The inability of the authorities of the bailiwick of Grüningen to cope with the rapidly spreading and highly popular movement and the urgent appeal of the Grüningen authorities to the Zürich Council to arrange for a disputation in which the points at issue should be freely discussed, with the request that Zwingli be admonished to allow the poor people to express their minds freely and not by his overbearing demeanor to make their words "stick in their throats," resulted in the appointment of a disputation for November 6-8, 1525. Arrangements were made for a full representation of the Anti-pedobaptists and of their opponents. That good order might be preserved in the debates and the utmost freedom of utterance be secured, the Abbot of Cappel, the Commander of Küssnacht, Dr. Hofmeister of Schaffhausen, and Dr. Vadian of St. Gall, were appointed presidents. Zwingli, Judae, and Grossmann were the principal disputants on the one side and Grebel, Manz, and Blaurock on the other. Hubmaier was expected but did not appear, owing no doubt to the critical situation at Waldshut.

The disputation was begun in the great council chamber with open doors, but the large number of Anti-pedobaptists present became so demonstrative that it was thought advisable to remove it to a room in the Minster Church and to restrict the attendance. The debate lasted for three days and the points at issue were ably and fully argued on both sides.

The authorities decided that the victory lay on the side of Zwingli. As might have been expected the Anti-pedobaptist leaders resolutely refused to submit to this decision, denied that any scriptural ground for infant baptism had been adduced, and insisted that their opponents had taken advantage of the fact that they enjoyed the favor of the authorities to deny them freedom of speech. A number of Anti-pedobaptists were now arraigned before the authorities at Zürich and in the Grüningen district. Some promised obedience, while others were heavily fined.

On November 18, Grebel, Manz, and Blaurock were imprisoned in the new tower on account of their anabaptistry and their "unseemly practices"; their food was to be limited to apple-sauce and bread and water, and they were to be wholly denied communication with their friends. The imprisonment was to last as long as the council should think fit. Ulrich Deck of Waldshut, who had for some time been laboring in Grüningen, Martin Ling of Schaffhausen, and Michael Sattler of Staufen, in Breisgau, were banished. Sattler we shall meet again as one of the ablest, most amiable, and noblest of the Anti-pedobaptist leaders and martyrs. Large numbers were imprisoned in Grüningen, and of these many persisted in their views and expressed their determination to be steadfast even unto death. They did not hesitate to declare that infant baptism was of the devil. The authorities claimed that the Anti-pedobaptists had been given the amplest opportunity to defend their principles and practices in the disputation at Zürich; that they had been fairly vanquished by Zwingli and his associates, and that their persistence in denouncing infant baptism and in rebaptizing involved disobedience to the constituted authorities, caused schism and the destruction of Christian love among Christian people, and could not be tolerated with safety to the community. The measures taken against them in Grüningen proved so ineffective that the sheriff (*Landvogt*) was in despair. "Truly, I know not where I should attack, so much disturbance besets me." "The Baptists make my head gray with their words and proceedings."

The long-threatened punishment of Waldshut occurred on December 9. The Waldshut authorities even in view of imminent doom had a few weeks before refused the demand of the Austrian authorities for the extradition of Hubmaier with eight other leaders of the disobedient party and the surrender of the city to be dealt with at the discretion of the government. Seeing that the possibility of maintaining the evangelical cause in Waldshut was at an end, with the permission of the Waldshut authorities Hubmaier withdrew on December 5, as he himself said, "a mortally sick man, who knows not whither he is to go." Forewarned that he was about to be seized, his flight was so precipitate that he was obliged to leave his clothing behind. His wife managed to get into his hands a small amount of money, and by the help of a neighbor he got safely across the Rhine. Many of his immediate followers escaped at about the same time. It was Hubmaier's intention to go first to Basel and thence to Strasburg; but the danger of arrest was so imminent that he thought it advisable to make his way to Zürich, notwithstanding his knowledge of the fact that his views were there under the ban.

The fall of Waldshut was lamented by the leaders of the dominant evangelical party in Switzerland, and their animosity was aroused quite as much against Hubmaier, whose radical teachings and procedures had been the immediate occasion of the catastrophe, as against the Austrian authorities, who would tolerate nothing evangelical. That an unfriendly reception awaited him at Zürich he no doubt fully expected; but the terribleness of the sufferings he was there to undergo for his fidelity to New Testament principles he could scarcely have foreseen.

Hubmaier arrived in Zürich ragged and wretched. He was entertained by a widow recently baptized by Aberli, now the most influential resident Anti-pedobaptist. He was shortly afterward imprisoned by the council, who naturally feared that the arrival of this great leader would cause a fresh outbreak of activity on the part of the radical religionists. Zwingli, Judae, Myconius, Hofmeister and others were appointed to confer with Hubmaier in regard to his teachings. A discussion took place on December 21, in which Hubmaier charged Zwingli with inconsistency in defending infant baptism, which he had earlier acknowledged to be without scriptural authority. Zwingli sought to prove from Acts 2 that infant church-membership existed in the apostolic church, and he quoted the passage in 1 Corinthians 10 about the baptism of the Hebrews by Moses in the cloud and in the sea, to prove that infants as well as adults were proper subjects of baptism. He proceeded to reproach Hubmaier violently for the disaster he had brought upon Waldshut. Feeble in health, and at the mercy of his opponents, Hubmaier is said to have promised to reconsider his views.

The Austrian authorities, chagrined that in the capture of Waldshut the chief object of their displeasure had escaped, urgently and repeatedly demanded the extradition of Hubmaier. That this was persistently refused was certainly to the credit of the Zürich authorities.

Zwingli made much of the favor thus shown, when afterward he was reproached for his cruel treatment of Hubmaier. It is not entirely clear whether the torture was literally applied to Hubmaier or not.[1] His own language does not necessarily imply more than that his recantation was extorted from him by the "great hardness and torment of the rigorous imprisonment, which" he "suffered against all right and in spite of his appeal to the confederacy, to the Zürich Council, and to the emperor himself." He claimed that the council had sought by violent means to compel him, a sick man who had just risen from a death-bed, to change his faith.

Zwingli is said at this time to have publicly advocated the execution of Hubmaier and the other Anti-pedobaptist leaders. Hubmaier's own account of his imprisonment is probably to be taken as accurate. He relates that more than twenty men, widows, delicate women, and maidens were thrown into a miserable prison, and were given to understand that during their lifetime they were to be permitted to look upon neither sun nor moon, and on a diet of water and bread they were to remain together, and die, and rot. Among the prisoners there were some (himself probably among them) who for three days did not take a bite of bread, in order not to let the rest hunger. Among Hubmaier's fellow-sufferers were Grebel, Manz, Blaurock, and a number of less prominent brethren, and Anna Manz, Anna Wiederkehr, and Elizabeth and Margaret Hottinger. Several of these women were among the most heroic confessors.

Most of the prisoners were sentenced on March seventh. In the process of March 5, Hubmaier is said to have promised to desist from rebaptizing. Blaurock did not hesitate to confess that he, along with his brethren in Christ,

---

[1] Of recent Swiss writers, Baur and Usteri are of the opinion that physical torture in the technical sense was employed; Egli thinks the evidence indecisive.

Grebel and Manz, had introduced believers' baptism, and to charge that Luther and Zwingli, no less than the pope, were thieves and murderers, inasmuch as they did not enter the sheepfold by the proper door, but sought to climb up some other way.

On March 7 a mandate proceeded from the council affixing the penalty of death by drowning, without any grace, to rebaptism. As regards those already imprisoned it is enacted that they be discharged in case they will confess that rebaptism is wrong and infant baptism right, and on their pledging themselves to abandon all effort for the promulgation of Anti-pedobaptist views. In case of relapse they are to suffer the death penalty by drowning. From this time onward no quarter was given to the advocates of believers' baptism.

The great majority of the imprisoned persisted in maintaining that since infant baptism is not commanded in Scripture it " must be rooted out," as must everything " which the Heavenly Father has not planted."

It was the design of the authorities by securing his recantation to demoralize the Anti-pedobaptist hosts, who looked upon him as the greatest defender of their principles. If torture in the technical sense was actually applied it was with this highly important end in view. Probably in the early days of March he was induced to sign a form of recantation, and it was arranged that he should personally appear in the two principal churches on the following Sunday and read it to the assembled multitudes.

The recantation begins:

I, Balthasar Hubmaier, of Friedberg, publicly confess with this my autograph that I have not otherwise known nor understood all Scriptures pertaining to water baptism, than that preaching should first take place, then believing, and thirdly, baptism. Upon this I finally took a firm stand. But now there has been shown to me through Master Ulrich Zwingli the covenant of God made with Abraham and his seed, also circumcision as a sign of the covenant, and how baptism takes the place of circumcision, which I have not been able to solve; and so also there has been held before me by others, as Master Leo, Dr. Sebastian, and Myconius, how love should be a judge and umpire in all the Scriptures, which I have taken deeply to heart, and so I have thought much of love and have finally been moved to relinquish my contention that infants should not be baptized, and acknowledge that I have erred in the matter of rebaptism.[1]

He repudiates the charge that he rejects magistracy and insists that he has ever taught obedience to the constituted authorities and the right of Christians to exercise magistracy. He denies that he has ever taught community of goods; he has simply insisted on the requirement of Christian charity to impart freely of one's substance for the relief of hungry, thirsty, naked, and imprisoned believers. He repudiates the charge that he thinks himself without sin and confesses that he is a poor sinner, conceived and born in sin, and will remain a sinner even until death. He entreats the authorities in consideration of his severe illness, adversity, banishment, and poverty, and of the great anger and cruelty that his adversaries have conceived against him, to deal graciously with him and not to suffer him to fall into the hands of his enemies, "for," he continues, "I am a weak man and can in this weak body not renounce bodily solicitude."

Hubmaier soon bitterly repented that in his weakness and despair he had so far compromised his position as to set his hand to this document; yet he knew full well that those who required this act of him were not deceived thereby. The instinct of self-preservation was undoubt-

---

[1] Stähelin ("Zwingli," Vol I., p 516), is of the opinion that this is the recantation Hubmaier promised to make in December, 1525, and not that which he was finally tortured into making in March and April, 1526. The same form of recantation may have been repeatedly employed.

edly stronger in him than in most of his brethren, who could be induced neither by "bodily solicitude" nor by torture even momentarily to depart a hair's breadth from what they believed to be the truth. Yet if we consider the circumstances few of us will feel justified in casting reproach upon this great and good man for so far manifesting fleshly weakness. It is gratifying to know that he soon rose superior to the carnal desire for self-preservation. When, according to arrangement, he was taken to the Minster Church to read publicly the document he had signed, he began instead to defend believers' baptism. The people murmured, Zwingli was obliged to restore order, and Hubmaier was remanded to prison.

The increased rigors of his imprisonment and the decision of the council to let their impenitent prisoners "die and rot"[1] in the tower finally overcame him and he consented, April 11, to do what was required of him. After performing his recantation, on his promise to depart from the Zürich jurisdiction and to refrain from activity in the Anti-pedobaptist cause while in the jurisdiction, he was released. Some kindly disposed citizens put into his hands ten gold pieces to aid him in his journeyings, without the approval of Zwingli, who was not above imputing to the man who had suffered such hardship and was evidently in the depths of poverty the most sordid motives. He went first to Constance and after a short visit departed for Augsburg, where an extensive Anti-pedobaptist movement was in progress. Here he met and conferred with Hans Denck, the high-minded mystic, with some of whose views he by no means agreed. Before June 21 he had found a home at Nikolsburg in Moravia, where he was to labor for more than a year with wonderful assiduity and success.

Grebel, Manz, and Blaurock were soon released with

---

[1] These words are official.

the injunction to abstain from Anti-pedobaptist teaching and practice. We find them soon impelled by their consuming zeal to renew their activity and their cause continued to flourish in the Grüningen district, the scene of their labors. If the Zürich authorities were reluctant to carry out the mandate in accordance with which drowning was to be the penalty of rebaptizing and evidently intended it more as a deterrent than as a law to be strictly executed, the local Grüningen authorities positively refused to execute the inhuman law and appealed in support of their refusal to certain old privileges that had been bestowed upon the district by the house of Austria.

In Grüningen the Anti-pedobaptist cause struck its roots deeper than anywhere else in the canton of Zürich. Many influential families were among its adherents. The heavy fines that were imposed on baptizers and baptized proved ruinous to the estates of many and interfered seriously with the economic well-being of the district. The authorities complained bitterly of the disturbances thus caused and urged the Zürich Council not to pay too much heed to the clergy, who were the chief informers against Anti-pedobaptists, "since some of them [the clergy] are lying and worthless." It would seem from the complaints of the Grüningen authorities as well as from the constantly recurring charges of the Anti-pedo baptists, that the great mass of the Swiss clergy were not only lacking in vital godliness but were even scandalously vicious. Such men were the objects of attack on the part of the Anti-pedobaptists and such in turn felt that their means of living were jeopardized by the pointed denunciations of the zealous sectaries. As a result of the firm footing which the Anti-pedobaptists had gained in Grüningen and the comparatively favorable attitude of the authorities, they were able to carry on

CHURCHES ORGANIZED

their work with vigor and success despite the zeal of the sheriff of the district and the rigorous and frequently reiterated mandates of the Zürich Council.

Of the seventy Anti-pedobaptist organizations in the canton of Zürich from the beginning of the movement till its almost complete suppression about 1535, twelve were in Zürichberg, seventeen in Oberland and adjacent regions, twenty-seven in Unterland, twelve in Weinland, and three in Kronaueramt. Of those in Zürichberg only two remained after 1527 and none after 1531. Of those in Oberland, all but two of which were formed during the years 1525-27, only four survived the year 1527, and only one (not mentioned in the earlier lists) remained to be extinguished after 1531. In Unterland eleven organizations were effected 1525-27, nine of which survived the latter date, while during 1527-31 fourteen new organizations were effected; of the older organizations twelve remained to suffer extermination between 1531 and 1535 and two were first formed during this period. Of the Weinland churches one was formed 1525-27, two during 1527-31, and nine during the years of extermination, 1531-35. All the Anti-pedobaptist communities in the Kronaueramt seem to have been organized during the later period. These figures show to some extent the rapidity with which the movement spread in the Zürich dependencies and how ineffective were the efforts of the Zürich authorities to suppress the popular party that insisted on a complete return to New Testament Christianity.

About the beginning of 1527 Manz and Blaurock were again arrested in the Grüningen district and brought to Zürich for trial. Reluctant as the council was to inflict the death penalty, it had come to feel that the case of Manz was a most aggravated one and that an example should be made of him. There is every reason to believe that the council acted on the advice of Zwingli when it decreed that this zealous and godly man should have his hands tied together and put over his knees, a stick inserted between his arms and legs, and should be thrown from a boat into the Rhine at a designated spot. This judgment was duly executed. The preamble of the sentence bases the action of the council on the fact that Manz "confesses that he has said that he and others who would accept Christ's leadership and follow the word, also walk according to Christ, would gather themselves together and unite themselves with him through rebaptism and let the others remain in their faith; accordingly now he and his followers have separated themselves from the Christian community and under the appearance and pretext of a Christian assembly and church will resuscitate and equip a self-constituted sect, factions, and assemblies of their own." Manz is further accused of maintaining that no Christian may exercise magistracy, or judge others with the sword or put to death or punish any one. That for such teaching and practice a man should be put to death with the approval of Christian teachers like Zwingli and his associates is strange indeed, and readers unacquainted with the spirit of the age and the circumstances of this particular case may be prompted to exclaim that men guilty of such intolerance were no Christians. This is not, however, the judgment of men who understand the spirit of the times and appreciate the difficulties that seemed to be involved in allowing each individual to choose his own manner of worshiping God and freely to propagate his views. To Zwingli and his associates nothing but disaster seemed likely to result from toleration. It would seem that Zwingli at last became so embittered against his opponents that he rather gloried in their sufferings.

Blaurock was tried the same day and was pronounced

equally guilty with Manz; but one victim sufficed, and in consideration of the fact that he was a foreigner he was sentenced to be beaten on the naked back through the streets until the blood should flow. On his promising to withdraw immediately from the Zürich jurisdiction and with the assurance that he would be drowned in case he returned, he was released. He soon returned, however, to the Grüningen district and resumed his ministry.

The unwillingness of the Grüningen authorities to execute the mandates of the Zürich Council was a source of much perplexity, especially as the advocates of believers' baptism were rapidly gaining ground and spreading into the surrounding regions. Early in June, 1527, the Zürich Council peremptorily demanded the drowning of a number of prisoners. On the refusal of the local authorities to comply, the Zürich Council threatened to secure the intervention of Berne and to take measures for enforcing obedience.

Inasmuch as Anti-pedobaptism was spreading from canton to canton and was in the opinion of the authorities menacing civil and ecclesiastical order, the Zürich Council thought it advisable to invite the confederated cantons of Berne, Basel, Schaffhausen, Chur, Appenzell and St. Gall to a conference to be held on August 13, to agree upon concerted and vigorous measures for the extermination of Anti-pedobaptism, which was declared to have for its aim the destruction "not only of the true right faith of Christian hearts, but also of outward and human ordinances and institutions of Christian and ordinary magistracy, against brotherly love and good morals." Correspondence was also inaugurated with Augsburg and Ulm, where Anti-pedobaptists were known to abound, and from the close commercial relations in which they stood to Switzerland having many interests in common with the latter.

By December 16, 1527, arrangements had been completed for a more thorough inquisition of heresy than had yet found place. At this time the council issued a mandate to the sheriffs of the canton requiring them to suppress all private meetings for religious purposes, and to arrest and bring to Zürich for imprisonment in the Wellenberg all participants in such meetings, who are to be released only on payment of five pounds.

The result of this mandate was the arrest and examination of large numbers, especially in the Unterland district. In these investigations the Anti-pedobaptists laid chief stress on the moral corruption of the clergy and the lack of proper discipline in the churches of the standing order. The authorities could not deny that the charges were well founded and remedial measures were adopted.

After Easter, 1528, synods were established, one of whose most important functions was to discipline unworthy clergymen. In these synods the gravest charges were made by representatives of several of the congregations against their pastors. The pastor of Steinmaur was removed for adultery. The Wetzikon Church accused its pastor of backbiting and theft. Wangen charged its pastor with drunkenness and gambling. The Bulach pastor was charged with absenting himself from church services when other ministers preached, with avarice, and with failure to train his children aright. He is required to go to Zürich for a course of study. The Russikon, Zell, Wildberg, and Turbenthal pastors were found guilty of drunkenness, tavern-haunting, and fighting. The pastor of Laufen was charged with covetousness, that of Ottenbach with drunkenness and wife-beating, and that of Stallikon with drunkenness. Of these some were removed, while others were sharply censured and on promise of amendment allowed to retain their

EXECUTION OF FALK AND REIMANN

positions. Thus an indirect effect of the Anti-pedobaptist movement was the inauguration of a somewhat vigorous discipline in the churches of the dominant party.

Already in 1526 baptismal registers had been introduced into the churches by the authorities, in order that it might be authoritatively ascertained whether any particular person had been baptized. Evasion of the law by opponents of infant baptism was thus rendered more difficult. Under the new disciplinary arrangement of 1528 provision was made for a close scrutiny of the lives of the members of each community, in order that those out of sympathy with the standing order might be the more readily detected. Thus the organization of the dominant party became more and more complete, the enforcement of conformity to the established order more and more rigorous, and the persecution of dissent more and more exterminating.

At Grüningen a number of Anti-pedobaptists had lain in prison for a year and fifteen weeks. In August, 1528, they were taken to Zürich for examination and subjected to great hardship, a small quantity of bread and water being the only nourishment allowed. Two of the leaders, Jacob Falk and Henry Reimann, persisted in their Anti-pedobaptism, and were sentenced to death by drowning on September 5. Others were induced to admit that infant baptism was right and rebaptism wrong and were released. One of the prisoners lay sick in the tower for several months and was swollen from head to foot. He preferred to die in the tower with his companions rather than in the castle outside.

The law against entertaining or in any way showing favor to Anti-pedobaptists was from this time onward rigorously enforced. The local authorities throughout the canton were held to their duty as never before. Grüningen after long and determined resistance was compelled by the intervention of Berne to yield obedience to the Zürich Council. Aggressive work on the part of the sectaries had become well-nigh impossible. Most of the leaders of the movement were either dead or in banishment. Moreover, a land of promise had been discovered in Moravia, and thither flocked thousands of the most aggressive Anti-pedobaptists from Switzerland, Southern Germany, Silesia, the Tyrol, and other countries. By 1529 the Anti-pedobaptist cause in Switzerland showed a marked decline; by 1535 only a few congregations remained. These were mostly in the canton of Berne, where they increased very rapidly from 1527 onward, and where they became so firmly rooted that they have been able to survive in considerable numbers to the present time. The Bernese brethren represented the purest type of sixteenth century Antipedobaptism. So closely were they related in doctrine and in practice to the Waldenses of the earlier time that a recent historian of the movement insists upon their direct derivation from the mediæval evangelicals who are known to have abounded in this region in the fifteenth century. In no other way is he able to account for the persistence with which they have held on their way in the face of bitter persecution. He thinks that if the Bernese Anabaptists had been a product of the Reformation their zeal would have soon subsided, and that like other spasmodic movements this would have speedily vanished.[1]

It scarcely need be said that in Roman Catholic countries Anti-pedobaptism was regarded as the most radical and dangerous type of Protestantism, and was from the

---

[1] E. Meyer, Gesch. d. Bernischen Täufer, 1895. The author has brought to light a vast amount of documentary material illustrative of the earlier as well as the later history of the Bernese Anti-pedobaptists from the public archives of the canton and other sources. While he may be unduly confident as regards the historical connection of this party with the older evangelical parties, he has presented the facts in favor of this view in a most impressive manner.

first proscribed. In April, 1529, an Imperial mandate, given at the diet of Speier, required, "that rebaptizers and rebaptized all and each, male and female, of intelligent age, be judged and brought from natural life to death, without antecedent inquisition of the spiritual judges." This law was obligatory upon Protestant and Catholic princes alike, and few of either considered it too severe. The rigor with which the edict was enforced depended, of course, upon the disposition of the individual princes, some of whom, like Philip of Hesse, were inclined to moderation; but that it was for the most part zealously carried out the multitude of recorded martyrdoms attest. It is stated by a contemporary historian,[1] that by 1530 two thousand Anti-pedobaptists had been executed, nearly all outside of Switzerland.

Anti-pedobaptists had become as widely diffused throughout Europe as the Waldenses and related parties had been during the thirteenth and following centuries. There were few communities in which they did not appear in greater or smaller numbers; while in many places they met with wonderful popular acceptance and could be suppressed only by long-continued and rigorous inquisitorial procedures. Of these multitudes a very large proportion owed their impulse to the Anti-pedobaptists of Switzerland and of Waldshut, who from 1525 were widely scattered by persecution. The influence of Münzer and Storch can also be traced with some distinctness in scattered chiliastic Anti-pedobaptist teachers and congregations. Hans Hut was the principal propagator of this type of doctrine in Austria and Southern Germany. Doubtless many individuals came independently to Anti-pedobaptist views from a study of the Scriptures. That a considerable proportion of the great Anti-pedobaptist host which in an incredibly short time

---
[1] Sebastian Franck.

was arrayed against Protestantism as decidedly as against Roman Catholicism had been previously under the influence of mediæval evangelical teaching, a comparison of the doctrines and the manner of life and work of the two parties renders highly probable.

To give in detail the history of this important and interesting movement in all its branches and during the entire period of its persistence is manifestly impracticable. Contemporary documentary materials abound and are being continually made more available by the zeal of European scholars, both Protestant and Catholic, and by the liberality of governments, municipalities, and societies. We shall be compelled to restrict ourselves to a few of the great centers of Anti-pedobaptist activity, and in these to the briefest statement of the more essential facts.

Literature: Pertinent works (as in Bibliography) of Egli, Strickler, Heberle, Strasser, Nitsche, Burrage, Schaff, Baur, Keller, Usteri, Stähelin, E. Müller, Loserth, Kessler, Gast, Bullinger, Füsslin, Beck, Cornelius, Hosek, Schreiber, Zwingli, and Hubmaier.

CHAPTER XII

SILESIA

SILESIA, bounded by Poland, Moravia, Bohemia, Brandenburg, and Saxony, had been greatly influenced by mediæval evangelical movements (Hussites, Bohemian Brethren, and Waldenses), and was sure to be among the earliest regions to adopt the more radical phases of the Protestant revolution. It is probable that Nicholas Storch spent a few months at Glogau and in the surrounding regions soon after the disastrous termination of the Peasants' War in May, 1525.

Lutheranism had already gained a considerable following in Silesia, and Storch is said to have begun his work by teaching the evangelical truths that he held in common with Luther, reserving his peculiar doctrines until he should have gained sufficient prestige to assure their popular acceptance. His influence is said to have extended to Fraustadt, which afterward became the center of his activity. Here as elsewhere the labors of Storch are said to have occasioned considerable commotion, and he was not able to remain long in the same place; but so great was his enthusiasm and such claims did he make for his teachings that multitudes are said to have accepted his leadership.

While in the succeeding years occasional indications of the influence of the Storch-Münzer type of teaching appear, the preponderating element in the important Antipedobaptist movement of 1525 onward was undoubtedly of the Swiss type. That the Swiss brethren, who had Silesians among them at an early date (1526) and who were widely scattered by persecution, from 1526 onward, should have had representatives in Silesia was what might have been expected.

Before entering upon a discussion of the Anti-pedobaptist movement that was to furnish its thousands of recruits to the great Moravian brotherhood, mention should be made of the mystical reforming movement led by Caspar Schwenckfeldt.

Of the influence of this Silesian nobleman in causing a widespread departure from the Lutheran type of teaching and a general adoption in evangelical circles of Anti-pedobaptist views we can speak with far more confidence than of Storch's Silesian activity. Schwenckfeldt belonged to an ancient noble house at Ossig. He studied in several universities, finishing his studies at Cologne. Like Luther he was an ardent student of the old-evangelical mysticism of Tauler, the German Theology, etc. While residing at the court of Duke Charles of Münsterberg he came under the influence of the teachings of Huss. When Luther came out boldly for reform, Schwenckfeldt was ready to accept his leadership.

In 1521 he retired for a season of profound Scripture study. In 1525 he became convinced that Luther was astray on baptism, the Lord's Supper, justification by faith, and a number of other points. A conference with Luther failed to result in harmony of views. Not only was he at variance with Luther in reference to doctrine, but he took sharp issue with him as regards the manner of bringing about reform. Reformation should proceed from within outward, without the intervention of the civil authorities.

He soon came to feel that the tendency of Luther's teachings was to bring about a state of carnal security in those who accepted them, and that his doctrine of justification by faith alone and that of assurance were immoral in their tendencies. His observation of Lutheran evangelical life led him to the conviction that Lutheran faith was a dead faith, that Luther's doctrine of Scripture was a doctrine of the letter and not of the spirit, that his teaching respecting baptism and the Supper was unscriptural and out of accord with the principles of spiritual Christianity. He maintained, moreover, that Luther had departed widely from the position he had occupied when he first appeared as a reformer.

He held that only the spiritually enlightened man can properly understand the Scriptures, and he distinguished between the word of God and the material Scriptures that contain this word. Faith he regarded as the personal appropriation of Christ, and it necessarily involved a complete transformation of character. Baptism he regarded as symbolical of the great inner transformation that has occurred in regeneration, and hence as utterly inapplicable to infants. The Lord's Supper he took to be symbolical of the spiritual partaking of Christ, and communion with his sufferings and death.

The Duke of Leignitz, one of the most influential of the Silesian nobility, sympathized with Schwenckfeldt's anti-Lutheran views of reform. There soon resulted a general falling away from the Lutheran position and large numbers openly adopted Anti-pedobaptist views.

Schwenckfeldt was too much of a mystic to be willing to be the leader of a radical reforming party or to lay so great stress upon external ordinances as was involved in the Anti-pedobaptist position, but he continued to the end of a long life in friendly relations with the Anti-pedobaptists, and his influence during the earlier time in Silesia, as well as during his later life when he made Strasburg his home, was highly favorable to the popular acceptance of their principles. "Hoffmann and the Anabaptists," he said on one occasion when accused of undue intimacy with that great leader,

I patronize not more than is in accord with the spirit of Christ. . . . That I now subject myself to no party and sect, neither to the Papists, Lutherans, Zwinglians, nor Baptists, has many causes and brings me not a little persecution and ill-will from them all. But I pray the Lord he will keep me in this position and not allow me to despise what is good, right, and well pleasing. Yet I see in one party much more of God than in the rest, more divinely given blessedness and imitation of the crucified Christ; this I cannot deny.

There can be no doubt as to the party to which he gave so decided a preference. He justified his separation on the ground,

That it is a necessity to the Christian that he touch no unclean thing, and that he be not yoked together with unbelievers, nor have communion with the works of darkness.

Schwenckfeldt had no thought of forming a sect, but a considerable number of those who had been dominated by his teachings gathered themselves after his death into a society for the circulation of his writings and the conservation of his influence. In 1734 a number of families settled in Pennsylvania, where they still have four congregations with a membership of about three hundred and six. Schwenckfeldt died in 1562.

The encouragement given to Anti-pedobaptism by Schwenckfeldt and the noblemen who supported him, and a natural predilection of the masses for radical types of religious thought, resulted in a very rapid growth of the cause. Hast (following Meschovius) doubtless grossly exaggerates when he states that by 1526 Silesia had become almost entirely Anti-pedobaptist; yet we have abundant evidence that thousands adopted Anti-pedobaptist views and that congregations were organized in many of the most important towns as well as in many villages and rural communities.

By far the most important leader at this time (1526-28)

was Gabriel Ascherham of Schärding. This Bavarian evangelist, of whose earlier antecedents little or nothing is known, was instrumental in the conversion of hundreds, if not thousands, of Silesians to Anti-pedobaptist views and in the organization of many congregations. When persecution arose (1527-28) he led a large party to Rossnitz in Moravia. He was followed later by hundreds more, the number of his Silesian followers in Moravia having reached, according to some accounts, about two thousand. The strife that arose between Gabriel and the Hutherites has resulted in an unjust loss of reputation for the Silesian leader, as the accounts that have been preserved emanated from his opponents. That he was strong-willed, somewhat arbitrary, and over-violent in his polemics, may be freely admitted; but the same might be said of most of the great leaders of the age.

Among the influential teachers of this time were Oswald and Hess in Breslau, where a congregation seems to have been organized. This community seems to have been visited by Hans Hut in 1527. Congregations existed in and around Leignitz, Glatz, and Glogau. These bore marks of the influence of Storch.[1] In Glatz and Schweidnitz the Anti-pedobaptists came forward in 1529 as a "League of Jesus Christ," and asked the princely and local authorities for the opportunity to explain and defend their principles under a safe-conduct. This request was refused and served only to increase the vigilance of the authorities and to sharpen the measures already being employed for the extirpation of the party.

According to a manuscript in the Vienna Court Library, Clemens Adler, the most important Silesian leader of the time, was executed at Glogau in 1636. According to the Presburg manuscript, he was master of three languages,

---

[1] Dr. Loserth is of the opinion that these had nothing to do with those Anti-pedobaptists who went to Moravia under the leadership of Gabriel.

Latin, Bohemian, and German. For some time he was engaged as a preacher in Bohemia. Moved by the Lord he came one day into the church at Glatz, silenced the preacher and himself preached for an hour. He was however driven from the city. Another leader of the Anti-pedobaptists in the city of Breslau and its environs was Hans Reck (Giganteus), well known through the controversy that he had with Dr. Hess, in connection with which he wrote (in Latin) his "Judgment on the Faith of Infants, to Dr. Joh. Hess." He also wrote a refutation of Justus Menius' strictures on the Anti-pedobaptists.

Andrew von Nespe is spoken of as an apostle of the Silesian Anti-pedobaptists. He labored successfully at Heilbron on the Neckar, in Wirtemberg, and in Bavaria, and finally suffered martyrdom at Neustadt on the Danube. The most important individual contribution of Silesia to the Anti-pedobaptist cause was undoubtedly Peter Reidemann, who, after laboring for a time in upper Austria, removed to Moravia and became head of the Hutherite connection. He wrote the best systematic exposition of the doctrines and practices of the party.

After 1528-29 the persecuting measures of the Silesian authorities were too exterminating in their nature to allow of the building up of vigorous church organizations, but fostered by the brethren in Moravia the cause was long kept alive. Schwenckfeldt was himself obliged to quit Silesia in 1528, the noblemen who favored his cause being no longer able to protect him.

Literature: Meschovius, Bachmann, Erbkam, and Hast, as in the Bibliography. For some of the details the writer is indebted to Professor Dr. J. Loserth, of the University of Graz, Austria, who in a private communication generously imparted much information not otherwise procurable.

CHAPTER XIII

THE AUGSBURG CENTER

AUGSBURG was one of the great commercial centers of the Reformation time. It was favorably situated for trade with Italy, Austria, and all parts of central Germany. Its merchants were among the most enterprising in the world and had their ships on all the seas. Augsburg profited largely by the discovery of the new world and the great increase of commerce with the Orient. Manufactures kept pace with foreign trade. In a population of about thirty thousand there were nearly fifteen hundred master weavers. As in the Middle Ages Augsburg was an important center of old-evangelical life, so in the Reformation time, side by side with Strasburg, it was a refuge for the persecuted and a place where any radical teacher might hope to gain followers. The bitter and long-continued conflict in Augsburg between the Lutheran and Zwinglian types of doctrine prevented the establishment of any complete or vigorously administered church order. Among the evangelical ministers no man arose who was able to mold the religious life of the city.

Augsburg received into its bosom at an early date representatives of the movement led by Storch and Münzer and those who had received their training in Anti-pedobaptist principles in Switzerland. Of mystical and fanatical types it had its full share. In no city of upper Germany was there so large an aggregation of Anti-pedobaptist life. Not only did Augsburg receive from abroad large numbers of representatives of the great Anti-pedobaptist movement, but its own inhabitants, among whom the artisan classes abounded, showed remarkable readiness to accept what claimed to be pure apostolic Christianity. Situated on the road between Strasburg and Moravia, two other great centers of the movement, it formed a sort of distributing point for the Anti-pedobaptist life of the time. Most of the prominent leaders spent more or less time here, and several of them made a profound impression on the religious life of the city. Among those who barely touched the city with their personal influence was Hubmaier, who spent a few days there on his way to Moravia. Among those who made Augsburg a definite field for labor may be mentioned Hans Denck, Jacob Gross, Hans Hut, and Eitelhans Langenmantel. Not only did Augsburg furnish a place of refuge for persecuted sectaries, but it was also a center from which streams of influence went forth.

Among the earliest laborers in the Anti-pedobaptist cause in Augsburg were Hans Denck and Ludwig Hetzer. The latter though not yet an avowed Anti-pedobaptist was already a somewhat zealous propagator of Anti-pedobaptist views. We have met him before in Zürich, where for some time he worked diligently with tongue and pen side by side with Zwingli in the cause of evangelical reform. At a later date we find him among those who were banished by the Zürich Council for opposing infant baptism. He had a profound sympathy for the poor and oppressed and was eager for social no less than for religious reform. He was befriended during his earlier visit to Augsburg by Georg Regel, a wealthy gentleman temporarily resident there. His wife Anna, under Hetzer's influence, afterward became an Anabaptist and it was on the pretext of suspicious relations with this woman that Hetzer was beheaded at Constance in 1529. During his later residence in Augsburg he supported himself chiefly by serving as a corrector of the press and by literary work. He translated from time to time a number of books written in Latin by leading Reformers, besides publishing a number of original works.

It was probably in the autumn of 1525 that he published his famous pamphlet on "Evangelical Cups." This is one of the strongest pleas for abstinence from intoxicants that appeared during the Reformation time. Undoubtedly excessive drinking was common among the evangelical clergy. In assemblies which they called evangelical the social cup was freely, often immoderately, indulged in. "No Christian," writes Hetzer, "should suffer that to be called evangelical which is antagonistic to the gospel. Many indeed think that 'moderate drinking' is quite allowable. If one does not vomit at the table he is said to have 'drunk moderately' even if he has drunk three measures of wine." He thinks that Bacchus and not Christ is the influence that brings them together in such assemblies, and that the utterances at such meetings are often inspired not by the Spirit of God but by the emptied beer glasses and cups. In such gatherings there may be volubility, but no true eloquence. By way of contrast he describes the gatherings of true Christians. He lays much stress upon the love-feasts of the early Christians in which rich and poor sat down together to food provided by the rich. "Now we should know that Christian life and faith are a mere sham . . . where there is no love or this is cold in us. Faith deals with God, but also through expression in works of love toward our neighbors."

Hetzer's disinclination toward infant baptism was due quite as much to his observation of the evil results of its adoption as to its lack of scriptural warrant. "The pope's book," he says, "in which I read that they have ascribed blessedness to external water baptism, led me to reject infant baptism." "Oh, how many pious mothers have been made miserable who have had no other thought than that unbaptized infants are damned. . . Also the special places of burial where unbaptized infants are not buried along with other people simply because they shall no more see God's face! Oh, the knavery!"

His position was one of wavering and indecision. We find him in September, 1525, seeking to re-establish himself in the confidence of Zwingli. He was then at Augsburg where he was zealously defending the Zwinglian view of the Supper against the Lutherans. Expelled from Augsburg we find him in November in Basel with Œcolampadius, whom he seems to have convinced that he was not an Anti-pedobaptist, and whom he induced to write to Zwingli to this effect. Yet he continued to labor in a somewhat secret way against infant baptism.

The influence of Hans Denck, his intimate friend and associate in Bible translation, it is easier to estimate. Next to Hubmaier we must regard Denck as the foremost leader of the Anti-pedobaptists. In scholarship and the profundity of his grasp of truth he was probably Hubmaier's superior. We first meet with him in Basel, where he was employed by one of the leading publishers as a corrector of the press, and where he was intimately associated with Œcolampadius. In 1523, on the recommendation of the latter, he was appointed rector of the St. Sebaldus school of Nürnberg. It is probable that he met Münzer on the occasion of his first visit to Nürnberg, and may have been somewhat influenced by this enthusiastic spirit. Besides being one of the foremost masters of the Hebrew and Greek Scriptures, he was like Luther, Carlstadt, Münzer, Schwenckfeldt, and many other leading men of the time, deeply imbued with the evangelical mysticism of the Middle Ages. In fact, he was a mystic himself of the highest type; but his mysticism was tempered by the profoundest knowledge of Scripture and the profoundest reverence for its teachings. At Nürnberg he fell into controversy with the famous Lutheran theologian Osiander on the doctrine of the Supper; but the doctrines of Scripture, sin, the righteousness of God, the law, the gospel, and baptism, ultimately came forward as matters of dispute. His highly spiritualistic conception of the Divine nature, of Scripture, of faith, and of the ordinances, were taken by his opponents to involve a practical setting aside of historical Christianity. He was accused, moreover, of denying that obedience was due to the civil magistracy and of maintaining the right and duty of a Christian man or woman to put away an unbelieving spouse and to marry a believer. Arraigned before the authorities at the instigation of the intolerant Osiander, he asked to be allowed to set forth his views in writing. His "Protestation and Confession" embodied the chief points on which he found himself at variance with Lutheranism. In this important document we find the germs of the system that he afterward wrought out with such beauty and eloquence. Driven from Nürnberg, he seems to have spent some months in retirement, maturing and giving careful expression to his views.

We next meet him in St. Gall in the following June, while the Anti-pedobaptist movement was at its height, but he seems to have taken no public part in the agitation. He made a strong impression upon Vadian, who wrote to Zwingli: "In Denck, that most gifted youth, all excellences were truly so present that he even surpassed his age and seemed greater than himself, but he has so abused his genius as to defend with great zeal Origen's opinion concerning the liberation and salvation of the damned."

At this period he seems to have been so carried away

by the thought of God's infinite love and mercy and to have urged this aspect of truth so eloquently upon those with whom he came in contact, that they could scarcely resist the conviction that the final salvation of all might be in accord with the Divine purpose. To give a detailed account of Denck's writings and of his system is manifestly impracticable in a work like the present.

A few quotations will suffice to give some idea of the quality of his theological thinking:

> Faith is obedience to God and confidence in his promise through Jesus Christ. Where this obedience is lacking this confidence is false and illusory. But the obedience must be genuine, that is, heart, mouth, and act must go together as far as possible.
> He who has known the truth in Christ Jesus and is obedient to it from the heart is free from sin, though not from temptation. He is not able to run in the way of God further than he is strengthened by God. He who runs more or less fails in truth, obedience, and freedom. He who surrenders his will to the will of God is both free and fettered. Whose servant one is, the same makes him free in doing what he will in his service. God compels no one to remain in his service whom love does not compel. The devil is able to compel no one to remain in his service who has once known the truth. Therefore it makes no difference whether we speak of free or fettered will, so long as we recognize the distinctions on both sides.
> God will give to every man according to his works, to the evil eternal punishment according to his righteousness, to the good eternal life according to his mercy. Not that he is under obligation, if he should reckon rigorously. But he pays us out of the promise that he has given to us beforehand. He looks upon faith and good works, regards them as well-pleasing, and rewards them. Not that they originate with us, but that we have not received in vain or rejected the grace which he has provided for us. It is all of one treasury, which is truly good, namely, from the Word which from the beginning was with God and in the last times has become flesh.
> The Holy Scripture I esteem above human treasures, but not so highly as the Word of God, which is living, powerful, and eternal, which is separate and pure from the elements of this world, since it is God himself, spirit and not letter, written without pen and paper, so that it can never be blotted out. Therefore also blessedness is not

bound up in Scripture, however useful and good it may always be in that direction. It is not possible for Scripture to make better a bad heart; but a pious heart is bettered by all things. A man who is chosen by God may attain to blessedness without preaching, without Scripture.

The broken law God himself has fulfilled. Perfect resignation to God's will, so that when we ask for wisdom we shall be willing that God should give us foolishness, is necessary to any proper conversion. So long as we will not leave blessedness out of our own hands it cannot come to us. So long as we strive to escape condemnation it continues to hang about our necks. Should one say, I am willing for God's sake to forego blessedness and to have damnation, yet God could not show himself toward him otherwise than he is, namely, good, and must give him the best and noblest that he has, that is, himself.

The voice of my heart, of which I assuredly know that it renders the truth, says to me that God is righteous and merciful, and this voice speaks in every good heart distinctly and intelligibly, the more distinctly and clearly the better each one is.

His ideas as to the righteousness and mercy of God did not permit him to believe that God would remain forever unreconciled with his enemies or would punish them eternally. Punishment in this life and the life to come he looked upon as designed to convince men of their folly and to bring them into the path of obedience.

It might have been expected that Denck's mysticism would make him indifferent to external ordinances, and that he would decline, like Schwenckfeldt, to throw himself heartily into the separatist movement; yet he was thoroughly convinced that infant baptism was not only unscriptural, but was also one of the principal bulwarks of the State-church systems that so obstructed Christian freedom. He became, after Hubmaier's departure to Moravia, the most influential Anti-pedobaptist leader. Bucer calls him the Anabaptist "pope"; Urban Rhegius their "abbot." Haller designates him "the Anabaptist Apollo"; Gynoræus, "the head of the Anabaptists."

At Augsburg, where Denck seems to have arrived in October or November, 1525, he enjoyed the friendship of the young nobleman, Sebastian von Freiburg, and of Georg Regel. His powerful personality soon drew around him a large number of those who had predilections for evangelical mysticism, and were out of sympathy with Romanism, Lutheranism, and Zwinglianism, which were strenuously contending with each other for the mastery. Hetzer seems to have left Augsburg before Denck's arrival. It is certain that most of those upon whom he had brought his influence to bear became followers of Denck and constituted the nucleus of the organization that was soon to be formed. Denck supported himself at this time by giving instruction to the sons of burghers in Latin and Greek, and must have devoted considerable time to writing. His most important work on "The Law of God" was probably written, or at least completed, after his arrival in Augsburg.

It was probably through the influence of Hubmaier, who visited Augsburg about June, 1526, on his way to Moravia, that Denck decided to organize the Anti-pedobaptist life of the city into a church. It is likely that Hubmaier influenced others during this visit. He conferred with the leading evangelical ministers, Gynoræus and Urban Rhegius, and no doubt sought to win them to his position. According to the report of the first of these, Hubmaier found little satisfaction in Denck's mystical views. The organization under Denck's leadership was formed soon after Hubmaier's visit, for it is mentioned in a letter from Gynoræus, August 22, as already an accomplished fact. The efforts of Rhegius and others to convince Denck of his errors in doctrine and in practice were eminently unsuccessful. After discussing with them the points at issue for some hours he suddenly broke off, convinced that no useful result could be reached. When it was proposed to have him appear before the council to answer charges made against him, he quietly departed. This occurred in the autumn of 1526. The Anti-pedobaptist community seems already to have numbered some hundreds. He was to return to Augsburg after a period of similar labors in Strasburg and Worms.

Hans Hut was probably the first who received baptism at Denck's hands in Augsburg. As early as 1521, Hut, who was then sacristan to the knight Hans von Bibra, was imprisoned for refusing to have his babe baptized. He afterward spent some time in Nürnberg, where he learned bookbinding and one or two other trades, and where he seems to have become acquainted with Denck. We next find him in Wittenberg engaged in the book business. He entered the camp of the peasants' army under Münzer just before the disastrous battle of Frankenhausen and was taken prisoner by the Hessian troops. Claiming to have been among the peasants not as a soldier but as a bookseller, he was released. It is probable, however, that he had already adopted Münzer's chiliastic views and that his real purpose in going to Frankenhausen was to have part in what he expected would be a great manifestation of Divine power on behalf of Münzer and the peasants. After leaving Frankenhausen he went to Bibra, where he is said to have preached, in the spirit of Münzer, that the subjects should smite all magistrates to death. He believed himself to have been specially commissioned by God to interpret the prophecies to the people of his time, and to proclaim the approaching end of the age and the setting up of a kingdom of righteousness through the slaughter of the ungodly.

With consuming zeal he labored for the propagation of his views. While he did not during his later ministry counsel the people to take up the sword and proceed immediately to slay the ungodly, he taught them to be ready to obey whenever God should make known to them that the appointed time had come. He possessed a striking and powerful personality and easily gained the enthusiastic confidence of the oppressed classes, who believed him to be endowed with supernatural powers and readily accepted his grotesque interpretation of the Scriptures. His labors extended over a vast territory.

In Moravia he attempted to gain the Nikolsburg Church, of which Hubmaier was pastor, to his views. He was vanquished by Hubmaier and speedily withdrew. Styria, Tyrol, Breslau, Salzburg, Würzburg, and other localities, were profoundly moved by his personal labors. So irresistible was his influence that a few hours' stay in a place often sufficed to establish a community pledged to his principles. In the intensity of his zeal and the fervor of his eloquence he has been compared with the Old Testament prophets. The terribly corrupting influence of this man on the Anti-pedobaptist cause can be readily surmised.

Hut's influence on the Augsburg Anti-pedobaptists was considerable ; but it is not to be supposed that those who had become deeply imbued with the evangelical mysticism of Denck, or the soundly biblical teachings of Hubmaier, were carried away by this wild enthusiasm. Hut did not remain long at a time in Augsburg, but visited the city often enough to keep his hand on the movement.

In October, 1527, he was thrown into prison by the Augsburg Council. It was asserted at the time that he made a desperate effort to escape by firing his cell and then giving the alarm. The fire advanced so rapidly that he was mortally burned before the guard arrived. He died a few days after ; but his trial proceeded, he was duly condemned, and his dead body was burned on December 7, 1527. We have laid more stress upon the errors of Hut than upon those evangelical elements in his teaching that were common to him and the sounder Anti-pedobaptists of the time.

If Thomas Münzer's influence was kept alive and multiplied by the enthusiastic labors of Hut, that of Denck was perpetuated in Augsburg not only through his published writings but also through a number of faithful disciples. The most noted of these was Eitelhans Langenmantel, a member of one of the oldest and most distinguished patrician families and son of one of the most illustrious citizens. After spending years abroad he returned to Augsburg and became early an enthusiastic defender of Zwingli's doctrine of the Supper in opposition to Luther's. He seems to have been baptized by Hut early in 1527. Without the learning and the profound philosophical grasp of Denck, or the wonderful popular power of Hut, his social position and his enthusiastic devotion to the Anti-pedobaptist cause constituted him one of the most influential leaders of the party. His anti-Lutheran writings showed a strong leaning toward the Anabaptist position. His view of the Supper differs from that of Zwingli in being more mystical, or in laying more stress upon the personal attitude of the believer toward Christ. He objected strongly to having the ordinances administered by the evangelical clergy for money. The ministers of the word should rather learn to trust in God. In 1526 he declared the "new papists" to be worse than the old. He accused the evangelical clergy of avarice. Not the slightest service will they render, he said, without pay, even for the very poor.

As an Anti-pedobaptist he came out boldly in defense of his principles. His work entitled, "A Divine and thorough Revelation of the true Anabaptists," was addressed to the brethren and sisters of the whole world.

The treatise is, like his earlier writings, strongly polemical against the evangelicals, and sets forth the views of the Anti-pedobaptists in the spirit of Denck rather than in that of Hut, yet without the excessive mysticism of the former.

Early in September, 1527, Denck returned to Augsburg, having spent the intervening months in Strasburg, Zabern, Landau, and Worms, in quietly propagating his principles and, in company with Hetzer, translating from the Hebrew the prophetical books of the Old Testament. This translation was published in Worms shortly before Denck's departure, and so great was its popularity that in three years not fewer than thirteen editions appeared. Its fidelity to the original and its literary excellence give it a high place among versions, and although Luther discouraged its circulation he was not above making considerable use of it in the preparation of his own version.

Soon after Denck's return to Augsburg the Anti-pedobaptist cause may be said to have reached the height of its prosperity. Its numbers reached at this time about eleven hundred. Baptism by immersion is said to have been regularly practised, the houses in which it was administered being indicated by bathing dresses hung out in front.

Shortly after Denck's return we find an extraordinarily large number of Anti-pedobaptist leaders in the city. Indeed, it was commonly believed and is highly probable that a great convention was held in Augsburg at this time. Among the visitors were the following: Hetzer; Kautz, a highly educated and eloquent young evangelical preacher who had been won for the Anti-pedobaptist cause by Denck and Hetzer at Worms, and who carried some of Denck's unsound views to harsher expression than would have been possible for Denck himself; Hut; Jacob Gross, of Waldshut, a faithful disciple of Hubmaier, whose labors in the Grüningen district of Zürich have already been noticed; Sigmund Salminger, an ex-monk from Munich, one of the pastors or bishops of the Augsburg community; Jacob Dachser, an ex-monk from Ingolstadt, who had also attained to a leading position among the Augsburg Anabaptists; Hans Gulden, of Biberack; Ulrich Trechsel; Peter Sheppach; Gregory Maler, of Chur; and Hans Bechelknecht, of Basel.

At about the same time the council, under the influence of the principal evangelical minister, Urban Rhegius, and under strong pressure from without, began to take energetic steps against the now flourishing and aggressive Anti-pedobaptist party. On August 25 Jacob Dachser was imprisoned. On September 15 a meeting was raided and Gross, Salminger, and Hut were seized. Through information extorted from some of these many more were soon afterward imprisoned, among them Langenmantel.

Of the large number arrested some were dismissed on promising to abandon their Anti-pedobaptist activity. About forty were steadfast. Among the prisoners were two members of the council, Vischer and Widholz. On September 6 Rhegius had published a reply to Langenmantel's polemic. On October 9 the council issued a sharp mandate against the withholding of infants from baptism, rebaptism, unauthorized religious assemblies, and the harboring of foreign Anti-pedobaptists.

Several of the prisoners were tortured in order that evidence of evil deeds and purposes on the part of the sectaries might be secured. It was probably under torture that Hut gave the full account of his activity that has been preserved. Damaging evidence against the imprisoned was industriously gathered from other cities. Beyond the facts that have already been mentioned regarding Hut's somewhat fanatical procedures, little that was discreditable could be discovered. It was commonly believed that Hut had established a secret league among his followers, and that he was industriously making preparations for the slaughtering of the ruling classes and for the setting up of a kingdom of righteousness and equality. During the early months of 1528 many arrests were made, the penalties for the most part being fines and banishment.

In Swabia, Bavaria, and Franconia exterminating measures against the Anabaptists were enacted in February, 1528. The Swabian League determined that each of the four quarters should maintain one hundred men for their suppression. The edict of Speier, with its sanguinary requirements, followed in April, 1529.

The tragic fate of Hut has already been mentioned. Langenmantel was allowed to go into banishment, but in his retirement he was seized and executed, with his attendants, May 12, 1528. Denck and Hetzer withdrew before the outbreak of the persecution. Denck went to Basel early in October, 1527, ill and discouraged. He died a few weeks later at the house of Œcolampadius, after having made a conciliatory statement of his views, sometimes erroneously represented as a recantation.

The party was too firmly rooted in Augsburg to succumb at once to persecuting measures. Of the banished more than one hundred sought refuge in Strasburg, where exterminating persecution was longer delayed. Many found their way to Moravia. For years there was a remnant of Anti-pedobaptist life that from time to time came to the notice of the authorities; but as a movement it was practically at an end by 1530.

Literature: Works of Denck, Hetzer, and Urbanus Rhegius; pertinent monographs and articles of Jörg, Roth, C. Meyer, Keim, Keller, Hagen, Erbkam, Winter, Will, Heberle, Trechsel, Frank, and Cornelius ("Die Münster, Aufruhr"), as in the Bibliography; Döllinger, Die Reformation, I., 195–201; and Uhlhorn, Urb. Rhegius.

CHAPTER XIV

HUBMAIER'S MORAVIAN LABORS (1526-27).

THE western provinces of Austria, including Styria, Salzburg, Carniola, the Tyrol, and the Passau region had, since the thirteenth century, been permeated with old-evangelical life. Whatever of reforming sentiment appeared in Northern Italy, Switzerland, Southern Germany, Bohemia, or Moravia, was pretty sure to find its way into these provinces through which ran some of the main roads from north to south and from east to west. From Switzerland, Southern Germany, and Bavaria Antipedobaptist influence was brought to bear upon these provinces as early as 1525-26. In few lands did it find a more responsive soil, or prove so persistent in the face of persecution that was meant to be exterminating.

From 1526 onward Moravia became the center of the movement for the entire Austro-Hungarian realm, a refuge for the persecuted and a supplier of men and means for the carrying forward of the work in the more severely persecuted regions.

It may be worth while to inquire why Moravia was about 1526 "a goodly land," where those who were striving to renew apostolic Christianity could "live cheaply and without persecution." As a result of more than a century of religious and political conflict in Bohemia, with which country Moravia was closely connected, Moravia had come to have an exceedingly heterogeneous population. Being somewhat removed from the center of conflict and the center of government, a large proportion of the more radical representatives of mediæval evangelical religion had removed thither from

Bohemia and other persecuting countries. Catholics, Hussites (Utraquists), and Bohemian Brethren were all strongly represented among the nobility, and all existed side by side in mutual toleration. The rights of the Utraquists were guaranteed by treaty. The Brethren (*Unitas Fratrum*) had gained toleration only after fearful sufferings for their faith.

So firmly had the Brethren become established that the famous edict of St. James (July 25, 1505) forbidding their religious services, the sale of their books, the administration of the ordinances by their ministers, the harboring of them by the nobility, etc., and aiming at their extirpation, while it was accepted by the Bohemian Diet and ruthlessly executed, was rejected by the Moravian. A number of the most influential nobles were supporters of the *Unitas Fratrum*. Many others were so far indifferent to the points at issue among the various parties that they were unwilling to disturb the tranquillity of their domains, and to deprive themselves of their most valuable subjects for the sake of gratifying king and pope.

The royal authority was remarkably feeble and ineffective from 1516 to 1526. Louis II., ten years of age, came to the Bohemian-Hungarian throne in 1516, and after years of unsuccessful warfare with the Turks, was slain at Mohacz in August, 1526. The Archduke Ferdinand, who had married a sister of Louis, claimed the throne in her right, but it was some time before his authority was fully recognized. Under such circumstances the nobles did each what was right in his own eyes, and it is gratifying to know that many of them made good use of their freedom.

Moravia was still a somewhat sparsely settled and undeveloped country, and had ample room for the thousands of skillful and industrious Anti-pedobaptist workmen who from 1526 onward streamed into it from Switzerland, Germany, Bavaria, the Tyrol, Styria, Carniola, and even from Italy. As the authority of Ferdinand increased, the immunity of the Anti-pedobaptists from persecution proportionately diminished, and we shall see that even in this New Jerusalem they had no occasion to forget that they were pilgrims and sojourners on earth.

Hubmaier, after his fearful sufferings at Zürich and short visits to Constance, Augsburg, and a number of other places on the way, arrived at Nikolsburg, in Moravia, about the first of July, 1526. From the beginning, whether by virtue of some prearrangement or otherwise we are not informed, he enjoyed the favor of Leonard and Hans of Lichtenstein, great landed proprietors in whose domains Nikolsburg was situated. It is probable that the Lichtensteins had been influenced to a considerable extent by Hussitism in one of its forms. From 1524 they took a deep interest in the movement led by Luther and fostered in their domains the new evangelical teaching.

The chief evangelical preacher in Nikolsburg, when Hubmaier arrived, was Hans Spitalmaier, a Bavarian, who had as his assistant Oswald Glaidt, a fellow-countryman. Glaidt had occupied himself zealously and with some success in efforts to secure a good understanding between the old and the new-evangelical parties.

In March, 1526, the Moravian nobleman, John Dubcansky, with the co-operation of several other noblemen, had secured a meeting (at Austerlitz) of representatives of the Utraquists, Bohemian Brethren, and Lutherans, for the purpose of seeking a basis of union. Glaidt took prominent part in this meeting, but the most influential theologian present was Martin Göschel, formerly suffragan bishop at Olmütz, but at this time provost of a nunnery at Kanitz, which position, because of its emoluments, he continued to hold after his adoption of evangelical views.

In 1525 he had married one of the nuns. When compelled in 1526 to give up the office, he contrived to put the control of the property of the cloister into the hands of officials who were ready to serve his interests. He labored zealously for the promotion of the new-evangelical teaching and for the union of all evangelical parties. The bishop of Olmütz proceeded energetically against him in April, 1526, and finally succeeded in severing his connection with the nunnery and its property. He betook himself to Nikolsburg, where he arrived at about the same time as Hubmaier, with whom he soon entered into very cordial relations, and with whose cause he identified himself.

Oswald Glaidt hospitably entertained Hubmaier on his arrival at Nikolsburg, and was soon afterward baptized by him. The lords of Lichtenstein were soon won to Hubmaier's scheme for the restoration of primitive Christianity and in all humility received baptism at his hands.

It is probable that Anti-pedobaptists were already in Moravia in considerable numbers before the advent of Hubmaier, but we have no definite information with regard to their activity.

In Hubmaier the evangelical cause secured a leader who in point of learning, character, and personal attractiveness was without a peer in any of the religious parties of Moravia. Multitudes followed the example of Lichtenstein and Glaidt, and in a short time from six thousand to twelve thousand in Nikolsburg and the surrounding regions had submitted to believers' baptism. The fame of Hubmaier's successful work and of the religious liberty that was accorded to Anti-pedobaptists in Moravia spread throughout Europe, and large numbers soon left the regions in which persecution prevailed for this land of promise.

Here also Hubmaier developed a remarkable literary activity. Froschauer, a Zürich publisher, took refuge as an Anti-pedobaptist in Nikolsburg. Here he was welcomed by Leonard of Lichtenstein, under whose patronage he set up a plant for the publication of Hubmaier's writings. Hubmaier seems at this time to have entertained the hope that many others of the evangelical nobility would follow in the footsteps of the Lichtensteins. To these noblemen one after another he dedicated his books in courtly style. Besides making the fullest (almost flattering) recognition of the services of Hans and Leonard of Lichtenstein, he dedicated works to Johann of Pernstein and Helfenstein, the governor-general of Moravia, to Arkled of Boskowitz, the chief treasurer, and to John Dubcansky,

He writes in the spirit of a man who has the utmost confidence in his cause, and encouraged by the acceptance that the truth has already received hopes to secure its general recognition throughout the land.

In a little more than a year he published not fewer than fifteen distinct works. A considerable number of these treat of baptism. The first of his Nikolsburg publications, issued soon after his arrival, was a critique of Zwingli's book on baptism, in which he gave a full account of his transactions with Zwingli, and of the cruel treatment he had received at the hands of the Zürich reformer. The argument is in the form of a dialogue between Zwingli and Hubmaier. Our readers are already sufficiently familiar with Hubmaier's method of dealing with this subject. It is in every respect one of the noblest defenses of believers' baptism ever written. He closes the book with an eloquent appeal to Zwingli:

Thou givest to the godless ground to say: See, they bend and gloss the Scripture according to their pleasure. With what dost thou yet tax the poor brethren and sisters, that thou shouldst fight against them with such groundless weapons? With what dost thou tax thine own conscience, which tells thee otherwise? With what dost thou tax Christ, that thou shouldst put in the place of his words thine own inventions? . . Confess the truth, thou art a captive. Abolish the miserable prisons, cease from hunting down pious brethren and sisters, from prisons and stocks, from blocks and from drowning. God grant thee grace that thou mayest again, as once thou didst, apprehend his plain, clear, pure word, and mayest walk according thereto.

Shortly afterward he published a pamphlet entitled "Judgment of Ancient and Modern Teachers, that Young Children Should Not be Baptized until they have been Instructed in the Faith." This he dedicated to the Provost Martin Göschel, of whose relations to the author mention has already been made. Of ancient writers, he cites Origen, Basil, Athanasius, Tertullian, Jerome, Cyril, Theophylact, Eusebius, and the *Corpus Juris Canonici*; of moderns, Erasmus, Luther, Œcolampadius, Zwingli, Judae, Hofmeister, Hagendorf, Hetzer, and Cellarius. His dedication contains a sober but forceful arraignment of the Roman Catholic Church, of whose terrible corruptions he and Göschel alike had the amplest personal knowledge. The book contains a summary in catechetical form of what a person should know before baptism. In compliment to Leonard and Hans of Lichtenstein he introduces their names as questioner and answerer, and calls them "lovers of the holy gospel." "Where water baptism according to the ordination of Christ has not been again instituted, there one knows not who is brother or sister, there is no church, no fraternal discipline or correction, no exclusion, no Supper," etc. The Supper is declared to be

A public sign and testimony of the love through which Christians oblige themselves before the church, just as they together break the bread and drink the cup, so also to give up their lives and their blood for each other, and this according to the example of Christ, whose suffering they memorialize in the breaking of the bread. Bread and wine are not the body and blood of Christ, but mere memorials of the suffering and death of Christ for the remission of our sins, the greatest sign of his love that he has left us.

Christians should fast daily, that is, should eat and drink in moderation with thanksgiving and without distinction of foods. All opprobrious words are to be avoided by Christians. As regards Sabbath observance, man's whole life should be a continuous Sabbath. The idea of sacred times and seasons found no place in his system.

His next writing was entitled "Ground and Reason that every Person Who has been Baptized in His Infancy is Under Obligation to be Baptized According to the Ordinance of Christ, though He Were a Hundred Years Old." The aim of the writing was to influence the multitude of Christians who acknowledged that there is no scriptural ground for infant baptism and yet declined to submit to believers' baptism, and who were, as he says, hanging like Absalom between heaven and earth, to take the decisive step in obedience to Christ's command.

His answer to Œcolampadius, prepared before he left Waldshut, was now for the first time published, as was also his "Twelve Articles of the Christian Faith," written while in prison at Zürich. Another writing published at this time was his "Apology or Vindication to all Christian Men," being an answer to the slanderous charges that were circulated to his disadvantage and to the hindrance of the progress of the gospel. He emphatically denies that he speaks contemptuously of the mother of Christ and of the saints, that he rejects prayer and confession, and that he despises the holy fathers and councils. He explains his real attitude in these matters in a thoroughly evangelical way. He repudiates the charge that he is an Anabaptist. The only true baptism is the baptism of believers, which he holds should be administered once for all. He can prove by thousands of witnesses that he has always taught obedience to the civil magistracy as instituted by God and entrusted by him with the disciplinary sword. The work is largely autobiographical and is of great value. Before the close of 1526 Hubmaier published two other writings, "A Short Pater Noster," or exposition of the Lord's Prayer, and "A Simple Exposition of the Word: 'This is My Body,' in Christ's Supper." In his dedication of this latter work to Leonard of Lichtenstein he comments in a highly complimentary manner on the composition of his name. Leonard expresses strength, truth, and steadfastness (*leo*—lion), so that even the grim lion of this world cannot frighten him; Lichtenstein says that light is come into the world which the good love and the evil hate. The word *stein* (stone) in the name is that stone upon which the wise man in the Bible built his house. He knows no place on earth where the light of the gospel is shining forth with such brightness as in the Lichtensteins' domains, where Spitalmaier and Glaidt are placing it on the candlestick.

During 1527 he published somewhat elaborate forms for baptism and the Supper, two works on "The Freedom of the Will," a work on "Brotherly Correction," a work on "Christian Exclusion" (excommunication of unworthy members), a catechetical work "including what every man should know before he is baptized in the water," and a work on "The Sword."

Hubmaier's form of baptism is satisfactory to Baptists in nearly every particular except that it does not require immersion as the act. His practice in relation to baptism was to have the candidate kneel and to pour water upon him. This practice was invariably followed, so far as we are informed, by the Moravian Anti-pedobaptists and by the entire Austrian brotherhood. This form is definitely prescribed in Peter Reidemann's "Account of our Religion," which from about 1547 onward was recognized by his brethren as an almost authoritative work. Yet Hubmaier frequently used the expression "baptizing in the water."

As regards the will, he held with Peter Chelcicky and with the old-evangelical party in general, as well as with the entire Anti-pedobaptist brotherhood, the anti-Augustinian view, practically equivalent to that which has become so widely prevalent in modern evangelical Arminianism. His very able discussion, which it would require too much space to summarize, may be set forth in the following sentences from another of his works: "Man has lost his freedom through sin and has received it again through the sacrificial death of Christ. He who sins is unfree, until Christ destroys the power of flesh and sin, death, devil, and hell. To this end unceasing prayer is necessary."

It is needless to say that Hubmaier laid the utmost stress on fraternal correction and upon the exclusion of unworthy members:

> After the people have received the word of God and through water baptism in the presence of the church have put themselves under obligation to God to live according to the word, and if they are ready to walk in newness of life and henceforth not to let sin reign in the mortal body, they still have need of medicine, because men are by nature children of wrath, evil and incapable, whereby the foul and stinking flesh together with the poisoned members may be somehow cut off, in order that the whole body may not be dishonored and corrupted.

The very essence of Hubmaier's position lay in the requirement of the strictest application of discipline according to the precepts of Christ and his apostles. He regarded the preaching of the gospel, baptism, and the

Supper as vain and useless apart from discipline, and sin, shame, and abomination as the inevitable consequence of its neglect.

In his treatise on the sword he puts himself at variance with the old-evangelical brotherhood and with the great majority of his Anti-pedobaptist contemporaries. His judgment is based upon a very full and careful examination of the Scriptures and is in entire accord with that of modern Baptists. He defends magistracy as a Christian institution and vindicates for Christians the right to exercise magistracy and to bear the sword. He discusses the fifteen proof-texts that his brethren of the mediæval time and his Anti-pedobaptist contemporaries were in the habit of urging against magistracy, attempting to show that fidelity to Scripture does not necessitate the conclusion reached, and caps his argument with the passage: "Let every man be subject to the higher powers," etc. "This Scripture alone, dear brethren, is itself sufficient confirmation of magistracy against all the gates of hell."

He maintains that Paul's injunction is with reference to magistracy in general, whether it be believing or unbelieving, God has not ordained magistracy against himself. If magistrates seek to punish the evil and summon Christian subjects to their aid, they are bound by the salvation of their souls to render the needed help:

> Subjects, however, are to prove well beforehand the spirits of their magistracies whether they are not moved more by vanity, pride, passion, animosity, hatred, and avarice, than by love for the common utility and the peace of the land: for this is not to bear the sword of God according to the ordinance. But if thou knowest that the magistracy punishes the evil solely in order that the pious may come to rest and remain unharmed, then help, then counsel, then assist, as often as it is required of thee. But if a magistracy should be childish or foolish, yea, wholly unfit to rule, it may be with propriety abolished and another chosen that is good, since on account of an evil magistracy God has often punished a whole

country. But if this cannot be done conveniently and with peace, also without great injuries and revolution, then it may be endured.

In conclusion he makes an earnest appeal to his brethren to which few in that generation were ready to respond:

> Therefore in fidelity I advise you, brethren, turn, prove yourselves. You have struggled hard and done much that was ill-advised against God and brotherly love under an appearance and a pretext of humility. Were Christian magistrates and subjects seen to hold together in a manly, brotherly, and Christian way, many a tyrant would desist from his oppression and compulsion against God and all that is proper and would sheath his sword. Even if there were no Scripture, yet our own conscience tells us that we should help the magistracy.

Hubmaier correctly discerned that one of the greatest obstacles to the progress of New Testament Christianity in his time was the rejection of magistracy, which caused Anti-pedobaptists everywhere to be looked upon as enemies of civil government and their presence as a menace to law and order. He made a strong but ineffective effort to remove this barrier.

Equally at variance with the great majority of his brethren was Hubmaier in relation to the doctrine of property. The preponderating sentiment of the Antipedobaptists was in favor of community of goods. The example of the early Christians in Jerusalem, who sold their goods and laid the proceeds at the apostles' feet, calling nothing their own, was thought by them to be in entire accord with the spirit of Christianity, and anything short of this absolute renunciation of private ownership, to savor of selfishness and worldliness. Hubmaier and many of the early Swiss Anti-pedobaptists maintained that while the spirit of Christ requires the utmost liberality on the part of believers in succoring needy believers and in carrying forward the work of

Christ, it does not require the relinquishment of private ownership.

The prosperous and promising cause at Nikolsburg was not to be permitted long to enjoy the peace and unity that the favorable external circumstances and the wise and considerate leadership of Hubmaier would seem to have promised. Hans Hut, whose career has been already sketched, appeared at Nikolsburg before the close of 1526, and here, as everywhere, soon made his influence profoundly felt. Not only did Hubmaier strongly object to his fanatical teaching with reference to the speedy setting up of a carnal kingdom of Christ, but the views of the two men came into the sharpest collision regarding magistracy. Hut, as we have seen, was one of the most radical opponents of magistracy as a permanent divine institution. While he believed that the time would soon come when under Divine direction believers would be called upon to take up the sword for the slaughter of the ungodly, and especially of the ruling classes, he denied the right of Christians to engage directly or indirectly in carnal warfare under the leadership of secular princes. A considerable proportion of those who had adopted Anti-pedobaptist views under Hubmaier's influence, including Oswald Glaidt and several other ministers, were carried away by Hut's enthusiasm. Even Göschel seems to have taken sides with Hut against Hubmaier. Two disputations failed to secure the desired unity, and Hut's teaching and conduct were regarded by Lichtenstein as so revolutionary in their nature as to warrant his exclusion from the community. We need not suppose that all who sided with Hut in this controversy accepted his more fanatical views. The chief points at issue were, as we have seen, magistracy and warfare, and on these points Hut was in accord with old-evangelical tradition and with the views of the great majority of contemporary Anti-pedobaptists, while Hubmaier was in the position of an innovator in these matters.

Before Hut's arrival a considerable party had appeared, represented by Jacob Wiedemann, Jäger, Schlegel, and Burkhardt, who not only denied that Christians could personally engage in warfare, but who insisted that it was just as little allowable to pay taxes for the support of warfare. Such taxes they stigmatized as "blood-money." These, of course, arrayed themselves on Hut's side in the controversy with Hubmaier.

Jacob Wiedemann (commonly called by his brethren "One-eyed Jacob") had come from the land of the Enns (Salzburg), and before the close of 1527 had begun to agitate most persistently in favor of community of goods. Spitalmaier, one of the Nikolsburg evangelical ministers who had been won to the support of Hubmaier's cause, continued faithful to the moderate principles of Hubmaier, and as pastor or chaplain of the Lichtensteins, contended zealously against Wiedemann and his party.

In the summer of 1527 the Austrian Government began to take cognizance of the Anti-pedobaptist movement that was rapidly spreading over Southern Moravia. The widely circulated writings of Hubmaier brought the movement into great prominence. Attention was called to the fact that the same Hubmaier who had been the cause of so much trouble at Waldshut, and whom the Austrian authorities had vainly endeavored to get within their power, was, with the full protection and support of an Austrian subject, bringing multitudes of people to the adoption of his heresies.

We need not dwell upon the steps by which the Lichtensteins felt themselves compelled to deliver their spiritual father into the hands of his enemies. Ferdinand was all the more desirous to put an end to the activity of Hubmaier from the fact that accounts were about this time continually coming to him of the growth and aggressiveness of the Anti-pedobaptist movement in Upper and in Lower Austria.

Hans Hut had been preaching publicly in Steyer, and his activity since leaving Nikolsburg had been unceasing and effective. So strong a foothold had the movement secured in the Salzburg region that the local officers assured the government of the necessity of proceeding with the utmost caution in efforts to suppress it. A number of people of consideration were involved and riot might follow an effort to punish them. In Lower Austria too, largely as a result of Hubmaier's influence, Anabaptist communities were appearing in many places.

The demand for Hubmaier's extradition seems to have been based on his supposed treasonable attitude toward the government during his Waldshut career. Whether the Lichtensteins could have protected him for any considerable time against the demands of the government it is not easy to determine. That they yielded with unseemly readiness is a conclusion that can scarcely be avoided.

In July, 1527, a little over a year after his arrival at Nikolsburg, he was seized, along with his devoted wife, by the Austrian authorities.

While Hubmaier was in prison at Greitzenstein, his old friend, Dr. Johann Faber, spent several days discussing with him in a friendly way the points at issue and seeking to win him back to the communion of the church. Hubmaier prepared on this occasion an elaborate confession, in which he stated his position in the most conciliatory manner that his conscience would allow; but he was too radically at variance with Roman Catholicism to satisfy his persecutors.

After a long imprisonment, he was burned at the stake on March 10, 1528. Three days later, his wife was drowned in the Danube and her body burned. Göschel, Hubmaier's distinguished colleague, was seized at about the time of Hubmaier's death. At Prague he was seven times subjected to the most excruciating tortures, and finally induced to recant. In consideration of the fact that he had been a Catholic bishop and of the intercession of some of the Moravian nobles he escaped the stake to die in prison shortly afterward of the hardships he had suffered.

Thus the Moravian Anti-pedobaptists were deprived of their greatest leader and the cause of radical evangelical reform of its ablest and soundest advocate. In point of ability and character Hubmaier deserves a high place among the evangelical leaders of the church universal.

Literature: Hubmaier's writings, and the pertinent works of Loserth, Hosek, Schreiber, Veesenmeyer, Wolny, Cornelius, Stern, Faber (Fabri), Kessler, Hagen, and Beck (Geschichtsbücher) as in the Bibliography.

CHAPTER XV

THE TYROL

THE Tyrol was happily designated by one of the emperors "the eye and the shield of Austria." No portion of Europe was more likely to be strongly influenced by the Anti-pedobaptist movement, and in few did it meet with a heartier reception or strike deeper its roots. The Tyrol is essentially a series of valleys, and at that time the mountain regions were covered with dense forests. Even in times of direst persecution Anti-pedobaptist teachers trained, like the Waldenses of the earlier time, in all the arts of evading their persecutors, were able to carry forward effective work. They were familiar with all the secret refuges and byways used by the persecuted people, and some of the leaders who had been singled out for destruction by the authorities were able for years to elude the vigilance of the police, who had every inducement to seize them.

One of the principal passes of the Alps was in the Tyrol. The Waldenses, whose principal centers during the thirteenth and following centuries were Lombardy and the western Austrian provinces, were continually passing through this region, and had many congregations within its bounds. Its contiguity to Switzerland and Southern Germany made it inevitable that Anti-pedobaptists fleeing from persecution or impelled by missionary zeal should make known to the Tyrolese what they considered the pure gospel.

Lutheranism had secured a considerable following at an early period, Urban Rhegius, the noted Augsburg evangelical leader, having for some time (1522-23) labored zealously for reform at Hall. The authorities were soon able to suppress all public evangelical teaching; but the people, whose religious sensibilities had been quickened by what they had learned of the gospel, gave a hearty reception to such evangelical preachers as were willing to risk their lives to make known the truth.

As early as 1525-26 there was at least one Anti-pedobaptist congregation in the Inn Valley. Hans Hut related that a certain Caspar from the Inn Valley told him (May, 1526) of some brethren who had been baptized there, and induced him to seek baptism at the hands of Denck, at Augsburg. The origin of this community is unknown. Its most distinguished member was Pilgram Marbeck who, in 1525, had been appointed by the Austrian authorities magistrate for miners, and of whose career as a loyal Anti-pedobaptist and as a civil engineer at Strasburg we shall hereafter learn.

In 1527, according to contemporary documents, these native Anti-pedobaptists were largely reinforced by refugees from Switzerland, Bavaria, Salzburg, and Carniola. It is said that "the teachers and ministers of the word" came down on both sides of the Brenner, traversed the land in all directions, and frequented the huts of the peasants, the houses of the citizens, and the castles of the nobles.

The cowherd Wolfgang, of the Sarn Valley, is said to have been "a messenger of Anabaptism." The esquires at Clausen had urged him by no means to be deterred from the preaching of the gospel, and a majority of them had attended his services. The warden of Guffidaun had sent for him, and there he had preached four times in private houses. If he had desired to preach in a church he might have done so. In Bozen, Taufers, and other places, he had enjoyed the favor of people of high social standing, including some priests. During the early part of 1527 the government received information of the existence of Anti-pedobaptists in Rattenberg, Glurns, and Mals. In May a mandate was issued for the imprisonment of all persons of high or low estate, native or foreign, spiritual or secular, who should impugn the sacraments of the church.

The most notable persons affected by the mandate were Anton von Wolkenstein and Helena von Freiberg. The former, whose house was said to be "an asylum of sectaries," was arraigned before the authorities, but was discharged on his promise to cease to have anything to do with the sectaries and their books. Far more loyal to the persecuted Anti-pedobaptists was Helena von Freiberg. She endured much loss and suffering on behalf of the cause that was very dear to her, but finally felt herself obliged to renounce her views (1534).

The first to suffer martyrdom in the Anti-pedobaptist cause in the Tyrol was Leonard Schiemer, who is spoken of as the "first Anabaptist bishop" in upper Austria. A full record of the trial has been preserved. A number of writings produced during his somewhat extended imprisonment are also extant. He was evidently a man of high culture and of remarkable force of character. A Bavarian by birth, his earlier years of service in the Anti-pedobaptist cause seem to have been devoted to his native land. His labors in the Tyrol had been of short duration, but singularly fruitful. The fields were evidently white unto the harvest, and any zealous preacher of the gospel could reap abundantly. Schiemer could not be induced to compromise his position in the slightest degree. He expressed his regret that he had not accomplished more than he had been permitted to do in the good cause. He was condemned to the stake, but was mercifully executed by the sword and his body burned, January 14, 1528.

When we remember that by 1531 one thousand Antipedobaptists had suffered martyrdom in the Tyrol and in Görtz, and six hundred at Ennisheim, we need not to be informed either of the great vigor with which their work was carried forward or of the terrible zeal with which the government pursued them. In almost every community a large proportion of those who were arraigned were induced so far to deny their faith as to secure release, and many escaped the vigilance of the authorities. Probably thousands of these dissenters from the Tyrol and Austrian provinces made their way to Moravia, and most of the leaders had their training among the Moravians.

To go into the details of the persecution is manifestly impracticable. To describe the work in its various localities would be to deal with the entire land; for probably no locality escaped the influence of the evangelism that was carried on with marvelous energy and success.

The Inn and the Danube furnished the means of communication between the upper Austrian provinces and Moravia. While boatmen trafficking on these streams were strictly enjoined by the government not to furnish transportation to heretics, and to assist the authorities in arresting them, and while a large special police force was appointed to prevent the intercourse that was known to exist between the Tyrol and Moravia, little was accomplished in this direction. Many were arrested, but their places were speedily taken by others who counted not their lives dear unto them.

It seems certain that a considerable number of the officials whose business it was to arrest and convict Antipedobaptists were themselves strongly in sympathy with the persecuted people. Some of them were suspected by the government and were punished. That many of them were faithful to the government the vast number arrested, convicted, and executed bears ample witness.

Among the first of the congregations to be taken in hand by the authorities were those of Freundsberg, Rattenberg, and Kitzbüchl. The prison of the first of these places was soon so overcrowded that that of Schwaz had to be called into requisition. Kitzbüchl was the chief resort of the Salzburg fugitives. The arrest of a certain local ex-priest, who called himself Paul, and around whom a large number of persons had gathered, was a special object of desire on the part of the authorities. For favoring and protecting him Helena von Freiberg incurred a deepening of the suspicion in which she was held.

The next prominent leader to be seized, tried, and executed was Hans Schlaffer, who had been in Moravia and Southern Germany, and who numbered among his friends and acquaintances such men as Wiedemann, Kautz, Hut, Hetzer, and Denck. He bewailed the sins that he had committed as a priest, and gloried in the work that he and his brethren had been permitted to do by way of restoring the pure gospel. He thought it just as unreasonable to put straw into the fire and forbid it to burn as to expect anything but corruption from the priests under existing conditions.

In 1528 a little book was discovered in circulation in which "Anabaptism was painted for those who could not read."

Ferdinand was continually writing to the local officials where heresy had been detected and urging them to use their utmost diligence in executing his mandates. Large numbers were put to death; many more were compelled by tortures and hardships to deny the faith. It was found that a large proportion of those, who under stress of torture were induced to promise to abandon the Antipedobaptist way, relapsed soon after their release.

In April, 1528, a special ordinance was enacted for the

burning or demolition of houses that had been used for dissenting services, and many such were destroyed. The carrying out of this ordinance affected disadvantageously many of the faithful whose houses had been thus used without their consent, and who bitterly complained of the loss inflicted. A further mandate prohibited the entertainment of these so-called heretics by innkeepers, etc.

Persecution having broken out in Moravia during this year, a considerable number of Tyrolese brethren returned to their homes and thus added to the perplexity of the authorities, who saw the numbers of the heretics rapidly increasing in the face of the rigorous execution of the royal mandates. One of the greatest difficulties with which Ferdinand had to contend was the extreme reluctance of local magistrates and jurors to press the persecution to extremes. Especially was this the case at Guffidaun and Sterzing. At Kitzbüchl large numbers were put to death and one hundred and six renounced Anabaptism.

Georg Zaunring, who at an earlier date was the associate of Reublin in his contest with Jacob Wiedemann, baptized multitudes in the summer of 1528. One of his disciples named Kirschner took up the work and preached throughout an extended region. He had baptized over a hundred when he was seized at Kitzbüchl, in April, 1529, and summarily executed.

A mandate of February, 1529, renews the provisions of the earlier mandates and complains that some magistrates are pronouncing judgment not according to the royal mandates, but according to their own opinions. Such conduct is strictly prohibited as being against their vows and oaths in accepting office. It is ordered that henceforth all Anabaptist processes be held in the cities and seats of justice, in order that the laxity likely to prevail in less responsible courts may be avoided. The imperial edict of Speier, which was promulgated at this time, sharpened the procedures in the Tyrol. Fifty mounted patrolmen and three inquisitors were employed to hunt out the noxious sectaries throughout the country.

Sterzing, Hall, and Kitzbüchl were at this time the principal centers of the movement. Among its adherents were citizens, peasants, and gentry. The prisons were perpetually filled to overflowing. Large numbers of orphaned children had to be cared for at the public expense. Spies were employed to insinuate themselves into their confidence by pretended conversion to their views and thus to ascertain their secret meeting places, the names and abodes of their leaders, etc.

At Brixen the priest Benedict denounced the butchery of the pious people and soon afterward identified himself with them. The jurors at Bozen protested against the bloodshed in which they were required to involve themselves, and especially against the sending to Bozen for trial of persons from outside their special jurisdiction.

In the Michaelsburg district persecution raged more fiercely than elsewhere. Here we first meet with Jacob Huter as an Anabaptist worker. Born in the Puster Valley, he received a fair education at the Bruneck school. He then went to Prague to learn the hatter's trade (whence his name). It is probable that there, if not earlier, he came under the influence of the old-evangelical teaching. As a journeyman hatter he visited many places, and finally took up his abode at Spital in Carniola. There seems to be no foundation whatever for the report of Meschovius, followed by some later writers, that Huter was a disciple of Nicholas Storch, and that he was a leader along with Gabriel Schärding of the great Anti-pedobaptist movement in Silesia. There is no evidence that he had ever visited Silesia. Just when and where he united with the brotherhood is unknown. His first labors seem to have been in the Puster Valley in the latter part of 1528 or early in 1529. When one of his meetings was raided in May, 1529, fourteen of those present were seized, but Huter along with some others escaped. The severity of persecution increasing, Huter was sent by his brethren to Moravia to consult with the brethren there as to fellowship and refuge for the persecuted. Returning to the Tyrol fully satisfied as regards the desirableness of emigration to Moravia he sent thither under the guidance of Georg Zaunring one company of people after another, with all their movable means, to enter into fellowship with Wiedemann's party.

During his absence in Moravia, Georg Blaurock, with the quality of whose Christian character and work we are already familiar, came to the Tyrol in company with Hans Langecker, a weaver. No evangelical preacher had awakened in the Tyrol anything like the widespread popular interest aroused by "Strong Georg." We find him laboring at Glurns, Schlaunders, Klausen, Guffidaun, and in many other localities. He moved rapidly from place to place, and thus for some months was able to escape the police. He labored as a man who realized that his time on earth was short, and the people everywhere thronged his ministry. On August 14, along with Langecker, he was arrested and thrown into the Guffidaun prison The two were burned alive on September 6, 1529.

The stress of persecution in the Tyrol drove a considerable number into the diocese of Trent, and the Venetian authorities were warned that some seemed to be making their way thither. It is highly probable that they succeeded, for a few years later the Venetian territory abounded in Anti-pedobaptists. Yet they continued to maintain themselves with unabated zeal in all the principal Tyrolese centers. The king continued to press on the persecution with the utmost vigor, and complaints are frequent of the remissness of officials, who are in some cases accused of favoring the heretics.

The practice of examining them publicly and disputing with them was found to encourage rather than deter from heresy, and its discontinuance was ordered. Persecution itself had no terrors for the zealous people. The Tyrolese officials reminded the king that "in two years scarcely a day has passed in which they have not dealt with Anabaptist matters, and more than seven hundred men and women in this earldom (Tyrol), in many different places, have been condemned to death, others have been driven from the land, still more have miserably fled, leaving their goods, and in some cases their children as orphans." They advise the king to send a special injunction to the upper and official classes all over the land to see to it that those who are charged with bringing heretics to justice do their duty. They complain of the

> madness that is now commonly found among the people, that they are not only not terrified by the punishment of others, but they go, where they are at liberty to do so or desire to go, themselves to the imprisoned and show themselves as their brethren and sisters, and when the magistrates waylay and surprise them, they confess readily and willingly without torture, will listen to no instruction, and rarely can one of them be converted from their unbelief, their only desire for the most part being to die speedily. And if indeed one recants, not much confidence is to be put in him; so that neither good teaching nor severe punishment will help among the people. We hope your royal majesty will, from these our true accounts, graciously understand that we have in no respect allowed our industry to flag.

It was exceedingly mortifying to Ferdinand to find his persistent and earnest efforts for the suppression of the Anti-pedobaptists so futile, and he probably derived little satisfaction from the assurance that the Tyrolese authorities had done their very best to carry out his wishes. In fact he could not be persuaded that his mandates had been energetically executed, and continued to sharpen his requirements and to look carefully after their execution. July 1, 1530, he issued further directions for the detection of Anti-pedobaptists, and offered a reward of thirty to forty florins to any one who would detect a brother and secure his arrest.

In the meantime Jacob Huter was laboring with unremitting zeal. From valley to valley throughout the Tyrol he went, encouraging the persecuted brethren, and where it was impossible for them to remain in their homes without great danger, arranging for their emigration to Moravia. His continued activity, notwithstanding the extreme anxiety of the authorities to get possession of his person, was possible by reason of his own rare skill in avoiding the officers of the law and the fidelity of his brethren, who could be induced by no tortures to betray him. Of Huter's successful efforts to heal the divisions that had arisen among the brethren in Moravia we shall hereafter become aware.

The persecution did not reach its height until 1532–33. We have some interesting indications of the meeting places of the brethren during these troublous times. At Rattenberg they met in a colliery; at Schwaz in an abandoned gallery of a mine; in Klausen, Huter held an assembly of one hundred and fifty in a pit and administered the Supper. At Albeins and at Prugg meetings of fifty to sixty were held in the smelting works.

On February 6 a mandate was issued prohibiting the housing or harboring of Anabaptists, who are declared to be "more noxious than murderers, and enemies of the land, whom every one should be willing to throw down and take prisoners." A few weeks later a fresh mandate was issued reminding all the people of the earlier ones and bewailing the fact that "in spite of all precautions it (the Anabaptists' sect) will have no cessation, but still propagates itself in many places."

A fresh mandate against those who harbor Anabaptists was issued April 24. These mandates proving inadequate for the immediate extermination of the party, a far more sanguinary one was issued on May 12. It is provided, among other things, that those who house, harbor, or in any way render assistance to Anabaptists shall be arrested and questioned under torture as to their relations to the Anabaptists; and even if their connection with the sect cannot be established, they shall nevertheless be punished in body and goods.

One of the chief sources of vexation to Ferdinand was the failure of the heretic hunters to seize the leaders, especially Huter, Hans Tuchmacher, Hans Amon, and Onofrius, who were known to be holding meetings here and there, but who long eluded their pursuers.

In June, 1533, Ferdinand offered a reward of sixty, seventy, or one hundred florins (according to circumstances) for the apprehension of any one of the Anabaptist ministers, and ordered that a number of men be secretly appointed to seek admission by baptism into the Anabaptist fellowship, learn all they could about their leaders, methods, meeting places, etc., and betray them to the authorities. Meanwhile the prisons were full, and torture, butchery, and burning went on with ever-increasing vigor.

In May, 1533, the government directed the warden at Guffidaun to pour some consecrated water into the drink of the obstinate prisoners and to cook their food with consecrated salt; to do this for some days and to see what would come of it.

Huter retired to Moravia for a season, in August, 1533,

having already sent multitudes of his brethren to this land of promise. His promotion to the head pastorship of the party that came to bear his name soon followed.

The trial of Anton von Wolkenstein and his family, identified with the Anti-pedobaptist cause since 1527, did not occur till 1534. With his wife and several other members of his household he was cast into prison, and every effort was made to induce them to recant. Both husband and wife persisted for some time in their refusal. It looked as if Lady Wolkenstein would persevere to the end and wear the martyr's crown. Anton yielded first, and through the importunity of her children, whose prospects in life would be utterly blighted by her execution for heresy, she was finally induced to sign a form of recantation. Young Sigismund von Wolkenstein with great difficulty emerged from the inquisition through the influence of friends and his agreement to enter the army.

Persecution having broken out violently in Moravia, many Tyrolese Anti-pedobaptists returned to their native land, among them Huter himself. Soon after his arrival, he wrote to brethren left behind an account of his work and its prospects. He is not able to advise or discourage the return of other brethren. Each must take the responsibility for himself. "The Lord has abundantly prospered our way, and has brought us safely to the Puster valley and the Etsch land." He is already at work in mountain and valley, visiting those who are hungering and thirsting after the truth. "But the godless tyrants and the enemies of the truth, who have the power to slay, do not yet know, as we suppose, of our being here. God from heaven grant that they may be blinded and may not for a long time be made aware of our presence." This letter unfortunately fell into the hands of the authorities, and the hunt for its author was renewed with intensified zeal.

The authorities used the utmost diligence in seizing the fugitives from Moravia, and many fell into their hands. From April to July, 1535, Huter's presence in the country seems to have been concealed from his enemies. From this time they were in hot pursuit of him. Three letters written to his brethren in Moravia shortly before his death are full of foreboding as to the future, but also breathe the spirit of pious resignation. That he should write with some degree of bitterness of those who had destroyed so many of his brethren and like "cruel hell-hounds" were seeking his own life was no more than might have been expected. He says:

> The godless, Sodomitic sea roars and rages. I fear indeed that there will be no rest until the pious Jonas is cast in and the cruel whale has swallowed him. The whale is the cruel tyrant and enemy of the truth, Ferdinand, with all his following, and the accursed pope, with his accursed hell-hounds. But God will command this sea and his own shall be delivered from the power of godless men. Dearly beloved brethren, we now expect daily, hourly, momentarily the catchpoles of the magistrate, and the servants of the executioner, and all tribulation. . . The Lord grant us power and strength to abide in his truth.

He was seized about November 19, 1535, and after suffering unspeakable tortures, was burned at the stake. His bearing throughout the whole process, like his life, was most heroic.

The Anti-pedobaptist cause, it is needless to say, suffered irreparable loss in the death of its ablest leader. Hans Amon, now at the head of Huterite Church in Moravia, sent Hieronymus Käls, an educated schoolmaster, with two companions, to encourage the sorely persecuted brethren in the Tyrol, January, 1636; but they were seized on their way at Vienna and there executed. Leonard Seiler was next sent, but he also was thrown into prison at Moding, where he lay for nearly a year. To attempt to enter upon evangelical work in the Tyrol or in any part of Austria at this time was most hazardous and required heroism of the highest order; but there was no lack of men who were willing to enter the breaches as they occurred.

Huter's successor in the Tyrolese work proved to be Onophrius Griesinger. For nearly two years he was able to elude the vigilance of the authorities and to carry forward the work in Huter's own spirit. He possessed courage amounting almost to audacity, but combined with this a rare skill in concealing his movements from the police acquired by years of experience as an evangelist in the Tyrolese valleys. A Bavarian by birth he had held an honorable civil position in Salzburg. Since his conversion (1532) his labors had been chiefly in the Tyrol. Arrested in April, 1536, he had effected an escape. The authorities offered one hundred florins for his apprehension, but this was not accomplished until August 26, 1538.

Associated with Griesinger were a considerable number of zealous evangelists who did not suffer the good work to languish. We still hear of large assemblies of the persecuted people in many places. The vigor of the work carried on at this time as well as later was due to the well-directed efforts of the Moravian brethren, a large proportion of whose members knew from experience what it was to attempt to follow Scripture and conscience in the Tyrol.

The zeal of Ferdinand and his advisers was unabated and vast numbers continued to suffer for their faith. Side by side with these persistent efforts for the extermination of heresy was a recognition of the corruptions of monastic and clerical life and a somewhat vigorous effort by bringing about needed reforms to remove one of the chief grounds for evangelical dissent.

From 1539 to 1548, although their ranks had been considerably thinned by persecution and emigration, the Anti-pedobaptist cause was energetically maintained largely through the encouragement of the Moravians. While persecution continued we see signs of relaxation. Executions became less summary, and more earnest efforts than heretofore were made to win the heretics, now recognized as deluded rather than malignant, from their errors. Ferdinand did not see his way to follow the recommendation of the Innsbruck government (September, 1529) that Anabaptists who persisted in their errors should be given a limited time within which to dispose of their property and leave the land, but he did not repel the suggestion with such decision as he would probably have done at an earlier time.

The ecclesiastical authorities at Brixen complained to the king (November 10, 1539) of the great expense involved in the attempt to exterminate the Anabaptists and the ineffectiveness of persecution. While within a few years more than six hundred have been executed, the sect has been thereby from day to day more and more enkindled and raised up. Attention is further called to the fact that many of those who have been appointed to try and condemn heretics have conscientious scruples against condemning the Anabaptists to death. While every effort is being made by them (the Brixen authorities) to enforce the royal mandates, they ask Ferdinand to take into consideration the addition of a provision for the sale of goods and removal from the land of such as persist in their errors. Evidently the Tyrolese people were growing weary of bloodshed.

Ferdinand renewed the earlier mandates a few weeks later and insisted on their rigorous enforcement. Yet by 1543 even Ferdinand relented and did not hesitate to declare that he had " a horror " of this continual slaughter and complained of the rigorous execution of the imperial and princely mandates against the poor and misguided people. The utmost importance continued to be attached to the apprehension of the leaders.

The most prominent leader during this time was Leonard Lanzenstiel (or Seiler), a Bavarian, who had spent some time in Bohemia and Moravia. He was nominated by Hans Amon as his successor in the leadership of the Huterite connection in 1542, and died at the stake in Salzburg during the same year. Closely associated with Lanzenstiel in Tyrolese work was Leonard Lochmayer, an ex-priest from Freisingen, converted to Anti-pedobaptism in 1527. He removed to Moravia in 1528 and became one of the most zealous and successful of evangelists. His field embraced Hungary and several parts of Austria. In the Tyrol he was considered by his opponents more dangerous than Huter. He suffered for his faith in 1538.

There is no more striking proof of relaxation in the execution of the mandates against the Anti-pedobaptists than is to be found in the career of Hans Mändl (1537-61). A native of the Tyrol, he was baptized by Griesinger in 1537. Soon afterward he was thrown into prison at Sterzing, where he lay for six months. In 1544 he was imprisoned for twenty-two weeks at Landeck. He regarded his deliverance on these two occasions as providential. By 1548 he was the chief leader of the Tyrolese Anti-pedobaptists and remained such until his death in 1561. Soon after he had assumed the leadership he was again arrested and imprisoned (November, 1548). He was treated with much kindness and consideration by a priest commissioned to convince him of his errors and managed to escape. After a career of great activity and success,—he is said to have himself alone baptized about four hundred and as leader exerted a widespread influence,—he was seized, condemned, and burned in 1561.

During this period the exodus to Moravia was constant and the work in the Tyrol was carried on largely under the direction and with the support of the Huterite connection in that land.

In the trial of Mändl the government had great difficulty with the jurors, who were required to swear that they would render judgment strictly according to the royal mandates and not according to their own consciences. Much time was consumed in dealing with three jurors who declared "that they could not burden their consciences with such a case and that they would sooner endure therefor any punishment whatever." They were thrown into prison.

The reign of the Emperor Maximilian II. (1564-76), was one of comparative toleration. The position of the Moravian Anti-pedobaptists was during this period, as we shall see, one of great prosperity. After Mändl's execution along with two other ministers, the exodus of the Tyrolese brethren to Moravia became greater than it had been for a number of years; yet in spite of the diminution of numbers the work was carried zealously forward.

Before the close of the sixteenth century, however, the Jesuits had begun to gain an ascendency over the Hapsburg rulers, and from this time onward the Anti-pedobaptists throughout Austria and its dependencies were systematically and persistently persecuted. We are familiar with the methods by which they conducted their crusade against evangelical religion of every type and of the process by which Hussites, Bohemian Brethren, Anti-pedobaptists, and Protestants, were almost utterly exterminated (1618-1648).

Literature: Pertinent works of Loserth, Kripp, and Beck, as in the Bibliography.

CHAPTER XVI

AUSTRIA

THE term "Austria," sometimes used to designate the archduchy of Austria, may be here employed in a broader sense so as to embrace Styria, Salzburg, Carniola, and Carinthia. The Tyrol has demanded a separate chapter.

The diocese of Passau, which embraced territory now partly in Bavaria and partly in Upper Austria, was a chief center of mediæval evangelical life. About 1260, as has been earlier mentioned, as many as forty distinct congregations were located by the authorities in this region. Notwithstanding the rigor of the inquisitorial processes carried forward at this time, they persisted in large numbers. Many were arraigned in Steyer in 1311. In the region between Traiskirchen and St. Polten resident heretics were found about this time in thirty-six localities, and one hundred and twenty-nine were burned at the stake. Many more recanted and many fled. A Waldensian bishop named Neumeister was burned in 1315, who confessed to having eighty thousand adherents in the archduchy of Austria alone. He represented the number of Waldenses in Bohemia[1] and Moravia as beyond computation. These statements seem exaggerated and may have been extorted; but the inquisitors must have believed that they were in accord with the facts.

The city of Steyer and its environs long continued to be a stronghold of dissent. The inquisitor Peter, who made Steyer his residence from 1395 onward, found mul-

---
[1] Among the errors attributed to the Bohemian heretics by Pope John XXII., in 1318, was Anabaptism.

titudes of Waldenses. A contemporary document places the number of suspects at more than one thousand. About one hundred were burned in 1397. We have abundant evidence of the activity of the Waldenses throughout the various provinces of Upper Austria during the early part of the fifteenth century.

This region formed part of the territory traversed and cultivated by the famous Waldensian bishop, Frederick Reiser, who was in close touch with the Taborite movement in Bohemia. A large proportion of the old-evangelicals of Upper Austria seem to have taken refuge in Bohemia and Moravia; but the inquisition was not entirely abandoned and occasional heretical processes occur. Waldenses were persecuted as witches in many parts of Europe during the latter half of the fifteenth century, and Waldensianism came to be practically synonymous with witchcraft.

The readiness with which Lutheranism found acceptance in Upper Austria, would seem to show that though its outward manifestation had long been suppressed the old-evangelical spirit had survived. By 1525 a majority of the local diet of Upper Austria had declared in favor of reform. Steyer, which had been a chief center of old-evangelical life, was also foremost in its enthusiastic adoption of Protestantism. The efforts of the Austrian government to secure the co-operation of the local authorities for the suppression of Lutheranism proved ineffective up to 1527. The aggressiveness of Anti-pedobaptism had by this time become so marked that special attention was now given to this phase of dissent and many princes and officials were ready to join hands with the king in efforts to extirpate so dangerous a heresy.

In August, 1527, Ferdinand issued a mandate in which he complained that not only was Lutheranism steadily increasing in strength, but that " new, fearful, unheard-of doctrines . . . are emerging. Among these the renewal of baptism and the abuse of the highly venerable sacrament of Christ's holy body are included." Erroneous teaching with respect to baptism, the mass, and extreme unction are to be punished with imprisonment, banishment, or in some other way; but whosoever shall have "preached up among the common people the false doctrine of Christian freedom, as if all things should be in common and there should be no magistracy . . . is to be capitally punished."

The Steyer Council complained that the clergy and monks will allow no learned man to labor there, "but if God should lead such an one here, they would have no rest or repose until he should be removed." The acceptance given to Hans Hut's preaching was in their opinion due not to any evil purpose but to love for God's word. The town clerk, Pruckmüller, quoted in favor of non-interference with the Anti-pedobaptists, Gamaliel's words: "If this work is of man's hand it will come to naught, but if it proceeds from God you cannot suppress it."

On September 10, 1527, Ferdinand issued full directions to the Steyer authorities for dealing with the disciples of Hut. They are to be required to abjure and ever afterward keep themselves free from all of Hut's errors, regularly attend the services of the church, and submit themselves to all its ordinances to the end of their lives, to do public penance on three successive feast days in a way prescribed, etc.

It is certain that, apart from the persistence of old-evangelical modes of thought and the preparation furnished by the widespread acceptance of early Lutheranism, Anti-pedobaptist life had invaded the Austrian provinces as early as 1525–6. The persecutions in Switzerland and the bordering States at this time scattered the persecuted flocks very widely and these regions were at this time among the most inviting. It is probable that Hans Hut found considerable numbers of radical evangelicals and some pronounced Anti-pedobaptists in most of the places that he visited in the memorable summer of 1527. We cannot easily account for the readiness with which his teachings were everywhere accepted and the rapidity with which he was able to organize churches of baptized believers without supposing that the preparation for his labors had been of a somewhat direct and very effective kind. But it was this great enthusiast who first inaugurated a vigorous and comprehensive propaganda of Anti-pedobaptist principles.

As early as 1525 there seems to have been an Anti-pedobaptist organization in the city of Steyer,[1] the stronghold of mediæval evangelical life. Even the names of the members of this little body of earnest Christians have been preserved and we are not left in ignorance of the handicrafts by which they gained their support. It is remarkable that a very large proportion of the Anti-pedobaptists of the sixteenth century, as of the Waldenses of the earlier time, were artisans. Their ability to support themselves, even in times of bitter persecution, was due largely to the fact that they enjoyed the privileges of journeymen and members of the trade guilds that formed so prominent a feature of the industrial life of the time, and so were able, when driven from one locality, readily to find entrance into another.

Some time before Hut's visit two brethren from this region, one of whom was to attain to a position of leadership in the land of his adoption, had taken up their abode in Moravia. These were Jacob Wiedemann and Philip Jäger, through whose advocacy the doctrine of community of goods came to prevail among the Moravian Anti-pedobaptists.

---

[1] Czerny, "Bauernkrieg." p. 58.

A recent Austrian writer[1] has made an elaborate effort to prove that the Anti-pedobaptists of Upper Austria represent a direct development out of the persistent Waldensian life of the mediæval time and were wholly independent of Swiss influence. He seeks to show that the type of Anti-pedobaptist teaching that prevailed here before Hut's visit was widely different from the Swiss and that it was closely conformed to the mediæval life and teaching that so widely prevailed in these regions during the thirteenth and following centuries. This effort can scarcely be pronounced a complete success. The materials for a comparison with the Swiss brethren are not abundant, and Anti-pedobaptists in general had so much in common with mediæval evangelical parties that it is not easy to discern in the position of those of Upper Austria any material difference.

Hans Hut, whom we have met as an influential leader in Augsburg, and whose widespread and highly effective activity as an evangelist has been referred to, was in 1527 at the height of his popularity. The Nürnberg Council described him in March of this year as follows: "The highest and most eminent patron of the Baptists is Johannes Hut, a well-informed and clever fellow, of tolerably good physical proportions and of a boorish person, with light-brown cropped hair and with a pale-yellow little beard. His dress is a gray and sometimes a black riding coat, a gray, broad-brimmed hat and gray stockings."

He had just been driven from Nikolsburg, where he had strongly attacked warfare as a Christian occupation, and had almost wrecked the church over which Hubmaier and Hans Spitalmaier presided, and of which the

---

[1] Nicoladoni, in his "Joh. Bünderlin." See Jäkel's able *critique* of Nicoladoni in his gymnasial address, "Zur Frage über die Entstehung d. Täufergemeinden in Oberösterreich."

Lords of Lichtenstein were members and patrons. He labored for some days in Vienna, and baptized fifty converts; but the pastor of the Anti-pedobaptist congregation, the ex-bishop Martin Göschel, resisted him with such decision as to cause his speedy departure. He awakened much interest in Mölk, where he probably found a body of Anti-pedobaptists, and was accompanied by two prominent and well-to-do citizens[1] of that place to Steyer. At Mölk he baptized about fifteen. At Steyer he received marked distinction. The chaplain and castle preacher of the burggrave introduced him into the houses of distinguished citizens, in some of which he was permitted to preach. He evangelized from one notable house to another under the patronage of Chaplain Jacob Portner, who was deeply impressed by Hut's understanding and exposition of Scripture.

After a few days he retired to the country for baptizing and administering the Supper. This aroused the authorities against him, and he was obliged to flee. His adherents were arrested, and the city incurred the severe censure of the king for so far encouraging this dangerous heretic. Chaplain Jacob, having embraced Hut's views and received baptism at his hands, went as a missionary to Freistadt.

The provincial authorities invited the six cities of the province to send each a delegate to sit in council with the Steyer authorities for judging the accused. Of those arrested some disclaimed adherence to Hut, and secured release. Those who proved steadfast disclaimed any spirit of disloyalty toward the government. They were accustomed to pray for the king. They sought to obey the scriptural injunction to subject themselves to every human ordinance for the Lord's sake. Their meeting

---

[1] These were probably Hieronymus Hermann, of Mänsee, and Carius Binder. The former was sent forth by Hut as a missionary from Steyer.

together in brotherly love had no revolutionary design; their doctrine was not new, but the doctrine of Christ.

After several efforts to secure their recantation had failed, the burgomaster, Zuvernumb, of Steyer, gave his opinion to this effect: "It is clear that either the accused are heretics or himself and all present are. As such they should be burned, but as an act of mercy they should be first executed with the sword." A large majority of the council favored milder measures and imprisonment until conversion was finally decided upon.

The provincial authorities appealed to Vienna against this decision, and Ferdinand issued a mandate (March, 1528) requiring the execution and burning of those who remained obstinate, and insisting that royal mandates shall be regarded as laws to be executed without regard to the consciences of those who sit in judgment.

A number of executions followed. One of the prisoners testified that Hut had introduced nothing new save the sign by which brethren could recognize each other. If a strange brother came he greeted them "in the Lord," and they thanked him "in the Lord," and they asked him whether he came "before or after the Lord." If he were a genuine brother his answer would be: "Neither before nor after but with the Lord." It was also ordered that houses in which Anabaptist meetings had been held with the consent of the owners be destroyed.

According to the testimony of Hieronymus Hermann, of Mänsee, a priest who had allied himself with Hut, the latter, while at Steyer, cast lots for four evangelists to be sent forth for proclaiming "the faith of Anabaptism." Hermann himself was one of the four chosen; Leonard Schiemer, a well-educated monkish preacher, afterward a prominent Anti-pedobaptist, was the second; a German priest (name not given) the third; and Jacob Portner, the burggrave's chaplain, the fourth.

Cuntz Schmaus testified that he had been won to the brotherhood by Hut, and in company with him had gone from Vienna to Waldeck, and that in fourteen days they had won one hundred converts to their brotherhood. These facts are given to show the rapidity of Hut's movements, the overmastering enthusiasm that enabled him to gain to his cause not only multitudes of intelligent artisans, but educated priests and monks as well, and his wonderful ability to imbue his converts with his own missionary spirit and to send them forth as propagators of his principles.

The enthusiasm aroused by Hut at this time was doubtless due in some measure to his prophetic utterances with reference to the millennium. His little book on "The Seven Seals" set forth his views in a way that powerfully impressed the discontented masses. His idea seems to have been that three and a half years after the Peasants' War, that is in 1528, the godless of Europe would be destroyed by a Turkish invasion, while the true believers would take refuge in various places, and be in readiness for a new reign of righteousness. That he had any purpose to resist and overthrow the magistracy he denied to the end. The Hutite propaganda went forward, from this time onward, with astonishing rapidity, and within a few months had covered the whole of Upper Austria.[1]

After the partial suppression of the Anti-pedobaptist cause at Steyer, Linz became the chief rallying point of the brethren. Hut visited the city in July. He gathered around him those already in partial or complete agreement with his views, baptized a considerable number,

---

[1] A recent Austrian writer, Nicoladoni, says (p. 35): "At the end of the year 1527 there was no city and no market-town in the land of Upper Austria in which confessors of the Baptist doctrine had not permanently or transiently taken up their abode; nay, Baptist churches proper must have been formed about this time in almost every larger place."

filled the little body with his enthusiasm, and set them to work preparing for the kingdom of God soon to be established.

A considerable number of the severely persecuted brethren of Steyer sought homes in Linz, and for a time the cause prospered. We have the names and occupations of many of the Linz members. More important than the local was the missionary work that this community was able to accomplish in the surrounding regions. Few communities furnished to the Anti-pedobaptist cause a larger number of distinguished leaders.

Among the more prominent leaders at Linz were Leonard of Wels, a schoolmaster; Hans Fischer, former secretary of a nobleman; Jacob Portner, who after his departure from Steyer had led the Anti-pedobaptists of Freistadt, but who at a later date labored for some time in Linz; and Wolfgang Brandhuber, a tailor who had lived and labored for a time at Passau. His activity is said to have embraced the whole of Upper Austria proper and the diocese of Passau. He is regarded as one of the most influential leaders of the time and his execution, early in 1531, along with about seventy of his brethren and sisters, was a great calamity. Peter Riedemann, a Silesian, afterward to become a great leader in Moravia, labored at this time in a neighboring community, Gmunden, and suffered a long imprisonment for his faith.

One of the most interesting characters among the Linz Anti-pedobaptists was Ambrose Spitalmaier. Although his labors were largely in other communities, it seems best to introduce here some account of his teachings. The record of his very thorough examination by the Erlangen authorities has been preserved and constitutes the best extant statement of the views of the Upper Austrian brethren at this time. Baptized by Hut at Linz in July, 1527, and set apart by him as a preacher of the gospel, he seems to have labored in and around Linz till September. Driven from his home he journeyed from place to place everywhere preaching and baptizing. He visited Augsburg, went thence to Nürnberg, where he was entertained by the saddlers' guild, and passing through Schwabach and Gunzenhausen came to Erlangen where he hoped to find a certain family to whom he had been directed by Hut.

He was arrested at Erlangen about September twelfth, was examined repeatedly with the utmost care, torture being employed to some extent, and after a few months of imprisonment was executed in February, 1528.

Spitalmaier was a man of marked intelligence, deep Scripture knowledge, and thorough grasp of religion in its inner spiritual sphere. We cannot believe that his religious convictions and experiences, and his study of the Bible, were matters of recent origin. They show a degree of maturity that must have been the result of years of evangelical life and thought. That he had been under the influence of the Lutheran movement is certain, that he had early imbibed the traditions and modes of thought of the mediæval evangelicals is not improbable. He says:

If any one desires to know our faith, we show him the will of God clearly in every creature, to each according to his occupation through his own tool, as Christ has taught that man through his handiwork, as through a book which God has given him, can recognize his will, as a woman through the flax that she spins and through the household work in which she is engaged. To sum up, our doctrine is nothing else than that we teach all men to recognize the will of God through the creature, as invisible things through the visible things that God has placed before our eyes. The chief result of such recognition of the will of God is the leading of a Christian life. This is the fundamental command of his teaching. . . Our teaching is nothing else, [he says again,] than from the eternal, pure word of God. Thus if I (or another) come to one who is not of this faith, I ask him first of all whether he is a Christian, what his Christian walk is, how he bears himself toward his brethren, whether he in association with others has all things in common, whether any one among them suffers want in respect of food and clothing, whether they practise mutual brotherly admonitions.

Brotherhood he regards as involving a mutual obligation on the part of believers to exhort each other and to guide each other in the right way, if one or the other is found astray; to avoid all unseemly strife; and to have all things in common, including spiritual as well as temporal gifts. We have this:

He who as a member of Christ would enter into the heavenly kingdom on the day of judgment must live, suffer, and die in such a manner as Christ the head has died for us; he who suffers not with him will not inherit with him; he must drink the cup that he has drunk. But he who will not suffer here must there suffer in eternal fire.

A real, genuine Christian should not have upon the whole earth so much as standing room for one foot. By this it is not meant that he should have no shelter and should sleep in the woods, that he should call his own no farm or meadow and should not labor, but only that he should not believe that what he has he must use for himself alone or say, the house is mine, the farm is mine, the penny is mine. He must rather believe that his possession is that of all his brethren.

His Christology has some points of interest. He says:

We hold and believe, that Christ here on earth became a real, essential man, such as we are, of flesh and blood, a son of Mary, who conceived him, however, without human seed. . . But according to his deity he was a natural Son of God from eternity to eternity, born in the paternal heart through the Word. . . With his sufferings he has quenched the eternal wrath of the Father against us and has procured for us his complacency.

Again: "Christ did not make satisfaction for the sins of the whole world; else no one would be damned." In this he would seem to be at one with the Particular Baptists of the later time, and at variance with most of his contemporaries. Less satisfactory is the following statement, which moreover it is difficult to reconcile with the statement already quoted about the deity of Christ: "As often as Christ is mentioned in Scripture by this name he is to be understood as a mere man with flesh and blood, corporeal and mortal as ourselves; therefore that he is not God but a man, an instrument through which God has made known to us his word." He would seem to have denied the real union of the divine and the human in the person of Christ, and the germs of the later anti-trinitarianism may have inhered in his somewhat confused thinking.

Infant baptism he regarded as not only superfluous, but as "a blaspheming of Christ." The administration of believers' baptism he described as follows: "They require no other words than, 'I baptize thee in the name of the Father, of the Son, and of the Holy Ghost,' and they take water in a dish or a cup, dip two fingers in it and make with them a cross on the brow of the candidate."

He charges with jugglery and legerdemain those who maintain that in the bread and wine of the Supper the body and blood of Christ are contained. They are deceivers of men and murderers of souls.

Mariolatry is condemned with the utmost decision. True believers have no special places of assembly and no ecclesiastical officers with authority over the bodies of believers.

Spitalmaier persistently denied any hostility to magistracy as such, and any purpose to attempt its abolition by violent means. He admits that magistracy is a divine institution, but that "it has not remained in God, since it has overstepped its proper function and does so still to-day." He regarded the magistracy with which he was familiar as "blind and a leader of the blind, since it seeks only its own and not that which belongs to God, and therefore its judgment is false." True Christians, "being meek in heart, need no magistracy, no sword, or constraint, for they do voluntarily that which is righteous. To the upright no law has been given, and only those Christians who are such merely in word require magistracy for their piety, else they would gouge out each others' eyes; which compulsory piety however is not well-pleasing to God." He intimates that the work of true Christians is to proclaim the truth, and to secure its acceptance by as many as possible. If they were ten to one in any community they would do nothing further than to pray for the ungodly minority that they also might be enlightened with the divine light.

Hut's eschatological views had evidently made a deep impression on Spitalmaier. He regarded all the political and religious troubles of the time, including Turkish invasions, as penal judgments of God. The last day he regarded as imminent, and interpreted the prophetic Scriptures in accordance with this view. Enthusiasm was given to his preaching of repentance by his conviction that the time was short. Yet he seems not to have attempted to fix the exact date of the great catastrophe.

Another citizen of Linz who attained to great prominence abroad was Johannes Bünderlin.[1] From 1515 to 1519 he studied in the University of Vienna. Here he came under the influence of Humanistic modes of thought and was prepared for his later radical career. Returning to Upper Austria he seems to have taken part in the evangelical movement that advanced so rapidly from 1520 to 1525. For some time he was a preacher in the service of Lord Bartholomäus, of Starhemberg (about 1526). It is probable that Bünderlin came under the influence of Anti-pedobaptist teachings while engaged in this service, his patron's secretary, Hans Fischer, being among the earliest Anti-pedobaptists of this region. He

---
[1] See Nicoladoni, "J. Bünderlin."

was baptized in Augsburg, probably in 1526, and after spending some time in Nikolsburg, Moravia, under the protection of Lichtenstein, he betook himself to Strasburg, where he appeared in 1529. Strasburg was at this time the resort of all types of Anti-pedobaptists and Mystics. Persecuting measures of a mild form were now, perforce, being introduced, and Bünderlin was called upon to give an account of himself. Here he published several works in which he set forth mystical views far more radical than those of Denck, and in some respects less evangelical than those of Schwenckfeldt.

The first of these works was on the contents of Holy Scripture, the second on the incarnation, and the third (published in 1530) was on baptism. The aim of the last was to show that "water baptism, together with other external usages practised in the apostolic churches, are continued by some of this time without God's command and the testimony of Scripture." His thought was that baptism was given to the apostolic church by way of accommodation to the Jews, "who still clung to the letter of the law. Christians need neither baptism nor the Supper." "Christ baptizes in the Holy Ghost and in fire, as from the beginning of the world this has taken place in every believing heart."

Thus by 1530 Bünderlin had abandoned the baptism to which he had submitted some years before, and for which he had thought it worth his while to suffer, and had gone beyond Denck and beyond Schwenckfeldt in spiritualizing Christianity and in disparaging external ordinances. His position at this time was similar to that of Faustus Socinus in the latter part of the sixteenth century and of the Society of Friends in the seventeenth.

Freistadt also seems to have been invaded by radical forms of evangelical life before Hut's visit, about August, 1527. It is probable that Hans Schlaffer, an Upper Austrian priest, who renounced popery in 1526 and afterward spent some time with the Lord of Zelking in the neighborhood of Freistadt, exerted some influence in the town. This is rendered probable by the fact that a tract of his has been preserved among the inquisitorial acts of the town council. Schlaffer visited Augsburg, Nürnberg, Regensburg, and Nikolsburg (1526–7), and became acquainted with most of the Anti-pedobaptist leaders of the time. He suffered martyrdom in the Tyrol early in 1528. A number of his writings have been preserved.

Here, as elsewhere, Hut baptized a considerable number (ten or twelve) almost immediately after his arrival, and organized the body for aggressive work. Jacob Portner, whom he had set apart for missionary work at Steyer, was left in charge of the work at Freistadt, and may be regarded as the pastor of the church.

Soon after Hut's departure persecution began, a number were seized, and others escaped. Those tried for heresy were here, as elsewhere, artisans. This persecution was instigated by King Ferdinand who, as early as August 12, had learned of the procedures of Hut and his associates, and who looked upon their presence as fraught with danger, involving "conspiracy and secret evil practices that lead to uproar and insubordination." Six had been arrested by August twenty-second. The most prominent of these was Georg Schoferl, whose confession of faith has been preserved. Much to the displeasure of Ferdinand, the examination of the accused was deferred until October.

Schoferl and his companions strenuously denied that they had derived their doctrines from Hut, Zwingli, or Luther, and insisted that they had "taken them from God's word." They repudiate the charge that they have submitted to a "second baptism." They know of only one baptism authorized by Scripture, and this is the baptism of believers. If they err they are willing to be instructed.

Schoferl's exposition of the Christian life represents a pure evangelical mysticism, like that of Ambrose Spitalmaier, in which great stress is laid on the renunciation of self and all selfish ends, and a complete surrender of the entire being to God. Blessedness comes only through suffering. "Christ taught the common people the gospel in their own handicrafts, and did not have much to do with books, but for the sake of the stiff-necked scribes he used Scripture, for which purpose also Scripture must still be used, and not for the sake of the common man: for the common man can be more successfully instructed in the creatures." In this we have another indication of the strong mystical tendency of Upper Austrian Anti-pedobaptist thought.

Here, as elsewhere, the persistent demands of Ferdinand led to the gradual suppression of the movement, and by 1530 few traces of it remained. It may be remarked that most of those originally arrested were induced to purchase their freedom by renouncing their faith.

Hut visited a number of other places and sent missionaries into communities that he could not personally reach. During the years 1527-8 Anti-pedobaptist congregations, greater or smaller, more or less completely organized, existed in Wels, Gmunden, Lambach, Haag, Ried, Schärding, Brunau, Obenberg, St. Florian, Grein, Vöcklapruck, and probably in many other places in Upper Austria.

In close sympathy with the movement in Upper Austria and the still more important and persistent one in the Tyrol, Styria, Carniola, and Salzburg were from 1527 onward seriously affected by this type of teaching.

Royal mandates and remonstrances, royal commissions for the inquisition of heresy, executions and banishments were here, as elsewhere, the order of the day.

As the Anti-pedobaptist communities were transient in their nature, and as few leaders of outstanding influence appeared in those regions, such details as have come to light add little to our knowledge of their thought and life.

Moravia became the great place of refuge for the persecuted people of these and of other lands; and if from time to time in later years Anti-pedobaptist life reappeared, it was for the most part due to the active encouragement of the vigorous and well-organized brotherhood that so long prospered in that goodly land.

Literature: Pertinent works of Nicoladoni, Jäkel, Beck, Preger, Czerny, Loserth, as in the Bibliography.

CHAPTER XVII

MORAVIA AND BOHEMIA (1528 ONWARD)

SOON after Hubmaier's removal from Nikolsburg the controversy between Wiedemann and Jäger on the one hand and Spitalmaier on the other became acute. The conduct of the Lichtensteins in delivering up Hubmaier to death had certainly not tended to weaken the party that rejected magistracy and insisted on community of goods. The unfaithfulness of this Anti-pedobaptist noble, as seen in his readiness to sacrifice his brethren to appease the royal fury and make secure his possessions, was an object-lesson of the most effective kind.

With Wiedemann and Jäger community of goods was of the very essence of Christianity. Their agitation of this question in season and out of season brought commotion into the community. Spitalmaier publicly requested his followers to have nothing to do with Wiedemann and Jäger and applied to them contemptuous epithets. Lichtenstein could not tolerate schism, and while he was sorry to lose so large a number of valuable settlers, or to do anything that savored of intolerance, he felt constrained to send away those who could not conscientiously abide by the existing order. Yet he did everything in his power to insure them against loss and unnecessary hardship, and personally accompanied them to the river that bounded his territory, urging them meanwhile to return and live at peace with the Nikolsburg pastor. They were inexorable, however, and proceeded on their way toward Austerlitz.

When they had reached Neusslaw they sent a deputation to the Austerlitz authorities to lay before them a frank statement of their views and wishes. They were cordially invited to settle and were assured that a thousand such would be welcome. Wagons were sent to convey the weary pilgrims to the city, where they were treated with the utmost kindness. They were provided with a desirable site for a communal house and with building materials.

With the approval of the authorities, brethren were sent into other lands, especially the Tyrol, for reinforcements. The severe persecution in the Tyrol, Salzburg, and in Upper Austria in general (1529-33), made their mission an easy one. Jacob Huter was sent by his Tyrolese brethren toward the close of 1529 to confer with them as regards doctrine and practice. His report was so favorable that large numbers soon emigrated. Huter himself remained in the Tyrol looking after the persecuted flocks until 1531 when he made a second visit to Austerlitz, which as we shall see was of the utmost importance in the history of the movement.

As early as 1527-28 we find Anti-pedobaptist communities at Znaim, Eibenschitz, Brün, and Rossnitz. At Rossnitz, Gabriel Schärding (Ascherham), a Bavarian furrier, had gathered the people and was acting as their minister. On the arrival of Philip Blawermel, a Swabian weaver, who seems to have enjoyed in a large measure the confidence and esteem of the majority of the community, especially of those who had come from Swabia, Hesse, and the Palatinate, Gabriel withdrew from the position of leadership in his favor. The community having grown inconveniently large and difficulties having arisen between Philip and Gabriel and their adherents, Philip removed to Auspitz with a colony of five or six hundred adults. Gabriel was now at the head of a community of about twelve hundred adults and afterward attained to a still more influential position as pastor of the united communities of Rossnitz, Auspitz, and Austerlitz. The reconciliation of parties and the union of communities was due to the influence of Jacob Huter and marks an epoch in the history of Moravian Anti-pedobaptists.

Between Huter's first and second visits (1529-1531) a lamentable schism had occurred in the Austerlitz community. In the expressive words of the chronicler: "In the meantime it came about, inasmuch as the devil does not rest but goes about the house of God like a roaring lion, seeking on all sides opportunity to introduce division and to destroy the unity of the Spirit in order that he may destroy that which is godly, he attacked it in the most favorable place, namely in the elders of the church, because the life of the whole people stands in them."

The occasion of the trouble was Wilhelm Reublin, whom we have learned to know as one of the earliest, ablest, most eloquent, and most successful of Anti-pedobaptist preachers. One-eyed Jacob had lost none of his zeal for community of goods and his zeal for sole leadership was just as marked. Jacob was one of those narrow, unamiable, stern, domineering ministers, whom people grow weary of, but from whose authority they find it difficult to escape. It might have been expected that with so large a community on his hands he would have invited the zealous and accomplished Reublin, who had suffered so much for the faith, to assist him. But no! Though absent much of the time he positively and persistently refused to have another share his work. Murmurings naturally multiplied.

Some of the young sisters had shown a reluctance to enter into matrimonial relations with the marriageable brethren. One-eyed Jacob in his usual energetic style had told the sisters that if they persisted in their obstinacy he "would be obliged to give the brethren heathen wives," and thereby had scandalized many. The sisters also complained that he "troubled them with strange questions," that he gave them lessons to learn, and that "those who succeeded in learning them and answered the questions skillfully were praised, while the simple and stupid, but yet true and pious, were thereby held up to ridicule and shame." Much sighing, complaining, and murmuring arose among the people in consequence of the failure of some of the members to conform strictly to the rigorous rules of the community. Some were obliged to withdraw to other houses for lack of room in the communal house. Some were known to have "gone to market and to have purchased whatever they desired," and to have "sent food and drink to each other." The Tyrolese brethren complained that the teaching was not so edifying as that to which they had been accustomed. Many objected to the communistic method of bringing up children.

Under such circumstances it could hardly have been expected that Reublin should wholly abstain from exercising his gifts, notwithstanding the fact that "he had not been called to the office of teacher" in the community. One-eyed Jacob, who was absent when Reublin began to hold meetings for the exposition of Scripture, did not fail on his return to resent this encroachment on his authority. He promptly called together "all the elders in the land," and with their concurrence, publicly denounced Reublin for this breach of church order. Reublin entreated them "for God's sake to give him an opportunity to reply." This was peremptorily refused, and forty or fifty of Reublin's friends refused to have anything further to do with the majority until this righteous request should be accorded.

Georg Zaunring, a minister in the church, was among

Reublin's most zealous supporters. One-eyed Jacob warned the people against Reublin and Zaunring in language so intemperate that about one hundred more went over to their side. But Jacob was master of the situation, for he had absolute control of the entire commissariat. The starvation argument has rarely been applied with more heartlessness. "Zaunring and Reublin, together with the people, appeared before the house quite sad at heart. Then Reublin shook off the dust from his shoes over all that remained with Jacob for a testimony of their false and unrighteous judgment."

With about one hundred and fifty followers, Zaunring and Reublin made their way to Auspitz. There "they were obliged to endure great hunger and need, and often had to live and labor on " water and a morsel of bread the whole day." Robbers also attacked them and beat some of them to death. "Deep calleth unto deep," is the reflection of the chronicler.

The Auspitz and Austerlitz churches each sent two delegates to the brethren in the Tyrol with the request that the latter would appoint two of their number to investigate the difficulties that had arisen and to adjudicate on them. Jacob Huter and Sigismund Schützinger were appointed. A pitiful charge against poor Reublin was trumped up, to the effect that when he had fallen into a severe illness he was found to have "reserved forty florins that he had brought with him from home." On the strength of this charge and that of his alleged irregularity in setting himself up as a teacher without due authorization, Huter and Schützinger excluded him as "a lying, unfaithful, malignant Ananias." Such treatment did one of the noblest of ministers receive at the hands of his brethren.[1]

---

[1] Reublin's name disappears entirely from the Chronicle from this time. Recently an order of the Emperor Ferdinand (Feb., 1559) was discovered by Bossert in the Inns-

Reublin humiliated and driven out, the attention of the church was soon called to the "fleshly freedom" contained in the teachings of Avan Schlegel. This "fleshly freedom" seems to have been nothing more serious than a mild protest against the communism that Jacob Wiedemann was enforcing. Schlegel was promptly deposed from his office and forbidden to teach, as was also his principal supporter Burkhardt von Ofen. These complained of the treatment they had received and were thereupon excommunicated. Bohemian David brought upon himself the censure of the church by " promising to pay and paying the authorities of Nicholshitz for some guards" to protect his party from robbers on their way to Auspitz. George Zaunring was deposed from his office and excluded from the church for receiving back his wife who had committed adultery.

As a natural result of so reckless an exercise of discipline the church soon found itself "destitute of pastors and teachers" and with only "ministers of temporal need," or deacons. The Tyrolese brethren were then requested to "come to their help with ministers." Huter and Schützinger again visited them and secured the reunion of the three churches, Rossnitz, Auspitz, and Austerlitz. Schützinger remained as pastor of the Austerlitz division, Gabriel continuing at Rossnitz as head pastor of the tripartite church and Philip retaining leadership at Auspitz.

Huter returned to the Tyrol, whence he sent "one crowd of people after another to Schützinger and the church." In 1533 Huter himself, with many others, re-

---

bruck archives, in which it is stated that Wilhelm Reble (this was a common way of writing his name) had made a long journey to lay before the emperor a request for aid in securing his inheritance at Rottenburg. He is spoken of as very old and his residence is given as Znaim, Moravia. How he spent the intervening twenty-eight years, we know not. An Anti-pedobaptist church of the Swiss type is known to have persisted at Znaim until 1591. It is probable that he quietly ministered to this body.

moved to Auspitz, where he was most cordially received. To Schützinger and the rest of the brethren that greeted him he said that he had "not come as to strangers but as to dear brethren." He was asked to assist in the pastoral care of the church, which he was by no means reluctant to do. For the past two years he had been recognized as the foremost leader of the entire connection in Austria and its dependencies, and had practically ruled the Moravian and the Tyrolese churches. Being still at the height of his zeal and activity he could not be expected, as a member of the triparite church, to remain in a subordinate position. Gabriel could not begin to cope with him as regards administrative ability or popular power. He soon found occasion to exclude from the church his former colleague, Schützinger, along with his chief sympathizers, for failure to conform strictly to the principle of community of goods.

Philip and Gabriel resisted Huter's high-handed measures and a complete division ensued between the Huterites and the Philippists. "The Philippists would neither work, sit, eat, nor drink with the Huterites." The latter, owing to the great force of character and administrative ability of their leader, soon became the principal party and gradually absorbed the Gabrielite and Philippist factions.

In 1535 began the first great persecution of the Moravian Anti-pedobaptists. The edict of Speier had not been executed with much rigor in Moravia, but the abominations of the Münster Kingdom (1534-35) had intensified the alarm that already prevailed among the rulers of Europe in consequence of the spread of Anti-pedobaptism. There was no longer any excuse for toleration. The Moravians and related bodies professed, to be sure, the utmost abhorrence of the Münster procedures, but their own social ideas were completely out of harmony with the views of civil government that prevailed, and the general prevalence of their principles and views would mean the complete subversion of the existing order, to say nothing of the possibility that under favorable circumstances they might attempt to set up the kingdom of God in Münster fashion.

The Moravian nobles, highly as they prized the Antipedobaptists as peaceable and industrious subjects, could no longer resist the demand of King Ferdinand for their extermination. Many of the unhappy people were destroyed. Their communities were ruthlessly broken up and under circumstances of the greatest hardship their members were scattered far and wide. Yet their scattering was not disorderly. On the contrary, the members were systematically divided up into small groups of eight or ten, each with a director, and wherever a group settled they were in a position at once to form the nucleus of a new community. Huter returned to the Tyrol, where, as we have already seen, he was arrested toward the end of the year and after suffering terrible tortures was burned at the stake, February 25, 1536. Thus died one of the ablest and most energetic of the leaders of the party, after ten years of highly fruitful service in the Tyrol and Moravia.

The fierceness of persecution soon subsided, as the Moravian nobility were careful not to go beyond what the exigencies of the case required. Hans Amon became the leader of the Huterite party after the departure of Huter and retained the position until his death in 1542. During his leadership many new "households," as the communistic churches were called, were formed in Moravia, and several in Austria and Bohemia. It was their communism more than anything else that stood in the way of their securing toleration, yet they "were resolved, by God's help, to die rather than give up community of goods." In 1542 Hans Amon, "a true evangelical servant of Christ and superintendent of the whole church of God, after he had suffered many conflicts and trials, after he had imparted to us, his fellow-believers, much wholesome doctrine, with peaceful heart fell asleep in the Lord at Stäckowitz in Moravia." He designated as his successor Leonard Lanzenstiel, with whom the brethren soon associated Peter Riedemann, the ablest literary exponent of their principles. To him we are indebted for an admirable statement of the doctrine and practice of the party.[1]

Besides the Huterites, Philippists, and Gabrielites, there were still in 1543 several congregations of "Swiss Brethren," or followers of the early Swiss leaders and of Hubmaier. These rejected community of goods, paid the "blood-tax," and, according to their opponents, were neglectful of discipline. During Riedemann's able administration of the Huterite party many of the Philippists, Gabrielites, and Swiss Brethren[2] united with the more vigorous party. In 1550 there were seventeen "ministers of the word," thirty-one "ministers of need," and about twenty-five "households" in the Huterite connection.

The years 1547-54 are called by the chronicler "the time of great persecution." Previous persecutions were as nothing compared with this. Many took refuge in Hungary, where some of the nobles received them kindly, but most of them returned to Moravia in 1549

---

[1] See Riedemann's "Rechenschafft unserer Religion," reprinted in Calvary's Mittheilungen, Vol. I., pp. 256-417.

[2] These were the followers of Hubmaier, who under the protection of Lichtenstein and others had congregations at Bergen, Pohlau, Wisternitz, Voitsbrunn, Tasswitz, Urban, Seletitz, Jamnitz, Muschau, and Znaim. Oswald Glait, one of Hubmaier's earliest and ablest Moravian converts, labored in this interest till his death at Vienna by drowning in 1545. A body of Swiss Brethren existed at Znaim in 1591, and one at Eibenschitz persisted till 1618 or later. See Beck, "Geschichts-Bücher," p. 152.

when the fierceness of persecution had somewhat abated. The narrative of this persecution is full of mournful interest and bears ample witness to the steadfastness of the brethren. It is remarkable that they rapidly increased in numbers even during this time of great suffering. "Many became pious, amended their lives, took the cross upon them, more than often afterward in good times."

With 1554 began what the chronicler calls "the good time of the church," and it continued with slight interruptions till 1592. During this long period the brethren enjoyed unbounded prosperity. Their churches and ministers multiplied. When the Emperor Maximilian urged the Moravian nobles to renew the persecution in 1567, they replied that the country would suffer great loss from being thus deprived of its best mechanics and laborers. When he insisted that they must be expelled within a year, the nobles protested that this was impossible, as the people would sooner be beaten to death than go forth they knew not whither. Maximilian was not noted for persecuting zeal and was not inclined to press the matter to extremes.

According to contemporary accounts the Moravian Anti-pedobaptists were highly skilled in the various mechanical arts as well as in agriculture and stock-raising. Their cutlery, linens, and cloths are said to have been the best of their kind. Their courts were called the beehives of the land. Order, cleanliness, sobriety, and earnestness are said to have been manifest in their whole demeanor. Their widows and orphans were carefully provided for and pauperism was unknown. The nobles gladly frequented their baths, of which they maintained a number. The best of horses came forth from their stables. They had almost a monopoly in several branches of manufacture. The Moravian landlords,

Catholic and others, were glad to put them in charge of their farms, mills, wine cellars, etc.; for they were known to be not only capable but strictly trustworthy. The communities became wealthy; but they used their surplus means in succoring needy brethren in other places and such as were constantly coming to live among them.

Even during this prosperous period they were heavily taxed and depredations were frequently made upon them. Times of scarcity, almost of famine, are recorded now and again; but they made little of providential afflictions or of slight annoyances. About 1622 they are said to have numbered in all Moravia seventy thousand.[1]

From 1592 onward their history is that of misfortune and gradual decline. The Jesuits were on their track, and we know full well what that meant. The Thirty Years' War devastated the land, though not to the same extent as Bohemia. After suffering indescribable hardships during those perilous times, these hardy, industrious Anti-pedobaptists still constituted a vigorous party at the close of the war in 1648.

From 1651 onward they were utterly ruined by invasions of Germans, Turks, and Tartars, and by 1665 they had been reduced to such misery that they felt constrained to petition the Mennonites in the Netherlands for aid. Many of them were taken captive by the Turks and conveyed to the far East. The Roman Catholic authorities, urged on by the Jesuits, massacred them mercilessly. According to the chronicler, "Some were torn to pieces on the rack, some were burned to ashes and powder, some were roasted on pillars, some were torn with red-hot tongs, some were shut up in houses and burned in masses, some were hanged on trees, some

---

[1] See Merian, "Topographia Bohemiæ, Moraviæ, et Silesiæ," p. 46, quoted by Loserth.

were executed with the sword, some were plunged into the water, many had gags put into their mouths so that they could not speak and were thus led away to death. Like sheep and lambs crowds of them were led away to be slaughtered and butchered. Others were starved or allowed to rot in noisome prisons. Many had holes burned through their backs and were left in this condition. Like owls and bitterns they dared not go abroad by day, but lived and crouched in rocks and caverns, in wild forests, in caves and pits. Many were hunted down with hounds and catchpoles," etc.

"Whence does it arise," wrote one of their Roman Catholic persecutors, "that the Anabaptists so joyfully and confidently suffer the death penalty? They dance and spring into the fire, they behold the glittering sword with undaunted hearts, they speak and preach to the people with smiling mouths, they sing psalms till the soul goes out, they die with joy as if they were in a festive company, they remain strong, confident, steadfast even unto death." Like Luther, Faber attributed these phenomena to Satanic influence.

"The holy land into which God brought them" no longer afforded them a refuge. Many of them escaped to Hungary and Siebenbürgen where they maintained themselves in gradually diminishing numbers until they became extinct about 1762. A number of families removed to Wischeuka in Southern Russia, where they persisted until the present century. The remnant removed in 1874 to South Dakota, where, to the number of three hundred and fifty-two communicants, in five organizations, they still maintain the faith and the customs of Jacob Huter.[1]

The historical documents of the Moravian Anti-pedobaptists show us a people of marvelous steadfastness and

---
[1] See Carroll, "The Religious Forces of the United States," p. 213.

undaunted courage. No more heroic martyrology exists. They evidently had not the slightest misgivings as to their position, and they considered the smallest of their peculiarities well worth dying for. Side by side with this unswerving loyalty to conviction and intimately related to it we find a certain narrowness and punctiliousness, an incapacity to bear with each other in minor differences, a willingness to throw a whole community into turmoil and thus to hinder religious work and jeopardize their toleration by the authorities on account of some slight personal disagreement or some slight breach of discipline.

Unable to tolerate each other in minor differences, we could not expect to find among them any due appreciation of the religious character of those who were at variance with them on fundamental points. Their extreme bigotry could not fail to make them hateful to those who did not share their peculiar views.

Community of goods, as we have seen, was regarded by them as fundamental. It constituted one of the chief grounds of suspicion against them and encouraged to the utmost extreme separatism and bigotry. It involved a surrender of personal freedom not conducive to the highest spiritual development. It rendered it possible for the head pastor and other officials to tyrannize over their brethren. It gave occasion to jealousies and murmurings and an unwholesome disposition to pry into each other's affairs. It practically destroyed family life by separating infants from their mothers and bringing them up together in communal nurseries. It excluded from the community the nobility and the gentry, many of whom openly sympathized with them in their main positions, but did not feel called upon to surrender property and rank and to enter into communal life.

On the other hand, this feature of their system was highly attractive to the poor and oppressed and doubtless attracted a far larger number than it repelled. It gave to the brethren a certain solidarity and harmony of action that enabled them to hold together and to multiply in the face of bitter persecution and readily to meet the charitable demands made upon them by the constant influx of persecuted and impoverished brethren from the West. Apart from their communism, their treatment by the civil authorities being supposed to be the same, it is difficult to see how they could have maintained a separate existence at all during the seventeenth century.

Their doctrinal position was in general identical with that of the great Anti-pedobaptist body and with that of the principal mediæval evangelical parties. They accepted heartily the Apostles' Creed; they seem to have been free from chiliasm; and they were decidedly anti-Augustinian in their anthropology. Their views of the will, original sin, universal redemption, and related doctrines, were similar to those of evangelical Arminians. As regards the subjects and the aim of baptism they were entirely at one with modern Baptists, but they did not come to see the importance of immersion as the apostolic mode. They were uncompromising in restricting the Lord's Supper to those who had been baptized into their fellowship and were in good standing. Their views on oaths, magistracy, warfare, capital punishment, etc., were those of the mediæval evangelical parties, of nearly all the Anabaptists (including the Mennonites), and of the later Society of Friends.

Their church polity, apart from the communistic organization already described, was as follows: The entire Huterite brotherhood, with its local organizations or households, was presided over by a head pastor or bishop (in this also they followed the Waldenses and the Bohemian Brethren) appointed by representatives of the entire body. Under the head pastor were in each local congregation "ministers of the word" and "ministers of need." These officers, while they are commonly designated as artisans of one sort or other, in prosperous and aggressive times devoted themselves largely to religious work, sometimes traveling into remote regions to minister to persecuted and scattered flocks and to labor for the conversion of souls.

Like the mediæval parties already referred to and most of the other Anti-pedobaptists, they were somewhat narrow and one-sided as regards occupations. Merchandizing, money-lending, and inn-keeping, were strictly prohibited as immoral or as inconsistent with the simplicity of the gospel; while physical labor was exalted and every member of the community was taught to work. A more industrious community probably never existed.

In Bohemia the Anti-pedobaptist cause never attained to important proportions. The proclamation of Thomas Münzer in 1521 in the Bethlehem chapel at Prague, no doubt caused considerable commotion at the time and met with some response from those who had been under Taborite influence; but there is no evidence that his visit resulted in any organized effort for the carrying out of his scheme. Hans Hut's labors in Upper Austria in 1626-27 undoubtedly made some impression on the neighboring parts of Bohemia. A congregation had been organized at Krumau some time before 1529, when, under the stress of persecution, eighty of its members went to Moravia and united with the Huterite party. They were led by Hans Amon, who as we have seen, afterward became the head pastor of the connection.

The repudiation of Anabaptism by the Bohemian Brethren in 1534, in order to escape the operation of the laws against Anabaptists and to distinguish themselves from this aggressive form of Christianity, was from one point of view a hindrance and from another a help to the

Anti-pedobaptist cause in Bohemia. It was thenceforth more difficult for the Anti-pedobaptists to carry forward their work undetected. It undoubtedly caused a considerable number of the Brethren who resented the abandonment on grounds of expediency of one of the original practices of the connection, to unite with the more consistent and more aggressive body.

Among the most noted of the Bohemian Anti-pedobaptists of the latter part of the sixteenth century was Georg Zobel, the physician, who from 1581 to 1599 was frequently called upon to practise his profession in the imperial court and from whose skill the emperor himself is said to have derived great benefit.

Chiefly through the encouragement of the Moravians individual congregations maintained themselves in Bohemia till the close of the sixteenth century; but persecution was so continuous and severe, and it was so easy for persecuted bodies to make their way to their more favored brethren in Moravia, that the building up of a strong cause in Bohemia was impracticable.

Literature: Pertinent works of Beck, Loserth, Cornelius (" Münst. Aufr."), Wolny, Czerny, and Dudik, as in the Bibliography.

CHAPTER XVIII

THE STRASBURG CENTER

SITUATED on the Rhine, the medium of communication between the East and the West, at a point that commands the commerce of the valleys of several of the tributaries of the Rhine, and on the great route of commerce between the North and the South, Strasburg was at the beginning of the sixteenth century an important manufacturing and distributing center. It was at the same time one of the most prosperous and one of the most cosmopolitan cities of the age. In the mediæval time it had been a stronghold of evangelical life and thought. Like many other cities it had secured for itself a large measure of independence. Its reputation for justice, moderation, and toleration was worldwide. The death penalty was rarely inflicted. Yet it was shrewdly remarked by a contemporary that better order prevailed there than in cities where the greatest severity was employed.

To the Anti-pedobaptists, hounded to death on all sides by persecutors, Protestant and Catholic, it became a veritable Eldorado. The large aggregation of artisans of all kinds offered the material from which the Anabaptists, like the Waldenses before them, assimilated most freely. Many of the evangelists were artisans and there was no city where they were more sure to find work, or failing this, hospitality. The liberality with which the citizens of Strasburg provided for the poor and distressed was extraordinary. New-comers, even when applying for aid, seem not to have been questioned about their faith, and as long as they conducted themselves so as not to disturb the public peace, citizens and strangers were free to believe what they would. The evangelical pastors were men of marked liberality. It was only after the growth of the Anti-pedobaptist cause had become so marked as to threaten seriously the existing order that Bucer assumed a persecuting attitude. Later, when he saw Capito, his chief colleague, on the point of being carried away by this new influence, he became somewhat intolerant. Distinctly more tolerant was Matthew Zell, who never could be induced zealously to antagonize the sectaries. "Whoever recognizes Christ as his Lord and Saviour shall have part at my table and I will have part with him in heaven." In accord with this motto was his bearing toward the Anti-pedobaptists and other opponents of the standing order. Schwenckfeldt spent two years in his home.

Wolfgang Capito was, if possible, still more friendly to the separatists. For years his attitude toward the Anti-pedobaptists was such as to cause the gravest anxiety to Zwingli, Bucer, and others. The position of Bucer in regard to infant baptism is succinctly expressed in the following sentence: "But if any one would postpone water baptism and could do so without the destruction of love and unity with those among whom he lives, we would ourselves not quarrel with him nor condemn him, for the kingdom of God is just as little water baptism as it is eating, drinking," etc.

As late as December, 1531, Bucer denied that there was any just cause for the Anabaptists' renunciation of communion with himself and the evangelicals of the city, and expressed a willingness to offer them the "sincere love that is known to be germane to the disciples of Christ . . . even if they persist in the abolition of infant baptism."[1]

---
[1] See letter of Bucer to Ambrose Blaurer in Cornelius, Vol. II., p. 261.

In 1526 or 1527 Capito began to show a strong inclination toward the Anti-pedobaptist position. At this period he was greatly influenced by Cellarius, Hetzer, and Denck, all like himself advanced Hebraists, and while differing in other matters agreeing in rejecting infant baptism as unscriptural and unwarranted. In 1528 Bucer regarded Capito as theoretically an Anti-pedobaptist. Cellarius offended Bucer and Capito took sides with the former. In his commentary on Hosea, Capito took occasion to refute Zwingli's and Bucer's arguments for infant baptism. He repudiated the idea that baptism sustains any relation to circumcision and could see no merit in the New Testament arguments used by Zwingli and Bucer in support of their position. He defined the church in such a way as to exclude infants, a profession of faith being a condition of membership. "In which symbols (baptism and the Lord's Supper) those rightly participate who participate in the first-fruits of the Spirit," expresses his idea of the proper use of the ordinances. Writing of the Anti-pedobaptist martyrs he says: "Those who under the harshest tyranny confirm Anabaptism with the confession of Christ, sin without malice if they sin." He could scarcely be dissuaded by Bucer (about December, 1531) from marrying the widow of an Anabaptist martyr.[1] For years Bucer tried in vain to deliver Capito from the influence of his Anti-pedobaptist associates and at times almost despaired of him. Yet in his later years even Capito became embittered against the people that were everywhere spoken against.

Nowhere was the separatist life so varied as at Strasburg. The bare mention of the names of the more influential leaders that for a longer or shorter period brought their influence to bear upon the religious life of

---

[1] Augustin Bader, who suffered at Stuttgart. See letter of Bucer to Blaurer in Cornelius, Vol. II., p. 262.

the city will illustrate this statement. The list includes the names of Storch, Carlstadt, Cellarius, Denck, Hetzer, Kautz, Bünderlin, Reublin, Sattler, Wiedemann, Schwenckfeldt, Franck, Servetus, and Hoffman.

Nicholas Storch is said to have visited Strasburg in the summer of 1524. With his mastery of the letter of Scripture and his extraordinary enthusiasm he soon made a deep impression, and as was everywhere the case, caused so much commotion that he was soon obliged to leave the city. That he left behind him those who formed the nucleus of a chiliastic Anti-pedobaptist community can scarcely be doubted.

Carlstadt, driven from Orlamünde through Luther's efforts, visited Strasburg in October, 1524. At this time Carlstadt stood for the most complete individualism in matters of religion. To him the essential thing was the mystical union of the believer with God. All outward forms and ceremonies were of entirely subsidiary importance. "If one should not receive the sacrament forever, he would yet be blessed, if he were otherwise justified." Infant baptism was, in his view, without scriptural authority and without value for the Christian life. He favored its entire abolition. Yet he never became an Anabaptist, and after a few years of suffering he thought it advisable to hold in abeyance his views on baptism and to accept a professorship in the University of Basel. But at this time he represented a radical type of reform and repudiated the idea that, to avoid scandal and maintain unity, idolatry and other unscriptural and baneful things should be even temporarily retained in Christian churches. He had already taken issue with Luther on the doctrine of the Lord's Supper and was the forerunner of the Swiss theologians in holding to the memorial view. He was exceedingly bitter against Luther, whom he regarded as a cruel persecutor and a perverter of Scripture. Luther's influence was sufficient to secure the prohibition and confiscation of Carlstadt's books and soon afterward the banishment of their author, who by the end of November had secured a considerable following and whose presence was thought to be fraught with danger. Yet Strasburg accepted Carlstadt's view of the Supper in preference to that of Luther and a breach with Luther soon followed.

During 1526 large numbers of Anabaptists from all parts of Alsace, Southern Germany, and Switzerland, streamed into Strasburg. Among the most influential of these were Wilhelm Echsel and Jacob Gross. The former had been baptized in the canton of Zürich and had been banished thence; the latter was one of Hubmaier's most faithful Waldshut followers, and since the fall of Waldshut had labored with zeal and success in the Grüningen district. In Strasburg he soon had a large following. A furrier by trade he baptized, among others, a fellow-workman from St. Gall, named Matthew Hiller, and Georg Tucher of Weissenburg. In his conference with the authorities he expressed himself entirely in accord with Hubmaier's views as regards magistracy. In reference to warfare his conscience would not allow him to engage personally in smiting people to death, but he would not object to standing guard, providing food for the soldiers, etc. Like most of the Anti-pedobaptists he steadfastly opposed oaths. His arguments against infant baptism are such as have already become familiar to us. He was imprisoned and afterward banished.

The Anti-pedobaptist life of Strasburg was first organized and made aggressive through the efforts of Hans Denck, who arrived in October, 1526. Here he was able almost immediately to gather around him and to impress with his peculiar modes of thought the unorganized material that had for some years awaited the advent of such a master spirit. Even the tolerant Capito could write a few weeks after Denck's arrival complaining of the disturbances that the latter was creating. He understands not the spirit of such men, but he is assured that they are not of God who take away from us that which is distinctive in Christianity, nor leave any confidence in the suffering of the Lord. A colloquy with Bucer, Capito, and others, December 22, left a highly unfavorable impression on the minds of the evangelical leaders and confirmed them in the conviction that they had to deal with an exceedingly able, but erratic and dangerous man.

Denck's residence in Strasburg was of short duration. In response to an order of the council he departed on December 25. He spent some days at Zaubern, and at Landau held a disputation on infant baptism with Johann Bader, an evangelical pastor. Bader published a full report of the discussion under the impression that he had effectively defended the Pedobaptist cause; but some years afterward he yielded to the force of Denck's arguments, rejected infant baptism, and became a follower of Schwenckfeldt. Denck next took up his abode at Worms, where he conducted himself quietly but exerted a strong influence in favor of radical Anti-pedobaptist reform.

While in Strasburg he had been closely associated with Hetzer, with whom he was zealously engaged in Bible translation. The latter still resided at the house of Capito and did not openly declare himself an Anti-pedobaptist; but he soon followed Denck to Worms, where he more openly espoused the Anabaptist cause.

Another Anti-pedobaptist visitor to Strasburg was Michael Sattler, an ex-monk, who had labored in Switzerland and had been banished some time before. Even his opponents are lavish in their praise of his learning, amiability, and piety. He must have had a singularly attractive personality. He was entertained by Capito and after a short but not unfruitful stay departed in a perfectly peaceable way. He did an important work in Rottenburg and its vicinity, was probably the author of the Schleitheim Confession of February 24, 1527, and suffered martyrdom shortly afterward (May 20) at Rottenburg. Even Bucer could speak of him as a "martyr of Christ," who, "though he was a leader among the Baptists, was much more reasonable and honorable than some of the rest." According to Capito, he manifested "a great zeal for the honor of God and the church of Christ, which he wished to have pure and irreproachable and free from offense to those who are without."

In view of the rapid growth of the Anti-pedobaptist cause at Worms and the encouragement that the Strasburg radicals were deriving from this source, the Strasburg preachers addressed a "True Warning" to the authorities at Worms (July 2, 1527) calling attention to the doctrinal unsoundness of Denck and urging that measures be taken against the party. Under the advice of the ministers the Strasburg Council issued a rigorous mandate against the Anabaptists on July 27. All residents of the city and land were strictly enjoined to guard themselves against Anabaptist error and prohibited from housing, harboring, supplying with food and drink, or giving secret encouragement to the sectaries. Undoubtedly it was the great influence of Zwingli that led the tolerant Strasburg ministers and council to assume a persecuting attitude.

A few arrests were made and some were banished, but the council soon revoked its mandate so far as the banishment of the followers of Denck was concerned, and in November Capito could write to Zwingli: "Daily new Anabaptists arise, likewise they bring in new views upon new, which stand outside of any connection with the honor of God." He laments their extreme persistence in holding to their views even when they seem to have been argumentatively worsted. Yet he thinks he sees some improvement.

Although a mild form of persecution continued they did not cease to multiply. When it became unsafe to hold large gatherings in the city they resorted to a neighboring forest where hundreds sometimes worshiped together. A difficulty in dealing with the Anti-pedobaptists lay in their conscientious objection to taking an oath. By arguments that do not now seem particularly cogent, Capito succeeded in convincing many of them of the lawfulness of oaths and Bucer was able to report in February, 1528, that all the Anabaptists had taken the oath.

At Worms, Jacob Kautz, a brilliant and enthusiastic young preacher, who had enjoyed the fullest confidence of the Strasburg ministers, was won by Denck and Hetzer to the Anti-pedobaptist cause. On July 9, 1528, he set forth his position in seven articles. These contain, along with the ordinary Anabaptist view of the ordinances, the most objectionable features of Denck's system, expressed in a manner that would doubtless have offended the latter. The external word is declared to be "not the true, living, eternally abiding word of God, but only the witness or indication of the inner." It is declared that in Christ will be more richly restored all that was lost through the first Adam, nay, that in Christ all mankind shall become alive or blessed.[1] "Jesus Christ of Nazareth" is declared in no other way to have suffered or made satisfaction for us, than that we should stand in

---

[1] Like Denck, he was accused of teaching that "the devil together with all the impicus would be saved." See letter of Bedrotus to Ambrose Blaurer, in Cornelius, Vol. II., p. 261.

his footsteps and traverse the road that he has beaten, and follow the command of the Father as did the Son.

This clear and dogmatic statement of erroneous doctrine was the occasion of severe persecution by order of the Elector of the Palatinate. In company with William Reublin, Kautz betook himself to Strasburg. Soon after his arrival he asked for a public disputation with the ministers on the doctrines for which he stood; but the authorities decided that he and Reublin should rather be dealt with privately by the ministers, inasmuch as their errors were "so fundamental." It was ordered, moreover, that the discussion take place in writing. On January 15 Kautz and Reublin presented a statement of their views. In the first part they expounded their baptismal views, in the second they sharply criticised the Strasburg church order, or rather lack of order. Private conferences proved ineffective and both parties pressed for a public disputation. In the meantime the Anti-pedobaptist cause was becoming daily stronger and more aggressive. The ministers were all the more eager for a public disputation because of the impression which was coming to prevail in Anti-pedobaptist circles that they feared the light. The edict of Speier (April, 1529) caused the council to refuse the demand; for unless it was prepared for a wholesale butchery of the Anabaptists the less noise made about them the better.

Kautz and Reublin had been imprisoned at an early stage of these procedures. Kautz having sickened was transferred to the hospital, where he enjoyed the ministrations of his wife. In October, Capito and Schwenckfeldt requested the council to "leave Kautz to them for four weeks," promising to return him at the end of this time if he should remain unconverted. He persisted in his views and was banished. Reublin also became "miserably sick and lame" through long imprisonment, and was banished. Having appeared again in an Anabaptist gathering he was again banished, with the threat of drowning, after the Zürich fashion, in case he should be found again within the jurisdiction.[1]

Cellarius, the associate of Storch and Münzer, resided for years in Strasburg. Being a distinguished Orientalist and Old Testament scholar, he gained for a time almost complete ascendency over Capito. He was strongly opposed to infant baptism, though he did not identify himself with the Anabaptists. At this period he seems to have laid more stress upon his millenarian views than upon Anti-pedobaptism. He was one of the most enthusiastic and scholarly millennialists of the time, and his interpretation of the prophetical Scriptures was largely in the interest of these views.

Reference has already been made to Capito's sympathy with Anti-pedobaptist views and his strong disinclination to the persecuting measures that Bucer advised. In 1528 or 1529 he wrote to Musculus: "The reckless proceedings of my colleagues against them (the Anabaptists) frighten me." He expresses his hearty accord with Musculus in his compassionate and gentle treatment of the Anabaptists. He attributes to Bucer the cruel measures that the authorities are employing against them. "I oppose, because in the sight of God the matter is to be dealt with, who indeed commands that the truth be left unmolested, but has not as yet seen fit to give any instructions as to whether errors should in any way be abolished and abjured." "I doubt not," he continues, "that with us everything would have remained entirely quiet if we had taken stricter account of the consciences of men and their exigencies. Often one proceeds not otherwise than

---

[1] In 1532 Kautz begged for permission to reside in Strasburg, which was refused. In 1636 we meet him again as schoolmaster at Iglau, in Moravia. See notice by Bossert in "Jahrbuch der Geselsch. f. d. Gesch., d. Prot. in Oesterreich," 1892, p. 54 *seq.*

as if profane things were being dealt with, and this takes place indeed through such as resting upon the judgments of others crassly condemn that of which they themselves have no proper understanding."[1] While he does not favor the abolition of infant baptism at the present time, he knows very well that the "considerations brought forward in support of infant baptism are without argumentative force."

The imperial edict of Speier introduced a new era in Anabaptist history. In the countries of the Swabian league and, in fact, in most countries belonging to the empire, Anabaptists were henceforth hunted down like wild beasts, and thousands were mercilessly destroyed. Nearly all of the original leaders had passed away. Strasburg now became more than ever the western center of the movement. From Bavaria, Baden, the Palatinate, the Tyrol, Würtemberg, Holland, Zealand, and other countries, Anabaptists flocked to Strasburg. Many of them had already suffered for the gospel. Immersion may in some instances have been practised here at this time.[2] Large numbers were thrown into prison and examined, some of them under torture. The object of the application of torture was to ascertain whether the Anabaptists practised community of wives, and whether they were plotting revolution. Among the leaders at this time were Pilgram Marbeck, Melchior Hofmann, Hans Bünderlin, and Andreas Hüber, an ex-priest of high standing.

---

[1] He probably refers to Bucer's dependence on Zwingli's judgment in such matters.

[2] Gerbert ("Stras. Sectenbewegung." p. 93) states that baptism occurred at this time "before the Butchers' Gate, probably in a branch of the Rhine." He refers to confessions of Anabaptists recorded in Wencker's MS. "Actensammlung." Röhrich quotes from the Acts a confession of Bertel and Esinger, that they were "baptized before the gate by a shoemaker." Others at the same time mentioned houses in which they had been baptized ("Zeitschr. f. Hist. Theol.," 1860, p. 48). Whether being "baptized before the gate" implies immersion, is a question that cannot be answered with confidence without further information as to the location of the gate referred to, etc.

Marbeck was, after Denck, by far the most important personage among the Strasburg Anti-pedobaptists. A Tyrolese by birth, and a member of a monastic order, he embraced Anabaptist views some time before 1527. Driven by persecution from his home he resided for some time (1527-8) in Augsburg. He removed to Strasburg in October, 1528. He was a skillful engineer and an enterprising business man. The city was suffering from an insufficient supply of fuel. Marbeck advised the council to purchase forests in the Ehn and the Kinzig valleys, and directed the rafting of the wood. Owing partly to his business engagements he did not assume the leadership of the party till 1530 or 1531. The Anabaptists, according to Bucer, "worshiped him like a god." Margaretha Blaurer, sister of the famous Ambrose Blauer, and one of the most eminent Christian women of the time, took a profound interest in Marbeck, whose influence over her Bucer vainly endeavored to destroy. She reproached Bucer for his harsh and rough treatment of the Anti-pedobaptists, his unseemly prejudice against them, and his lack of a proper understanding of their position. His prestige as a business man and the friendship of such personages as Margaretha Blaurer enabled Marbeck for some time to carry forward his work with comparative freedom.

In October, 1531, he published two books in defense of his principles. This was made the pretext for his imprisonment. After fruitless conferences with Pollio and Capito, he was allowed to discuss with Bucer before the council the points at issue. An abbreviated but apparently careful record of the two days' discussion has been preserved in the Strasburg archives. In these procedures Marbeck conducted himself with much dignity, and his defense of his position was, from a Baptist point of view, eminently satisfactory.

In the beginning of the discussion he states that he appears before the council not because he recognizes the authority of any human judgment in matters of faith, nor to discuss with the preachers alone, but rather that he may speak with all Christians. He expresses a willingness to follow Bucer in case he should be overcome in argument, and asks that Bucer follow him in case the former be vanquished. He rebukes the spirit of hatred and strife that exists between the papists and the followers of Bucer, and between Luther and Zwingli, and urges the council to put away all respect of persons as among papists, evangelicals, and Anti-pedobaptists. If this shall take place, good will result; if not, matters will grow worse. Like Kautz and Reublin, he complains that there is no proper church order in Strasburg. "Every Christian should subject himself to the biblical word and the work of Christ, not that works have anything to do with the matter, but that every one should give himself up to the obedience of Christ, which is accomplished in him through the grace of God. . . Moses at God's command used the staff, which was changed into a serpent not in the power of the staff, but from the power of God's command. So also I have accepted baptism as a witness of the obedience of faith, not that I have regard to the water, but only to God's word." Bucer admits that there is no special command to baptize infants, but insists that there is also no special command to baptize adults. The discussion followed well-beaten paths on both sides.

The council decided in favor of Bucer and decreed the banishment of Marbeck. He obtained permission to remain a few weeks to arrange his affairs, but after making an earnest plea for the suspension of persecution and the granting of toleration and support to "those miserable men who have no abiding place in the whole world, and who flee to you," he was obliged to depart early in January, 1532. Marbeck's plea for liberty of conscience deserves to be placed by the side of that of Hubmaier.

After spending some time at Ulm he again took up his residence at Augsburg. Until his death, about 1546, he was the guiding spirit of an Anti-pedobaptist movement that had many congregations scattered throughout the region between Ulm and the Neckar, and that from 1535 onward, owing in part to the lamentable corruption of the evangelical churches, grew from year to year. He seems to have kept up a regular correspondence with the brethren in Moravia. Among his influential supporters were the noblewomen Marpurga Marschalk of Pappenheim and her kinswoman Magdalena. These seem to have been active members of an Anti-pedobaptist church. He was intimately acquainted with Lady Helena Streicher, a disciple of Schwenckfeldt, whom he sought to win to the support of his cause. In 1542 he published an exposition of his teachings regarding baptism, sin, hereditary sin, divine worship, magistracy, the Supper, etc.[1] A copy of this work he sent to Helena Streicher, whose polemical zeal for Schwenckfeldt's views was aroused thereby. She replied that she could not agree with him nor accept the views of the "Baptists." They have an external water baptism without the Spirit. "You are washed through your baptism, but not sanctified." She regarded the "Baptists" as "bodily pious people," but not as "children of God." "They make of the cross an idol" and "degrade Christ to a servant according to the flesh." She exhorts Marbeck to free himself from the outward elements. Marbeck rejoined in a letter of twenty pages, in which he sought to correct

---

[1] "Vermahnung auch ganz klarer gründlicher und unwidersprechl. Bericht zu wahrer Christlicher ewig bestandiger Brüder-Vereinigung."

her misapprehensions respecting the views of his brethren. He knows only "of one baptism . . . that is the baptism of the Lord, the washing away of my sin . . . If you know of two baptisms, show me the Scripture therefor." He agrees that mere water baptism, without the Spirit, is a vain work, but he repudiates the charge that the baptism of his brethren is such. This letter, with the printed book, Helena put into Schwenckfeldt's hands, who, after private correspondence had proved unavailing, wrote a sharp polemic against Marbeck and Magdalena Marschalk. Marbeck replied to Schwenckfeldt's "Judicium" with considerable bitterness, charging him with making "false accusations," whereby he would "fill with doubts the consciences of the weak, perplex the zealous, blind the eyes of the simple, and throw suspicion on the covenant's witness with Christ." The congregations under Marbeck's charge seem to have been considerably disturbed by Schwenckfeldtian mysticism, and shortly before his death he thought it necessary to make discussion with Schwenckfeldt a matter of church discipline.

Few Anti-pedobaptist teachers were permitted to labor so long or so fruitfully as Pilgram Marbeck, and no one maintained a more unblemished reputation. The writings of his opponents abound in recognitions of his high character and of his ability as a Christian teacher.[1]

From 1531 the authorities were careful to suppress any attempt at aggressive work on the part of the Anti-pedobaptists, but remnants of the party long existed.

Literature: Pertinent works of Gerbert, T. W. Röhrich, G. W.

---

[1] For the facts about Marbeck's career after his banishment from Strasburg I am indebted to Prof. Dr. J. Loserth, who on the basis of materials contained in the Beck Collection has recently published "Two Biographical Sketches" ("Zwei Biographische Skizzen"), of which one is occupied with Marbeck. He informs us that a collection of Marbeck's writings (presumably in English) is to be published in America.

Röhrich, Keller ("Ein Apost."), Baum ("Capito u. Butzer"), Erbkam, Hagen, Heberle, Keim, C. Meyer, Cornelius ("Münst. Aufr."), Trechsel, Nicoladoni, Loserth ("Zwei Biog. Skizzen"), Arnold, and Göbel, as in the Bibliography; the contemporary writings (including correspondence) of Zwingli, Bucer, Capito, Franck, Schwenckfeldt, Hetzer, Denck, Kautz, Bünderlin, Marbeck, and the "Getrewe Warnung d. Prediger."

CHAPTER XIX

MELCHIOR HOFMANN AND STRASBURG

TWO years and a half before the banishment of Pilgram Marbeck from Strasburg there appeared upon the scene a man who was to exert a momentous, nay, a disastrous influence on the Anti-pedobaptist cause. This was Melchior Hofmann, a native of Hall in Swabia and a furrier by trade. Like Nicholas Storch he was profoundly versed in the letter of Scripture and supposed himself to be in possession of a key to all the mysteries of the sacred book. Naturally he was deeply interested in the prophetical Scriptures and the book of Daniel and the Apocalypse had for him special attractions. These he interpreted with reference to his own times and he reveled in thoughts of millennial glories about to be revealed. He seems to have accepted Luther's views at an early date, and about the middle of 1523 we find him zealously laboring for reform at Wolmar in Livonia.

The fact that he was an artisan no doubt gave him greater influence with the masses than he could otherwise have attained; but his eloquence and enthusiasm and his extraordinary Bible knowledge would have awakened profound and widespread interest under any circumstances. If he had enjoyed the advantages of a regular education Hofmann would certainly have taken rank with the foremost men of his age. He was after a time imprisoned and banished by the head of the Teutonic Knights, who held control in those regions.

In the summer of 1524 we find him laboring in Dorpat with such zeal and success, that when the bishop's sheriff attempted to arrest him the people would not permit his imprisonment and in retaliation for the affront offered to their preacher they raided the churches and destroyed images, pictures, etc. In the riot that followed lives were lost on both sides.

The authorities soon afterward gave full recognition to Lutheranism, and had not suspicion been aroused as to his orthodoxy Hofmann might have remained in Dorpat; but his allegorical method of interpreting the Scriptures and the fanatical tendency of his chiliastic teachings led the authorities to require, as a condition of his further engaging in religious work, a certificate of orthodoxy from theologians of repute. At Riga he secured such a certificate, but the suspicion was too profound to be allayed by any lower authority than that of Luther himself. So to Wittenberg he went, June, 1525, and though Luther was not without misgivings he did not feel free to withhold the desired testimonial.

While at Wittenberg Hofmann published his first book in the form of an address to the church at Dorpat, in which he expressed himself on most points quite in accord with Luther's views and condemned fanaticism of the Münzer type (the Peasants' War had just ended disastrously). Yet in its allegorizing and its prophetical forecasts it contained the germs of much of his later extravagance.

Returning to Dorpat he found that even Luther's endorsement had not sufficed to remove the dislike and suspicion of the clergy and the secular authorities. The fact that he was a mere mechanic without theological education, and that he gloried in preaching the gospel without cost while supporting himself by his handicraft, was no doubt one reason for the aversion of the clergy; the peculiar and over-confident type of his teaching was certainly another. He was soon involved in controversy with the Lutheran ministers, and Luther called himself a fool for having commended him. The controversy resulted in Hofmann's banishment.

We next find him in Sweden, where the Reformation had already made considerable progress, but the contest with Roman Catholicism was still acute. He arrived at Stockholm about the beginning of 1526 and soon secured recognition as a preacher of the gospel. Here he published " A Short Exhortation to the Assembly of Believers in Livonia." A chiliastic interpretation of the twelfth chapter of Daniel was embodied in this work. From this time onward chiliasm formed the mainspring of Hofmann's activity. As a specimen of his exegesis his interpretation of the four beasts (Ezek. 1 and Rev. 4) may be cited. The lion is the law, the calf stands for the " figures " or typical passages in the Old Testament. The twelve wings of the two beasts designate the twelve tribes of Israel. In the New Testament the human countenance and the eagle prevail. By the former he understands the parables and similitudes which Christ expressed in the spirit of man. Among them " lies the eagle enswathed, which the children of God taste and feel in their hearts." By the eagle he seems to understand the Holy Spirit. Equally fantastic is his interpretation of the Apocalypse.

Soon afterward he published a fuller exposition of Daniel 12, together with a scriptural justification of lay preaching, a discussion of the Supper, of confession, and of the office of the keys. He still held fast to the Lutheran doctrine of justification, predestination, and the will.

In his doctrine of the Supper he departed from the Lutheran doctrine of the real presence and adopted substantially the Carlstadt-Zwinglian view. The believer partakes of Christ through faith in his word or under the sign and seal of the sacrament. " The bread which thou in faith and in the power of the word receivest, this is to thee the body, and the drink is to thee the blood of Christ."

The church he regarded as a democratic organization in which all members have equal rights. The clergy are shepherds and not lords and have no further power than to preach the word. Every layman moreover has the full right to exercise his gifts. Every one is under obligation to contribute his being to the kingdom of God.

Magistracy he regards as intended only for evil-doers. If all were Christians there would be no need for it. Oaths he rejects unconditionally as prohibited by Christ himself.

He now undertook to fix the time of the end of the dispensation by computation from prophetic data, and 1533 was the result reached.

Thus we see this remarkable man already equipped with the allegorical and chiliastic system of the mediæval Franciscan sects (Joachimites, etc.) and with the old-evangelical views of magistracy, oaths, lay evangelism, etc. Was Hofmann a product of the sect-life of the pre-Reformation time, or did he derive his peculiar views from various sources after he became interested in Lutheranism ? His perfect familiarity with the letter of Scripture and the thoroughness with which he was imbued with allegorical methods of interpretation and with chiliastic modes of thought make it probable that these were not recent acquisitions, but that he acquired them in his youth. That they were the products of his own mind cannot for a moment be accepted as probable. The influence direct or indirect of Storch, Münzer, and Carlstadt, and that of the Swiss Anti-pedobaptists must in any case be recognized.

In Stockholm, as elsewhere, Hofmann's preaching seems to have been provocative of disorderly and iconoclastic procedures. Leaving Stockholm early in 1527 he went to Lübeck, where he at once awakened much popular interest, and where the usual riotous demonstrations attended his ministry.

King Frederick I., of Denmark, became greatly interested in the artisan preacher toward the close of 1527 and invited him to Kiel, not precisely as court preacher, but rather as a general evangelist. Here he labored for about two years, keeping his chiliastic views constantly to the front. Amsdorf published against his views of prophecy in 1528, and other of the Lutheran leaders, including Luther himself, encouraged by their letters the growing local opposition.

He continued to publish largely in defense and in exposition of his views, having purchased with the proceeds of his handicraft a printing plant for this purpose. His exposition of the tabernacle, in which each minutest part is supposed to have a profound spiritual significance, contains most of the features of the method current among the Plymouth Brethren. His polemical writings are denunciatory, but scarcely more so than those of his Wittenberg opponents. Having been drawn into a controversy on the Supper he took distinctly anti-Lutheran ground, and after a disputation with the Lutheran preachers he was banished.

He maintained that Luther's earlier teaching (1523) was in accord with his own, and that the former had since changed his position. But he had little regard for the authority of man. "If all emperors, kings, princes, popes, bishops, cardinals, stood in one heap, the truth should and must be confessed to the honor of God." He was now in communication with Carlstadt, who visited him in Holstein and who no doubt influenced him considerably in his view of the Supper.

Plundered of his goods (to the value, as he estimated,

of one thousand florins), he left Holstein for East Friesland in company with Carlstadt. Luther's doctrine had gained wide acceptance in East Friesland, but a reaction was setting in under the leadership of Aportanus in favor of the Zwinglian view of the Supper and related doctrines. Carlstadt is said to have thrown himself into the anti-Lutheran movement with the most passionate zeal. Hofmann occupied himself at first with preparing his account of the disputation which had resulted in his banishment. It is probable that during his short sojourn he formed connections which were of value to him in the great work that he accomplished there at a later date.

Hofmann reached Strasburg in June, 1529, where he was heartily received by the ministers as one who had suffered for his defense of the Zwinglian view of the Supper. It would seem that he had already reached the conclusion that the human nature of Christ was not derived from Mary, but that it only passed through her body like water through a tube. This view, along with his chiliasm, formed henceforth an important part of his teaching and he was able to give it such currency that it became a feature of later Mennonite theology. Like the Gnostics of the earlier time and the Cathari of the Middle Ages, he supposed it a degradation of Christ to assert that he partook of our corrupt nature and thought to exalt Christ by denying his true humanity.

The Strasburg ministers soon discovered that they had a dangerous visionary on their hands and advised him to give up preaching and return to his trade; but he was too thoroughly convinced that he was under the direct guidance of the Holy Spirit and that God had a great work for him to do to act upon this advice. Of all men he thought himself best qualified to expound the Scriptures and to tell the world what it needed to know. He formed at this time intimate relations with Schwenckfeldt, though it does not appear that either greatly influenced the other.

During this visit he published a number of writings in exposition of his prophetic views, including a somewhat detailed exposition of the Apocalypse, in which he applies the prophecies to the events of history in such a way as to show that they have nearly all been fulfilled and that the final catastrophe is at hand. The thousand years of the Apocalypse Hofmann regarded as already past, yet his carnal view of the kingdom of Christ fully justifies us in calling him a chiliast. We can sympathize with Hofmann's recent biographer, F. O. Zur Linden, when he says in reference to Hofmann's attempt to interpret the Apocalypse as contrasted with Luther's attitude of reserve: "Oh, that he too had let this book alone, how much confusion and misfortune would the world and especially our Low-Dutch lands have been spared!"

Hofmann, like the other dissenters of the time, came to look upon Luther as an arch-persecutor and murderer of God's people, as a Judas, nay, a Satan.

At Strasburg Hofmann formed the acquaintance of Leonard Jost and his wife Ursula, who supposed themselves to be the recipients of divine revelations, and in 1530 he published one of Ursula's visions, with an interpretion of Rev. 12, which he applied to the emperor in a way that the council regarded as treasonable. At about the same time he made bold to petition the council for the use of one of the churches. It is probable that he now formally entered into relations with such Anti-pedobaptists as were in accord with his views, and was himself baptized.

Driven from the city on the ground of the publication before mentioned he returned at once to Friesland where the controversies that were raging between Lutherans and Zwinglians gave him ready access.

His wonderful work in the Netherlands and in Westphalia during the next three years will be narrated in a future chapter. Suffice it here to say that largely through his efforts these countries were covered with enthusiastic Anti-pedobaptists, who by reason of the chiliastic teachings of Hofmann were ready to be led by some of his fanatical disciples into the fearful excesses of Münster. He seems to have made a secret and flying visit to Strasburg in November, 1530.

Some time after he had broken with Lutheranism concerning the Supper he continued to hold with the Lutherans as regards predestination, the will, and related subjects. With his rejection of infant baptism he now put himself into accord with Anti-pedobaptist modes of thought on these points as well.

He returned to Strasburg early in 1533, under the impression that this city was to be the New Jerusalem whence the conquering hosts of God would march forth to destroy the enemies of the truth. In this course he supposed that he was acting under immediate divine direction. He scrupulously avoided appearing in public as a teacher, and on days when he was likely to be visited at his lodging to such an extent as might furnish occasion for suspicion he prudently absented himself. A complete change seems to have come over the bold, reckless preacher.

He was closely associated with Leonard Jost, whose prophecies he compared to those of Isaiah and Jeremiah, and with a number of prophetical women. Since the banishment of Pilgram Marbeck and other moderate teachers it is probable that a larger proportion of the Strasburg Anti-pedobaptists were ready to listen to the dreams of a Hofmann than was the case when he first visited the city. Moreover, the terrible fate that had befallen their brethren throughout most of Europe through the execution of the imperial edict of Speier had done much to prepare the minds of Anti-pedobaptists to receive hospitably any assurance that a special divine interposition was at hand for the deliverance of the persecuted host. Hofmann's reputation as a mighty evangelist must have given weight to his utterances. Still he had the ear of only a section of the Strasburg Anabaptist community.

Claus Frei, a disciple of Hofmann, had left his wife and eight children, under the supposed prompting of the Spirit, and was living with a widow who felt herself drawn to him by the same influence. He was repudiated by Hofmann and the Anti-pedobaptists in general. On his refusal to abandon his adulterous life, after having been repeatedly ordered to do so, he was drowned by order of the council in 1534.

It may be said of Hofmann that while there is every reason for believing that he was sincere in his prophesying and his entire religious life, and while he never supposed himself commissioned to command Christians to take up arms against the enemies of God or to commit any immoral act, his reliance on visions and his general method of teaching were such as could not fail to lead others less fundamentally sound than himself to take their own fleshly inclinations for the promptings of God's Spirit and to commit all kinds of enormities in the name of religion. The Münster Kingdom was a natural outgrowth of Hofmann's teachings, however shocking the atrocities of Münster must have been to him.

One of the prophetesses saw in a vision on a river a white swan that sang with wonderful sweetness. She interpreted the vision to mean that Hofmann was the white swan and the true Elias who was expected before the end of the age. At another time she saw the walls of the city studded with dead men's heads. She searched and found the head of Hofmann. It smiled at her in a friendly way; whereupon all the rest of the heads came to life.

Before Hofmann left Friesland an aged brother had prophesied that he must return to Strasburg, suffer six months' imprisonment, and then lead the children of God to universal victory. He patiently awaited the fulfillment of this prophecy.

Meanwhile he published a number of works, among them a treatise on "The Sword," in which he denied the right of the civil magistracy to jurisdiction in religious matters, and a prophecy with reference to the imminent inauguration of the new dispensation at Strasburg. He was thrown into prison (May, 1533), where he died ten years later.

There is something highly pathetic in the patience with which he endured his imprisonment and in his faith in his own prophecies and those of his associates which could not be shaken by failure of fulfillment. He seems to have continued to the end of his life to fix the date of the beginning of the new order of things a short time ahead. When the time arrived, instead of abandoning the prophesying, he would go over his computations anew and remove his date forward a stage. The close connection of his modes of thought with the Münster Kingdom (1535) made it impracticable for the Strasburg authorites to release him, and intensified the bitterness with which Anti-pedobaptists were everywhere persecuted.

Literature: Gerbert, Zur Linden, Krohn, T. W. Röhrich, Cornelius ("Münst. Aufr."), as in the Bibliography, and Hofmann's writings.

CHAPTER XX

HOFMANN AND THE NETHERLANDS

THE Netherlands, which in the time of the Protestant revolution belonged to the imperial domains, possessed during the Middle Ages a large measure of evangelical light. During the latter part of the fifteenth century and the early years of the sixteenth, large numbers of Waldenses were discovered by the officers of the Inquisition, compelled by the most cruel tortures to confess to the most abominable teachings and deeds, and were then burned at the stake. Among these were a number of men and women of high rank. The Brethren of the Common Life with their evangelical mysticism and their earnest devotion to Bible study and to the promotion of popular education had here their chief stronghold. From 1477 onward the Bible was widely circulated in the vernacular and zealously studied. A vast amount of ascetical and mystical devotional literature was circulated during the early years of the sixteenth century. This was nearly all Catholic, it is true, but its circulation shows that Christian life was energetic and it prepared the way for evangelicalism of a more thorough-going type. The density of the population, the large number of prosperous cities, the presence of a large and influential artisan class, the facilities for travel furnished by the natural and artificial waterways, well fitted the Netherlands for the activity of radical types of evangelical life.

Luther's earlier reformatory writings were widely circulated and eagerly read. Zwinglianism had come into conflict with Lutheranism from 1526 onward and the strife had reached an acute stage by 1529.

Carlstadt and Hofmann availed themselves of this controversy in 1529 to diffuse with their own substantially Zwinglian view of the Supper their more radical schemes of reform. Neither Lutheranism nor Zwinglianism had at this time gained sufficient foothold among the people to be able to resist the strong popular influence of Hofmann, who with all the enthusiasm and confidence of a prophet proclaimed the approaching end of the age and warned men to flee from the coming wrath.

A few representatives of the earlier Swiss and German Anti-pedobaptist movements had no doubt taken up their abode in the Netherlands and disseminated their views within narrow circles long before the appearance of Hofmann. It is probable that out of the evangelical life of the earlier time, under the impulse of the great Protestant movement individuals here and there, or even small communities, had come independently to Anti-pedobaptist views. But it remained for Hofmann to inaugurate an enthusiastic propaganda of these principles in combination with his chiliastic perversions.

It is stated on the authority of eye-witnesses that Hofmann did not proclaim himself an Anti-pedobaptist immediately on his return to Emden in May, 1530. He is said to have still posed as a Zwinglian and thereby to have gained such an influence over the entire anti-Lutheran element as enabled him successfully to promulgate his more radical views a little later. He found a portion of the evangelical clergy ready to adopt his Anti-pedobaptist views as soon as he saw fit to announce them. Friesland was at this time a refuge for the persecuted evangelicals of Holland as well as from Catholic German countries. The local government was tolerant and enforced the imperial decrees as little as possible, whereas in Holland persecuting edicts were at this time remorselessly executed. The evangelical element in Friesland was likely, therefore, to represent a somewhat radical type of Protestantism.

The contemporary accounts of Hofmann's activity in East Friesland are conflicting. The Lutheran authorities have evidently wished to exaggerate the extent to which their Zwinglian opponents were carried away by Anabaptist fanaticism; the Zwinglians for obvious reasons have sought to minify the extent of the defection. It is certain that some of the Zwinglian ministers opposed Hofmann, while others defended him. Among his opponents was Aportanus, the most influential of them all, through whose influence the Count Enno had been brought to favor Zwinglianism as against Lutheranism and who died a few months after Hofmann's arrival. It seems certain that Hofmann for a time had the use of a room in the church, where he publicly baptized. He is said within a short time to have baptized at Emden about three hundred.

Difficulties having arisen in Emden which interfered with the further prosecution of his work, he left the church he had organized in the care of Jan Trijpmaker, and about the first of October went forth as an apostolic herald to proclaim the gospel covenant and to gather out from the multitudes the "lovers of the truth."

About this time he published one of the most remarkable of his works, entitled "The Ordinance of God," in which he sets forth the programme of his great enterprise. By the ordinance of God he means the baptismal command of Christ (Matthew 28 : 18 *seq.*), which he adopts as the motto of his book and expounds clause by clause. He understands the passage to teach that the redemptive work of Christ is universal, and that the obligation rests upon contemporary believers to make a universal proclamation of the gospel. He takes occasion to repudiate the Lutheran doctrine of justification by faith alone, and insists upon a "faith that brings forth its true fruits." "Where the power and the truly good works of righteousness are not present, there also is no justification." Like the old-evangelical party, he lays great stress on the imitation of Christ in his life of holiness and self-sacrifice.

So in the matter of baptism. "Jesus came to the Jordan, bound himself there through the water-bath of baptism with God, and offered up to him in all submissiveness his own will. Thereupon God opened the heavens and sent down upon Jesus all his power, his Spirit, his heart, and his will, and received him as his dear son." In all points should the children of God and the brethren of Jesus be imitators of him. He designates baptism "the true sign of the covenant." This should be received by believers publicly without fear of men as the act whereby we entrust ourselves to Christ and unite ourselves with him in order that henceforth we may be obedient to the will of the Father, the Son, and the Holy Spirit alone. By the reception of water baptism we become incorporated into the body of which Christ is the head. Hofmann's view of the Supper, as here presented, is thoroughly spiritual and, like his view of baptism, from the Baptist point of view unobjectionable.

After a journey back to Strasburg, in which he probably did much missionary work, he went to Holland. Here also Lutheranism had been introduced to a considerable extent some years before, and had been successfully combated by Zwinglianism, which seems to have been more in accord with Netherlandish modes of thought. Persecution of evangelical Christianity had prevailed from 1525 till 1531, and wonderfully prepared the minds and hearts of the people for the gospel that Hofmann was about to proclaim, with the speedy setting up of the kingdom of God and the destruction of God's enemies.

In 1525 some Anti-pedobaptists from upper Germany are said to have gone to Holland, but their influence can scarcely be detected. In 1527 we meet with a party of separatists who had formed themselves into a brotherhood to await the advent of Christ. In the same year, Jan Walen and two of his brethren from Krommeniesdijk, in Waterland, were burned as Anabaptists in Holland.

Trijpmaker, whom Hofmann had left at Emden, removed to Amsterdam about November, 1530, where he carried forward the Hofmannite propaganda with great zeal and success. While making Amsterdam the center of his activity he itinerated widely among the cities of Holland, organizing in many places churches of "the lovers of the truth," who accepted at his hands the "sign of the covenant."

Hofmann appeared in Holland early in 1531, and of course took the leading part in the aggressive work. His numerous writings were no doubt very widely circulated and must have been highly influential. Trijpmaker had labored quietly and secretly and so had not come in conflict with the authorities. Hofmann was less circumspect and soon had to flee from Amsterdam to escape arrest. Trijpmaker himself fell into the hands of the authorities and, along with eight of his fellow-believers, was beheaded in December, 1531. They showed wonderful heroism and devotion to their principles.

Hofmann now promulgated an order that baptism be suspended for two years, just as the building of the temple under Zerubbabel was suspended for two years, and intimated that at the end of this time there would be a wonderful manifestation of God's power on behalf of the lovers of the truth. The effect of Hofmann's thus fixing the date of the advent of Christ and the setting up his kingdom on earth was truly wonderful. His disciples were filled with the enthusiasm of those who are assured that they have a great mission to fulfill, and that the time is strictly limited. They must indeed work while it is called to-day. There was no longer any uncertainty as to the future. Two years of enthusiastic service would bring them into a glorious inheritance. From this time forward the growth of the Hofmannite party in Holland was very rapid. Lutheranism and Zwinglianism almost completely vanished, and from this time until 1566 evangelical teaching was almost exclusively of the Anti-pedobaptist type. From Holland the movement extended throughout the Netherlands and into the surrounding countries, as well as into England.

Before leaving Holland Hofmann published his work on "Fettered and Free Will." This is one of his ablest works. As he had already put himself on record against Luther's teachings regarding the Supper, predestination, and baptism, he now combats with acuteness and warmth his doctrine of the will, and thus put himself in one additional particular in accord with the theological system of the mediæval evangelical parties and of the various parties of the Anti-pedobaptists.

In this, as in several writings that followed, he adopted as a Scripture motto, "He that hath ears, let him hear." While he holds fast to the view that salvation is only of grace and only through Christ, he insists on the universality of Christ's redemptive work. To every man, after enlightenment has been received through the preaching of God's word, is given free power of choice between life and death. God compels no one to come into his kingdom. His doctrine of the will, as all other points of his teaching, he illustrates strikingly from the Old Testament through the application of the allegorical method.

Hofmann seems to have made another journey up the Rhine at the end of 1531, for he appeared in Strasburg in

December, where he soon afterward issued two other works. In one of these he vigorously combats what he takes to be the Lutheran doctrine of Satan, death, hell, sin, and eternal damnation, which he maintains have not their origin in God, but are the outgrowth of self-will. If there had been no self-will there would also be no Satan, no hell, no death, no pain, and no damnation. He denounces the view of "the false apostle" (Luther) that some men were created unto damnation. Not God but Adam is the originator of sin, and through his fall his posterity have come into the power of sin, death, and damnation, so that only God through the incarnation of his Word can erase the injuries wrought through the first man. While in these doctrinal treatises his chiliastic views are kept in the background, they have by no means been lost sight of.

In a work entitled "The Joyful Witness of the True, Peaceable, Eternal Gospel," published at this time, Hofmann gives us some means of judging of the degree of acceptance that has been accorded to his teachings in upper Germany. He complains that after the truth has been taught for three years he still sees no people who will hear. "O God, what a dreadful time is this, that I still see no true evangelists, yea, even know no writer in the whole of Germany who has borne witness to the true faith and the everlasting gospel."

It would seem that up to this time the great majority of the Strasburg Anti-pedobaptists looked upon him with distrust, and so narrow and bigoted was he that he was incapable of recognizing anything as truth and gospel that was not in entire accord with his own views. In fact, he seems to have regarded with the utmost hatred, and as due to Satanic influence, the teachings of all who were at variance with himself. In this, to be sure, he followed the example of some of the leading Reformers.

Hitherto he had spared the Zwinglians in his polemics. He now denounced them as "miserable, treacherous thieves of God's honor.'

In 1532 appeared his work on "The true, all-glorious, sole Majesty of God, and of the true Incarnation of the Eternal Word and Son of the Most High." In this treatise he sets forth dogmatically the view that he had for some years been teaching as to the flesh of Christ, the true humanity of which he denied. It is probable that Hofmann had already (1532) touched Hesse with his personal influence. It is certain that soon afterward large numbers of Anabaptists were to be found there who agreed with him in his characteristic views.

His last missionary journey to the Netherlands occupied part of 1532 and part of 1533. His work was largely that of giving encouragement and direction to his faithful evangelists and visiting the various flocks. Yet he was not without opposition among his own people. We find that his authority to suspend the administration of baptism for two years was called in question by Jan Matthys, who had been baptized by Trijpmaker, and whose influence was soon vastly to exceed that of Hofmann himself.

It was probably at this time that Hofmann made his missionary tour through West Friesland, where he already had many disciples. It was the heroic martyr death of Sicke Snyder, a West Frieslander who had been brought under the influence of Hofmann's views at Emden, and had there received baptism, that led to the conversion of Menno Simons.

In 1533 he published his exposition of the Epistle to the Romans, in which he seeks to explain the ninth chapter of the epistle in accord with his own view of universal redemption, and puts himself on record in favor of the civil magistracy as an institution ordained of God. In this latter point he may have had in view the revolutionary utterances and acts of Jan Matthys that were already giving cause for the gravest anxiety and that were so speedily to precipitate the Anti-pedobaptist life of the Netherlands, Westphalia, and neighboring countries into the horrors of Münster.

Of Hofmann's return to Strasburg to await the inauguration of the new dispensation and of his imprisonment during the remainder of life, mention has already been made.

Literature: Zur Linden, Leendertz, Krohn, Cornelius ("Nederl. Wiedert." and "Münst. Aufr."), De Hoop-Scheffer, Brons, Göbel, as in the Bibliography; and the writings of Hofmann.

CHAPTER XXI

HESSE, JÜLICH-CLEVE, AND WESTPHALIA

THE Landgrave Philip of Hesse was, with all his moral delinquencies, by far the most tolerant of all the princes of Germany. In spite of the entreaties and remonstrances of such neighboring princes as Duke John George, of Saxony, and of such Protestant leaders as Luther, Melancthon, and Bucer, and in spite of the imperial edict of Speier, he steadfastly refused to deal severely with the Anti-pedobaptists. The Peasants' War of 1525, which his contemporaries were wont to charge to their account, had involved his own domain and he had been personally engaged in suppressing this popular uprising, yet he not only refused to put the peasants to death, but he allowed a man who had been prominently engaged in the movement and who perpetuated many of Münzer's peculiar teachings, to labor for years in his territory when Anti-pedobaptists were being remorselessly butchered by nearly all the princes of the empire, and when his attention was constantly being called in the sharpest way to his delinquency and to the exceeding peril of toleration.

It is remarkable that while up to 1530 at least two thousand of the sectaries had been executed in the empire, not one execution had taken place in Hesse. In 1529, in response to a remonstrance from the Elector of Saxony, he wrote: "We are still unable at the present time to find it in our conscience to have any one executed with the sword on account of his faith."

Even after the Münster catastrophe, when other princes were slaughtering Anti-pedobaptists indiscriminately as all alike revolutionary and capable, under favorable circumstances, of the atrocities of Münster, he insisted on making a distinction between fanatics of the Münster type and evangelical advocates of believers' baptism. "Some of them are simple, pious people," he writes to John Frederick, of Saxony, who was urging him to exterminate Anabaptists without discrimination, " and must be treated with moderation."

He admits that those who have taken the sword may be suitably executed by the sword, but insists that those who simply err in their faith should be dealt with moderately and won back to the truth through loving ministry. In case they do not yield to such treatment and give trouble in their community, they may be banished. " But to punish capitally, as has happened in some principalities in the land, those who have done nothing more than err in the faith, cannot indeed be justified on gospel grounds."

The Saxon princes under the influence of Luther and Melancthon gave no quarter to Anti-pedobaptists of any type, and it was regarded by them as a serious grievance that Philip so obstinately refused to co-operate with them in the work of extermination.

The most noted and influential of the Hessian Antipedobaptists was undoubtedly Melchior Rinck, who, on account of the identity of their first names and the similarity of some of their views, has been confounded by many writers with Hofmann. Rinck was a man of distinguished scholarship who, probably by reason of his mastery of the Greek language, was often called "the Greek." According to some early writers he was one of the Zwickau prophets who visited Wittenberg in 1521, but this is probably a mistake. We find him in Hersfeld in 1523, as schoolmaster and chaplain. Along with Heinrich Fuchs he came into conflict with the concubinary pastor. The latter was worsted to the delight of the Wittenbergers.

He seems about this time to have come under the influence of Thomas Münzer and to have become a prominent agitator side by side with Münzer and Pfeiffer. When he entered into relations with Münzer he was pastor at Echardshausen. Escaping with his life from the battle of Frankenhausen he was for some time a fugitive and we are unable to trace his career. We find him at Worms in 1527 signing a challenge for a disputation on baptism along with Denck, Hetzer, and Kautz. He seems soon afterward to have settled down in the neighborhood of Hersfeld where he formed an Anti-pedobaptist church and to have exerted a considerable influence throughout Hesse.

He was often arrested and the most determined efforts were made by Hessian officials and foreign princes and theologians to induce the Landgrave to authorize his execution. According to Balthasar Raidt, whom Philip appointed to labor with him, Rinck maintained that all who follow Luther and teach as he does are leading the people to the devil, denied that any are damned for hereditary sin who have not come to the age of intelligence and personally acquiesced in sin, maintained that all who receive the sacrament according to Luther's view receive a devil every time they do so, denied predestination, maintained that infants baptized in the Lutheran or popish way are sacrificed to the devil, insisted upon believers' baptism, denied the real presence in the Supper, and held that man can through the denial and renunciation of his works, of the creature, and of himself, through his natural powers, prepare himself for faith and come to the Spirit of God.

The harsh expression about the sacrament he afterward denied having used, but he certainly looked with great disfavor on Luther's doctrine of the real presence. In this account of Rinck's doctrines no mention is made of his chiliastic views; but in this regard he is known to have been in sympathy with Münzer, and he is said to have been in Münster in 1533 a short time before the outburst of fanaticism.

No further trace of him can be found. Some have supposed that he met his end in the Münster conflict, but he certainly did not appear among the leaders and it is likely that he left or died before the city came into the hands of the Anti-pedobaptists.

Rinck's labors extended into many places in Saxony and Thuringia, where, however, persecution was so persistent as to be from the beginning practically exterminating. In these countries nothing like an organized existence with continuity of effort was possible. Many Anti-pedobaptists appeared from time to time and churches were organized in many places; but the Wittenberg theologians were too alert to leave them long undetected and they constantly urged upon the civil rulers the duty of using the utmost severity toward those who would restore primitive Christianity.

We have seen that through the labors of Hofmann Anti-pedobaptism of the Hofmannite type was during the years 1530-33 widely diffused throughout the Netherlands and the neighboring countries. Mention has also been made of the baleful influence exerted by Jan Matthys. Hofmann, under divine direction as he supposed, had ordered the suspension of baptism for two years. He was himself Elias, Enoch would appear later and be revealed to the faithful. In two years the saints would gather at Strasburg, the new Jerusalem, and to the number of one hundred and forty-four thousand would go forth in the name of the Lord to set up his kingdom. Hofmann had gone to Strasburg to await the great event and in accordance with a prophecy was lying in prison. As the end of 1533 drew near expectation was at its height and the wildest excitement prevailed throughout Hofmannite circles, now become very wide.

The city of Münster and Westphalia in general, after the suppression of the peasant uprising of 1525, had excluded Protestantism in all forms with the utmost rigor. Münster was a great ecclesiastical center and was governed by a most dissolute prince-bishop, whose opposition to Protestantism was on personal and political far more than on religious grounds. The clergy were indifferent to the wants of the people and incapable in any case of supplying them.

The spirit of liberty had not been destroyed when the peasants were crushed, neither was it possible to keep from the knowledge of the people the evangelical work that was going on all around them. The intensest eagerness for evangelical teaching arose and soon became irrepressible.

In 1529 Bernard Rothmann, a brilliant young clergyman who had been educated at Deventer in the school of the Brethren of the Common Life, and who had come somewhat under the influence of Lutheranism and of Zwinglianism, began to preach evangelical sermons at St. Mauritz Church, near Münster. Despite the opposition of magistrates and clergy the Münster people thronged his ministry. He was suspended for a year in order that he might go to Cologne for further studies or for the correction of his errors. He seems to have spent his year in becoming more deeply imbued with evangelical teaching and returned to his work in 1531 to labor for reform.

While it was the working people that were chiefly attracted by his ministry, a number of influential citizens, magistrates among them, soon appeared among his supporters. Seeing his way clear to carry out a measure of evangelical reform, he made a visit to Wittenberg to confer with Luther and his associates. Returning in July he assumed a still more aggressive attitude and met with ever-increasing popular favor.

When the bishop inhibited his preaching and attempted to banish him from the diocese, instead of going into banishment he took up his abode in the city, where he had a large following.

The social democracy of the city which had since the suppression of the peasant uprising remained comparatively quiet, had at its head Bernard Knipperdollinck, a man of ability and standing, who is said to have come in contact with Melchior Rinck some time before and who was no doubt already in sympathy with the social-democratic, if not with the mystico-religious and chiliastic views of Münzer. An alliance was formed between the radical Lutheran element and the social democracy. Rothmann appeared in 1532 as the enthusiastic advocate of the rights of the common man and the opponent of the privileged classes.

He resumed his preaching in February, 1532, in the court of St. Lambert Church. A few days later he secured the use of the church itself, while the foremost guild of the city accorded to him the use of the guildhouse as a dwelling.

Bishop Frederick was powerless to interfere with the progress of the popular evangelical movement, which was by this time strongly represented on the council. The retirement of Frederick and the succession of Erich as prince-bishop (March 27, 1532), checked for a time the progress of the radical party, inasmuch as the moderate evangelicals looked upon him as evangelically disposed and hoped that he would carry forward the work of reform in a safe and legal manner.

Rothmann was ordered by the council, with the approval of the heads of the guilds, to suspend his preaching. Supported by the masses he refused to obey.

The death of Bishop Erich in May and the succession of Count Franz von Waldeck in June put an end to hopes for reform through the constituted authorities. Count von Waldeck was not only notoriously immoral and irreligious, but his political connections were such as would certainly prevent him from showing any sympathy with evangelical teaching. An attempt on his part to execute a mandate of Charles V. for the immediate removal of all anti-Catholic preachers and the punishment of all disturbers of the existing order brought him into sharp collision with the municipal authorities, who declared their determination with property and life to maintain the preaching of the gospel. Attempting to enforce obedience, the bishop was driven from the city and its neighborhood and many of his aristocratic supporters were imprisoned. This occurred December 26, 1532. The bishop appealed to the neighboring Catholic princes, while the evangelical citizens of Münster received promises of support from the Landgrave Philip of Hesse and Duke Ernst of Lüneburg.

Peace was made in February, 1533, on terms highly advantageous to the evangelicals. The success of the evangelical movement aroused the wildest enthusiasm not only in the city and diocese, but throughout the lower Rhenish regions. Under Rothmann's direction the council adopted a scheme of church order in accordance with which the choice of pastors was to be left to each congregation. The monasteries were closed. The Catholic priests, deprived of popular support and of the means of livelihood, were obliged to leave the city. Arrangements were made for evangelical education, general and theological, and for the care of the poor.

A similar evangelical movement had for some time been going forward in the lower Rhenish provinces, especially in the Cleve-Jülich duchy. In the summer of 1532 the Clevish authorities banished the evangelical leaders. These had figured as Lutherans, but under the influence of the Hofmannite movement several of them seem already to have reached Anti-pedobaptist views. The most noted of these was Heinrich Roll, an ex-monk from Haarlem. In 1532 he published a work on the Supper, in which he took substantially Zwinglian ground, but laid great stress on the spiritual communion of the believer with God. The work is remarkably free from violence and bitterness and takes a most charitable view even of the enemies and persecutors of the truth, who persecute because they know no better. "If they knew the flesh and blood of the true body of Christ, they would rather die than revile that which they now revile."

Roll appeared in Münster in the summer of 1532. One after another nearly all his fellow-laborers followed. Among them were Dionysius Vinne, Johann Klopriss, Hermann Staprade, and Henry Schlactscaef. Several of these were to play prominent parts in the Münster upheaval that was soon to follow.

Roll became an avowed advocate of believers' baptism soon after his arrival in Münster. Under his influence Rothmann took the same position in May, 1533. Rothmann had by this time attained to a commanding influence. He had married the widow of a syndic, had the full support of the council and the guilds, and could readily have carried out any but the most radical scheme of reform.

When Rothmann declared himself against infant baptism, his Lutheran friends remonstrated with him and begged him to desist from the agitation of such questions. This proving ineffective, the council summoned him and his Anti-pedobaptist followers and commanded him to avoid such revolutionary teaching. But he had become too completely mastered by his views on baptism to be able long to hold the matter in abeyance. He was soon preaching against infant baptism more violently than ever. He insisted that in matters of faith the assembled church and not the magistracy has authority. Staprade, now a pronounced Anti-pedobaptist, was soon afterward called by the congregation of St. Lambert to be Rothmann's assistant. Staprade was the first in Münster publicly to declare infant baptism an abomination in the sight of God.

The syndic van der Wieck exerted himself to the utmost to save the city from the domination of the Anti-pedobaptists. Failing in other measures, he arranged a disputation for August 8, 1533, in which the celebrated Humanist van dem Busche was the chief Pedobaptist spokesman, and in which Rothmann represented the Anti-pedobaptist party. Rothmann quietly allowed his opponents to state their position, and then in a speech of over an hour presented the arguments against infant baptism with great fullness and clearness. So profound was the impression he made that no one of his opponents was willing to undertake a refutation of his arguments.

Notwithstanding the advantage that the Anti-pedobaptist party had gained in the disputation, the council undertook to compel Rothmann, Roll, Klopriss, Vinne, Stralen, and Staprade, all of whom were now ardent rejecters of infant baptism, to resume the administration of the rite. Two members of the council required Staprade to administer baptism to their own infants. On his refusal he was banished. The alternative was given to the other five to administer baptism to infants or go into banishment. They replied that they must obey God rather than men, and were willing with goods and life to defend the truth. They insisted that jurisdiction in matters of doctrine belongs not to the council but to the churches. If the council has anything against them, it should bring the charges before the assembly of believers to be dealt with. They warn the council most earnestly against incurring the Divine judgment by interfering with the ministers in their proclamation of the truth.

The council proceeded to order the closing of the churches of the disobedient ministers and to depose Rothmann. A great popular demonstration secured for Rothmann the right to preach in another church, on condition that he should be silent on the matters in dispute. He promised to conform to the requirement until such time as the matter should have been made clear and the Lord should have given further intimation as to his will.

Thus far there had been nothing fanatical in the conduct of the Anti-pedobaptist cause in Münster. There was much disorderly excitement among the evangelicals in their struggle with the Roman Catholic authorities and considerable iconoclasm; but among the Anti-pedobaptists as such we see only a firm resolve to follow the dictates of conscience and to restore Christianity to the form in which it was given by Christ and his apostles.

In a "Confession on the Two Sacraments," published by Rothmann, Klopriss, Staprade, Vinne, and Stralen, November 8, 1533, we have the following definition:

> Baptism is an immersion in water, which the candidate desires and receives for a true sign that he has died to sins, being buried with Christ, has been thereby raised into a new life, henceforth to walk not in the lusts of the flesh but in obedience to the will of God. . . In this [obedience to the will of God] is blessedness placed and this it is also that is required in baptism. . . Those who are baptized thereby confess their faith, and in the power of faith are inclined to put off the entire old man and henceforth to walk in newness of life. . . Accordingly baptism is a gate or entrance into the holy church and a putting on of Jesus Christ.

They regarded the baptism of unintelligent, will-less, and speechless children, as an abominable perversion and as "the source of the desolation and of the complete apostasy of the holy church."

In an earlier paragraph "water sprinkling" is given a place in the definition of baptism side by side with immersion.

Literature: Bouterwek, Cornelius ("Münst. Aufr."), Hochhut. Erbkam, Göbel, and Schauenburg, as in the Bibliography.

CHAPTER XXII

THE MÜNSTER KINGDOM

WE left Melchior Hofmann in prison at Strasburg patiently awaiting the divine trumpet blast that should usher in the new dispensation. His disciples in the Netherlands, Westphalia, and the provinces of the lower Rhine, had been laboring with great secrecy but with remarkable enthusiasm in the full expectation that the new age would be ushered in according to his prediction in 1533. Baptism had been suspended for two years at Hofmann's command in order that the propaganda might be the more secret and effective.

Jan Matthys, a Haarlem baker, had come to the front as under Hofmann the inspired leader of the party. In Matthys we see a wholly different spirit from that which animated Hofmann. With all his extravagancies Hofmann never abandoned the great fundamental truths of Christianity. God continued with him to be a God of love. While he uttered some bitter words against his opponents, he seems never to have been dominated by the spirit of hatred. He expected the godless to be destroyed, but he never reached the point of commanding believers to take up the sword of Gideon and to slaughter them.

In Matthys we see the spirit of the Taborites and of Thomas Münzer revived, and that in an intensified form. Münzer was too much of a scholar and had been too much under the influence of evangelical mysticism to be as utterly fanatical as Matthys became. He seems to have been consumed with hatred of the upper classes, whom he regarded as the oppressors and persecutors of the poor people of God. God to him was in relation to the ungodly a God of vengeance. The dealing of Jehovah with the Canaanites was the basis of his idea of the way in which the new dispensation was to be established. Christians are to take up arms and to blot out the ungodly from the face of the earth.

Weary of waiting for the promised inauguration of the new age at Strasburg, he proclaimed himself a prophet of God, nay the prophet Enoch who, according to Hofmann's scheme, was to appear just before the great event. It was revealed to him that baptism should be resumed. Near the end of 1533 he sent forth a number of his faithful followers two by two to visit the Hofmannite congregations and to inform them that the promised Enoch had appeared and that baptism was to be resumed as a preparation for the great event.

They seem to have been generally successful in arousing enthusiasm. Not only were vast numbers of the working classes baptized in the communities where congregations had already been established, but a rapid propaganda was carried forward by those who had already accepted Anti-pedobaptist views throughout the cities and villages of the Netherlands and neighboring countries. The social democracy seem to have been everywhere ready to receive the new gospel, so agreeable was it to their aspirations after freedom and abundance. In an incredibly short time many thousands must have been introduced into the covenant by baptism and have committed themselves to the carrying out of the great revolution that Matthys had planned.

The news of the overthrow of Roman Catholicism in Münster and of the rapid growth of the Anti-pedobaptist cause soon reached the Netherlands and all the regions in which Hofmannite communities had been planted. As a result multitudes from these regions flocked to Münster, where they hoped to find protection and succor.

On December 8, Jan Schröder, one of Rothmann's disciples, publicly discussed in the court of St. Lambert's Church the points at issue between the council and the Anti-pedobaptists. The council having threatened to withdraw the protection that had been conditionally accorded to Rothmann, he replied that he had no need of its protection; God and his people would protect him.

Rothmann resumed preaching on disputed points on December 14. Schröder was imprisoned on December 15. The next day the whole of the smith guild, to which Schröder belonged, besieged the council house and demanded his release. The magistrates were obliged to yield, and the released prisoner was borne in triumph through the streets. The Anti-pedobaptist party, thus combined with the social democracy, was now conscious of its power and became bold and aggressive.

About January 5, 1534, two missionaries from Matthys reached Münster and made known to the Anti-pedobaptist leaders that Enoch had appeared in the person of Matthys, that the millennial kingdom was at hand, and that the baptized and redeemed should henceforth under the dominion of Christ lead a blessed life, with community of goods, without law, without magistracy, and without marriage. Baptism was at once to be resumed. Rothmann, Roll, Vinne, and Stralen were baptized, and through them during the next eight days fourteen hundred submitted to the ordinance and were thus prepared to take part in the new *régime*.[1]

Those who were baptized renounced the wickedness and the heathen ways of the world, and promised in all fidelity to fulfill the will of Christ. Brotherly love, com-

---

[1] Notwithstanding the definition of baptism as immersion, quoted in the last chapter, the authors of the definition seem not to have been immersed themselves or to have practised immersion. According to the evidence of eye-witnesses, the method of baptizing that prevailed in Münster was the pouring of three handfuls of water on the kneeling candidate. See Cornelius, "Augenzeugen," p. 20.

munity of goods, the renunciation of rents and interest, the cancellation of notes, mortgages, etc., and the abandonment of extravagance and display in dress, were among the features of the new kingdom. No communion was to be had with the godless. Unbelievers were not to be admitted to their religious meetings.

These first emissaries from Matthys seem not to have fully expounded the means by which the kingdom was to be set up. The full revelation was soon to be made. On January 13 appeared two men who had been especially commissioned by Matthys to remain in Münster and to lead in the great work. These were John of Leyden and Gert tom Kloster. The former was a highly gifted young man about five and twenty years of age. Of only a moderate education, he had learned the tailor's trade and had traveled widely as a journeyman. He had spent some time in England. He had come first under the influence of the teaching of Hofmann and latterly had been completely carried away by the enthusiasm of Matthys.

Rothmann hesitated for a time to fall into line with the sanguinary programme of Matthys and John of Leyden, but he was overborne by the popular enthusiasm and soon accepted the leadership of the young fanatic.

The city authorities were utterly powerless to stay the progress of this wild enthusiasm. Evangelicals and Catholics fled. The monasteries and religious houses of all kinds were seized and their inmates obliged either to leave the city or to be baptized. Many of them accepted the latter alternative and entered with great heartiness into the abominations that were to follow. The same alternative was presented to the citizens in general. John of Leyden and his followers soon had possession of the entire city with all its wealth.

In February, 1534, persecution was renewed with

great severity in Holland. Learning of the success of his emissaries in Münster, Matthys reached the conclusion, by divine revelation as he claimed, that Münster and not Strasburg was the new Jerusalem. Strasburg had failed of the honor because of its sins. He dispatched messengers in all directions to bear some such message as this to the faithful:

> Dear brethren, you are to journey to ——. There you are to be before midday. This must be. The 24th of March you must be there, before midday. See that no one selfishly remains behind, or vengeance will without fail overtake him.

This message spread through the land like wildfire. The poor people had no intimation as to their destination or the object of their leaving their homes and their all. The command came to them as the voice of God himself, and they obeyed unquestioningly. They were met at the appointed places by Matthys' confidential agents and directed as to their further course.

Thousands of the wretched, deluded people were seized in the principal ports of the Netherlands and many were cruelly executed. In some of the cities the fanatics attempted to gain control. There are cases recorded, probably authentic, in which men and women ran naked through the streets proclaiming the vengeance of God. Thousands of Netherlanders and others reinforced the thousands of the inhabitants of Münster who had been drawn into the fanaticism.

Matthys himself was soon in Münster, where he continued to play the rôle of chief prophet. The city was now organized as a theocracy. Matthys secured the appointment of seven deacons with absolute authority. An indignant citizen rebuked the leaders. Matthys condemned him to death; John of Leyden stabbed him, and Matthys finished the slaughter. Matthys is said to have proposed the slaughter of all the ungodly who remained in the city, but was opposed by Knipperdollinck, who knew full well that such a procedure would arouse the indignation of Christendom and prove destructive to the hopes of the theocracy.

The bishop found great difficulty in securing the aid that was necessary for the suppression of the movement. The Protestant princes were not anxious to see the Roman Catholic dominance restored and the neighboring Catholic princes were not in a position to render immediate and adequate succor. Well equipped with arms and provisions and filled with fanatical zeal the Münsterites were by no means easy to dislodge from their stronghold.

Messengers were sent out in all directions to proclaim the establishment of the new Jerusalem and to invite all the faithful to come to Münster and to participate freely in the good things which were there in abundance. It is in accordance with the principles of human nature that the needy and vicious classes should accept the invitation without much reference to their religious convictions, and that they should readily accept a gospel that conveyed so immediate and material advantages.

The city was soon besieged by the bishop's forces and such allies as he was able to secure, but for some months the siege was by no means complete, and the inhabitants of Münster were able to communicate somewhat freely with the outside world.

In April Matthys went forth with a small band under supposed Divine guidance to attack the besiegers, and after a desperate struggle was slain.

To John of Leyden now belonged the undisputed supremacy. He proceeded to organize the new Israel after the model of the old. Twelve elders were appointed with power of life and death. A new code of laws based upon the Mosaic was promulgated. The elders were to sit in judgment twice each day. Knipperdollinck was made executioner. One of the provisions of the new code was that every one belonging to the new Israel shall unhesitatingly observe (that is, abstain from or obey) whatever Scripture either forbids or commands. This ordinance undoubtedly had chief reference to the Old Testament, and the design of it apparently was to give place to polygamy. Rothmann and the rest of the preachers soon began to preach polygamy with an effect upon the people that can be easily imagined.

John's attention was drawn to a prophecy in accordance with which a king should arise in Israel who should have dominion over the whole earth. It was revealed to him that the promised king was none other than himself. "God has chosen me to be king over the whole world. But I tell you, dear brethren, that I had rather feed swine or follow the plow than be king. Yet what I do I must do, for God has appointed me thereunto."

Knipperdollinck, Rothmann, and the rest of the prophets, became the king's functionaries and counselors. As David had his harem, so John provided himself with wives at his pleasure and slew with his own hands such as displeased him. Old marriage relations were completely ignored. Women were in many cases forced to unite with men who felt it a sacred duty to have a plurality of wives. It was truly a reign of terror, in which the wildest license on the one hand and the most absolute despotism on the other prevailed.

In December, 1534, the leaders of the theocracy published "The Book of Vengeance," the aim of which was to vindicate and glorify the kingdom of God in Münster. It is addressed to the "true Israelites and members of the covenant in Christ Jesus, all and each," and seeks to show by copious quotations from the Old and New

Testaments that the promised kingdom has been set up, and that the day of wrath for the ungodly is at hand.[1]

For more than a year the wretched fanatics were able to resist the bishop and his troops. The scenes enacted during this year are indescribable. Rebellion was suppressed in the most summary manner. There was not the slightest regard for the sacredness of human life and the leaders reveled in blood.

Toward the end of the period the blockade was made complete and provisions grew scarce. The last few months were a time of fearful suffering. Knowing full well that massacre would follow conquest the besieged held out as long as possible. The scene ended in a horrible massacre and in the most revolting torturing of the leaders.

The massacre was not confined to Münster, but extended over the whole territory that had been affected by the movement. Multitudes of those who were sympathetic with the aims of the new Jerusalem had been destroyed before the fall of Münster. Throughout nearly the whole of Europe the persecution of Anti-pedobaptists in general was greatly intensified.

Philip of Hesse, as before remarked, was the only prince in Western Europe who still ventured to discriminate between wild fanatics and those who quietly opposed infant baptism and sought by purely spiritual means to restore Christianity to its primitive position.

Princes and religious leaders who from the beginning had considered the Anti-pedobaptist movement fraught with danger and had felt compelled to persecute it, saw in the Münster episode a justification for their fears and their severity, and some of those who had sought to exercise moderation felt that their leniency had been ill bestowed.

---

[1] "Das Büchlein von der Rache" is reprinted in full by Bouterwek, p. 66, *seq.*

The Münster Kingdom was regarded for centuries as a great object-lesson, showing the natural working out of the principles involved in the Anti-pedobaptist position. If all Anti-pedobaptists were not so atrocious as Matthys, John of Leyden, and Knipperdollinck, it was because all did not have the same opportunity to exhibit themselves in their true character. If some taught and practised absolute non-resistance and abstinence from the use of the sword, this was supposed to be a shrewd device on their part for escaping persecution and for avoiding the burdens of citizenship.

In England and in America the opponents of the Baptist movement long persisted in holding up the Münster Kingdom as a sample of what might be expected should its advocates be allowed to grow strong enough to show their colors. No episode in history has done so much to impede the progress of Baptist principles as that of Münster. Its influence is still quite marked in Germany and other European countries.

What then are the lessons of this frightful episode? Where rests the responsibility for the Münster Kingdom? Primarily it rests with the oppressors of the working classes, or rather with the institutions that made such oppression possible. This grinding oppression had become intolerable long before the Reformation time and fanatical leaders had frequently appeared with visionary schemes for the emancipation of the oppressed. The early reformatory utterances of Luther and others had aroused anew the hopes of the common man. The wide diffusion of the Scriptures and of evangelical teaching had convinced the people that the treatment they were receiving was unjust and unchristian. The violent suppression of the great peasant uprising had not destroyed the seeds of discontent. In fact it had been increased by the atrocities committed.

But the immediate cause of the particular form of revolution that found its culmination in the Münster Kingdom was chiliasm, combined as it always is in times of social and religious fermentation, with prophetical mysticism. The prophetico-mystical chiliasm of Nicholas Storch and Thomas Münzer was perpetuated by Hans Hut, Melchior Rinck, and Melchior Hofmann. The unrelenting persecution to which Anti-pedobaptists were nearly everywhere subjected and the utter hopelessness of their cause from a human point of view put the people in such a state of desperation that they were ready to listen to any one who, claiming to be divinely illuminated, proclaimed to them that in fulfillment of prophetical Scriptures a new era was about to be inaugurated in which the cruel persecutors of the people of God should be destroyed, in which magistracy, that seemed to them to stand so much in the way of the prosperity of the cause of Christ, should be abolished, and in which the people of God should live a glorious and blessed life in the full enjoyment of the liberty and equality that they despaired of ever receiving under existing conditions.

Hofmann taught obedience to the magistracy, but encouraged the expectation of the speedy inauguration of the glorious kingdom of Christ through direct Divine agency. It was but a step farther to the position of Matthys, that God would have his people destroy the ungodly and set up a kingdom of righteousness, as under the Old Testament dispensation, by their own right arms. The more revolting features of the Münster Kingdom followed naturally from the position that Matthys had taken. Fanaticism once in power knows no bounds, and if the Old Testament system is a model in some respects, why not in all?

It should be observed that only a portion of the great Anabaptist party was involved in chiliastic heresy, and that a large element of the party was wholly free from complicity or sympathy with the Münster uproar.

Literature: Cornelius, Keller, Dorpius, Hast, Erbkam, De Bussière, Rhegius, Kerssenbroick, Kielstra, Bouterwek, Pearson, and Rothmann, as in the Bibliography.

CHAPTER XXIII

MENNO SIMONS AND THE QUIET ANTI-PEDOBAPTISTS

IT is certain that there were Anti-pedobaptists in the Netherlands before the advent of Melchior Hofmann. It is equally certain that Hofmann's type of teaching became so far the prevailing type that for a number of years there is no record of any Anti-pedobaptist opposition. The enthusiasm of the Hofmannite movement seems to have drawn to itself all the social-democratic and radical-religious elements. It would be going too far to say that from 1528 to 1534 there were in the Netherlands no Anti-pedobaptists who were free from the extravagant chiliasm of Hofmann; but if such there were they seem not to have lifted up their voices in protest.

When Jan Matthys went beyond Hofmann and claimed to have received a divine intimation that the time had come for believers to take up the sword and smite the ungodly, there was some not very effective protesting; but the great mass of Anti-pedobaptists were swept irresistibly into the maelstrom of chiliastic fanaticism. That a considerable number refused to follow blindly the prophetic guidance of Matthys there can be no doubt. In the very nature of things the names and numbers of those who held back would for the most part escape publicity. Many who were for a time involved in the current fanaticism were cured of their chiliasm by the course of events.

Among the most noteworthy of those who refused to follow the lead of Jan Matthys were Dirk and Obbe Philips and Leonard Bouwens, of Emden in East Friesland. It was at Emden, as will be remembered, that Hofmann began his labors in the Netherlands. Here more than elsewhere Anti-pedobaptists and evangelicals in general had enjoyed partial toleration. It was probably due to the degree of toleration enjoyed by the Anti-pedobaptists of this region that so large a proportion of them were able, notwithstanding the chiliastic teaching to which they were subjected, to withhold themselves from fanaticism.

Menno Simons, who was to gather out of the wreck caused by the outburst of chiliastic fanaticism of 1534–35 the sound evangelical elements and to carry forward along old-evangelical lines the work of restoring primitive Christianity, was born at Witmarsum, in West Friesland, about 1492. He was educated for the priesthood and entered upon his duties as parish priest in the neighboring village of Pingjum about 1519.

According to his own account, he had at this time little or no knowledge of the Bible and was entirely devoid of right religious convictions and motives. He performed the duties of his office in a purely perfunctory manner and lived a life of self-indulgence.

In the third year of his incumbency, while he was on one occasion administering mass, the thought came to him with irresistible force that the elements he was handling could not be the body and blood of Christ. He at first attributed this mental disturbance to the devil, sighed, prayed, and confessed; but his skepticism held its ground. It is probable that he was already to some extent familiar with the Protestant agitation, and his doubts may have been due to this source.

Once led to question the correctness of the traditional system, he could not resist the impulse to investigate the new teachings that were causing such a stir in the religious world. He began reading assiduously the writings of Luther and other evangelical teachers. There is evidence that from 1523 onward the writings of many of the

German and Swiss Reformers were extensively circulated in the Netherlands.

Like most of the religious thinkers of the time, he was soon brought face to face with the question of infant baptism. He had been taught as a Catholic that by means of baptism infants are washed of original sin. He tested this view by Scripture and decided that it was against the blood of Christ. Afterward he went to Luther, who taught him that infants should be baptized upon their own faith. This also, he saw, was not in accord with God's word. In the third place he went to Bucer, who taught him that infants should be baptized in order that the obligation to bring them up in the way of the Lord might be more carefully observed. This theory also he found without scriptural basis. In the fourth place he went to Bullinger, who claimed that infant baptism was a sign of the new covenant as circumcision was of the old. This view also failed to satisfy him. He was impressed with the fact that these views were mutually contradictory and that not one of them had a scriptural foundation.

Instead of abandoning at once the church of whose falseness he had become convinced, he remained for a long time in his priestly office and even received promotion to a position in his native town. His convictions had not yet become overmastering, and he was still content perfunctorily to fulfill the requirements of his position and to spend his time in a profound study of the questions that were agitating the religious world.

In 1533 persecution drove a number of Anti-pedobaptists from Flanders to West Friesland. The martyrdom of one of these, Sicke Frierichs by name, made a profound impression on Menno's mind; but he still hesitated to take the decisive step and to subject himself to the operation of the terrible imperial edicts that were being so ruthlessly executed.

The fanatical movement culminating in the Münster Kingdom (1534-35) soon followed and brought such shame to the Anti-pedobaptist name that he felt constrained still to hold his convictions in abeyance.

It is probable that as early as 1534 Menno entered secretly into relations with the Anti-pedobaptists, while still maintaining publicly his position as priest. However this may be, he attempted in vain to dissuade members of the fanatical party from carrying into effect their ruinous programme. But the spirit of vengeance in the name of God had taken too firm a hold on their natures to be dislodged by such argument as he was able to adduce.

In February, 1535, a body of these fanatics numbering three hundred men with women and children had entrenched themselves in a monastery in the neighborhood of his home. Most of them fell in the conflict, and of those who were taken captive nearly all were executed. Among those who were slain was Menno's own brother. This event aroused Menno's conscience as nothing else had done.

> I thought within myself, wretched man that I am, what do I remaining in this position and not confirming by my life the word of the Lord and the knowledge that I have received? If I do not lead the ignorant, misguided sheep who are so anxious to do what is right, as much as in me lies, to the true fold of Christ, how then will the blood shed in error rise up against me in the judgment of Almighty God? My heart trembled in my body at this contemplation of myself. I implored God for grace and the pardon of my transgressions, and besought the Almighty that he would create in me a pure heart, that he would endow me with frankness and manly power in order that I might preach his unfalsified word.

His prayer was answered. Immediately he conferred not with flesh and blood, and his subsequent life was one of single-minded devotion to what he believed to be God's truth. Few men in all history have approached nearer to the life of the great apostle to the Gentiles than did Menno Simons. First of all, he began to preach and write with all earnestness against John of Leyden and the Münster Kingdom, denouncing the leaders as false prophets.

In 1536 he openly renounced the Roman Catholic Church. How he spent the following year we do not know; but we see him in 1537, after much hesitation on account of distrust of his ability to lead the Anti-pedobaptist cause in such trying times, yielding to the earnest entreaty of a deputation of quiet Anti-pedobaptists that he should come forward and assume the leadership of the shepherdless flock, "who in obedience to Christ stood ready to lead a life in the fear of God, who served their neighbors in love, willingly bore their cross, sought the welfare and safety of all men, loved righteousness and truth, and fled from unrighteousness."

He now began to write in defense of his position. On baptism and the Supper his views were in accord with those we have met in the great Anti-pedobaptist movement of the earlier time. As regards oaths, magistracy, warfare, and capital punishment, he was in agreement with the evangelical parties of the Middle Ages and with the great majority of the Anti-pedobaptists with whom we have already become acquainted.

In view of the terrible disaster that had come upon the Anti-pedobaptist cause through the chiliastic fanaticism of Matthys and John of Leyden, he laid special stress, as did the Waldenses of old, on the duty of Christians to resist not evil under any circumstances. He exalted the doctrine of the new life in Christ, agreeing with the rest of the Anti-pedobaptists of the time in repudiating the Lutheran doctrine of justification by faith alone and insisting on the imitation of Christ in his life of utter self-abnegation.

As with the old-evangelical party in general the Sermon on the Mount was, in Menno's view, fundamental.

> We must be born from above and transposed out of the evil nature of Adam into the good way of Christ, from which a new life follows. The poor, ignorant people are vainly consoled through external works and exercises. Let each one be warned no longer to trust in the fact that he is a baptized Christian, nor upon the long usage of the times, nor upon papal decrees, nor upon imperial edicts, nor upon the wit of the learned, nor upon human counsels and wisdom.

He defies lords, popes, cardinals, and bishops to prove with a single word of Scripture "that a perverse, carnally minded man, without the new birth from God's Spirit, has been saved or can be saved merely because he vaunts his faith in Christ, or hears mass, or goes to church, or makes pilgrimages." "For us," he says, "a counsel has been made in heaven, to which alone we listen and which alone we must follow. This counsel stands,—it stands, I tell you,—and the gates of hell shall never prevail against it."

He published soon afterward a strongly polemical work against the corruptions of the Roman Catholic Church, entitled "The Contradictions of Babylon," and various apologetical works, in which he sought to induce the authorities to distinguish between the wild fanatics of Münster and the quiet, non-resisting, benevolent people with whom he had identified himself.

The authorities were soon seeking his life and offering a reward for his arrest. With great caution he had been able to labor in West Friesland until 1542. In the city of Groningen he found a comparatively safe retreat owing to the tolerant disposition of Duke Charles of Gelders, who ruled the city. The bishop of Utrecht was also inclined to toleration. Yet even here Menno and his more prominent associates felt themselves unsafe after a time and betook themselves to East Friesland, where the Countess Anna, regent of the province, had long been known as the friend and protector of evangelical Christians.

While from 1530 onward it had not been possible wholly to avoid persecution of the Anti-pedobaptists, so vigorously pressed throughout the empire, it was never carried to the cruel extreme here as in most other regions. The countess had entrusted the direction of religious affairs to the noted reformer John a Lasco, a Polish nobleman and ex-priest, who was far more liberal in his attitude toward the Anti-pedobaptists than were most of the Protestant leaders. After the suppression of the Münster Kingdom, East Friesland became a refuge for the persecuted from the rest of the Netherlands, Switzerland, France, and England. Here were to be found about 1543 the quiet, non-resisting followers of Dirk Philips, the disciples of Battenburg, the leader of the Dutch Münsterites, and those of David Joris, the pantheistic Anti-pedobaptist leader. The Countess Anna and John a Lasco, like Philip of Hesse, and unlike most rulers and theologians, Protestant and Catholic, recognized the distinction between the quiet Anti-pedobaptists and the chiliastic fanatics.

It is probable that Menno had already established relations with Dirk and Obbe Philips and Leonard Bouwens before his removal to East Friesland. At any rate, soon after his arrival at Emden we find him closely associated with these leaders, whose followers were somewhat numerous in Emden and its vicinity. At Leer and Norden and in many villages and country places communities of quiet Anabaptists are known to have existed at this time.

Thus Menno is to be regarded as in no sense the originator of the religious denomination that bears his name, but rather as the organizer and leader of a people already somewhat numerous and only waiting for a master spirit to lead them out into aggressive and fruitful work.

Unfortunately, as it seems to us, Menno had adopted, along with the sounder elements common to the old-evangelical party and to the Anti-pedobaptists, Melchior Hofmann's view of the incarnation, involving denial of the true humanity of Christ. Upon this dogma he laid the utmost stress, and he spent in its defense a vast amount of time that might have been far better employed. At the same time he needlessly aroused much antagonism by advocating a view that seemed to the great majority of evangelical Christians out of harmony with Scripture teaching and with the great doctrines of grace. It may be said that this view has been abandoned by the majority of Menno's own followers. Undoubtedly it was a hurtful excrescence on Menno's system.

He soon became involved in controversy with John a Lasco on the incarnation, the two natures of Christ, hereditary sin, sanctification, the Christian ministry, etc. John a Lasco proposed a public disputation, to which Menno readily agreed. It was held in January, 1543, and lasted for three or four days. As usual, both parties claimed the victory and each leader published in defense of his position.

Menno's first work growing out of this controversy was on the incarnation, his second on church polity, and his third on baptism.[1] In the last he set forth clearly the

---

[1] It seems almost certain that Menno did not require or practise immersion. In his "Foundation Book" (p. 22, folio Dutch edition of his works) he refers to the act of baptism as receiving "a handful of water." The passage in his treatise on "Christian Baptism" (p. 409) sometimes supposed to assert the exclusive validity of immersion, cannot possibly be so interpreted. The author is simply insisting upon believers' baptism as "the only baptism in the water that is well pleasing to God" to the exclusion of infant baptism. Yet in this same treatise he speaks repeatedly of "baptizing in the water" and of baptism as "a water-bath," and he does not hesitate to employ the symbolism of burial and resurrection in connection with the ordinance. On p. 419 he repudiates the idea of the "miserable world" (referring to his Pedo-

grounds on which he felt himself justified in continuing to strive for the restoration of primitive Christianity, rather than co-operate with evangelical bodies that retained infant baptism and maintained unjustifiable relations to the civil powers.

Like most of the polemical writing of the time, Menno's would have been improved by the introduction of more "sweetness and light." His influence was doubtless lessened by the irritation that he must have caused by the sharpness of some of his utterances. His denunciations of a salaried ministry were particularly odious to those who felt themselves justified in living by the gospel. Undoubtedly Menno's attitude of pronounced hostility to a regularly educated and paid ministry and the acceptance of this view by his followers, while it may have attracted the illiterate of his time, was a source of permanent weakness to his denomination. This came to be felt after a while by his followers and efforts were made to overcome it.

Before the close of 1543 we find Menno in Cologne, where the Archbishop-Elector Hermann von Wied had adopted Protestantism and had just introduced a plan of reformation under the advice of Melancthon and Bucer. Here Menno labored quietly, but apparently with large results, for two years. It is probable that during this time he visited many other places and that through correspondence and otherwise he was encouraging and directing the work in the Netherlands and throughout the Rhenish regions of Germany.

A large community of Anti-pedobaptists in sympathy with Menno's views was already in Cologne and its neighborhood. Here also Menno proposed to hold a pub-

baptist opponents, Catholic and Protestant) that "a plunging (*Duycken*) in the water" is equivalent to "the new birth." While perfectly familiar with immersion as the primitive form of baptism he was probably content with affusion, the practice of the later Mennonites as well.

lic disputation on the incarnation and other points of doctrine on which he was at variance with the evangelical ministers. The theologians of Bonn and Wesel would have accepted his proposal, but were influenced by John a Lasco to decline.

By 1546 the Catholics had secured the deposition of Hermann von Wied and had regained ecclesiastical control in Cologne and its dependencies. Menno, with his sick wife, was obliged to seek elsewhere a retreat and a center for his evangelistic activity.

For the next nine years Wismar afforded him a home and the East Sea region was the chief field of his labors. He continued to publish largely in defense of his views and was engaged in several controversies with prominent theologians during this period. The most noteworthy of these were with John a Lasco, Gellius Faber, and Martin Micronius.

In 1547 he made a visit to Emden for the purpose of conferring with Obbe and Dirk Philips, Gillis of Aachen, Henry of Vrenen, Antony of Cologne, and Leonard Bouwens, with reference to the future work of the denomination. These were all general evangelists (head-elders or bishops), and had been for some years engaged in a wonderfully successful evangelistic work. Besides these, there were two brethren present who were out of harmony with the rest on fundamental points: Adam Pastor, who was inclined to anti-trinitarianism, and Francis Cuyper, who was too much disposed toward Roman Catholic views.

The chief questions discussed at this conference were those regarding the incarnation of Christ and the exercise of the ban. On the latter point a serious difference of opinion that finally led to a division of the body appeared. Menno, Dirk Philips, Gillis of Aachen, and Bouwens, agreed in insisting on the most rigorous application of discipline, the rest contended for more of moderation. The specific question on which division occurred was with reference to marital avoidance. Menno contended that the believing husband or wife of a church-member excluded for improper conduct should refuse to cohabit with the excluded party. Here again Menno seems to us to have spent his strength in vain. From this time onward a large part of his time was consumed in advocating this extreme view, and the attempt to enforce it was the cause of endless trouble in the churches as well as of a schism in the connection.

Menno saw all the greater reason for the use of rigor in the application of the ban from the fact that Münsterites were seeking to gain entrance into the churches and that the good name of the connection depended on their rigorous exclusion.

"I know of a surety," he wrote in a circular letter after his return to Wismar, "that if we had not used our utmost endeavor by means of the ban to keep clear of the adherents of the Münster fanatics, we should not now be so free from the abominations of the perverse sect, to which we can now bear witness before the whole world. Without the ban our churches would have stood open to all errorists, all scoffers and wanton sinners, while now the pure, clear light of the gospel in this time of anti-Christian abomination is revealed to us."

If the question had been between discipline and no discipline, between the exclusion of unworthy members for sufficient cause with the guarded admission of applicants on the one hand, and the indiscriminate reception of all who might apply for membership with the toleration of open sin and heresy on the other, there would have been point in Menno's contention. It is possible that the opponents of Menno favored a degree of laxity that was unwholesome and that did not sufficiently guard the purity and the good name of the connection; it is certain that Menno's position was rigorous in the extreme and it is probable that it occasioned more of scandal than it prevented. The marriage tie is too sacred a thing to be ruthlessly broken on account of misconduct that makes exclusion from church-membership proper, and it seems clear that the New Testament neither requires nor permits such avoidance as Menno required.

Soon after the division mentioned above, Obbe Philips abandoned the Anti-pedobaptists and henceforth labored zealously against them. Dirk Philips long continued to labor side by side with Menno. Next to Menno he was the chief literary leader of the connection and his practical works are still highly prized in Mennonite circles. Leonard Bouwens probably surpassed both Menno and Philips in popular power. He continued to make Emden his center and evangelized with great zeal throughout the Netherlands, planting churches in many places and encouraging them by his visits. He is said in the course of a few years to have baptized ten thousand. It was with the utmost reluctance that Bouwens allowed himself to be made a head-elder (or bishop) along with Menno and Dirk Philips. His wife was strongly opposed to his assuming the responsibilities and incurring the dangers that belonged to the office and wrote to Menno entreating him to excuse her husband. Menno replied most benevolently, yet was inexorable in his insistence that Bouwens should assume the office to which he had been chosen and for which he was so eminently fitted. His chief co-laborer in the Netherlands was Gillis of Aachen.

As already suggested, Menno devoted a large part of his attention to literary work. In 1552 he published an earnest appeal to the civil rulers on behalf of his persecuted people, defending them against the charges that were made against them by their enemies and setting forth their pious and inoffensive character. A second apology was addressed to the evangelical ministers. In a third writing he set forth the views of his connection with reference to justification, ministry, baptism, the Supper, and oaths. The tone of Menno's apologetical writings was too polemical to be highly effective, and it is doubtful whether they produced any favorable result.

John a Lasco had been obliged to leave Emden in 1547, when, owing to the treachery of Maurice of Saxony, the emperor seemed for the time to have the Protestant princes at his mercy, and had resolved to crush out every vestige of Protestantism in his hereditary possessions. Lasco took refuge in England, where he ministered for a number of years to a congregation of Polish Protestants. Persecution under Mary drove him thence. With two other ministers, Utenhofen and Micronius, and about one hundred and seventy-five others, he came by ship in stormy weather to seek protection from the king of Denmark. After being much tossed about and suffering fearful hardships, they succeeded in gaining an audience with the king. He finally decided, after long consultation with his Lutheran preachers, that he could not allow such as denied the real presence in the Supper to remain in his land. They besought him, in view of their misery and the fact that winter was at hand, to allow them to remain for the winter. But he was inexorable, and they were obliged without further delay to set sail.

The ship containing Lasco and the other ministers became fastened in the ice near Wismar. The Mennonites were the only persons ready to bear them succor. Lasco and the other ministers proceeded with little delay to Emden, while a number of their followers remained at Wismar. One of these, Hermes by name, soon began to agitate for a disputation with Menno. Menno's security at Wismar depended on his avoidance of any sort of publicity. He consented to a disputation on the distinct understanding that secrecy should be observed in the matter. Hermes sent to East Friesland for Micronius, who on February, 1555, disputed for eleven hours with Menno on the incarnation of Christ, baptism, the oath, and divorce. Without regard to Menno's interests, Micronius published an account of the disputation. Menno soon afterward published an extended reply to Micronius on the points at issue between them as well as a reply to Gellius Faber, who had published an ill-tempered attack on Menno and his views. The followers of Lasco were soon afterward banished from Wismar by the Lutheran authorities, toleration being still accorded to Menno and his followers.

In August, 1555, the six Lutheran cities of the Hanseatic League, to which Wismar belonged, decreed the banishment of all Anti-pedobaptists. Menno and his followers found a retreat at Wüstenfelde, in the possessions of Count Bartholomæus von Ahlefeldt, who had come to know the quiet Anti-pedobaptists in the Netherlands, and who treated Menno with the greatest kindness. Here he remained till his death in 1559. Bouwens had had chief charge of the work in the Netherlands, and Dirk Philips had been for some years assisting Menno in the East Sea region.

The advantage gained by the emperor over the Protestant princes in 1547 had soon been lost and the exterminating procedures against evangelical teaching in the Netherlands were temporarily suspended. Large numbers of the Mennonites had suffered martyrdom during this period of acute persecution in East Friesland and elsewhere. Anabaptism was made punishable with death, even in case of repentance. Heavy penalties were attached to harboring or in any way ministering to Anabaptists. Inquisitors were appointed to search them out and bring them before the tribunals. Some of the nobility suffered among the rest. Yet in spite of persecution the Mennonites rapidly increased and were soon the principal evangelical party in the Netherlands.

The question of the incarnation of Christ and that of the application of church discipline continued to agitate the minds of the brethren and to be productive of strife and division, by which Menno was deeply grieved. The German brethren, now quite numerous (1555), felt that the time had come when these and other questions that were the occasion of controversy among the quiet Antipedobaptists should be settled. To this end a conference was called at Strasburg, which had become an important center of the new connection. A statement framed by the conference with reference to the incarnation has fortunately been preserved. It is admitted that—

in many passages of Scripture it seems as if Christ brought his body with him from heaven, but in others, as if he received his flesh from Mary. Further, it seems also that he is the Father and also God himself. The confusion of tongues has come upon the brethren in this matter because they would know more than it was intended that they should know.

It is urged that more attention be given to keeping God's commandments than to prying into such mysteries. They should be content with the statement: "The Word became flesh and tabernacled among us." "To take from or to add to these words is not only disturbing, but it is criminal." It is further stated that godlessness and evil are to be overcome more through the example of a Christian life and walk than by means of words.

It is evident that this document involved a sharp censure of Menno and Philips. A copy of it was sent to Menno, who lost no time in framing an answer.

Menno and those immediately associated with him had

formulated nine rules of discipline, which they wished all the churches of the connection to follow. These forbade marriage outside of the church and required suspension of fellowship in case of such marriage until the life had been tested anew; forbade intercourse, beyond what was absolutely necessary, with apostates; and required marital avoidance in case of the evil life of husband or wife till amendment. In case of the separation of a married couple on account of religion, the party remaining in the church may not marry again unless the apostate party marry again or become immoral; children of believers shall not marry without their parents' consent; the payment of just debts may be required, but nothing ungodly must be done in collecting; military service and all bearing of arms are strictly prohibited; no one shall set himself up as a teacher or exhorter until he has been chosen thereunto by the church and ordained thereunto by the elders.

These rules caused great dissatisfaction in many quarters. Bouwens sought rigorously to enforce them in the churches under his immediate direction. Gillis of Aachen met with much opposition in executing them among the Waterland churches. The feeling was very general that the requirement of marital avoidance involved too serious an interference with personal liberty. The Franecker church was thrown into confusion by the efforts of the strict party to carry out Menno's rules.

Menno was deeply grieved by the remonstrance of his brethren assembled at Strasburg and by the failure of many in the Netherlands rigorously to execute his rules. He claimed that he and Dirk Philips had always favored making allowance for circumstances. He entreated his brethren to let the rule requiring marital avoidance stand, but to use due caution in executing it. If the innocent husband or wife feels bound by conscience to adhere to the sinful and excommunicated spouse and in the judgment of the brethren this can be done without endangering the Christian life of the innocent party, he makes no objection. Yet he would have each case individually investigated and passed upon by the elders. He claimed to know of three hundred cases in which through the guilt of one party both (husband and wife) have been brought to destruction. Evidently the cases that would escape the application of the rule by Menno and those who were like-minded would be few indeed. To make his position on this and other matters perfectly clear Menno published in 1555 his "Foundation Book," the most complete and mature exposition of his system. A deputation from the upper German brethren, consisting of the teachers Sylis, Lemke, and Heinrich, visited Menno at Wismar to discuss this question of marital avoidance and if possible to reach a basis of agreement which all the churches could accept. These brethren were to report to the German and Netherland churches; but so imperfectly did they agree among themselves and so varying was the coloring they gave to the conference with Menno, that greater confusion than ever ensued.

In 1557 another convention was held in Strasburg with representatives of the Anti-pedobaptist churches of Würtemberg, Swabia, Moravia, Alsace, the Palatinate, and Switzerland, the chief purpose being to discuss and if possible reach a conclusion on the questions of discipline that had been thrust upon the churches by the rules of Menno and Philips.

The conference addressed a letter to Menno in which they urged him not to be too rigorous and while expressing general agreement with the Wismar rules yet insisted on liberty to deal with individual cases on their merits and with due regard to the usages of the country in which a church is situated. Especially do they think that the utmost caution should be observed in the application of the rule requiring marital avoidance. The command as to marriage transcends that as to excommunication.

The right of the conference to address this remonstrance to Menno is grounded on the fact that some of its members bore on their persons the marks of torture for their faith, while in the house of one of them thirty years before an interview with Michael Sattler had taken place. Many of the members had traveled one hundred and fifty miles at great cost and sacrifice to be present at the meeting.

Mention is also made of a very large meeting of Anti-pedobaptists that had occurred at Worms, shortly before, in which the doctrines of hereditary sin and of spiritual and bodily sin were discussed and much confusion caused among the brethren in the Palatinate. The number said to have been at the Worms meeting (one thousand four hundred or one thousand five hundred) is suspiciously large; but it is evident that there was at this time in the Palatinate as well as in Alsace and in the lower Rhenish regions a large Anti-pedobaptist element that wished to maintain a good understanding with Menno, yet viewed independently the questions that from time to time arose.

It may be remarked that at this time there was considerable activity among the Anti-pedobaptists in Hesse, Westphalia, Switzerland, and in fact in most of the countries of Western Europe. This was due in part to the encouragment received from the successful movement in the Netherlands; but to a larger extent it was due to the revival of the religious life that had been so fearfully persecuted just before and for some time after the Münster catastrophe. The Münster affair was now well in the past and there was coming to be a slight realization among rulers that all Anti-pedobaptists were not Münsterites.

With a view to restoring unity and order in the churches Menno, now growing infirm with age and disease, made a visit to the churches in Friesland and afterward attended a conference at Cologne. The result was by no means according to his desire. Almost brokenhearted he returned to his home. The last few years of his life were embittered by the controversies in the churches of the connection which his influence was inadequate to allay. He died January 23, 1559.

Literature: Works of Menno Simons and Dirk Philips, "Mennonitische Blätter, "Doopsgezinde Bijdragen," and monographs of Brons, Cramer, Roosen, De Hoop Scheffer, Van Braght, Blaupot ten Cate, Schyn, Hamelmann, Upeij u. Dermout, and Van Slee, as in the Bibliography.

CHAPTER XXIV

THE LATER MENNONITES

BY 1559, the date of Menno's decease, those who agreed substantially with the great organizer of quiet Anti-pedobaptist life numbered many thousands. Lutheranism had long been practically extinct in the Netherlands. The Calvinistic type of teaching, soon to become dominant, had long since proved itself better adapted to the genius of the people and had supplanted it.

The great mass of the people had come to abominate the Spanish rule and the Catholic religion with which the gloomy and unscrupulous king Philip II. was so thoroughly identified. After the accession of Philip, Calvinism grew more aggressive. It soon became evident that the king would give no quarter to evangelical religion in any of its forms. The persecuting measures under the direction of the Duke of Alva (1567 onward) are too well known to need recounting here. It is probable that by 1572 nearly twenty thousand evangelical Christians had fallen a sacrifice to Philip's cruel zeal.

The effect of the persecution was to intensify the enthusiasm of the Calvinists. Their preachers did not hesitate to risk their lives in proclaiming the truth and thousands would gather to hear them. A large number of Mennonites suffered among the rest, but as they were on principle quiet and non-resisting and did not openly antagonize their persecutors they probably suffered less in proportion to their numbers than the Calvinists.

The conviction was growing upon the people of the Netherlands that the time was at hand when by a desperate struggle the galling Spanish Catholic yoke must be thrown off. The Mennonites with their radical opposition to warfare and their principle of absolute non-resistance could not under such circumstances hope to win to their cause the controlling life of the land. Men like William of Orange sympathized deeply with the Mennonites in many things; but if he and others who were like-minded had united themselves with their non-resisting friends they would all together, so far as we can see, have been led like sheep to the slaughter by the relentless Spaniards. It was in the very nature of things that militant Calvinism should carry the day.

In the forty years' struggle with Spain that began in 1568 the Mennonites occupied the somewhat inconsistent position of being liberal contributors to the expenses of the war and assisting the patriotic cause in every possible indirect way, and yet refusing on conscientious grounds to bear arms.

Before and during the war the Mennonites were as a body a most prosperous people. Industry and thrift insured to almost all a competency and to many large means. They were foremost in contributing to every benevolent cause, and in no way restricted their gifts to denominational channels. They became noted for their honesty and uprightness, and though they refused to take judicial oaths, their word was considered a sufficient guarantee for their faithful performance of all obligations. While even in their most prosperous times they insisted upon the utmost plainness in dress, they made up in a measure for this excessive plainness by requiring whatever they used to be the very best of its kind. So noticeable was their care in this regard that the term "Mennist-fine" came to be used in trade to designate the best that could be made.

The controversy on discipline that Menno himself had been utterly unable to prevent or allay continued after his death and increased in its violence. Party divisions, some of which have continued to the present time, soon became clearly marked. Four of these we note in the early time. The Waterlanders occupied the extreme liberal position laying much stress upon the freedom of the individual. Their churches were contemptuously nicknamed by their strict opponents "truck-wagons." The extreme position as regards disciplinary rigor was occupied by the Flemings, who made such matters as dress a ground for discipline, insisted on marital avoidance of an excommunicated member, and in general strove to carry out Menno's rules more rigorously than he himself would have thought of doing. Intermediate between these were the Upper German and Frisian churches and the "young" or "loose Frisians," the latter closely approaching the position of the Waterlanders.

There can be no doubt that among the stricter parties the rigorous exercise of discipline sometimes amounted almost to persecution and that the spirit of censoriousness was cultivated at the expense of brotherly love. An illustration of this tendency is afforded by the famous case of Bintgens, an elder in the Franecker church. Bintgens had purchased a house for seven hundred florins, which he allowed the seller for purposes of his own to value in the deed at eight hundred florins, deriving himself no benefit whatever from the misstatement. When this came to the ears of a brother elder he declared that Bintgens had sinned by being a party to a fraud. The matter was brought up in the local church where Bintgens expressed his profound sorrow for what had occurred, but maintained his entire innocence of any fraudulent intention in the matter. He would have sooner paid double the value of the house than wrong any one. The church seemed satisfied with his statement. Two of the elders, however, some time afterward began to agitate the matter afresh, and appealed to the elders of the neighboring churches for their opinion of the case. These refused to give an opinion without further knowledge of the circumstances.

Two parties were now formed in the church, the one demanding Bintgens' deposition from office, the other sustaining him. A council was called to adjudicate on the matter. Bintgens now claimed that while he had paid only seven hundred florins in money, he had given to the seller one hundred florins' worth of linen. No definite result was reached, but the prevailing sentiment seems to have been unfavorable to Bintgens.

A second council was called at which Bintgens' accusers demanded not only his deposition from office, but his exclusion from church fellowship. There was a difference of opinion as to whether the matter should be decided by all the churches or by some brethren especially appointed thereunto, or whether the procedure enjoined in 1 Tim. 5 : 19, 20 should not be followed.

A third council failing to agree, the Amsterdam and Haarlem brethren advised that the opinion of brethren in Groningen, Cologne, and Emden be sought. The council ended in bitter wrangling, some of the brethren accusing others of trying to cover up Bintgens' guilt. Bintgens' party refused to admit the right of the Groningen and Emden brethren to be consulted in the premises. The Amsterdam brethren pronounced against Bintgens and secured the concurrence of those of Emden and Groningen ; the Haarlem brethren took the side of the accused. The Haarlem church became so exasperated with that of Amsterdam as to withdraw from its fellowship. The dominant party persisted in condemning Bintgens and his adherents and stigmatized them as " House buyers " and " Bankrupts."

The transaction that occasioned the controversy took place in 1588. In 1590 the bitter divisions just mentioned were at their height. The vindication of the principle of absolute honesty was worth much, but it is doubtful whether it was worth what it cost in this case. The censure of the local church with Bintgens' expression of sorrow for what had occurred should, it seems, have sufficed. This is only a sample of divisions that were constantly occurring through undue rigor in the exercise of disciplinary functions.

From 1574 onward the Reformed (Calvinistic) church sought persistently to destroy the Mennonites, but they enjoyed the protection of William the Silent and afterward of Maurice of Nassau. The Synod of Dort in 1574 decided to exhort the government to tolerate no one who would not swear obedience to it, to compel the Mennonites to have their infants baptized, and in case of refusal to turn them over to the Reformed ministers to be dealt with. They also sought the right to intrude themselves into the assemblies of the Mennonites for the purpose of convincing them of their errors. In West Friesland they secured for a time the latter privilege and used it greatly to the annoyance of the brethren. Having gained the support of Count Leicester, who had come to the Netherlands as a representative of Queen Elizabeth, to aid the Dutch in their war with Spain, the Reformed ministers, though their membership constituted as yet only a small fraction of the population (one-tenth according to some authorities) sought to secure recognition as the established church of the land with power to coerce dissent. Maurice of Nassau, under the advice of Barnaveld, followed the example of his honored father, William the Silent, in protecting the Mennonites.

In 1596 a public disputation, lasting from August 16 to November 17 and embracing one hundred and fifty-five sittings, was held at Leeuwarden in Friesland between Ruardus Acronius on behalf of the Reformed and Peter of Cologne on behalf of the Mennonites. The aim of the disputation on the Reformed side was, apparently, by bringing out into publicity the teachings of the Mennonites to gain a pretext for their persecution.

The protocol of the disputation was published by the Reformed party, accompanied by a claim of complete victory and violent denunciations of the Mennonites. The preface, which occupies fifty-two closely printed quarto pages, concludes with an impassioned appeal to the authorities to withdraw all toleration from the Anabaptists, whose principles are declared to strike at the root of saving truth and of civil and religious order, and whose doctrine, founded in lying hypocrisy, eats as doth a gangrene.

Peter of Cologne was probably the most prominent of the Mennonite teachers of the time. Though seventy years of age, he conducted the Mennonite side in the prolonged disputation with marked ability and to the satisfaction of his brethren. Neither he nor his opponent adhered rigidly to the agreement to avoid all bitterness which, under any circumstances, would have been difficult.

The Reformed synods at Franecker and Harlingen sought to induce the magistracy to restrain Peter from preaching in Friesland.

About 1601 a book of Beza's defending the execution of heretics was translated into Dutch and published, the chief object being to prepare the public mind for the slaughter of the Mennonites. In the preface it is argued that to tolerate heresy is to make peace with Satan. Only one church must be tolerated in the State.

In answer to the objection that some might raise to the persecution of heretics on the ground of loss of trade, etc., it is answered that it is better to have a city desolate and uninhabited than a thriving city full of heretics. In some places the Mennonites were refused the privilege of doing business or of holding meetings and their ministers were fined and ordered to go into banishment.

In 1603 a Reformed synod asked the government to restrain the Mennonite bishops from traveling from place to place, preaching and baptizing; in 1604 the government was asked to prohibit the ordaining of young ministers by the Mennonites; in 1605 it was petitioned not to allow them to build any more chapels. The most determined efforts on the part of the Calvinists to crush out the Mennonites by the use of the civil power were continued almost without intermission during the seventeenth century. If the Mennonites were not destroyed root and branch, but were able to survive the calumny and persecution to which they were subjected, it was due to no lack of zeal on the part of the Reformed ministers, but rather to their power of endurance and the restraining influence of the government.

The Socinian wave that swept over the Protestant Netherlands during the last years of the sixteenth century and the early years of the seventeenth did not leave the Mennonites unaffected. In common with the rest of the Anti-pedobaptists and with the old-evangelical party of the mediæval time, the Mennonites had from the beginning been most pronounced in their opposition to the Augustinian system as it had been revived and modified by Luther and Calvin. They had much in common with the Socinians, who, as we shall see, were themselves rigid Anti-pedobaptists and insisted on the inspiration and authority of the Scriptures, while they gave to Christ a position not of co-equality with the Father, but yet of exaltation above all created things. His miraculous conception, his creative, providential, and redemptive work were unreservedly accepted. As regards original sin, the will, and justification, the Socinianism as expounded in the Racovian Catechism (1590), was not essentially different from that of the old-evangelical party as perpetuated by the Anti-pedobaptists in general and by the Mennonites.

Calvinism never assumed a more extreme type than it assumed in the Netherlands about the beginning of the seventeenth century. The mighty reaction against hyper-Calvinism under Socinian and other influences resulting in the rending asunder of the Reformed church and the formation of the Remonstrant or Arminian communion, with the years of strife and persecution that preceded and followed the Synod of Dort (1618), could not have failed to interest and influence the Mennonites. During the seventeenth and eighteenth centuries supposed sympathy with Socinianism on the part of some of the Mennonites was alike an occasion of internal strife and of attacks from their Calvinistic opponents.

About 1619 a movement originated at Rhynsburg, Holland, that not only sustains an important relation to the subsequent history of the Mennonites, but has also an interesting point of contact with English Baptist history. The brothers van der Kodde (John, Adrian, William, and Gisbrecht), by way of reaction against the religious strife of the time, began to hold meetings for Christian fellowship and prophesying. They repudiated creeds and eschewed all controversy. Their meetings were open to all true believers, each of whom had the fullest liberty of taking part in the exercises. Their assemblies were largely devoted to the edifying interpretation of the Scriptures whose authority they accepted. The breaking of bread, in commemoration of the incarnation and death of Christ and as a means of communion of believers, prayer, and the singing of hymns, formed prominent features of their meetings. The Christian ministry as a distinct office they thought unnecessary and harmful. The New Testament having been given, Christians had no need that any one should teach them, but all alike should draw from the revealed word as they might be able and each should be in his measure a teacher of others. They baptized into the fellowship of the saints by immersion. Their modes of religious thought were distinctly anti-Calvinistic. Socinianism was undoubtedly the chief source of their impulse, although they did not dogmatize as did the Socinians on the person of Christ, etc. It is highly probable that they were influenced to a considerable extent by the Mennonites, with many of whose views they thoroughly agreed and who certainly took a prominent part in the movement after its organization.

Deprived to a great extent of educational advantages the Mennonites utilized the meetings of the Rhynsburgers (or Collegiants) as means of improvement and edification. It is also probable that the introduction of immersion by the Rhynsburgers was due to Socinian influence, as the Socinians insisted on immersion while the Mennonites usually practised sprinkling or affusion. After a period of prosperity the movement gradually declined and became extinct early in the present century.

It does not fall within the plan of the present work to trace the history of the Mennonites beyond the first quarter of the seventeenth century, when they exerted an influence on the rise of the English Baptists.

Literature: Works of Menno Simons and Dirk Philips, "Mennonitische Blätter," "Doopsgezinde Bijdragen," and monographs of Brons, Cramer, Roosen, De Hoop-Scheffer, Van Braght, Blaupot ten Cate, Schyn, Hamelmann, Upeij u. Dermout, and Van Slee, as in the Bibliography.

CHAPTER XXV

ITALY AND POLAND

NO country of Europe was more hospitable to freedom of thought at the beginning of the sixteenth century than Italy. As the center of the Renaissance, with its repugnance to scholasticism and its devotion to classical modes of thought and expression, Italy was the theatre of a widespread departure from the old faith and the development of radical types of Christian thought.

Several of the popes of the latter part of the fifteenth and the early years of the sixteenth centuries are said to have been free-thinkers of the most pronounced type, and the Roman Curia was not likely under such circumstances to apply the inquisition of heresy with pristine vigor. Before the outbreak of the Protestant Revolution clubs of learned men of evangelical tendencies were in the habit of meeting in various places for the discussion of theological questions and for mutual edification.

There is no reason to suppose that the evangelical movement of which Lombardy had been since the twelfth century a chief center had been exterminated during the later Middle Ages. It is probable, on the other hand, that a large proportion of the evangelical Christians whom we meet in Italy during the fourth and following decades of the sixteenth century had earlier been under old-evangelical influence. From the Rhætian provinces of Switzerland and from the contiguous districts of the Tyrol the old-evangelical life of Northern Italy was no doubt reinforced and made aggressive by the Anti-pedobaptists who abounded in the former territories.

That evangelical Anti-pedobaptist views should have there become blended with the radical modes of thought, the later development of which we see in the Italico-Polish anti-trinitarian movement, is quite comprehensible. The tendency of Italian Humanism was to call in question, with the errors and corruptions of the mediæval church, the fundamental doctrines of the Christian religion; and the doctrine of the Trinity was sure to be assailed.

The writings of Luther and of the evangelical leaders of Switzerland and Southern Germany were somewhat widely circulated in Italy from 1520 onward. Anti-trinitarian tendencies were doubtless fostered to a considerable extent by the writings of the Spanish anti-trinitarian Michael Servetus, which are known to have been in circulation during the fourth decade of the century. Servetus was one of the most zealous of Anti-pedobaptists. He declared infant baptism to be "a figment of Anti-christ" and "a figment of Satan." He adduced twenty-five reasons why pedobaptism should be abolished. He insisted that as Adam was born thirty years old, as the Jews were permitted to enter the sanctuary only after the thirtieth year, and as Christ was baptized when thirty years old, so believers should be baptized at this age. He had a peculiar view of the right mode of administering the ordinance. The candidate should go down into the water and then have water poured upon his head. While he emphasized the importance of faith as a prerequisite to baptism and held that baptism without faith effects nothing, he was yet assured that baptism adds something to faith. If two believers prepared for baptism should die, the one baptized and the other unbaptized, the former alone would be free from the power and the pains of hell.[1]

---

[1] See "Restitutio Christianismi," pp. 228, *seq.*, 411, *seq.*, 560, *seq.*, 570, *seq.*, 484, *seq.*, 492, *seq.*, 616, *seq.*, etc.

The Republic of Venice had long been a place of refuge for political as well as religious fugitives and was able to resist the efforts of the Roman Curia to introduce the inquisition until 1551. Early Socinian tradition knew of a college or club of freethinkers at Vicenza in the Republic of Venice about 1546. It is not in accord with the purpose of the present work to investigate the rise of the anti-trinitarianism as such in Italy, and this movement claims attention only from the fact that it was closely connected with an important Anti-pedobaptist movement. One of the earliest representatives of this liberal Anti-pedobaptist tendency was the Sicilian, Camillo Renato, who was active as a teacher in Caspano, Traona, Chiavenna, and Vicosoprano, during the years 1542-45. He has been fitly characterized as a "Calvinistic Quaker." A rigid predestinarian, he held that the elect and only they have the spirit of God and so are immortal. Souls that have not the Holy Spirit die, those that have the Spirit only slumber in death to receive afterward a renewed, purely spiritual form of being. The child of the Spirit needs no external law. The sacraments are only symbols of truths that have already been realized in the heirs of the kingdom. The Supper is a memorial of Christ's death. Baptism is only an external sign that the old man has been put away.

In a controversy with Meinardo, who had adopted the Reformed view of the sacraments, he repudiated baptism received "under the pope and antichrist," in a special writing, and openly denied that infant baptism was in accord with the "doctrine of the gospel." He had no sympathy with the Reformed view that infant baptism takes the place of circumcision. He laid great emphasis on regeneration, which involves a complete transformation of our nature and constitutes us children of God and heirs of eternal life.

Camillo Renato was closely associated with a number of men who became prominent anti-trinitarians, among others with Lælius Socinus, then a young man, and Celio Secundo Curio. His correspondence with Bullinger of Zürich, with whose views of the Supper he was in substantial accord, was broken off as a result of his controversy with Meinardo on baptism. In his rejection of infant baptism he soon had a considerable following. Among the most noted of his first disciples were Francesco Negri, and the physician Pietro da Casali Maggiore, one of the most zealous Anti-pedobaptists of the time.

Greater by far than the influence of Camillo was that of Tiziano. Almost nothing is known of his antecedents. We first meet him about 1547 or 1548, fleeing from place to place to escape persecution. Camillo had declared himself opposed to infant baptism, but there is no evidence that he submitted to or practised believers' baptism. It is probable that he attached too little importance to external rites to think either worth while.

Pietro Manelfi, an ex-priest, was led by the teachings of the famous Capuchin friars Hieronimo Spinazola and Bernardino Ochino to believe that the pope was antichrist. He was baptized along with a number of other notable men by Tiziano in 1548 or 1549, and after serving for some years as a leader among the Italian Antipedobaptists became an apostate and a traitor. He attributed the following teachings to Tiziano: (1) Insistence of believers' baptism; (2) rejection of magistracy as inconsistent with the spirit of Christianity; (3) maintenance of the symbolical and memorial nature of the sacraments; (4) exaltation of the Scriptures as the only criterion of the faith; (5) denunciation of the Romish church as devilish and absolutely anti-christian. As ordinances administered by this anti-christian church are of no value he insisted on believers' baptism.

By 1550 about forty Anti-pedobaptist churches, scattered throughout Northern Italy and contiguous parts of Switzerland, were in fellowship with each other and were enjoying the periodical visitations of a general superintendent. Their connectional organization seems to have been very similar to that of the Waldensian churches of the earlier time.

The churches had become greatly agitated over the question "whether Christ is God, or man." To settle this question it was decided to secure the assembling of all the ministers of all the churches at Venice. No church was to send more than two representatives, yet there were about sixty delegates present. As many distant churches would not be likely to send a full delegation, it is probable that at least forty churches were represented. Among the delegates were Tiziano, Iseppo of Asola, Manelfi, Celio Secundo Curio, afterward to become famous as an advocate of freedom of conscience and as author of the "Tragedy of Free Will," Francesco Negri, and the ex-abbot Hieronimo Buzano, who had offered to his Anti-pedobaptist church the income of one thousand ducats a year from his office. It is gratifying to know that the church declined to receive anything "from the blood of the beast." An interesting feature of this convention is that the churches paid the expenses of their delegates.

Unfortunately the doctrinal beliefs of this large and respectable Anti-pedobaptist convention were far less satisfactory than their attitude toward the corruptions of Rome and their views on the ordinances. It was decided that the Scriptures of the Old and New Testaments were to be accepted as the fundamental authority. Thrice during the meeting the Supper was celebrated. The utmost devoutness seems to have characterized the entire proceedings of the convention. And yet after forty days of earnest discussion they reached the following conclusions: (1) Christ is not God but man, begotten by Joseph of Mary, but full of all divine powers. (2) Mary afterward bore other sons and daughters. (3) There are no angels as a special class of beings; where Scripture speaks of angels, it means servants—that is, men sent by God for definite purposes. (4) There is only one devil, namely, human prudence. By the serpent, who, according to Moses' account, seduced Eve, nothing else than this is to be understood. (5) The godless are not to be awakened at the last day, but only the elect, whose Head Christ has been. (6) There is no other hell than the grave. (7) If the elect die, they slumber till the day of judgment, when they shall all be awakened. (8) The souls of the godless pass into dissolution with their bodies just as in the case of the beasts. (9) Human seed has from God the capacity to propagate flesh and spirit. (10) The elect are justified through God's eternal mercy and love, without any sort of external work, that is, without the merit, blood, and death of Christ.

Such is the account of his brethren that Manelfi, who, having by years of personal visitation and intercourse secured complete information as to the connection, gave to the Inquisition. There is no reason to doubt its substantial accuracy, as its main features are otherwise known to be in accordance with the facts. It is possible that only those churches were included in the connection that were understood to entertain low views of the person of Christ. We have abundant evidence a few years later in the records of the Inquisition that side by side with the anti-trinitarian Anti-pedobaptists were some who rejected the anti-trinitarian and other errors to which the convention at Venice almost unanimously subscribed.

Manelfi's report to the Inquisition furnishes a full and

seemingly accurate account of the church organization of the anti-trinitarian Anti-pedobaptists of Italy and Switzerland. It seems to have been almost identical with that of the Waldenses of the Middle Ages. Each local congregation had its ministers ordained by the "apostolic bishops," or general superintendents. The functions of these latter were to "preach the word and to constitute ministers." A connection of churches had grown up before the time of the convention referred to, and this connection was fostered through the regular visitation of the congregations by the itinerant superintendents or bishops. A superintendent was usually accompanied in his itinerating by a less-experienced brother, who thus secured the necessary training in the arts of evading the authorities and of reaching successfully the scattered and persecuted flocks. For instance, Manelfi had accompanied Marcantonio of Asola in his visitation of the churches in Vicenza, Padua, Treviso, and Istria. He had visited the churches in the Romagna, in Ferrara, and in Tuscany, in company with the "bishop," Lorenzo Nicoluzzo, from Modiana. As a traveling companion of Pasqualino of Asola he had again visited the churches in Ferrara, Padua, and Vicenza.

From Manelfi we learn that the brethren practised a most effective method of warning each of approaching danger, through special messengers dispatched to the various threatened congregations. They were shrewd enough likewise to visit and console brethren in prison despite the rigid prohibition of the authorities. He himself had visited an Anti-pedobaptist brother in prison, and while there had converted and baptized a Lutheran prisoner. Manelfi was able to give the most detailed information with reference to the entire connection and with reference to individual congregations.

It was upon one of his tours of visitation in October, 1551, as he was passing through Ravenna on his way to Tuscany, that the conviction pressed itself upon him that he was an apostate from the true faith and that there was nothing left for him but to retrace his steps and seek as far as in him lay to undo the evil that he had accomplished during his years of apostasy. He forsook his companion, made his way to Bologna, threw himself at the feet of the inquisitors, and was restored to the fellowship of the Romish church.

It was natural that the authorities should insist upon his furnishing all the information he possessed for assisting the inquisitors in their work of exterminating heresy, and he showed no reluctance in betraying those with whom he had so long and so zealously labored and whose confidence he had so fully enjoyed. Of the large number of Anti-pedobaptists arraigned by the Inquisition through the information furnished by Manelfi the majority renounced their faith and promised to return to their allegiance to Rome. A considerable number fled to Moravia and Poland. Some of those who took refuge among the ever-hospitable and at that time highly prosperous brethren in Moravia were convinced by them of the errors of the Italian brethren with reference to the person of Christ, the future life, etc., and were filled with yearning to instruct their Anti-pedobaptist fellow-countrymen more perfectly in the way of the Lord and to induce as many of them as possible to take refuge in the goodly land where they themselves had been so kindly received and so richly blessed.

Among the most noteworthy of the Italian anti-trinitarian Anti-pedobaptists who were brought to evangelical views through intercourse with the Moravians was Giulio Gherlandi. Educated for the priesthood and already introduced into one of its lower grades, Gherlandi, while still a young man, was awakened by our Lord's warning, which he found in the Breviary: "Beware of false prophets," etc. His knowledge of the corrupt lives of the clergy led him to identify them with the false prophets that inwardly were ravening wolves. After much prayerful heart-searching he determined to leave the Romish church and to seek a people "who should be free through the gospel of truth from the bondage of sin and should walk in newness of life, a people that is God's holy, unspotted church, separate from sinners, without wrinkle and without blemish."

About 1549 he came in contact with the Anti-pedobaptists and was baptized at Treviso by Nicolao d'Alessandria. He became an active worker in the new fellowship and baptized a number of converts. Some time between 1551 and 1557 he went to Moravia and was soon brought into complete accord with the doctrines and the mode of life of the brethren there. In 1557 he was sent on a mission to Italy to warn his friends against "that pestilential doctrine"—denial of the deity of Christ. His aim was after instructing his brethren in right doctrine to lead them away to Moravia, "since there was no servant of the word to be found in Italy." This first mission he seems to have accomplished in safety.

In 1559 he was sent a second time to Italy. This time he was accompanied by two other brethren. They bore a letter from Francesco della Saga, an influential Italian Anti-pedobaptist convert to Moravian orthodoxy, to the Anti-pedobabtist church at Vicenza. The document begins:

We, the church sanctified through Jesus Christ and received into the communion of God the Father and of his Son Jesus Christ, together with the elders and ministers, desire for all those who are in Italy and would live perfectly in the truth, insight into the divine will: that with upright heart they may recognize Christ in his power, embrace him, yield themselves up to him, and thereby become partakers of his fellowship and of eternal life.

The writer is just as careful to warn his hearers against the opposite (Hofmannite) error of denying the true humanity of Christ by maintaining that he brought his flesh with him from heaven. Adverse reference is also made to other errors into which the Italian party had fallen, such as conditional immortality and denial of the existence of angels and of the devil; and the hope is expressed that if they still hold to such views they will soon abandon them and allow themselves to be led by the Spirit of God into the true church.

This short letter gives us a clear insight into the spirit that actuated the Italian brethren who in Moravia had been won to right views of the person of Christ in their efforts to deliver their fellow-countrymen from what they saw to be ruinous errors. In the efforts which they put forth in this direction they had the hearty co-operation of the entire Moravian brotherhood with whom they had become identified.

To facilitate their work in reaching the scattered brethren in Italy, Gherlandi and his companions had been furnished with a list of the names of brethren in various places, especially we may suppose of those thought to be most likely to respond to the sentiments of the letter and to the efforts of the missionaries. It seems to us little short of criminal that at such a time men with such a mission should have run the risk for themselves and for those whom they were seeking to bless that was involved in carrying on their persons such documents. To what extent they had accomplished their mission before they were arrested and their brethren throughout Italy betrayed into the hands of the Inquisition we are not in a position to determine. Some time before October 14, 1561, when he had his first hearing before the Inquisition, Gherlandi was seized in the Venetian jurisdiction and the documents referred to were used by the inquisitors for his own condemnation as well as that of those whose names appeared on his lists. The Counter-Reformation was now in full progress. The clues furnished by the document were utilized to the utmost; large numbers were seized and subjected to torture with a view of ascertaining the names and whereabouts of as many of their brethren as possible.

Gherlandi's admirable account of his life and of the principles and practices of the Moravian Anti-pedobaptists, with whom he was in complete and loving accord, has already been referred to.

Another Italian convert to Moravian orthodoxy claims our attention. Francesca della Saga, of Rovigo, born in 1532, while a student in the University of Padua was brought by a severe illness and the earnest words of an artisan to reflect upon his spiritual condition. Late in the fifties we find him among the Moravians, working at the tailor's trade and occupying a position of considerable influence. He made several journeys to Italy to look after his inheritance and to promote the welfare of his Italian brethren.

In 1562 we find him engaged in an earnest effort on behalf of his fellow-countrymen, in company with Antonio Rizzetto of Vicenza. Their efforts were being crowned with success when they were betrayed by a false brother and, just as they were setting sail from Capo d'Istria on their way to Moravia with a large company of coreligionists, were seized by the authorities. Among the prisoners was the physician Nicolao Bucella. Most of the members of the party came from a church that seems never to have affiliated with the radical Anti-trinitarian element.

Gherlandi was still in prison and, witnessing to the last most heroically to the truth, was sentenced to death by drowning in October, 1562. Saga's trial occurred at about the same time. His confession of faith, which the authorities allowed him to make in writing and which has been preserved, is in harmony with the highest and purest type of Anti-pedobaptist teaching. His letters to the brethren in Moravia and to the members of his own family, who had no sympathy with his religious views and who held completely aloof from him, reveal to us an extraordinarily pure and noble Christian character. After more than two years of imprisonment both Saga and Rizzetto were executed by drowning in 1565. We hear little or nothing henceforth of Anti-pedobaptists in Italy. It is probable that most of those who did not renounce their faith made their way to Moravia and Poland.

Humanism found its way early to Poland and in point of intelligence and tolerance the Polish nobles were at the beginning of the Reformation in advance of the same class in most other lands. A lively intercourse was maintained between Italy and Poland, and many free-thinking Italians found refuge and employment in the retinues of Polish nobles. Poland had been strongly influenced by the Hussite movement of the fifteenth century, for after the defeat of the Hussites in Bohemia and Moravia many had emigrated to this land of freedom. Anti-pedobaptists from Germany and Moravia had gone thither in considerable numbers during the fourth and fifth decades of the century. Lutherans and Reformed had each a considerable constituency. As no one party possessed overmastering strength toleration became a necessity even to those that were not tolerant on principle. Lutherans, Reformed, Bohemian Brethren, Anti-pedobaptists, and anti-trinitarians existed side by side, each having their special favorers among the nobility.

Lælius Socinus, who in his own person and through his less-learned but more aggressive nephew, Faustus Socinus, gave a great impulse to the anti-trinitarian movement in Poland that came to bear his family name, had been closely associated with Camillo Renato, the Italian Anti-pedobaptist. Lælius himself was suspected as early as 1555 of holding to Anti-pedobaptist views.[1]

Peter Gonesius, a Pole, after studying at Wittenberg and in Switzerland, where he came under the influence of the anti-trinitarian teachings of Servetus and of the Italian free-thinkers, returned to Poland and began zealously to propagate his views about 1555. He denounced the Nicene and Athanasian Creeds as human fictions, denied the consubstantiality of the Son with the Father, and repudiated the Lutheran doctrine of the communication of idioms, in accordance with which by virtue of union with the divine the human nature of Christ has been exalted so as to possess in their fullness all divine attributes.

In 1558 he presented to the Reformed synod a treatise against infant baptism, which he sought to prove neither scriptural, ancient, Christian, nor reasonable.[2] He was defended by Jerome Pieskarski and soon found many favorers among the nobles. His Anti-pedobaptist views were vigorously propagated by Martin Czechowitz; his anti-trinitarian views found a warm advocate in the brilliant but not over-scrupulous Italian physician, George Biandrata. Simler connected the growth of Anti-pedobaptist sentiments in Poland as well as of dissension in general with the advent of Bernardo Ochino, the great Capuchin preacher, who after his expulsion from Zürich came to Poland in his old age in 1564. It is by no means certain however that Ochino denied infant baptism.[3]

---

[1] See letter of Julius Mediolanus, minister at Peschlav, to Bullinger (November 4, 1555), printed in the "Museum Helveticum," Part XIV., p. 289. Julius warns Bullinger against Lælius, who had recently persuaded the Zürich pastor of his doctrinal soundness. "We have had sufficient experience of the fact that Servetians and Anabaptists do not easily put aside what they have once imbibed."

[2] See on Gonesius, Foch, "Der Socinianismus," Vol. I., p. 143, seq.

[3] Simler's charge against Ochino is quoted in "Museum Helveticum," Part XIV., p. 231, seq.

One of the most noted of the early Anti-pedobaptist and anti-trinitarian leaders of Poland was Gregorius Paulus, pastor at Cracow. John a Lasco represents him as thundering against God's essence and trinity, as proceeding to such further madness as to deny "that infants ought to be admitted to baptism as the fountain of life and the door of the church," and as insisting that those who had received baptism in infancy ought to "receive baptism anew." After he has impressed upon his people the doctrine that baptism should be given not to crying babes but to believing adults, "he leads them to the river and immerses them." He claimed that these things were "the first rudiments of the ancient religion about to be restored," and maintained that he was acting under the guidance of the Holy Spirit. An associate of his, Goncozius by name, had written against the use of the sword in the spirit of the old-evangelical sects and of the Anti-pedobaptists in general.

John a Lasco distinguishes between the religious condition of greater Poland, which borders on Silesia and Pomerania, where the "Waldensian Brethren" (Bohemian Brethren) are carefully guarding against the encroachments of heresy, and lesser Poland, whose religious condition owing to the prevalence of anti-trinitarianism and Anti-pedobaptism was utterly deplorable.[1]

By 1574 the anti-trinitarian Anti-pedobaptists had become a vigorous and aggressive party in Poland and in Siebenbürgen, closely connected with Poland and subject to the same influences. In 1574 a catechism was set forth in which baptism is restricted to adults and is defined as " the immersion in water and the emersion of a person who believes the gospel and repents, in the name of the Father, Son, and Holy Spirit, or in the name of Christ only, whereby he publicly professes that by the

---
[1] Letter to Beza, May 30, 1566, in "Museum Helveticum," Part XIV., p. 282, *seq.*

grace of God the Father, in the blood of Christ, through the operation of the Holy Spirit, he is washed of all his sins, in order that being inserted into the body of Christ he may mortify the old Adam, and be transformed into that heavenly Adam, with the assurance that after the resurrection he will attain to eternal life."[1] The utmost stress is laid upon the exercise of church discipline as a means to the maintenance of the purity of the church.

These anti-trinitarian Anti-pedobaptists were far removed from the religious indifferentism that has characterized much of the later Socinianism. They yielded to none in their zeal for the authority of Scripture and in their belief that in Christ and in him alone is salvation. Their view of the person of Christ, while wholly inadequate from our point of view, was coupled with the profoundest reverence for Christ and the completest trust in him. In rejecting the Nicene and Athanasian symbols they misinterpreted the teachings of the New Testament itself with respect to the God-Man. Directing their attention chiefly to those passages in the New Testament that seem to imply subordination they lost sight of, or misunderstood, those passages that identify the Son with the Father and imply his coequality and consubstantiality.

The "Racovian Catechism" was first issued in 1605,[2] when anti-trinitarian Anti-pedobaptism had become the controlling type of Protestantism in Poland, when it had an efficient and largely attended college and a well-equipped publishing house at Racov, and when it enjoyed the support of some of the most powerful of the nobles. It had been prepared in part by Faustus Socinus; but in many points it takes far more evangelical ground than

[1] See Foch, "Der Socinianismus," p. 152, seq., and Rees' historical introduction to his edition of the "Racovian Catechism," p. lxxi., seq. The catechism of 1574 is variously ascribed to George Schomann and to Gregorius Paulus.
[2] Composed about 1590.

this great leader had taken in his published writings. The inspiration and authority of the Scriptures are vindicated in the most orthodox way.

"The Lord Jesus", is said to have "been conceived of the Holy Spirit and born of a virgin, without the intervention of any human being." He is spoken of as "from his earliest origin the only begotten Son of God." He is said to have "been sent by the Father, with supreme authority, on an embassy to mankind." "He was raised from the dead by God, and thus as it were begotten a second time. . . . By this event he became like God immortal." It is recognized that he possesses "dominion and supreme authority over all things." He is said to have been "not merely the only begotten Son of God, on account of the divine power and authority which he displayed even while he was yet mortal; much more may he be so denominated now, that he has received all power in heaven and earth, and that all things, God himself alone excepted, have been put under his feet."

Yet his coeternity and consubstantiality with the Father are explicitly denied.

Baptism is defined to be,

A rite of initiation whereby men, after admitting his doctrine and embracing faith in him, are bound to Christ and planted among his disciples, or in his church; renouncing the world, with its manners and errors, and professing that they have for their sole leader and master in religion, and in the whole of their lives and conversations, the Father, the Son, and the Holy Spirit, who spoke by the apostles: declaring, and as it were representing by their very ablution, immersion, and emersion, that they design to rid themselves of the pollution of their sins, to bury themselves with Christ, and therefore to die with him, and rise again to newness of life; binding themselves down, in order than they may do this in reality; and at the same time, after making this profession and laying themselves under this obligation, receiving the symbol and the sign of the remission of their sins, and so far receiving the remission itself.

As regards the subjects of baptism it is said:

It does not pertain to infants, since we have in the Scriptures no command for, nor any example of, infant baptism, nor are they as yet capable, as the thing itself shows, of the faith in Christ, which ought to precede this rite, and which men profess by this rite. In answer to the question: "What then is to be thought of those who baptize infants?" it is replied: "You cannot correctly say that they baptize infants. For they do not baptize them—since this cannot be done without the immersion and ablution of the whole body in water; whereas they only lightly sprinkle their heads—this rite being not only erroneously applied to infants but also through this mistake, evidently changed."

It should be said that Faustus Socinus did not see eye to eye with the majority of the Polish anti-trinitarians with respect to baptism. He denied that our Lord intended to enjoin the perpetual observance of this rite. It was intended only for those to whom the Commission was originally given. Refusing to receive baptism as a believer he was for many years excluded from the fellowship of the Polish churches that historically bear his name.

The Polish anti-trinitarian Anti-pedobaptist movement is of great importance in Baptist history. From this party the English General Baptists derived much of their impulse, by it they have been greatly influenced, and between it and them there has always been a close affinity; from it, through the Rhynsburgers, or Collegiants, of Holland, the Particular Baptists of England seem to have derived their immersion (1641), having already come to the conviction that immersion and immersion only is New Testament baptism.

Literature: Works of Socinus, Servetus, Czechowitz, Ottius, Wissowaty, Benrath, Trechsel, Foch, Sandius, Bock, Tollin, Gordon, and the Racovian Catechism, as in the Bibliography.

CHAPTER XXVI

ENGLAND (to 1558)

EVANGELICAL Christianity, in the form of Lollardism, persisted in England and Scotland with considerable vigor until after the inauguration of the Protestant Revolution. Inquisitorial processes occurred from time to time from the time of Wycliffe onward.

In a Lollard book, found in circulation, along with others, in 1415, in the city of London, the pope is designated "that wicked Antichrist," who "hath sowed among the laws of Christ his popish and corrupt decrees"; the archbishops and bishops are said to be "seats of the beast Antichrist, when he sitteth in them, and reigneth above other people in the deep caves of errors and heresies." The bishop's license to preach is "the true character of the beast . . . and therefore simple and faithful priests may preach when they will, against the prohibition of that Antichrist, and without license." "The court of Rome is the chief head of Antichrist, and the bishops be the body; and the new sects [monastic orders, etc.] brought in not by Christ, but damnably by the pope, be the venomous and pestiferous tail of Antichrist."

Regenerate church-membership is insisted upon. Ornamental church buildings are condemned. "The followers of the humility of Jesus Christ ought to worship their Lord God humbly, in mean and simple houses." "The often singing in the church is not founded on the Scripture, and therefore it is not lawful for priests to occupy themselves with singing in the church, but with the study of the law of Christ, and preaching his word."

The memorial view of the Supper is strongly set forth in opposition to transubstantiation. Indulgences, priestly intercessions, pilgrimages, the veneration of images, and almsgiving as a meritorious work apart from the worthiness or the need of the object, are earnestly repudiated.

The owner of this and other English evangelical books brought to light at this time was John Claydon, a prosperous London currier, who was burned at Smithfield for his fidelity to principle. Many other heresy trials occurred at about this time. Lord Cobham, one of the noblest of martyrs, died at the stake in 1418. Between 1428 and 1431 one hundred and twenty men and women in different parts of England were arraigned for Lollardism, and many remained faithful even unto death.

Among the heresies brought to light in the various inquisitorial processes besides those already given, were the denial of the special sanctity of any days except Sunday; rejection of ecclesiastical fasts; insistence that prayer is to be offered to God alone, with the rejection of Mariolatry and the veneration of saints, images, relics, holy places, etc.; denial of the efficacy of offerings and intercessions for the dead; denial of the doctrine of purgatory; repudiation of ordinances administered by corrupt priests; rejection of sacerdotal celibacy and strong conviction as to its ruinous effects; repudiation of monastic vows; vigorous opposition to auricular confession; insistence on the utmost simplicity in living, luxury being regarded as contrary to the spirit of the gospel; and in general the acceptance of apostolic precept and example as the norm of faith and life. In all this the Lollards were at one with the best evangelical life of the Continent, and they seem to have been almost wholly free from the extravagancies that marred the teachings of some of the continental parties.

The Lollards were in agreement with the Waldenses

and related parties in their rejection of oaths, warfare, and capital punishment, though they seem to have placed less emphasis upon this set of views than their continental brethren. A Lollard party arraigned in 1428 was charged with maintaining "that it is not lawful to swear in private cases." This would seem to imply the lawfulness of judicial oaths. But in another trial of the same year a Lollard woman is charged with exhorting vehemently against any sort of oath as venomous to the soul.[1] As early as 1395 a large body of Lollards declared, in a memorial to Parliament:[2] "Manslaughter by war or pretended law of justice for any temporal cause, without a spiritual revelation, is expressly contrary to the New Testament, which is a law of grace and full of mercy."

As regards the ordinances they repudiated with the utmost decision the Roman Catholic view of the magical efficacy of priestly consecration, insisted that the Supper is a memorial rite, denied the necessity of baptism to salvation, and in general closely approached the Baptist position. Yet diligent research has failed to discover any case of Anti-pedobaptism among the English evangelicals before the incoming of Anti-pedobaptists from the Continent (1530 onward). While it would be rash to assert that these views, so common on the Continent during the later Middle Ages, had no representatives in England at that time, documentary materials thus far available by no means warrant a contrary assertion.

The fact is that the extant materials for the history of English evangelical life during the mediæval and early Reformation times are meagre and unsatisfactory. This is no doubt largely due to the happy circumstance that the Inquisition proper was never established in England, and that the systematic and persistent efforts of skilled detectives, examiners, and recorders, to which we are

---
[1] Foxe, Vol. III., p. 549.   [2] Lechler's "Wycliffe," p. 448.

largely indebted for the fullness of our information about the Waldenses and related bodies, were wanting here. We have reason to suspect that there was in England during the later Middle Ages vastly more of evangelical life than came into publicity; we may regard it as probable that some at least of those who had so firm a grasp of apostolic Christianity were not content with denying the magical efficacy of water baptism and asserting that unbaptized infants are saved, but went on to insist upon believers' baptism. Yet we must beware of asserting that such was the case.

To show that at the beginning of the Protestant Revolution Lollardism had lost nothing in clearness of view, strength of conviction, and aggressive opposition to the hierarchy, a Scotch and an English case may be cited. In 1494 the "Lollards of Kyle," to the number of thirty, were arraigned before the archbishop of Glasgow.[1] The list includes such names as Campbell, Shaw, Chalmers, Cunningham, and Reid. The charges against them, the correctness of which we have no reason to question, embraced nearly all of the views attributed to the earlier Lollards expressed with Scotch vigor. It is interesting to note their close adherence to old-evangelical traditions with respect to oaths, magistracy, warfare, etc.: "It is not lawful to fight or to defend the faith"; "Christ at his coming has taken away power from kings to judge" [in religious matters, was no doubt meant]; "In no case is it lawful to swear." Other striking statements are: "The pope is not the successor of Peter, but where he [Christ] said, Get thee behind me, Satan"; "The pope is the head of the church of Antichrist"; "The pope and his ministers are murderers"; "Every faithful man or woman is a priest"; "True Christians receive the body of Jesus Christ every day."

---

[1] Knox, "Reformation," Vol. I., p. 7, seq.

As it is not to be supposed that the Lollards of Kyle were without fellow-believers in various parts of Scotland, a knowledge of their sturdiness and aggressiveness helps us not a little to understand the rapidity with which a little later popery gave place to a thorough-going type of Protestantism.

From 1510 to 1527 forty Lollards were arraigned by the Bishop of London alone. Among the most noted of these was Richard Hun (1514), a man of intelligence and substance. He is charged with having "read, taught, preached, published, and obstinately defended, that bishops and priests be the scribes and Pharisees that did crucify Christ," that "bishops and priests be teachers and preachers, but no doers, neither fulfillers of the law of God; but catching, ravening, and all things taking, and nothing ministering, neither giving"; with "keeping divers English books prohibited and damned by law, as the Apocalypse in English, Epistles and Gospels in English, Wycliffe's damnable works," etc.; with defending "the translation of the Bible and the holy Scripture into the English tongue, which is prohibited by the laws of our mother, holy church"; with saying that "kings and lords, called Christian in name and heathen in conditions, defile the sanctuary of God, bringing clerks full of covetousness, heresy, and malice, to stop God's law, that it cannot be known, kept, and freely preached"; with damning "the University of Oxford, with all degrees and faculties in it . . . saying that they hinder the true way to come to the knowledge of the laws of God and Holy Scripture"; and with saying that "the very body of the Lord is not contained in the sacrament of the altar, but that men receiving it shall thereby keep in mind that Christ's flesh was wounded and crucified for us."[1]

---

[1] Foxe, Vol. IV., pp. 183-6.

It is natural to suppose that many of those who came forward as aggressive evangelicals under Henry VIII. had been under the influence of this older evangelical party. We should not expect here, any more than on the Continent, evidence of the passing over of individuals from the older to the newer forms of evangelicalism; but the speedy disappearance of the older form after the introduction of the newer is sufficient proof of the fact.

We are safe in saying that the deeply rooted principles of Lollardism lay at the basis of the Puritanism and the Independency of the later time, and along with other circumstances help us to account for the widespread acceptance of radical types of evangelicalism under Elizabeth and the Stuarts. The persistent influence of the older Lollardism could hardly have failed to co-operate to a greater or less extent with the foreign Anti-pedobaptist teaching that appeared in England about 1530 and was from this time onward always active.

The early persecutions in the Spanish Netherlands under Charles V. and the encouragement given to manufacturing enterprise by Henry VIII. caused a large immigration of Dutch artisans to England (1528 onward). By 1560 there were in England about ten thousand Dutch, and two years later the number had increased threefold. The Duke of Alva's persecutions (1568-73) raised the number to at least fifty thousand. There were many thousands of Dutch in London at this time. A majority of the population of the manufacturing city of Norwich in 1587 were Dutch and Walloons. Dover, Romney, Sandwich, Canterbury, Colchester, Hastings, and Hythe, had each a large Dutch population.[1] The great majority of these were Calvinists, who were tolerated by the government and had their own churches and pastors; but a considerable proportion were certainly

---

[1] Green, "History of the English People," Book VI., Chap. V.

Anti-pedobaptists, at first of the Hofmannite and later of the Mennonite type. The English, up to the time of the Dutch immigration, knew little of manufacturing, and the incoming of this large artisan population was an important source of wealth to the country.

A large proportion of the business men of Antwerp settled in London after the fall of their city (1576). The Dutch were at this time among the most highly educated people in the world. Ideas of civil and religious liberty had reached a degree of maturity in the Netherlands unknown elsewhere. It would be difficult to overestimate the extent of the wholesome influence exerted by the large body of intelligent Dutch refugees upon the political and religious thought of England. Dutch influence reached England in other ways as well. Both before and during the Spanish wars many Englishmen resided for longer or shorter periods in the Netherlands and there became imbued with Dutch ideas.

The first public notice of the presence of foreign Anti-pedobaptists in England is contained in a royal proclamation of 1534:

> Forasmuch as divers and sundry strangers of the sect and false opinion of the Anabaptists and Sacramentaries (Zwinglians), being lately come into this realm, where they lurk secretly in divers corners and places, minding craftily and subtilly to provoke and stir the king's loving subjects to their errors and opinions, whereof part of them, by the great travail and diligence of the king's highness and his council, be apprehended and taken, the king's most royal majesty declareth . . . that he abhorreth and detesteth the same sects and their wicked and abominable errors and opinions, and intendeth to proceed against such of them as be already apprehended.

All who had not been found were commanded to depart the realm within eight or ten days.[1]

This was followed by another proclamation, in which

---

[1] Wilkins, "Conc.," Vol. III., p. 777.

the king complains that many strangers who, condemning the holy sacrament that they had received in infancy, had presumptuously rebaptized themselves, had entered the realm, and were spreading everywhere their pestilent heresies "against God and his Holy Scriptures to the great unquietness of Christendom and perdition of innumerable Christian souls." Many have been convicted "and have and shall for the same suffer the pains of death." All such heretics are ordered to leave the realm in twelve days " on pain to suffer death " in case they be apprehended after the prescribed date.

It is evident that Anti-pedobaptists were at this time somewhat numerous and very aggressive in England.

There is no sufficient reason for regarding James Bainham, a barrister, who suffered martyrdom for his radical evangelical views in 1534 as an Anti-Pedobaptist. Like the Lollards and the Zwinglians he denied with great emphasis the necessity and the magical efficacy of water baptism and insisted upon repentance and faith as conditions of salvation.

Neither are we to regard the Lollard books that were condemned about this time, along with Tyndale's New Testament, as distinctively Anti-pedobaptist. The radical evangelicalism of Tyndale and Fryth had much in common with English Lollardism and with the old-evangelical position in general, as well as with the position of the early Anti-pedobaptists of the continent; but the same may be said with reference to many of the earlier writings of Luther, Zwingli, Œcolampadius, etc. A writer is not necessarily a Baptist for saying : " The water of the font has no more virtue in it than the water of the river ; the baptism lies not in hallowed water, or in any outward thing, but in the faith only ; "[1] or, " The water of baptism is nothing but a sign that we must be under the

---

[1] "The Sum of Scripture," fol. 6.

standard of the cross;"[1] or, "Men of war are not allowed by the gospel; the gospel knows peace and not war. . . Some texts of the canon suffer war, but the teaching of Christ forbids war;"[2] or, "The gospel makes all true Christian men servants to all the world";[3] or, "Christian men, among themselves, have nought to do with the sword, nor with the law, for that is to them neither needful nor profitable";[4] or, "A true Christian man never plaineth to the judge of the injury that is done unto him";[5] or, "The worst Turk living has as much right to my goods at his need as my own household or myself";[6] or, "Every man is lord of another man's goods. I am bound to love the Turk with the very bottom of my heart"; or, "Whosoever first ordained universities . . . was a star that fell from heaven to earth; there are brought in moral virtues for faith and opinions for truth. . . The universities are the confused cloud and open gate of hell, and this cloak of all other is most noisome, and does most hurt and damage."[7] These quotations represent a strongly mystical type of old-evangelical teaching and the authors of the books cited may have been Anti-pedobaptist, but of this we have no evidence.[8]

In 1535 we have a definite account of the arrest, trial, and burning of some Dutch Anti-pedobaptists. According to a contemporary chronicler:[9]

The five and twentieth day of May (1535) were in St. Paul's Church, London, examined nineteen men and six women, born in Holland, whose opinions were—first, that in Christ is not two na-

---

[1] "The Sum of Scripture," fol. 12. [2] Ibid, fol. 116 and 118. [3] Ibid, fol. 110.
[4] Ibid, fol. 110. [5] Ibid, fol. 113. [6] "Wicked Mammon."
[7] "The Revelation of Antichrist," fol. 31, 32, 33.
[8] These books seem to have been written or edited by Tyndale. The quotations are given in the garbled form in which they were brought forward by the inquisitors. Foxe gives the passages in full along with these abstracts ("Actes and Monuments," V., 570, *seq.*)
[9] Stow, p. 571.

tures, God and man; secondly, that Christ took neither flesh nor blood of the Virgin Mary; thirdly, that children born of infidels may be saved; fourthly, that baptism of children is of none effect; fifthly, that the sacrament of Christ's body is but bread only; sixthly, that he who after baptism sinneth wittingly, sinneth deadly, and cannot be saved. Fourteen of them were condemned, a man and woman were burnt at Smithfield. The remaining twelve were scattered among the towns there to be burnt.

These can have been no other than disciples of Melchior Hofmann, some of whose characteristic views, as on the incarnation, are here somewhat inaccurately set forth.

In 1538 Philip of Hesse wrote to Henry VIII., whose alliance with the Protestant princes of Germany was at that time being earnestly sought, informing him that an Anabaptist named Peter Tasch had recently been arrested, on whose person was found correspondence with brethren in England. From the correspondence it appeared that one of the latter had recently published a book on the incarnation which it was hoped would aid much in disseminating true doctrine. Tasch himself was planning to join his brethren in England. Philip, who was noted for his tolerant disposition, was too anxious to gain the good will of Henry to withhold this interesting bit of information. He even went so far as to represent the sectaries in the most unfavorable light. Henry did not require much stimulus in the direction of intolerance. On October 1 he ordered Cranmer and a number of his clerical colleagues to make a rigorous search for Anabaptists, their books and their correspondence. Such as should recant were to be liberated; such as should prove obstinate were to be burned along with their writings.[1] On November 16 the king issued a fresh proclamation against the importation or printing of unlicensed books and ordering the burning of the books of

---
[1] Wilkins' "Conc.," Vol. III., pp. 836-7.

Anabaptists and Sacramentaries. A few days later a number of arrests were made and two, a man and a woman, were burned at Smithfield.

In December the king issued a letter to the justices of the peace throughout England urging the utmost rigor against Anabaptists. Many fled to Holland. On January 5 thirty-one of them were beheaded at Delft, where a few months before twenty-seven of their brethren had died for their faith.

Violent measures having proved ineffective, it occurred to the king to issue a proclamation of grace to such as had been misled by "certain Anabaptists and Sacramentaries, coming out of outward parts into this realm" through "divers and many perverse and crafty means," and who "now be sorry for their offenses and minding fully to return again to the Catholic Church." "The king's highness like a most loving parent much moved with pity, tendering the winning of them again to Christ's flock, and much lamenting also their simplicity, so by devilish craft circumscribed . . . of his inestimable goodness, pity, and clemency, is content to remit, pardon, and forgive . . . all and singular such persons," etc. Yet if any in future "fall to any such detestable and damnable opinions," the laws will be mercilessly enforced against them.

This proclamation affords evidence of the most convincing kind of the numbers and aggressiveness of Anti-pedobaptism in England at this time and of the fact that these teachings were spreading among the native population.

In 1540 the king issued a general pardon to those who had religiously offended, but made a special exception against such as maintained that "infants ought not to be baptized," that "it is not lawful for a Christian man to bear office or rule in the commonwealth," that "every manner of death, with the time and hour thereof, is so certainly prescribed, appointed, and determined to every man by God, that neither any prince by his word can alter it, nor any man by his willfulness prevent or change it." This last specification does not strike one as characteristic of the Anti-pedobaptist teaching of the time, which made much of free-will.

There is no adequate reason for regarding Anne Askew, a gentlewoman of Lincolnshire, who was burned after suffering cruel tortures in 1546 because of her zeal against transubstantiation, as a Baptist, or even as an Anti-pedobaptist. Her intense antipathy to popish ceremonialism would seem to connect her with the earlier Lollardism; but Calvinism had become fully developed by this time and her zeal may have been of the Calvinistic type. Her profound knowledge of the Scriptures and her mastery of the arts of polemics would seem to show that she not only possessed intellectual powers of a very high order but that she had enjoyed educational advantages beyond what was usual for women at that time. She was far more than a match for the bishops in argument; but her repartees were sharper by far than good judgment would have dictated. There is no hint in contemporary literature that she held to any of the distinctive views of the hated Anti-pedobaptists.

Edward VI., son of Henry VIII. and Jane Seymour, ascended the throne when only ten years of age. He had been brought up under Protestant influence and his advisers were favorable to the complete abolition of Roman Catholicism. Cranmer had by this time come to be a thorough-going Protestant of the Melancthon type, and his influence as primate and religious director of the young king was paramount. A number of leading Protestant theologians of the Continent were prevailed upon to take up their abode in England and to assist in the work of shaping the polity of the English church. Among the most noted of these were Bullinger, Zwingli's successor at Zürich; Peter Martyr, a learned Italian, who had for years been associated with the Swiss Protestants; Martin Bucer, the great Strasburg theologian, who had labored zealously for the conciliation of Lutheranism and Zwinglianism and whose position was essentially Melancthonian; John a Lasco, an eminent Polish theologian of noble birth, who also represented a moderate type of Protestant theology; and Bernardo Ochino who, as Vicar-General of the Capuchins, had attained to a reputation as a pulpit orator almost equal to that of Savonarola in the earlier time, and having been converted to Protestantism in 1542, had since lived as an exile in Geneva and elsewhere.

It might have been expected that Cranmer's liberal programme would embrace toleration for evangelicals of a more radical type; but these liberal theologians were for the most part deeply prejudiced against the Anti-pedobaptists, with whose exclusive and uncompromising adherence to their principles they had had unpleasant experience. Bullinger had taken a foremost part in their exclusion from Switzerland and was to write voluminously against them. Of Bucer's increasing dislike for them we have had abundant evidence. Cranmer's father-in-law, Osiander of Nürnberg, was one of the earliest and most uncompromising opponents of Anti-pedobaptism. It was the conviction of all the leaders that the toleration of Anabaptists would imperil every social, religious, and civil institution, and that they must be excluded at whatever cost.

In 1547 an Anti-pedobaptist named Robert Cooke became a member of the court of Edward VI. as keeper of the royal wine cellar. He had spent considerable time in Switzerland, and was learned and accomplished. Besides opposing the baptism of infants, he is said to have held to Pelagian views on original sin and related doctrines. Skillful and aggressive in debate, he gave vast trouble to such court preachers as Coverdale, Turner, Parkhurst, and Jewel.

Turner was incited by Cooke's polemics to write "A Preservative, or Triacle, against the Poison of Pelagius lately renewed and stirred up again by the furious Sect of the Anabaptists" (1551). He quotes the opinions of his opponents (no doubt having Cooke's arguments in mind) on original sin and infant baptism in their relations to each other:

> By baptism alone is no salvation, but by baptism and preaching; and certain it is that God is able to save his chosen church without these means. But this is his ordinary way to save and damn the whole world, namely, by offering remission of sins and baptism to all the world, that thereby the believers may be absolved from all conscience of sin, and the disobedient and unbelievers bound still either to amend or to be damned.

Again:

> The remission of sins is offered to all, but all receive it not; the church sanctified by faith in the blood of Christ only receiveth, and unto them only baptism belongeth. Therefore none ought to receive it but such as have not only heard the good promises of God, but have also thereby received a singular consolation in their hearts, through remission of sin, which they by faith have received. For if any receive baptism without this persuasion, it profits them nothing.

Again:

> All the world hath sinned and is defiled in Adam. How, now, will water scour away the filth of this corruption? No; it is a wound received in the soul, and is washed away but with the only faith in the blood of Christ.

The Pelagianism here set forth is certainly of a very mild type, and the theory of baptism is quite in accord with the Baptist position.

Cooke was induced so far to withdraw his offensive opinions as to obviate the necessity of abandoning his position in the court. As late as 1573 we find him acting as one of the gentlemen of the queen's chapel.

In 1547 Ridley and Latimer were appointed to deal with certain Anti-pedobaptists in Kent, where many Dutch had settled.

After the rebellion of 1549 Parliament passed an act of grace and general pardon; but those were expressly excepted who held: "That infants were not to be baptized; and if they were baptized, that they ought to be rebaptized when they came to lawful age; that it was not lawful for a Christian man to bear office or rule in the commonwealth; that no men's laws ought to be obeyed; that it was not lawful for a Christian man to take an oath before any judge; that Christ took not his substance of our blessed Lady; that sinners after baptism could not be restored by repentance; that all things be or ought to be common, and nothing several."[1]

Early in 1549 an ecclesiastical commission was appointed, consisting of Archbishop Cranmer, Bishop Ridley, and a number of other prominent prelates and statesmen, with full powers to search out and punish Anabaptist and Arian heresy. At about this time a translation of a violent polemic against the Anabaptists, ascribed to Calvin, was published in England. The effect of it could only be to sharpen the zeal of churchmen and statesmen against the sect already sufficiently abhorred.

There is some reason for suspecting that Joan Boucher, of Kent, who suffered martyrdom in 1550 for persistently denying that our Lord derived his flesh from Mary, was an Anti-pedobaptist. This Hofmannite view seems to have been almost universally maintained by Dutch-Eng-

---
[1] Strype, "Mem." II. 1, 291.

lish Anti-pedobaptists and is not often encountered outside of this circle. She devoted herself assiduously to the secret circulation of Tyndale's New Testament and other religious books of an evangelical character. She is said to have enjoyed the friendship of Anne Askew and she had much in common with that heroic woman. Though illiterate, she was well versed in Scripture and was able to hold her own in argument with the learned prelates of the day. Like Anne Askew she gave needless offense by the harshness of her denunciations and the sharpness of her repartees.

Her manner of putting the Hofmannite doctrine of the incarnation is interesting:

I deny not Christ is Mary's seed, or the woman's seed; nor do I deny him to be a man. But Mary had two seeds—one seed of her faith, and another seed of her flesh and in her body. There is a natural and a corporeal seed, and there is a spiritual and an heavenly seed. . . And Christ is her seed; but he is become man of the seed of her faith and belief—of spiritual seed, not of natural seed; for her seed was sinful, as the seed and flesh of others.

Every effort was made by Ridley and others to persuade her to purchase her life by denying her faith on this point; but she was as firm as a rock. "It was not long ago," she said, "since you burnt Anne Askew for a piece of bread, yet came yourself to believe the doctrine for which you have burnt her; and now you will burn me for a piece of flesh, and in the end you will believe this also."

Little reliance can be placed on the tradition of the little Baptist church at Eythorne in Kent that its history as a Baptist church antedates the martyrdom of Joan Boucher and that she was a member. Of course it is possible that this and some other of the English Baptist churches that claim a very early date grew out of Dutch-English Anti-pedobaptist congregations of the sixteenth century, or out of still older Lollard congregations; but the evidence in no case seems complete. A critical investigation of the claims of these churches is a desideratum.

Kent continued to give much anxiety to the authorities on account of the continuance there of Anti-pedobaptist activity. The Bishop of Winchester (Gardiner) had to be taken severely to task on account of his lukewarmness in extirpating heresy. John Knox was highly recommended for the bishopric of Rochester "because he would be a great confounder of the Anabaptists lately springing up in Kent." Congregations, Anabaptist or Pelagian, or both, were discovered about this time in Essex and Kent. Many of their members were arrested and tried, but chief stress was laid on their free-will teaching and rejection of the doctrine of original sin.

Under Queen Mary (1553-8) Roman Catholicism was re-established and all forms of evangelical life were under the ban. Cranmer, Ridley, and Latimer, who had been so zealous for the burning of Anabaptists, themselves suffered at the stake. The government was so much occupied with larger game that the obscure Anti-pedobaptists were no doubt to some extent overlooked. It may be that they suffered less under "bloody Mary" than under the gentle, evangelical Edward.

Literature: Underhill, "Introduction to the Hanserd Knollys Soc. Pub."; Crosby, "Hist. of the Eng. Baptists," Vol. I.; Ivimey, "Hist. of the Eng. Baptists," Vol. I.; Evans, "Early Eng. Baptists," Vol. I.; Goadby, "By-Paths of Bapt. Hist."; Strype (various works); Foxe, "Actes and Monuments"; Fuller, "Ch. Hist."; Collier, "Eccl. Hist."; D'Anvers, "Treatise on Baptism"; Burnet, "Hist. of the Ref."; Knox, works, ed. Laing; Tyndale, works; Van Braght, "Blœdig Toneel"; Wilkins, "Concilia Mag. Br."; Walker, "Creeds and Platforms" and "Hist. of the Congreg. Ch. in the U. S."; Campbell, "The Puritans"; Hanbury, "Hist. Memorials"; and Dexter, "The Congregationalism of the Last Three Hundred Years."

CHAPTER XXVII
ENGLAND (1558-1602)

AT the beginning of her glorious reign, Elizabeth determined on political and other grounds to establish a Protestant form of religion; but the limits of toleration were sharply defined and an act of uniformity rigorously enforced. The great majority of the educated and influential churchmen who served Elizabeth had been trained, during the era of Mary, in the most rigorous form of Protestantism and would have preferred a Presbyterian establishment; but the will of the queen was supreme and great theologians were obliged to swallow their convictions as to what was best and content themselves with what was practicable. The idea of toleration was as foreign to the Calvinistic divines as to the Tudor queen. Only a few years before, the great Calvin had compassed and gloried in the burning of Servetus, and Theodore Beza, his colleague and successor, had recently written an atrocious work in favor of the punishment of heretics by the civil magistracy.

In 1560 John Knox, the great Scottish reformer, who had become noted during his English ministry under Edward VI. for his zeal against Anabaptists, published "An Answer to a Great Number of Blasphemous Cavillations Written by an Anabaptist, an Adversary to God's Eternal Predestination." The author of the book attacked was a former friend of Knox.

The spirit of the Anti-pedobaptist work may be judged from the following extracts:

> Your chief Apollos be persecutors, on whom the blood of Servetus crieth a vengeance, so doth the blood of others more whom I could

name. But forasmuch as God has already partly avenged their blood [referring, no doubt, to the burning of Cranmer, Ridley, etc., who had themselves been arch-persecutors], and served some of their persecutors with the same measure wherewith they measured to others, I will make no mention of them at this time. And to declare their wickedness not to have proceeded of ignorance and human infirmity, but of endured malice, they have for a perpetual memory of their cruelty, set forth books, affirming it to be lawful to persecute and put to death such as dissent from others in controversies of religion, whom they call blasphemers of God. Notwithstanding, afore they came to authority, they were of another judgment, and did both say and write, that no man ought to be persecuted for his conscience' sake; but now they are not only become persecutors, but also they have given, as far as lieth in them, the sword into the hand of bloody tyrants. Be these, I pray you, the sheep whom Christ sent forth in the midst of wolves? Can the sheep persecute the wolf? Doth Abel kill Cain? Doth David, though he might, kill Saul? Shortly, doth he which is born of the Spirit kill him which is born after the flesh? Mark, how ye be fallen into most abominable tyranny, and yet ye see it not. Thus I am constrained of conscience to write. That if it shall please God to awake you out of your dream, that ye may perceive how one error hath drowned you in more error, and hath brought you to a sleeping security, that when ye walk, even after the lusts, thirsting after blood, and persecuting poor men for their conscience' sake, ye be blinded, and see not yourselves, but say, "Tush! we be predestinate; whatsoever we do we are certain we cannot fall out of God's favor." [1]

This Anti-pedobaptist writer seems to have maintained that there was a logical connection between the Calvinistic theology, with its predestinarianism, and the persecuting spirit which in that age everywhere characterized the great Reformed body.

Knox answered this plain-spoken warning with reviling and threats rather than with argument:

You dissembling hypocrites cannot abide that the sword of God's vengeance shall strike the murderer, the blasphemer, and such others

---
[1] Quoted by Underhill in his "Historical Introduction."

as God commandeth by his word to die; not so, by your judgments; he must live, and may repent.

He accuses his opponent of blasphemy for suggesting that God had taken vengeance on Cranmer and others for persecuting his saints.

I will not now so much labor to confute by my pen, as that my full purpose is to lay the same to thy charge, if I shall apprehend thee in any commonwealth where justice against blasphemers may be ministered, as God's word requireth. And hereof I give thee warning, lest that after thou shalt complain that under the cloak of friendship I have deceived thee. Thy manifest defection from God, and this thy open blasphemy . . . have so broken and dissolved all familiarity which hath been betwixt us, that although thou wert my natural brother, I durst not conceal thine iniquity in this case.

He proceeds to justify the burning of Servetus and Joan Boucher by referring to Old Testament examples of the capital punishment of idolaters, etc.: "Your privy assemblies, and all those that in despite of Christ's blessed ordinance do frequent the same, are accursed of God."

From the above quotation it is manifest that Robert Browne was by no means the first to advocate in Britain the doctrine of soul-liberty. This writer deserves to be put by the side of Hubmaier in the early part of the fifteenth century, of the General Baptist authors of the tracts on liberty of conscience in the early part of the seventeenth century, and of Roger Williams and John Clarke a generation later, as one of the noble Anti-pedobaptist advocates of separation of Church and State and absolute freedom of conscience.

Referring to the beginning of Elizabeth's reign, Jewel wrote:[1] "We found a large and inauspicious crop of Arians, Anabaptists, and other pests, which I know not

---
[1] Zürich Letters, Vol. I, p. 92.

how, but as mushrooms spring up in the night and in darkness, so these sprung up in that darkness and unhappy night of the Marian times." There was at this time a great outcry from pulpit and press against the sectaries, chief stress being put upon their anti-Calvinistic teachings. In 1559 it was seriously proposed to imprison "incorrigible Arians, Pelagians, or free-will men" in "some castle in North Wales, or Wallingford . . . there to live of their own labor and exercise, and none other be suffered to resort unto them but their keepers."

Parkhurst, bishop of Norwich, was severely reprimanded for his failure to clear his diocese of Anti-pedobaptists. Norwich, as has been stated, was a great resort of Dutch immigrants and the Anti-pedobaptist element was large and aggressive.

In 1560 Elizabeth reinforced the Act of Uniformity by a special order to heretics (Anabaptists, etc.,) to depart the realm within twenty-one days on pain of imprisonment and forfeiture of goods. In the same year an anonymous supplication on behalf of those thus cruelly threatened for permission freely to exercise their religion was addressed to Bishop Grindal, of London. He suspected Hadrian Hamsted, one of the ministers of the Dutch church in London, of being its author, and addressed a letter to the Dutch ministers regarding the matter. Hamsted, when summoned before the bishop, acknowledged that he had spoken in a tolerant way of the error of the Anabaptists on the incarnation. The maintenance of such views he had held to be no bar to fellowship. Quarreling over such matters he had compared publicly to the disputing of the Roman soldiers over Christ's garments. Such errors he had said were as the wood, hay, and stubble, which would be consumed; but the souls of those who held them might be saved so as by fire. He had also advocated freedom on the part of parents to withhold their infants from baptism, or to present them, according to the dictates of conscience. Hamsted was deposed from his ministry by the bishop and soon afterward left England. Yet the matter of infant baptism continued to be agitated in the Dutch church, and the services of the bishop were four years later again called into requisition.

In 1567 the government ordered an inquisition to be made, especially in the diocese of Norwich whose bishop was suspected of winking at schismatics and Anabaptists, as to the character of the religious instruction imparted in the schools and as to the manner in which functionaries of the church were performing their duties. Special inquiry was to be made as to whether any taught or said that children being infants ought not to be baptized, that post-baptismal sins were not remissible by penance, that it was not lawful to swear, that civil magistrates may not punish certain crimes with death, or that it was lawful for any man without the appointment and calling of the magistrate to take upon him any ministry in Christ's church.[1]

The year 1568 was still more trying to the authorities. Vast numbers of Dutch were at this time fleeing before the fury of Alva and it was feared that among them might be "Anabaptists and such other sectaries." The government now ordered a special visitation to be made in all communities of foreigners with a view to ascertaining their mode of life, the length of their residence, the cause of their coming, the churches they attended, etc. All suspected persons were to be arraigned and those found guilty of erroneous teaching, unless they should yield to "charitable teaching," were to be compelled to depart the realm within twenty days or to expect severer punishment. Many Dutch Anabaptists are said to have been

---

[1] Underhill, "Hist. Introd. Broadm. Rec.," p. 53.

holding private conventicles in London at this time and to have perverted a large number of citizens.[1]

In 1572 Whitgift published, from Continental sources, a highly unfavorable account of the Anabaptists, the horrors of the Peasants' War and of the Münster Kingdom being represented as due wholly to their baneful teachings and as samples of what might be expected in England if such heresy were not remorselessly suppressed. For more than a century English Anti-pedobaptists had to bear the fearful burden of such obloquy, which from time to time was reiterated in the most unscrupulous and sensational way.

A body of dissenters discovered in the isle of Ely in 1573 had most of the peculiarities of the Anti-pedobaptists of the time, although rejection of infant baptism is not specifically charged.

On Easter-day, 1575, about thirty Dutch Anti-pedobaptists were seized in the suburbs of London while holding religious services in a private house. They were released on bail, but about the beginning of May were summoned before a royal commission, consisting of Bishop Sandys and a number of civilians and judges. Several Dutch ministers and a French Protestant minister were invited to sit with the commission.

Four questions were propounded to the accused: "(1) Whether Christ had not taken his flesh and blood of the Virgin Mary? (2) Ought not little children to be baptized? (3) May a Christian serve the office of a magistrate? (4) Whether a Christian, if needs be, may not swear?" The fullest accounts of these examinations have been left us by members of the accused party. To question 1. they answered: "He (Christ) is the Son of the living God." Question 2, they answered with a straight negation. Their answer to question 3

---
[1] Collier, Vol. VI., p. 462, and Strype, "Parker," Vol. I., p. 522.

was somewhat ambiguous: "That it did not oblige their consciences, but as they read, they esteemed it an ordinance of God." Their view on this point was evidently that of the great Anti-pedobaptist brotherhood of the sixteenth century. Their answer to question 4 was: "That it also obliged not their consciences; for Christ has said in Matthew, 'Let your words be yea, yea; nay, nay.'" Here also their position is manifest.

When they had given their answers the bishop declared that their misdeeds were so great that they could not enjoy the favor of God. They were informed that the queen and her council were resolved to compel all strangers to renounce these articles. If they would comply with this requirement, they might remain in the land free from taxes; if not, a frightful death awaited them.

There was no desire on the part of Elizabeth or her advisers to relight the fires of Smithfield, but Anabaptist heresy was too dangerous a thing to be tolerated. If it could be exterminated without bloodshed, so much the better; if not, it must at all cost be exterminated.

Master Joris (one of the Dutch ministers) came to us and said, if we would join the church, that is, the Dutch church, our chains should be struck off and our bonds loosed. The bishop, he said, had given him command so to do. But we remained steadfast to the truth of Jesus Christ. He is indeed our Captain, and no other; yea, in him is all our trust.

Five of their number were induced to recant and were set for a gazing-stock in St. Paul's church-yard, a fagot being bound on each one's shoulder to indicate that he deserved to be burnt. After repeated and strenuous efforts to overcome the scruples of the rest of the party, one woman only having been terrified into submission, fourteen women and a youth were led, bound together, to Newgate, where they remained some days in daily expectation of a horrible death. Finding them steadfast, and not relishing a wholesale slaughter of women, the queen commuted the sentence to banishment. They were put on board a ship, the youth having been tied to a cart and whipped through the streets. Separation from husbands, fathers, etc., and the probability that an ill fate awaited them on their debarkation almost annulled the satisfaction that escape from a fiery death in England would naturally have given.

The five principal members of the party had some time before been separated from the rest for harsher treatment. On June 2, just after the embarkation of the fifteen, they were again brought bound before their inquisitors. Threats of burning availed nothing. "It is a small matter thus to die," said Jan Pieters. "We must shave such heretics, and cut them off as an evil thing from the church," said the bishop. "How canst thou cut us off from your church," said Hendrik Terwoort, "seeing we are not of it?"

The rigors of their imprisonment were thenceforth greatly increased. So heavily ironed were their limbs and so hideously foul was their cell that they longed for a speedy death. "After eight days one of our brethren was released by death, trusting in God; his dying testimony filled us with joy." So great a horror of the Anabaptists had English churchmen conceived, that they were fearful lest the ordinary criminals in the prison should be corrupted by association with them.

One of the churchmen used occasionally to visit them in their dungeon and in the most solemn manner command the evil fiend to depart from them. Bishop Sandys thought the toleration of such opinions meant the expulsion "both out of church and commonwealth" of "all godliness, all peace, all honesty."

But there were many in high positions who looked with dismay upon the prospect of a return to the barbarous practices of the age of Mary. A vain effort was made to induce the queen to give her attention to an earnest supplication and a confession of their faith prepared by the condemned. Lord Burghley earnestly strove to stir up the compassion of Bishop Sandys for the miserable men. But bishop and queen were alike obdurate. John Foxe, the famous martyrologist, wrote a letter to Queen Elizabeth, pleading for a milder form of punishment than burning at the stake. Exile he thought a right sentence. "But I hear there are one or two of these who are appointed to the most severe punishment, viz., burning, except your clemency forbid. Now in this one affair I conceive there are two things to be considered; the one is the wickedness of their errors, the other the sharpness of their punishment." He admits the absurdity and the monstrosity of their opinions and says:

> It is certain they are by no means to be countenanced in a commonwealth, but, in my opinion, ought to be suppressed by proper correction. But to roast alive the bodies of poor wretches that offend rather through blindness of judgment than perverseness of will, in fire and flames, raging with pitch and brimstone, is a hard-hearted thing, and more agreeable to the practice of Romanists than the customs of the Gospeler.

He beseeches her majesty for the sake of Christ

> that these miserable wretches may be spared; at least that a stop may be put to the horror by changing the punishment to some other kind . . . that the piles and flames of Smithfield, so long ago extinguished by your happy government, may not more be revived.

Foxe's opposition to the holocaust that had been determined upon was evidently far more a matter of sentiment than a matter of principle. The queen hardened her heart even against this tender plea. One of the five died early in prison. Two were finally liberated. It was reserved for Jan Pieters and Hendrik Terwoort to rekindle with their writhing bodies the flames that were, in co-operation with other influences, so to quicken the popular conscience of England as sixty-five years later to destroy at a stroke ecclesiastical and civil despotism, to introduce into Britain an era of religious toleration and constitutional government, and to establish in America, after generations of conflict, absolute liberty of conscience, complete separation of Church and State, and government of the people, by the people, for the people.

A thoroughly sympathetic and highly instructive account of the sufferings of this party of Dutch Anti-pedobaptists has been preserved in a letter by Jacques de Somers,[1] a member of one of the Dutch churches in London, to his mother in Ghent. The facts he records substantially as given by the martyrs themselves. "It is with extreme reluctance that I write upon a subject of which you cannot even think without emotions of the deepest distress." He claims to have had full first-hand information, and he encloses copies of the confession and petition referred to above. "Their confession of faith was scriptural, and drawn up in such a manner that I would be free to subscribe to every tenet, with the exception of the article concerning oaths, in which they publicly confessed their belief that men should 'swear not at all.'" He gives the following personal details concerning the martyrs: "One of them, Jan Pieters, was a poor man, upward of fifty years old, and had nine children. His first wife was previously burnt at Ghent, in Flanders, on account of her religion; and he married a second wife, whose first husband had likewise been burnt at Ghent for his religious principles. . . The other, called Hendrik Terwoort, was a handsome and respectable man, about twenty-six years old, a goldsmith by trade,

---

[1] Translated from the Dutch Martyrology of Van Braght for Benedict's "History of the Baptists," and copied by Evans, "Early Eng. Bapt.," Vol. I., p. 159, seq.

and had been married eight or ten weeks before he was apprehended."

He gives the queen credit for signing the death warrants with reluctance, persuaded thereunto by "perverse men and enemies of the truth," who had grievously misrepresented the principles of the persecuted people. He continues:

> The Lord forgive those who were authors and abettors in this matter, and so misrepresented these poor people to her majesty, as you may judge from their confession, which they signed near me (in my presence), with their own hands; for though I do not assent to the whole, and am assured that they are in a mistake in regard to the article concerning the original conception of Christ and the origin of his flesh, yet as they made a Christian confession in express terms, and often confessed orally in my presence that Christ is very God and very man, like unto us in flesh and blood, and in all other respects, sin excepted, so be it far from me to acknowledge that they were worthy of death; nay, I would much rather acknowledge them as brethren.

He refers to two other young men of the party as still in prison. He has earnestly labored to secure their release, but thus far without success. He is aware of the fact that it seems strange and incredible to his mother and deeply distresses her "that those who formerly suffered persecution should now persecute other people on account of their religion, constraining the consciences of others with fire and sword, whereas they formerly taught, and which is the plain truth, that it is the province of no man to lord it over the consciences of others; and that faith is a special gift of God and is not implanted in men by any human power." He assures his mother that "some of the pious and learned, as well English as foreigners, who are here, did not approve of nor assent to it."

It would seem that the Dutch evangelicals who took refuge in England during the Elizabethan age had among them at least a fair proportion of those who, under Mennonite and Socinian influence, had revolted against the asperities and the intolerance of the prevailing Calvinism and who, early in the seventeenth century, under the leadership of Arminius, Uitenbogaert, Episcopius, etc., and supported by such statesmen and scholars as Grotius and Olden-Barnaveld, were to cause a tremendous upheaval in the Dutch Reformed Communion. It is probable that this liberal Dutch element that was tolerated by the government of Elizabeth exerted a more direct and pervasive influence in favor of religious liberty than the avowed Anti-pedobaptists, who were not only under the ban of the authorities, but were comparatively few in number, unlearned, and obscure. Many of these liberal Dutch Protestants sympathized with the Anti-pedobaptists in all but their extravagancies and were inclined to look upon these as comparatively harmless.

Meanwhile the pent-up fires of opposition to forms and ceremonies were beginning to break forth. Hooper had "scrupled the vestments." Jewel had wished that all "extraneous rubbish," including the linen surplice, might be abolished, and had stigmatized the liturgical ceremonies as "scenic apparatus," "fooleries," and "the relics of the Amorites."

Thomas Cartwright, of Cambridge, one of the ablest theologians of the age, was forced from his professorship (1570) by reason of his advocacy of the exclusive right of presbyterial church government and his uncompromising hostility to prelacy and to royal supremacy. In 1574 more than five hundred divines followed him in subscribing a Presbyterian book of discipline. Conventicles of non-conforming Puritans were established in many localities and many noblemen supported preaching of this type. Most of these non-conforming Puritans were quite as intolerant as were the churchmen of the time. What they contended for was a union of Church and State with the church in full control, as in the Genevan theocracy. They objected strongly to being persecuted themselves, but they held that it was the duty and right of the civil magistracy to punish all errors in doctrine and life and in general to execute the behests of the ecclesiastical authorities.

Some time between 1578 and 1580 Robert Browne, a highly connected and well-educated young man who for some years had been zealously laboring as a Puritan preacher and teacher, reached the conviction that Presbyterianism no less than prelacy is without scriptural warrant, and that according to apostolic precept and example the church is a pure democracy in which each member, by reason of his personal relation to the Lord Jesus Christ, the only Head of the church, has equal rights and privileges with every other. He insisted upon the right and duty of separation from a corrupt and apostate church. "The kingdom of God," he maintained, was "not to be begun by whole parishes, but rather of the worthiest, were they never so few." His zeal soon brought him into collision with the authorities. His irregular preaching was forbidden by the bishop. This seems to have further fired his zeal.

According to his own account "he took counsel still, and had no rest, what he might do for the name and kingdom of God. He often complained of those evil days and with many tears sought where to find the righteous, which glorified God, with whom he might live and rejoice together, that they put away abominations." Hearing that there were some in Norfolk who were "very forward" in religious reform, he "thought it his duty to take a voyage to them" in order that he might assist them in organizing separate worship. No doubt it was from Robert Harrison, a Cambridge graduate who had resided for some years as teacher and hospital master in Norwich and who agreed with Browne in regarding episcopal authorization as "trash and pollution," that he learned of the people's attitude toward reform. In many things Harrison was less advanced than Browne, but they labored together in Norwich, and in 1580 or 1581 a Separate church was organized.

To give a detailed account of the lives and labors of Browne and Harrison would not be in accord with the purpose of the present work. The question has arisen and has been much discussed whether Browne was indebted to the Dutch Anti-pedobaptists for his clearly conceived and ardently advocated views on the right and duty of separation from the ungodly, the abominableness of prelatical or civil interference with conscience, and the rigid limitation of the authority of the State to civil matters. That he was closely associated with the radical elements of the Dutch population in Norwich is admitted by all. There is an early tradition that his work in Norwich began among the Dutch.[1] Of this we cannot be sure; but it is certain that while in Norwich he had abundant opportunity to become familiar with the views of the Anti-pedobaptists which, on a number of points, were identical with his own.

His failure to follow them in the rejection of infant baptism and in their peculiar views with respect to the incarnation, oaths, magistracy, etc., is sufficient proof that he had not been dominated by their influence. We do not feel warranted, therefore, in going so far as certain recent Pedobaptist writers have done, who virtually attribute Browne's entire system, so far as it deviated from Puritanism, to Anabaptist influence,[2] but must con-

---

[1] Fuller, followed by Collier, Chambers, and others.
[2] D. Campbell, "The Puritan in Holland, England, and America," and W. E. Griffis, "The Anabaptist in the New World," December, 1895.

tent ourselves with the more reserved position of the ablest living authority on Congregational history, that

> Anabaptist modes of thought, imported with these Hollanders into their new English home, may have borne some fruitage, and may have unconsciously affected Browne himself in his conceptions of the church. Though no trace of a recognition of indebtedness to Anabaptist thought can be found in Browne's writings, and though we discover no Dutch names among the small number of his followers whom we know by name at all, the similarity of the system which he now worked out to that of the Anabaptists is so great in many respects that the conclusion is hard to avoid that the resemblance is more than accidental.[1]

It may be further said that the views of the Dutch Anti-pedobaptists were by this time too well known in England to allow the supposition that Browne was ignorant of them and too much abhorred for us to expect any unnecessary mention of indebtedness to them. Whatever of suggestion Browne may have received directly or indirectly from the Dutch Anti-pedobaptists, it was the recognized conformity of their views with Scripture and not the fact that they were advocated by a certain class of men that impressed him. It is by no means impossible that the martyrdom of Pieters and Terwoort, which awakened much interest at the time, produced a deep impression on the young Puritan preacher already zealous for reform and aided him in reaching the advanced position he came to occupy. But of this we have no evidence.

Finding that the bishop of Norwich and the archbishop of Canterbury were bent on the suppression of this little independent church, and learning no doubt from his Dutch friends that English dissenters would be welcomed in Zeeland, Browne emigrated with a portion of his fol-

---

[1] Williston Walker, "A History of the Congregational Church in the United States," p. 30, *seq.*

lowers and settled in Middelburg, probably near the close of 1581. Middelburg had long been in close commercial relations with England, and English merchants and others had some time before established there a congregation of Puritan proclivities. Here also Browne and his followers seem to have been intimately associated with the Mennonites. It was while resident in Zeeland that Browne set forth in a somewhat elaborate way his fully matured system of church reform. The titles of these works will give some idea of their contents: "A Treatise of Reformation Without Tarrying for Any, and of the Wickedness of Those Preachers, Which Will Not Reform Till the Magistrate Command or Compell Them"; and "A Book which Sheweth the Life and Manners of All True Christians, and How Unlike They are unto Turks and Papists, and Heathen Folks."[1] He was still careful to maintain the right and duty of baptizing infants.

The Middelburg church, under Browne's guidance, soon became involved in strife. Browne left it in disgust late in 1583, and after attempting in vain to labor in Scotland returned, broken in spirit and apparently shattered in intellect, to the Established Church. His later career was obscure and in every way discreditable. A portion of his Norwich congregation seem to have remained when Browne left for Middelburg, but little is known of their subsequent history. Some members of the Middelburg congregation are said to have united with the Mennonites. Browne's books were strictly prohibited in England (June, 1583) and two brethren were hanged for circulating them.

The congregation in London, led by Greenwood, Barrowe, and Penry, first came clearly into the light in 1586-7. These able and devoted men were arrested at

---

[1] See copious extracts from this work in Walker, "Creeds and Platforms," p. 18, seq.

this time, and after prolonged imprisonment, which some of them turned to good account in writing against the establishment, they were hanged in 1593. Their position was far less in accord with that of the Anti-pedobaptists of the time and with that of modern Baptists than was that of Browne. They advocated a moderate system of presbyterial government, and acknowledged the right and duty of the State to coerce heresy.

In 1591 Francis Johnson, a Puritan minister who had taken refuge at Middelburg, was converted by reading passages in one of Barrowe's tracts, the publication of which at Middelburg he was seeking to prevent. He returned to London, conferred with Barrowe in prison and became one of the ablest representatives of the presbyterial type of Congregationalism. Shortly after the martyrdom of Greenwood, Barrowe, and Penry, he led a party of Separatists to Amsterdam, where a strong church was established. He was soon joined by Henry Ainsworth, one of the most scholarly men of the time. Soon after the settlement of the company in Amsterdam "divers of them fell into the errors of the Anabaptists," which were "too common in these countries, and so persisting, were excommunicated by the rest." So wrote Francis Johnson in 1606.

In a polemical treatise published in 1589 against Greenwood, Barrowe, and Penry, Dr. R. Some sought to show that these Separatists were essentially Anabaptists. He compared the views of the two parties with considerable minuteness, and as both based themselves upon Scripture there could not fail to be much in common. He asserted that there were several Anabaptistical conventicles in London and other places, and that some of their members had been educated at the universities. He pointed out the grave dangers involved in tolerating dissent. "If every particular congregation in England might set up and put down at their pleasure, popish and Anabaptistical fancies would overflow this land; the consequence would be dangerous, viz., the dishonor of God, the contempt of her majesty, the overthrow of the church and universities, and the utter confusion of this noble kingdom."

In a writing by John Payne, published at Haarlem in 1597, Englishmen are warned against the "new English Anabaptists." He mentions one Maidstone as being in prison at Norwich for his Anabaptist teachings. He urges that the prisoner be not put to death, but banished, "by reason, our noble prince, judges, nor State, should not be so reputed of, with such hard terms, by Anabaptists and others, as I am loath here to express." He appeals to the prisoner himself not to suffer in so disreputable a cause.

The notices of Anti-pedobaptists during the remainder of Elizabeth's reign are few and insignificant. No doubt a very large proportion of these, as of non-conforming Puritans and Separatists, were driven from the country by the inquisitorial procedures of the government and had taken up their abode in the Netherlands where a large measure of freedom was accorded.

It should not be necessary to call attention to the fact that the document brought to light about 1866 and published by Dr. John Clifford in 1879 as the "Ancient Records" of "the church of Christ meeting at Epworth, Crowle, and West Butterwick, in the county of Lincoln," has been proved to be a miserable forgery. This spurious record begins in 1598-9. The elders of the church in 1599 were James Rayner, Henry Helwys, John Morton, William Brewster, and William Bradford. Believers' baptism is insisted upon in the covenant, and William Bradford is represented as baptizing in the river Torne at midnight. The last two names are famous as those of the leaders of the Mayflower party that had enjoyed the ministry of John Robinson. Thomas Helwys (not Henry) and Morton were members of the Anti-pedobaptist church founded by John Smyth in 1508. Many details are given in this forged document and the great mass of them have been proved to be completely out of accord with the known facts. As this document has been used in certain well-known books it is not surprising that it is often quoted as authentic by those who have not been informed of the exposure of the forgery.[1]

Literature: Underhill, "Introduction to the Hanserd Knollys Soc. Pub."; Crosby, "Hist. of the Eng. Baptists," Vol. I.; Ivimey, "Hist. of the Eng. Baptists," Vol. I.; Evans, "Early Eng. Baptists," Vol. I.; Goadby, "By-Paths of Bapt. Hist."; Strype (various works); Foxe, "Actes and Monuments"; Fuller, "Ch. Hist."; Collier, "Eccl. Hist."; D'Anvers, "Treatise on Baptism"; Burnet, "Hist. of the Ref."; Knox, works, ed. Laing; Tyndale, works; Van Braght, "Blœdig Toneel; Wilkins, "Concilia Mag. Br."; Walker, "Creeds and Platforms" and "Hist. of the Congreg. Ch. in the U. S."; Campbell, "The Puritans"; Hanbury, "Hist. Memorials"; Dexter, "The Congregationalism of the Last Three Hundred Years;" and Dexter, "John Smyth."

[1] See Dexter, "John Smyth," etc., p. 63, seq.

CHAPTER XXVIII

ENGLAND (1602-1609)

JUST before or shortly after the beginning of the reign of James I. (1602), a Separatist church was formed at Gainsborough, in Lincolnshire, under the leadership of John Smyth. As this church was a few years later to adopt believers' baptism and to become the mother of English General Baptist churches, it claims a place in this narrative.

Of Smyth's childhood nothing is known. As he matriculated at Christ's College, Cambridge, as a sizar, in 1571, we may infer that he was born somewhere between 1550 and 1555. On the completion of his course for Bachelor of Arts in 1575-6, he was chosen Fellow in his college and proceeded to the degree of Master of Arts in 1579. He seems to have been strongly inclined to Puritanism as early as 1585, for in this year he preached a lenten sermon on Sabbath-keeping that caused him some trouble. Somewhere about 1590 he was preacher in the city of Lincoln and was afterward beneficed at Gainsborough. After a long period of anxiety and questioning as regards the propriety of separating from the corrupt establishment and a conference on the subject with a number of his brother ministers, he withdrew from the Established Church about 1602 and organized a congregation of believers at Gainsborough.

Smyth and his followers covenanted together "to walk in all his ways, made known or to be made known unto them, according to their best endeavors, whatsoever it should cost them, the Lord assisting them."

This church was in every way a most remarkable one.

It embraced Helwys and Murton, along with Smyth destined to be the fathers of the General Baptist movement. John Robinson, the Father of the Pilgrims, who was to become pastor of a Separate church at Scrooby, in the neighborhood of Gainsborough, who, with his congregation, was to follow Smyth in his exodus to the Netherlands, and whose congregation, after years of discouraging experience at Leyden, was to try its fortunes in New England (1620 onward), united with Smyth's church about 1604. Among the other members to become men of foremost rank in Congregational history, and especially in the early religious history of New England, were William Brewster and William Bradford.

Harassed by continuous persecution and knowing that a congregation of English Separatists had long enjoyed toleration at Amsterdam, "the most were fain to fly and leave their houses and habitations and the means of their livelihood," and "to go into the Low Countries, where they heard was freedom of religion for all men."

Smyth and most of the Gainsborough congregation made their way to Amsterdam late in 1606 or early in 1607. Robinson and most of the members of the Scrooby congregation followed during 1607 and 1608. Arriving at Amsterdam Smyth and his company had not identified themselves with the older congregation of which Francis Johnson was pastor and Henry Ainsworth teacher, but proceeded on an independent basis as "the Second English Church at Amsterdam." That they should have proceeded along independent lines at Amsterdam was natural, seeing that their numbers were sufficient and that they had so learned and so highly esteemed a minister as Smyth, whose activity would have been hampered if with his congregation he had entered into the fellowship of a church already well organized and fully officered. It is probable that consciousness of important differences as regards church polity would in any case have prevented an organic union of the two companies.

For some time, however, the two congregations sustained the most cordial relations and full communion with each other. Shortly before or after Smyth's arrival at Amsterdam he published a tract under the title, "Principle and Inferences Concerning the Visible Church," which showed little or no deviation from the views of Johnson and Ainsworth, yet with the suggestion of sympathy with the more democratic system of Robert Browne. This position was more distinctly taken in a larger work entitled, "Separatists' Schism," which soon followed. He could still speak contemptuously of Anabaptists, classing them with Papists, Arians, and "any other heretics and anti-Christians," the acceptableness of whose "prayers and religious exercises" with God he emphatically denied.

His view of church government at this time is embodied in the following sentences:

> Christ's church, in several respects, is a monarchy, an aristocracy, a democracy. In respect of Christ the King it is a monarchy, of the eldership an aristocracy, of the brethren jointly a democracy or popular government. . . The body of the church hath all power immediately from Christ; and the elders have all their power from the body of the church, which power of the eldership is not exercised, nor cannot be used over or against the whole body of the church, for that is an anti-Christian usurpation. . . The definitive sentence, the determining power, the negative voice, is in the body of the church, not in the elders.

In this he took definite issue with the position of Johnson, but did not go much beyond that of Ainsworth.

It was not the question of baptism that first occasioned the breach of communion between the congregation presided over by Smyth and the older congregation at Amsterdam. Early in 1608 Smyth seems to have found himself at variance with his brethren of the older church on a number of points, some of which strike us at this time as rather trivial. The matter cannot be so well set forth as in his own summary of

"Our Differences from the Ancient Brethren of the Separation": (1) We hold that the worship of the New Testament properly so called is spiritual, proceeding originally from the heart; and that reading out of a book (though a lawful ecclesiastical action) is no part of spiritual worship, but rather the invention of the man of sin, it being substituted for a part of spiritual worship. (2) We hold that seeing prophesying is a part of spiritual worship, therefore in time of prophesying it is unlawful to have the book as a help before the eye. (3) We hold that seeing singing a psalm is a part of spiritual worship, therefore it is unlawful to have the book before the eye in time of singing a psalm. (4) We hold that the presbytery of the church is uniform; and that the triformed presbytery consisting of three kinds of elders, viz., pastors, teachers, rulers, is none of God's ordinance but man's device. (5) We hold that the elders of the church are pastors; and that lay elders (so called) are anti-Christian. (6) We hold that in contributing to the church treasury, there ought to be both a separation from them that are without, and a sanctification of the whole action by prayer and thanksgiving.

It is evident that up to this time the unscripturalness and unwarrantableness of infant baptism had not impressed itself upon the mind of this godly man who was seeking even in the minutest matters to bring his life and that of his church into entire conformity with New Testament precept and example, and who was even supersensitive as to any infringement on spiritual worship. His deep-seated prejudice against the Anabaptists undoubtedly had the effect of delaying for some time his application of the principle of the rigorous exclusion of all formalism and all unscriptural elements to the matter of baptism.

His objection to the use of the book in singing psalms and in prophesying, while it seems to us somewhat grotesque, was of the nature of an extreme application of the anti-liturgical principle of Puritanism. Spiritual worship alone is acceptable to God. The use of a book interferes with the freedom of the working of the spirit. Prophesying is utterance under the promptings of God's Spirit. The use of a book implies dependence on a human object instead of on the divine impulse. Much can be said in defense of his contention that church beneficence as an act of worship should be restricted to believers. At any rate, it was a logical inference from the principle of Separatism that lay at the basis of the older Amsterdam church as well as the newer. It is evident that Smyth had by this time reached the position of pure Congregationalism in church government, every vestige of Presbyterianism having been eliminated.

It is asserted by his contemporaries that Smyth at this time contended most pertinaciously for the position that translations of the Bible as being human productions are apocryphal, and are not to be used in the worship of God; but "that teachers should bring the originals, the Hebrew and Greek, and out of them translate by voice." It is claimed that this objection to the use of the translated Scriptures in worship was the primary cause of the breach of communion between the two congregations. Testimony to this effect is so full and so unanimous that it cannot with any propriety be called in question. This again was an extreme application of the principle that in worship nothing human should be allowed to intervene between the believer and God.

Having broken communion with the brethren of the older church on the ground of more questionable applications of scriptural principles, it was inevitable that the inconsistency involved in the position of the Separatists as regards baptism should sooner or later dawn upon Smyth and his followers. They had reached the position of being ready to carry out regardless of consequences the requirements of fidelity to Christ and to New Testament Christianity. In spite of their intense prejudice against the Anabaptists, the conviction forced itself upon them that neither they themselves nor those from whom they had separated were a true church of Christ. All alike had received their baptism in the apostate Church of England, and they had received this so-called baptism not in personal obedience to Christ's command and on a profession of faith in him, but as unconscious infants.

The exact date of Smyth's change of view as regards baptism cannot be accurately determined. It must have been late in 1608, or early in 1609, for in the preface to the "Character of the Beast," etc., evidently written after he had adopted Anti-pedobaptist views, he states: "I end writing this 24 of March, 1608," while a work entitled "Parallels, Censures, Observations," etc., evidently written before he had reached firm ground on the baptismal question, bears on its title-page the date 1609. An undated work by Smyth on "The Differences of the Churches of the Separation," in which he vindicates for himself and his followers the sufficiency of the grounds for separation from the older church, seems to have intervened. The date March 24, 1608, would be, according to the new style of reckoning, March 24, 1609. The "Parallels," though written before the "Character of the Beast," may not have issued from the press till 1609, which according to the old style began on March 25. These works must in any case have followed each other in quick succession. His adoption of Anti-pedobaptist views must have occurred some time before March 24, 1609 (N. S.), and probably some time before the end of 1608 (N. S.).

The procedures of Smyth and his associates are thus

described by their Amsterdam contemporaries: "After this," wrote Richard Clyfton, "they dissolved their church (which before was conjoined in the fellowship of the gospel and profession of the true faith) and Mr. Smyth being pastor thereof gave over his office, as did also the deacons, and devised to enter a new communion by renouncing their former baptism, and taking upon themselves another, of man's invention."

"Soon after this," wrote Henry Ainsworth, "God stroke him [Smyth] with blindness, that he could no longer find the door of the church out of which he was gone by schism, and which he had assaulted with error. . . . And now as a man benumbed in mind, he crieth out against us, contrary to his former faith and confession: 'Lo, we protest against them (saith he) to be a false church, falsely constituted in the baptizing of infants, and their own unbaptized estate,' etc."

Richard Bernard, after enumerating six earlier changes of views on Smyth's part, proceeds: "Seventhly, and lastly, if it prove the last, he hath (if you will believe him) recovered the true baptism, and the true matter and form of a true church, which now is only to be found pure among a company of Se-baptists," etc.

An anonymous contemporary writer puts the matter thus: "Soon after Satan drew him to deny the covenant preached to Abraham to be the covenant of grace, which led him to deny his baptism received in infancy."

Nothing was more natural than that Smyth's opponents should taunt him with inconsistency. He manfully met the charge in the following memorable words:

To change a false religion is commendable, and to retain a false religion is damnable. For a man, of a Turk to become a Jew, of a Jew to become a Papist, of a Papist to become a Protestant, are all commendable changes, though they all of them befall one and the same person in one year, nay, if it were in one month. So that not to change religion is evil simply ; and therefore that we should fall from the profession of Puritanism to Brownism, and from Brownism to true Christian baptism, is not simply evil and reprovable in itself, except it be proved that we have fallen from true religion. If we therefore, being formerly deceived in the way of Pedobaptistry, now do embrace the truth in the true Christian apostolic baptism, then let no man impute this as a fault unto us.

Be it remembered that the Separatists were at this time agreed in regarding the English Established Church as apostate, and in regarding any sort of communion with this church as wholly inadmissible. Be it remembered, furthermore, that the central point of their contention was for a pure church—a church of the regenerate. They had all received what they considered baptism in their infancy, at the hands of the priesthood of this apostate church ; they were themselves, by the practice of infant baptism, the regenerating efficacy of which they denied, introducing into the membership of the church those whose conversion even in the future was by no means assured. The wonder is not that Smyth should have come to an overmastering realization of the inconsistencies involved, but rather that any of them should have failed to see the untenableness of the position they had assumed. Men like John Robinson escaped the alternative that Smyth chose by receding from the position of extreme Separatism and adopting the position known as Semi-separatism, which involved a more friendly attitude toward the Church of England.

With Smyth and his followers conviction was the immediate forerunner of action. What action followed their conviction that infant baptism in general and Church of England baptism in particular was unwarranted and invalid has been stated in general in some of the extracts given above. Repudiating their former baptism and their church organization as unscriptural and unwarranted, they proceeded to introduce a new baptism of believers, and to organize themselves strictly according to New Testament precept and example, as understood by them, into a true church of Christ, whose members all claimed to have been regenerated by the Holy Spirit through faith in Christ.[1]

Being in an unbaptized estate, they must first of all obey Christ in the ordinance of baptism. How should they proceed in this matter? Who should take the initiative? As the spiritual leader of his people and their pastor, under the former organization, it could be no other than Smyth himself. Should he first administer the ordinance to another and then receive baptism himself at the hands of the person thus baptized? Helwys or Murton would naturally have shrunk from initiating the new baptism. It seems almost certain that what actually occurred was this: Smyth first baptized himself and then as a baptized believer proceed to baptize Helwys and the other members of the company. This is in accordance with the unanimous testimony of contemporaries who had the fullest opportunity to know the facts, and was uncontradicted, so far as we are aware, by any member of the party concerned.[2]

As this act of se-baptism was made a matter of reproach by Smyth's contemporary opponents, and has been similarly used in more recent times by the adversaries of the Baptists, some Baptist writers have vainly attempted to weaken the force of the evidence and to repudiate the charge as calumnious. A few of the testimonies of contemporaries will suffice for setting this transaction in its proper light.

---

[1] This occurred in all probability about October, 1608. See DeHoop-Scheffer, "De Brownisten te Amsterdam," p. 104.

[2] Dexter (" The True Story of John Smyth, the Se-baptist," pp. 26, seq.) has adduced the evidence in so convincing a manner as to render the question of Smyth's se-baptism no longer an open one.

Ainsworth wrote: "Mr. Smyth anabaptized himself with water... He anabaptized himself and then anabaptized others." John Robinson wrote: "As I have heard from themselves... Mr. Smyth baptized first himself, and next Mr. Helwys, and so the rest, making their particular confessions." Richard Clyfton, severely criticising both the act itself and the idea of the church that underlay the act, wrote: "If you [referring to Smyth] that baptize yourself (being but an ordinary man), may do this, then may another do the like, and so every one baptize himself."

Even more conclusive is Smyth's own testimony. The passage is valuable, moreover, as showing the grounds on which Smyth and his followers justified their action in introducing a new baptism and in organizing themselves afresh:

Whereas, you say that they [we] have no warrant to baptize themselves [ourselves], I say, as much as you have to set up a true church, yea, fully as much. For if a true church may be erected which is the most noble ordinance of the New Testament, then much more baptism; and if a true church cannot be erected without baptism... you cannot deny... that baptism may also be recovered. If they must recover them, men must begin so to do, and then two men joining together may make a church... Why may they not baptize, seeing they cannot conjoin into Christ but by baptism?... Now, for baptizing a man's self there is as good warrant as for a man churching himself. For two men singly are no church, jointly they are a church, and they both of them put a church upon themselves, so may two men put baptism upon themselves. For as both those persons unchurched yet have power to assume the church each of them for himself with others in communion; so each of them unbaptized hath power to assume baptism for himself with others in communion. And as Abraham and John Baptist, and all proselytes after Abraham's example (Exod. 12:48) did administer the sacrament upon themselves, so may any man raised up after the apostasy of Antichrist, in the recovering of the church by baptism, administer it upon himself in communion with others... And as in the Old Testament, every man that was unclean washed himself; every priest going to sacrifice washed himself in the laver at the door of the tabernacle of the congregation; which was a type of baptism, the door of the church (Titus 3 : 5). Every master of a family administered the Passover to himself and all of his family. The priest daily sacrificed for himself and others. A man cannot baptize others into the church, himself being out of the church. Therefore it is lawful for a man to baptize himself together with others in communion, and this warrant is a plerophory for the practice of that which is done by us.

Thus the fact of se-baptism seems to be fully admitted by Smyth himself. If Smyth and his associates were right in concluding that they were unbaptized, and that it was their duty to organize themselves on a New Testament basis as a church of Christ, it was evidently incumbent on them either to seek and find a church of believers in which true baptism could be secured or to introduce believers' baptism anew.

Why they did not seek baptism at the hands of the Mennonites, who were close at hand and were known by them to practise believers' baptism, it may not be possible to determine. The odium of the name "Anabaptist," by which the Mennonites, despite their most earnest protests, were commonly called, doubtless had some influence in deterring them from taking this step. The difficulty of making themselves thoroughly understood by the Mennonites owing to their lack of familiarity with the Dutch language was probably another reason for their proceeding independently in the matter.

As it regards the form of the new baptism introduced by Smyth, modern criticism has rendered it highly probable that it was not immersion but affusion. We need not go into a detailed proof of this proposition. A few considerations will suffice for our present purpose. In a letter addressed by leaders of the Mennonite church at Amsterdam to those of the church at Leeuwarden on the occasion of the application of Smyth and his followers for admission into the fellowship of the former, it is distinctly stated: "We ministers ... summoned these English brethren and again most perfectly examined them as regards the doctrine of salvation and the government of the church, and also inquired for the foundation and form of their baptism, and we have not found that there was any difference at all, neither in the one nor the other thing between them and us." There is no evidence, so far as we are aware, that at this time any party of Mennonites practised immersion. Like the great majority of the Anti-pedobaptists of the Reformation time, they contented themselves, as regards the act of baptism, with the practice that prevailed around them, the subjects of baptism and its sacramental efficacy being alone matters of controversy.

About ten years later (1619) the Rhynsburgers (Collegiants) introduced immersion under the influence of the Polish Socinian Anti-pedobaptists, who may have derived it from the Swiss and Augsburg Anti-pedobaptists.

The most competent Mennonite scholar of the present time[1] does not hesitate to assert that the universal practice of Mennonites of all parties about 1609 was affusion. It is not probable from the context that the term "form of their baptism" in the above quotation refers directly to the mode of applying the water. It probably refers rather to the words spoken in connection with the administration of the ordinance. But the absence of any intimation in the controversial literature of the time that Smyth had introduced an innovation as regards the mode of administering baptism, beyond that of se-baptism, seems quite decisive against the supposition that the believers' baptism that he introduced and insisted upon was immersion.[2]

---

[1] Dr. J. G. DeHoop-Scheffer.
[2] For a full discussion of this point, see Dexter, "J. Smyth," p. 10, *seq.*

The party that under Smyth's guidance adopted believers' baptism and formed themselves into a new church consisted of about forty-two men and women. The foremost among the brethren, after Smyth, were Thomas Helwys and John Murton, both of whom proved steadfast in their new faith.

About the beginning of 1609, or earlier, a division arose in the newly constituted body. In the meantime Smyth had become better acquainted with the Mennonites, and thoroughly imbued with their teachings, including the Pelagian or Socinian modes of thought that at this time widely prevailed among them. He had reached the conviction that he and his followers had made a prodigious blunder in ignoring this truly apostolic communion, and in introducing a new baptism and a new church order. What they had done in ignorance, or from culpable prejudice, it was their bounden duty to undo as promptly as possible. That he should soon have made himself intolerable in the little church, a portion only of whose members favored his latest proposal, was what might have been expected.

The minority, led by Helwys and Murton, felt it necessary to excommunicate Smyth and his supporters for the errors into which they had fallen. The following is their own justification of this procedure:

> That it may not be thought we lay imputations or cast reproaches upon Mr. Smyth unjustly, we thought good, in short, to set down some of the errors whereunto he is fallen, etc. (1) That concerning Christ the first matter of his flesh, he affirmed that all the Scriptures would not prove that he had it of the Virgin Mary, thus making Christ to have two matters of his flesh. (2) That men are justified partly by the righteousness of Christ apprehended by faith, partly by their own inherent righteousness. (3) That Adam's sin was not imputed unto any of his posterity, and that all men are in the estate of Adam in his innocency before they commit actual sin; and therefore infants were not redeemed by

Christ, but as angels and all other creatures. (4) That the church and ministry must come by succession, contrary to his former profession in words and writings, and that by a supposed succession he cannot show from whom, nor when, nor where. (5) That an elder of one church is an elder of all the churches in the world. (6) That magistrates may not be members of Christ's church and retain their magistracy.

Smyth and thirty-one others promptly sought admission into the Mennonite church in Amsterdam, whose pastor was the celebrated Lubbert Gerrits.[1] They "confess this their error, and repent of the same, viz.: that they undertook to baptize themselves contrary to the order laid down by Christ," and "now desire to get back into the true church of Christ as speedily as may be." Helwys, Piggott, Seamer, and Murton, on behalf of the church, addressed a letter to the Mennonite brethren (March 12, 1609)[2] beseeching them to proceed cautiously in the matter of receiving Smyth and his company and setting forth somewhat fully their position in the matter:

We are with much gladness and willingness stirred up to write to you, praying you, as you love the Lord and his truth, that you will take wise counsel, and that from God's word, how you deal in this cause betwixt us and those who are justly, for their sins, cast out from us. And the whole cause in question being succession (for so it is in deed and in truth), consider, we beseech you, how it is Antichrist's chief hold, and that it is Jewish and ceremonial, an ordinance of the Old Testament, but not of the New. Furthermore, let it be well considered that the succession which is founded upon neither the times, person, nor place, can [not] be proved to any man's conscience, and so herein we should ground our faith, we cannot tell upon whom, nor when, nor where.

The case of John the Baptist is cited to prove the right of an unbaptized person to introduce baptism.

---

[1] See the correspondence in Evans' "Early Eng. Bapt." Vol. I., p. 209, seq.
[2] Evans, supposing the date given to be O. S., has changed it to 1610. Dexter calls attention to the fact that the N. S. had been adopted in Holland in 1583, and insists upon the earlier date.

And whosoever shall now be stirred up by the same Spirit to preach the same word, and men thereby being converted, may, according to John's example, wash them with water, and who can forbid? And we pray that we may speak freely herein, how dare any man or men challenge unto themselves a pre-eminence herein, as though the Spirit of God was only in their hearts, and the word of God now only to be fetched at their mouths, and the ordinance of God only to be had from their hands, except they were apostles? Hath the Lord thus restrained his Spirit, his word, and ordinances, as to make particular men lordly over them, or keepers of them? God forbid. This is contrary to the liberty of the gospel, which is free for all men, at all times and in all places. . . And now for the other question, that elders must ordain elders; or if this be a perpetual rule, then from whom is your eldership come? And if one church might once ordain, then why not all churches always?

It might have been expected that the Mennonite church would receive with open arms this large body of zealous converts to their principles. But they had had too much experience of internal strife to be willing to incur the risk of introducing into their body a factious element, or of alienating sister churches by entering precipitately upon a course that might be called in question. The remonstrance of Helwys and his brethren may have furnished still further ground for hesitancy. The Amsterdam Mennonite church writes to the church at Leeuwarden, stating the fact that these English have been thoroughly examined by them, and have been found in perfect agreement with the Mennonite churches in every respect. They express the opinion "that these English, without being baptized again, must be accepted." It is stated that the English are willing to be baptized, if it can be proved to be necessary from Scripture and reason. If the Leeuwarden brethren think they ought to be rebaptized, they are entreated to come to Amsterdam, and to prove to their Mennonite brethren and to the English that the baptism the latter have received is invalid.

The Leeuwarden brethren were non-committal and indisposed to take any responsibility upon themselves in the matter. Yet they urge that nothing be done which might disturb the good fellowship of the connection.

A Mennonite brother, Jan Munter, provided Smyth and his associates with a room for worship in "The Great Cake House"; but the English brethren were not formally received into fellowship until 1615, about three years after Smyth's death.

Helwys and the rest of the anti-succession party returned to England about 1611, impelled by a deep conviction that flight from persecution "had been the overthrow of religion in this island, the best, ablest, and greater part being gone and leaving behind them some few who, by the others' departure, have had their affliction and contempt increased, hath been the cause of many falling back, and of their adversaries rejoicing."

The church of Helwys and Murton became the mother of the General Baptist churches. Although these leaders objected strongly, as we have seen, to most of the features that differentiated the Mennonites of the time from modern Baptists, including the Pelagian (Socinian) type of doctrine, these views soon gained general acceptance among their followers. Before 1624 controversy had arisen as to the deity of Christ, the lawfulness of oaths, magistracy, and warfare, and as to the obligatoriness of the weekly celebration of the Supper. Both parties to the controversy appealed to the Dutch Mennonites and sought to secure recognition at their hands (1624-6). A rich literature in defense of liberty of conscience emanated from this body of believers (1614 onward).[1]

It is worthy of remark that both Smyth and Helwys gave clear and forcible expression to this old-evangelical principle. In a long and elaborate confession of faith

[1] See "Tracts on Liberty of Conscience," Hanserd Knollys Society Publications.

prepared by Smyth about 1611,[1] he declares: "That the magistrate is not by virtue of his office to meddle with religion or matters of conscience, to force or compel men to this or that form of religion or doctrine, but to leave the Christian religion free to every man's conscience, and to handle only civil transgressions (Rom. 13), injuries, and wrongs of man against man, in murder, adultery, theft, etc., for Christ only is the king and lawgiver of the church and conscience (James 4 : 12)." Helwys wrote as follows: "The king is a mortal man and not God, therefore hath no power over the immortal souls of his subjects, to make laws and ordinances for them, and to set spiritual lords over them. If the king have authority to make spiritual lords and laws, then he is an immortal God and not a mortal man."

It is not the purpose of the present work to trace the history of Anti-pedobaptism beyond the date of the organization of the first English Baptist church of which we have any definite information. From this time onward the history of Anti-pedobaptism becomes almost coincident with that of the Baptists.

Earlier Anti-pedobaptism was for the most part so hampered by errors in doctrine and in practice and so remorselessly persecuted by Church and State, that it could not possibly embody itself in a great aggressive denomination adapted to all classes and conditions of men. Its narrowness and its erroneous views were doubtless due in large measure to the fierceness of the persecution to which its advocates were everywhere subjected. Magistracy as observed by them was for the most part hostile to pure religion, destroying those who sought to restore primitive Christianity; warfare was generally waged for selfish and cruel ends and involved

---

[1] A good English translation is given by Barclay in his "The Inner Life," etc. Appendix to Chap. VI.

untold misery; oaths were employed for the most part either profanely or with a view to extorting from Christian people information to which the authorities had no right. That they should have interpreted the Scriptures in accord with these prepossessions was most natural. Communism, so far as it was introduced among Antipedobaptists, struck at the root of modern civilization and doomed the parties adopting it to extinction. Separatism was sometimes carried so far as to make its subjects narrow and bigoted, and incapable of effectively impressing their views upon those outside their own communion.

Helwys and his followers escaped many of these narrowing influences, but not all. The Socinian form of anti-Augustinian theology, against which Helwys and Murton protested at the beginning, proved a great hindrance to the effectiveness of the party and in the eighteenth century almost wrecked it.

It remained for the Particular (Calvinistic) Baptists, formed by secession from a London Congregational church in 1633, to embody Anti-pedobaptism in a form that, when animated by the missionary spirit, has proved highly effective. In this form during the past century its progress has been marvelous, and there seems to be no limit to its possible achievements.

Literature: Underhill, "Introduction to the Hanserd Knollys Soc. Pub."; Crosby, "Hist. of the Eng. Baptists," Vol. I.; Ivimey, "Hist. of the Eng. Baptists," Vol. I.; Evans, "Early Eng. Baptists," Vol. I.; Goadby, "By-Paths of Bapt. Hist."; Strype (various works); Foxe, "Actes and Monuments"; Fuller, "Ch. Hist."; Collier, "Eccl. Hist."; D'Anvers, "Treatise on Baptism"; Burnet, "Hist. of the Ref."; Knox, works, ed. Laing; Tyndale, works: Van Braght, "Blœdig Toneel"; Wilkins, "Concilia Mag. Br."; Walker, "Creeds and Platforms" and "Hist. of the Congreg. Ch. in the U. S."; Campbell, "The Puritans"; Hanbury, "Hist. Memorials"; Dexter, "The Congregationalism of the Last Three Hundred Years" and "John Smyth"; Barclay, "Inner Life of the Rel. Soc. of the Commonwealth"; De Hoop-Scheffer, "De Brownisten te Amsterdam"; and Whitsitt, "A Question in Baptist History" (published since this work was written).

BIBLIOGRAPHY

Ante-Nicene Fathers, The. Am. Ed., 10 vols. New York.

Anschelm, V., Berner Chronik, ed. Stierlin. Bern. 2 vols. 1884-86.

Archiv für die Schweizer Reformationsgeschichte. 3 vols. Solothurn, 1868-76.

Arnold, G., Unparteyische Kirchen-und-Ketzerhistorie. 4 vols. 1699-1700.

Arx, J. von, Geschichte d. Kantons St. Gallen. 3 vols. St. Gallen, 1810-13.

Auss-Bundt, Das ist etliche schöne Lieder (Anabaptist Hymnal). Basel, 1838.

Bachmann, R., Niklas Storch, d. Anfänger der Zwickauer Propheten. Zwickau.

Bader, J., Brüderliche Warnung für den newen Abgöttischen Orden der Widertäuffer, 1527 (contains Bader's report of a debate on baptism between himself and Denck. The author became a Schwenckfeldtian some time afterward and suffered for his faith. A copy of this work is in the library of the University of Rochester, N. Y.).

Bahlman, Die Bibliographie zur Gesch. d. Wiedertäufer in Münster (Zeitschr. f. vaterland. Gesch. u. Alterthumskunde Westfalens, Vol. LI.).

Balan, P., Monumenta Reformationis Lutheranæ, Vol. I. Regensburg, 1884.

Barclay, R., The Inner Life of the Religious Societies of the Commonwealth. Third edition. London, 1879.

Basel, Chroniken, ed. W. Vischer. Leipzig, 1872.

Baum, J., Capito und Bucer. Elberfeld, 1860.

Baumann, F. L., Quellen zur Geschich. d. Bauernkriegs. 1878. (On Langenmantel, etc.)

Baur, A., Zur Einleitung in Zwinglis Schrift: In Catabaptistarum Strophas Elenchus (Zeitschr. f. Kirchengesch., Bd. X., p. 390, seq.).

Baur, A., Zwinglis Theologie. 2 vols. Halle, 1885-89.

Beck, J. von, Ein Beitrag zur Gesch. der. Wiedertäufer in Kärnten (Archiv d. hist. Vereins, Bd. XI.).

Beck, J. von, Geschichtsbücher d. Wiedertäufer in Oesterreich-Ungarn von 1526 bis 1785. Wien, 1883.

Beck, Collection of Anti-pedobaptist literature (probably the most extensive ever made, embracing copies of documents from the principal archives and libraries of Europe. See partial list of its contents in Loserth's Hubmaier, p. 10, seq., and Beck's own directory to the MS. sources in Gesch.-Bücher, pp. 23, 24. The collection is still in the possession of the Beck family, but has been most generously entrusted to Loserth and others for scientific use. Loserth's recent works on Anti-pedobaptist history have been based upon Beck's materials. The rich hymnological collection has been committed to Prof. M. von Waldberg, of Heidelberg).

Belling, H., Ueber Jovinian (Zeitschr. f. Kirchengesch., Bd. IX., p. 391, seq.).

Benrath, K., D. Wiedertäufer im Venetianischen um Mitte d. XVI. Jahrh. (Theol. St. u. Kr., 1885).

Bezold, F. von, Gesch. d. Husitenthums. München, 1874.

Biographical Sketches of many Anti-pedobaptist leaders in the Herzog-Plitt Real-Encyklopädie and in the Allgem. Deutsch. Biographie.

Blaupot Ten Cate, S., Gesch. d. Doopsgezinde. 5 vols. Leeuwarden, 1839-47.

Bock, F. S., Historia Antitrinitariorum. Regiomonti et Lipsiæ, 1774.
Bonwetsch, D. Gesch. d. Montanismus. Erlangen, 1881.
Bouterwek, K. W., Zur Literatur u. Gesch. d. Wiedertäufer, besonders in den Rheinlanden. Bonn, 1864.
Bouterwek Manuscript Collection (in possession of the Berg Hist. Union).
Braght, Tileman van, Bloedig Toneel of Martelaars-Spiegel. Amsterdam, 1685.
Brandt, G., History of the Reformation . . . in and about the Low Countries. Tr. by J. Chamberlayne. 4 vols. London, 1720-23.
Brenz, J., Bedenken etlicher, dass weltliche Obrigkeit der Wiedertäufer mit leiblicher Straf zu wehren schuldig sei. 1536.
Breyer, R., Die Arnoldisten (Zeitschr. f. Kirchengesch, Bd. XIII.).
Brons, A., Ursprung, Entwickelung, und Schicksale der Taufgesinnten oder Mennoniten. Norden, 1884. (The highly creditable work of a mother in Israel.)
Bullinger, H., Adversus omnia Catabaptistarum prava dogmata. Zürich, 1535.
Bullinger, H., Der Wiedertäufer Ursprung, Fürgang, Secten, etc. Zürich, 1560 (also Latin translation by Simler, same date).
Bullinger, H., Reformationsgeschichte. 3 vols. Frauenfeld, 1838-40.
Bullinger, H., Von dem unverschampten Fräfel, ergerlichen Verwyren und unwarhaften Leeren der selbstgesandten Wiedertäufer. Zürich, 1531.
Burrage, H. S., An Apostle of the Anabaptists (translated from Keller, Bapt. Quar. Rev., Jan., 1885.
Burrage, H. S., A History of the Anabaptists of Switzerland. Philadelphia, 1881.
Burrage, H. S., The Anabaptists of the Sixteenth Century (Papers of the Am. Soc. of Ch. Hist., Vol. III.).
Burrage, H. S., Baptist Hymn Writers. Portland, 1888 (pp. 1-25).
Burrage, H. S., Thomas Münzer (Bapt. Quar. 1877).
Bussière, T. de, Hist. de l'Etablissement du Protestantisme à Strasbourg et en Alsace. 1856.
Bussière, T. de, Hist. du Développement du Protestantisme à Strasbourg et en Alsace. 1859.
Bussière, T. de, Les Anabaptistes. Hist. du Lutheranisme, de l'Anabaptisme et du regne de Jean Bockelsohn à Münster. Paris, 1853.
Buxtorf, Die Reformationschronik des Karthäusers Georg. Basel, 1849.

Calvary, S., Mittheilungen aus dem Antiquariate, Bd. I. Berlin, 1870. (Contains portrait, sketch, and bibliography of Hubmaier, a reprint of his "Ein Form des Nachtmals Christi," and a reprint of the 1565 edition of Riedemann's "Rechenschafft unserer Religion."
Calvin, J., Brevis Instructio adv. Errores Anabaptistarum (Opera, ed. Amsterdam, Vol. VIII.).
Campbell, D., The Puritan in Holland, England, and America. 2 vols. New York, 1892.
Carlstadt, A. (His tracts are not so excessively rare as are those of most of the radicals of the Reformation time. Jäger in his life of C. has given copious extracts, including everything of much importance.)
Caspari, C. P., Alte und neue Quellen zur Gesch. des Taufsymbols u. der Glaubensregel. Christiana, 1879.
Caspari, C. P., Ungedruckte, unbeachtete, u. wenig beachtete Quellen zu Gesch. d. Taufsymbols u. d. Glaubensregel. 3 vols. Christiana, 1866.
Cate, S. Blaupot Ten, Geschiedenis der Doopsgezinden. 1839-47.
Chronik d. Stadt Schaffhausen. Schaffhausen, 1844.
Collier, Jer., Eccl. Hist. of Great Britain. 1708 (new edition, London, 1840).
Comba, E., I Nostri Protestanti, Vol. I. Firenze, 1895. (Sketches of Hippolytus, Novatian, Jovinian, Claude of Turin, Arnold of Brescia, Peter Waldo, Marsilius of Padua, etc.)
Comba, E., Storia della Riforma in Italia, Vol. I. Firenze, 1881.

BIBLIOGRAPHY

Comba, E., Hist. des Vaudois d'Italie, Vol. I. (also English transl., London, 1888).

Conant, T. J., Meaning and Use of "Baptizein" Philologically and Historically Investigated. New York, 1860.

Clifford, J. (editor), The English Baptists. London, 1881.

Cornelius, C. A., Antheil Ostfrieslands an der Reformation. 1854.

Cornelius, C. A., Berichte d. Augenzeugen über das Münsterische Wiedertäuferreich. 1853.

Cornelius, C. A., Die Münsterische Humanisten. Münster, 1851.

Cornelius, C. A., Gesch. d. Münsterischen Aufruhrs. Leipzig, 1855-60.

Cornelius, C. A., Die Niederländischen Wiedertäufer während der Belagerung Münsters. Münster, 1869.

Cornelius, C. A., Studien zur Gesch. d. Bauernkriegs (Abh. d. Bair. Akad. Cl. lii., Vol. IX.).

Cornelius, C. A. (Editor), Die Geschichtsquellen d. Bisthums Münster. Münster, 1851-6.

Cramer, A. M., Het Leven en de Verrigtingen van Menno Simons. Amsterdam, 1837.

Crosby, T., Hist. of the English Baptists, Vol. I. London, 1738.

Cunitz, Les Vaudois (Rev. de Theol., 1852).

Cutting, S. S., Historical Vindications. Boston, 1859.

Czechowitz, M., De Pædobaptistarum Errorum Origine, et de ea Opinione, qua infantes baptizandos esse, in primo nativitatis eorum exortu, creditur. Lublini, 1575.

Czerny, A., Die Erste Bauernaufstand in Oberösterreich, 1525. Linz, 1882.

Denck, J. (For full bibliography see Keller, Ein Apos. d. Wiedert., p. 241, seq. A reprint of his more important tracts was published at Amsterdam in 1680 under the title "Geistliches Blumengärtlein." The Crozer Theol. Sem. possesses a copy of this edition, and a MS. copy from this is in the Howard Osgood collection of the Rochester Theol. Sem.). Keller reprints several important documents in the appendix to his J. von Staupitz. Heberle has given copious extracts from some of the writings. The tract, Von der wahren Liebe, has been reprinted by the Mennonite publishing house, Elkhart, Indiana.

De Hoop-Scheffer, J. G., De Brownisten te Amsterdam gedurende den eersten Tijd na hunne Vestiging, in verband met het Ontstaan de Broederschap der Baptisten. Amsterdam, 1881.

De Hoop-Scheffer, J. G., Eene Geschiedenis van de Doopsgezinden, van hunne Geschillen en Hereenigingen, door een Doopsgezinde in 1647 (in Doopsgezinde Bijdragen, 1876).

De Hoop-Scheffer, J. G., Eenige Opmerkingen en Mededeelingen betreffende Menno Simons (in Doopsgezinde Bijdragen, 1864, 1865, 1872, 1881, 1889, and 1890).

De Hoop-Scheffer, J. G., Geschiedenis der Kerkhervorming in Nederland. Amsterdam, 1873 (Germ. transl. by Gerlach. Leipzig, 1886).

Demmer, E., Gesch. d. Reformat. am Niederrhein, 1885.

Denis, E., Huss et la Guerre des Hussites. Paris, 1878.

De Soyres, J., Montanism and the Primitive Church. Cambridge, 1878.

De Schweinitz, E., History of the Unitas Fratrum. Bethlehem, 1885.

Detmer, H., Ungedruckte Quellen zur Geschichte der Wiedertäufer in Münster (Zeitschr. fur vaterl. Gesch. u. Alterthumskunde Westfalens, Bd. LI.).

Deutsch, S. M., Drei Actenstücke zur Gesch. d. Donatismus. Berlin, 1875.

Dexter, H. M., The Congregationalism of the Last Three Hundred Years, as Seen in its Literature. New York, 1880.

Dexter, H. M., The True Story of John Smyth, the Se-Baptist, etc. Boston, 1881.

Dickius, L., Adv. impios Anabaptistarum errores. 1533.

Dieckhoff, A. W., Die Waldenser im Mittelalter. Göttingen, 1851.

Döllinger, I. von. Beiträge zur Sektengeschichte d. Mittelalters. 2 vols. München, 1890. (Vol. I. is a not very satisfactory "Hist. of the Gnostic-Manichaean Sects"; Vol. II. is a rich collection of documents on sects in general, embracing most of the important extant materials.)

Döllinger, I. von, Die Reformation. 3 vols. Regensburg, 1846-8.

Doopsgezinde Bijdragen, ed. Harting, Cool, and De Hoop-Scheffer. Leeuwarden, 1861 onward.

Dorpius, H., Warhafftige Historia wie das Evangelium zu Munster angefangen, und darnach durch die Widertäuffer verstört, wider auffgehört. Vorred D. Joh. Bugenhagii Pomer. Strassburg, 1536 (new edition by Merschmann, Magdeburg, 1847).

Dudik, B. Gesch. d. Buchdrucks in Mähren von 1486-1621. Brünn, 1879 onward.

Dudik, B., Mährens allgemeine Geschichte. 5 vols. 1860 onward.

Egli, E., Actensammlung zur Gesch. d. Züricher Reformation. Zurich, 1879.

Egli, E., Die St. Galler Täufer. Zurich, 1887.

Egli, E., Die Zuricher Wiedertäufer. Zürich, 1878.

Erbkam, H. W., Gesch. d. Protestant. Sekten. Gotha, 1848.

Erhard, C., Gründlich Historia der Münster. Wiedertäufer. München, 1589.

Evans, B., Early English Baptists. 2 vols. London, 1862.

Everts, W. W., Jr., Balthazar Hubmeyer (Bapt. Quar. Rev., April, 1881).

Faber, J., Ursach warumb der Widertäuffer Patron Hubmayer zu Wien verprennt sey. Wien, 1528 (reprinted by Loserth, B. Hubmaier, p. 210, seq.).

Fabri, J. Adv. Doctorem Balthasarum Pacimontanum, Anabaptistarum nostri sæculi primum authorem, orthodoxæ fidei Catholica Defensio. Leipzig, 1528.

Falkenheiner, W., Philipp der Grossmüthige im Bauernkriege. Marburg, 1887.

Fischer, A., Von der Wiedertäufer verfluchtem Ursprung. Bruck, 1604.

Fischer, C. A., Hutterischer wiedertäufer Taubenfolk. Ingolstadt, 1607.

Flacius, Matthias, Catalogus Testium Veritatis (various editions).

Fock, O., Der Socinianismus. Kiel, 1847.

Förstemann, C. E., Neues Urkundbuch zur Gesch. d. Evang. Kirchen-Reformation. Hamburg, 1842.

Foxe, J., Actes and Monuments, edition by Townsend. 8 vols. London, 1843-9.

Frank, Sebastian, Chronica. 1536 (and often).

Frantz, J. F., Die schwärmerischen Greuelscenen d. St. Galler Wiedertäufer. Ebnat, 1824.

Fredericq, Corpus documentorum inquisitionis Neerlandicæ. Ghent, 1889.

Fries, L. Die Gesch. d. Bauernkrieges in Ostfranken, ed. A. Schaffler and T. Henner. Würtzburg, 1883.

Fries, Patarener, Begharden, u. Waldenser in Oesterreich (Wiedemann's Oester.Vierteljahrsch. f. Kath. Theol., 1872).

Füsslin, J. C., Beyträge zur Erläuterung d. Kirchen-Reformationsgesch. d. Schweitzerlandes. 5 vols. Zürich, 1741, seq.

Füsslin, J. C. (editor), Epistolæ ab Ecclesiæ Helveticæ Reformatoribus vel ad eos scriptæ. Zürich, 1742.

Füsslin, J. C., Lebensgesch. d. Andreas Bodenstein von Karlstadt. Frankfurt, 1776.

Füsslin, J. C., Kirchen- und Ketzergesch. d. mittelalt. Zeit.

Füller, Th., Ch. Hist. of Britain. London, 1655 (new ed. London, 1868).

Gale, J., Reflections on Mr. Wall's Hist. of Inf. Baptism. London, 1711 (new ed. Oxford, 1862).

Gast, J. De anabaptismi exordio, erroribus, historiis abominandis, confutationibus adjectis Libri II. Basel, 1544.

Gast, J. Tagebuch, Uebersetzt von Buxtorf-Falkeisen. Basel, 1856.

Gerbert, C. Gesch. d. Strassburger

BIBLIOGRAPHY

Sectenbewegung zur Zeit d. Reformation, 1524-1534. Strassburg, 1889.
Gerdesius, D., Historia Reformationis. Groningæ, 1744-52.
Getrewe Warnung der Prediger des Evangelii zu Strassburg über die Artikel, so Jacob Kautz, Prediger zu Wormbs, kürtz hat lassen aussgehn. Strassburg, 1527.
Gilly, W. S., Vigilantius and his Times. London, 1844.
Gindely, A., Gesch. d. Böhmischen Brüder, 2d ed. Prag, 1861.
Gindely, A., Quellen zur Gesch. d. Böhm. Brüder (Fontes rerum Austr. ii., Vol. XIX.).
Gindely, A., Ueber die dogmatischen Ansichten der böhmisch-mährischen Brüder, nebst einigen Notizen ihrer Entstehung. 1854.
Goadby, T., By-paths of Baptist History. London, 1871.
Göbel, M., Gesch. d. christl. Lebens in der rhenisch-westphälischen Kirche. 3 vols. Coblenz, 1849-60.
Goll, J., Quellen und Untersuchungen zur Gesch. d. Böhmischen Brüder. Bd. I. und II. Prag, 1878-82.
Gordon, A., Miguel Serveto-y-Revés (in Theol. Review, 1878).
Gordon, A. The Sozzini and their School (in Theol. Review, 1879).
Griffis, W. E., The Anabaptists (The New World, Dec., 1895).
Gründlicher Bericht van der evang. Reformation d. Christliken Kerken in Ostfriesland van 1520 beth up den hüdigen Dag. Bremen, 1594.
Guidonis, Bern., Practica inquisitionis hereticæ pravitatis, ed. C. Douais. Paris, 1886.

Haddan and Stubbs, Councils and Eccl. Doc. relating to Great Britain and Ireland. 3 vols. 1869-78.
Hagen, C., Deutschlands religiöse u. litterarische Verhältnisse im Reformation-Zeitalter. 3 vols. Frankfurt, 1860.
Hagenbach, K. R., J. Oekolampads Leben und ausgewähte Schriften. Elberfeld, 1859.

Hagenbach, K. R., Oswald Myconius. Elberfeld, 1859.
Halbertsma, J. H., De Doopsgezinde en hunne Herkompst. Deventer, 1843.
Hamelmann, H., Disputatio Westphalica contra Anabaptistas, hoc est, Disp. habita Monsterii Westph. coram Senatu a. 1533, 7 et Augusti ab H. Buschio . . . contra B. Rothmannum . . . 1572.
Hamelmann, H., Opera genealogico-historica de Westphalia et Saxonia inferiori. Lemgo, 1711.
Hanbury, B., Historical Memorials relating to the Independents or Congregationalists. 3 vols. London, 1839-44.
Hartfelder, K., Zur Gesch. d. Bauernkrieges. Stuttgart, 1884.
Hase, K., Das Reich d. Wiedertäufer. Leipzig, 1860.
Hase, K., Neue Propheten, 2d ed. Leipzig, 1861.
Hatch, E., Bampton Lectures, and Hibbert Lectures.
Haupt, H., Die deutsche Bibelübersetzung d. mittelalterlichen Waldenser. Würtzburg, 1885.
Haupt, H., Deutsch-böhmische Waldenser um 1340 (Zeitschr. f. Kirchengesch., Bd. XIV., 1, seq.).
Haupt, H., D. Mährischen Wiedertäufer und ihre Kommunistische Verfassung (Beilage zur Allgemeinen Zeitung, Nos. 53 and 54).
Haupt, H., Die Religiösen Sekten in Franken vor der Reformation. Würtzburg, 1882.
Haupt, H., Die Waldensische Ursprung d. Codex Teplensis. Würtzburg, 1886.
Haupt, H., Waldenserthum u. Inquisition im südöstlichen Deutschland. Freiburg, 1890.
Haupt, H., Waldensia (Zeitschr. f Kirchengesch., Bd. X., p. 311, seq.).
Hausrath, A., Arnold von Brescia. Leipzig, 1891.
Hausrath, A., Die Arnoldisten. Leipzig, 1895.
Heath, R., Anabaptism from its rise at Zwickau to its fall at Münster, 1521-1536. London, 1895.

Heath, R., Early Anabaptism (Cont. Rev., Apr., 1895).

Heath, R., Hans Denck, the Anabaptist (Cont. Rev., Dec., 1892).

Heath, R., The Anabaptists and their English Descendants (Cont. Rev., March, 1891).

Heath, R., The Communism of the Anabaptists (Cont. Rev., Aug., 1896).

Heberle, Die Anfänge d. Anabaptismus in der Schweiz (Jahrb. f. deutsche Theol., 1858).

Heberle, Joh. Denck u. d. Ausbreitung seiner Lehre (Theol. St. u. Krit., 1558).

Heberle, Joh. Denck u. sein Büchlein vom Gesetz Gottes (Theol. Stud. u. Krit., 1851).

Heberle, W. Capitos Verhaltniss zum Anabaptismus (Zeitschr. f. d. hist. Theol., 1857).

Herzog, J. J., Das Leben J. Oecolampads u. d. Reform. d. Kirche zu Basel. 2 vols. Basel, 1843.

Herzog, J. J., Die Romanischen Waldenser. 1853.

Hochhut, C. W. H., Der Landgraf Philipp u. d. Wiedertäufer (Zeitschr. f. d. hist. Theol., Vols. XXVIII. and XXIX., 1858-59).

Hochhut, C. W. H., Die Wiedertäufer unter d. Söhnen Landgr. Philipps (Zeitschr. f. d. hist. Theol., Vols. XXIX., XXX., and XXXI., 1859-61).

Höfler, Geschichtschreiber d. Hussit. Bewegung in Böhmen. 3 vols. Wien, 1856-66.

Höfling, J. W. F., D. Sacrament d. Taufe. 2 vols. Erlangen, 1846-48.

Hoffmann, W., Taufe u. Wiedertaufe. 1846.

Hofmann, Melchior. (See full bibliography, with copious extracts from his extant works in Zur Linden and in Leendertz. His account of the Flensburg disputation is reprinted in Strobel's Beiträge z. Lit., Vol. II., pp. 443, seq.).

Hosek, F. X., Balthaser Hubmaier. Brünn, 1867. (Published in Bohemian. An English translation through the German, edited by W. W. Everts, Jr., was published in the Texas Hist. and Biog. Mag., Vols. I. and II.)

Hottinger, J. J., Helvetische Kirchengesch. 4 vols. Zürich, 1698-1729.

Hubmaier, Balthasar. (See full bibliography and copious extracts in Loserth, Hosek, and Schreiber. Two large collections of H.'s tracts have been brought to the U. S., the one made by Dr. Howard Osgood and possessed by the Rochester Theol. Sem., the other made by Dr. J. P. Greene, of William Jewell College, Mo.)

Ivimey, J., A Hist. of the Engl. Baptists. Vol. I. London, 1811.

Jacklin, Georg Blaurock (Jahresbericht d. hist. -antiq. Gesellsch. von Graubünden, 1891).

Jager, C. F., Andreas Bodenstein von Karlstadt. Stuttgart, 1856.

Jäkel, J., Zur Frage über die Entstehung der Täufergemeinden in Oberösterreich (Gymnasial programme). Freistadt, 1895.

Jäkel, J., Zur Gesch. d. Wiedertäufer in Oberösterreich u. speciell in Freistadt (Museum Francisco-Carolinum. Linz, 1889).

Jannsen, J., Gesch. d. Deutschen Volkes. Freiburg, 1880, seq.

Jehring, J. C., Grundliche Historia von denen Begebenheiten ... so unter den Taufgesinnten oder Mennoniten ... vorgegangen. Jena, 1720.

Jörg, J. E., Deutschland in der Revolutionsperiod von 1522-36. Freiburg, 1851.

Joris, D., T'Wonder-boeck, 1551 (also c. 1600).

Jostes, F., Die Waldenser u. d. vorlutherische Bibelübersetzung. Münster, 1885.

Jundt, A., Les Amis de Dieu au quatorzième Siècle. Paris, 1879.

Jung, A., Friederich Reiser (Zeitschr. Timotheus, 1822).

Jung, A., Gesch. d. Reform. d. Kirche in Strassburg. 1830.

Kadebach, O., Ausführliche Gesch.

BIBLIOGRAPHY

Kaspar von Schwenckfeldt u. d. Schwenckfelder. 1860.

Karapet, M., Die Paulikianer. Leipzig, 1893.

Kautsky, K., Die Gesch. d. Sozialismus von Plato bis zu den Wiedertäufern. Stuttgart, 1895.

Keim, Th., Ludwig Hetzer (Jahrb. f. d. deutsch. Theol., 1856).

Keim, Th., Reformationsgeschichte d. Reichstadt Ulm. Stuttgart, 1851.

Keim, Th., Schwäbische Reformationsgesch. bis zum Augsburger Reichstag. Tübingen, 1855.

Keller, L., D. Böhmischen Brüder u. ihre Vorläufer. 1894.

Keller, L., D. Waldenser u. d. deutsche Bibelübersetzungen. Leipzig, 1886.

Keller L., Ein Apostel der Wiedertäufer (Joh. Denck). Leipzig, 1882.

Keller, L., Gesch. d. Wiedertäufer u. ihres Reichs zu Münster. Münster, 1880.

Keller, L., Joh. von Staupitz u. d. Anfänge d. Reformation. Leipzig, 1888.

Keller, L., Wolfgang Ulimann (Art. in Deutsche Biographie, Vol. XXXIX., p. 187, seq.).

Keller, L., Zur Gesch. d. Altevangelischen Gemeinden. Berlin, 1887

Keller, L., Zur Gesch. d. Wiedertäufer nach dem Untergang d. Münsterischen Königreichs (Westdeutsch. Zeitschrift f. Gesch. u. Kunst).

Kerssenbroick, H. von, Gesch. d. Wiedertäufer zu Münster, in Westphalen, aus ein Latein. Handschrift übersetzt. 1771.

Kessler, J., Sabbata, ed. Götzinger. St. Gall, 1866-68.

Kielstra, T., Het Münstersche Oproer (in Doopsgezinde Bijdragen. Leiden, 1888).

Kirchhofer, M., Bertold Haller oder d. Ref. von Bern. Zürich, 1828.

Kiessling, J. R., 'ΑΝΕΚΔΟΤΑ de Ludivico Hetzero (Museum Helveticum, Parts XXI. and XXIII. Zürich, 1751).

Kiessling, J. R., Der Lehrgebäude d. Wiedertäufer, nach den Grundsätzen d. Martin Czechowitz. Reval u. Leipzig, 1776.

Kirchhofer, M. (editor), Schafhauserische Jahrbücher von 1519-29. Frauenfeld, 1838.

Kirchhofer, M., Sebastian Wagner genannt Hofmeister. 1808.

Klimesch, P., Der Codex Teplensis. Augsburg, 1884.

Knewstub, Confutation of the Errors of Henry Nicholas. London, 1579.

Knonau, Meyer von, Die Eidgenossenschaft gegenuber den deutschen Bauernkrieg von 1525 (Hist. Zeitschrift, 1878).

Knox, John, An Answer to a great number of blasphemous cavillations written by an Anabaptist, and Adversary of God's Eternal Predestination. 1560 (3d ed., 1591).

Kolde, Th., Joh. v. Staupitz, ein Waldenser u. ein Wiedertäufer (Zeitschr. f. Kirchengesch., 1885).

Kolde, Th. (editor), Aeltester Bericht über die Zwickauer Propheten (Zeitscr. f. Kirchengesch., 1881, p. 323, seq.).

Krasinski, V., The Rise, Progress, and Decline of the Reformation in Poland. 2 vols. London, 1838-40.

Kripp, Ein Beitrag zur Gesch. d. Wiedertäufer in Tirol. Innsbruck, 1857.

Krohn, B. N., Gesch. d. fanatischen u. enthusiastischen Wiedertäufer (Melchior Hofmann). Leipzig, 1758.

Krummel, L., Gesch. d. Böhmischen Reformation im XV. Jahrh. Gotha, 1866.

Krummel, L., Utraquisten u. Taboriten. Gotha, 1876.

Küssenberg, H., Chronik d. Reform. in d. Grafschaft Baden (Archiv. f. d. Schw. Ref.-Gesch., Vol. III.).

Langenmantel, Hans, Auslegreng des Vaterunser. Elkhart, Ind.

Lea, H. C., A Hist. of the Inquisition of the Middle Ages. 3 vols. New York, 1888.

Lechler, G., Joh. von Wiclif u. d. Vorgesch. d. Reformation. 2 vols. Leipzig, 1873. (Eng. translat. of part of the work by Lorimer: Joh. Wiclif and his Eng. Predecessors. London, 1878).

Leendertz, W. J., Melchior Hofmann (in Dutch). Haarlem, 1883.

Leib, K., Historiarum sui temporis ab a. 1524 ad a. 1548 annales (in Döllinger's Mater. z. Gesch. d. XV. u. XVI. Jahrh. Regensburg, 1863).

Liliencron, R. von, Zur Liederdichtung d. Wiedertäufer (Abhandl. d. Kön. Bair. Akad. d. Wissensch., 1877).

Lindner, G. B., De Joviniano et Vigilantio. Leipzig, 1840.

Loserth, J., D. Anabaptismus in Tirol (2 parts). Wien, 1892.

Loserth, J., D. Communismus d. Mährischen Wiedertäufer im XVI. u. XVII. Jahrh. Wien, 1894.

Loserth, J., Deutsch-böhmische Wiedertäufer (Mittheil. d. Vereins f. Gesch. d. Deutschen in Böhmen. Prag, 1892).

Loserth, J., Die Stadt Waldshut u. d. Vorderösterreichische Regierung in d. Jahren 1523-1526. Wien, 1891.

Loserth, J., Doctor Balthasar Hubmaier u. d. Anfänge d. Wiedertäufer in Mähren. Aus gleichzeitigen Quellen. Brünn, 1893. (By far the best work on the subject, almost superseding the earlier treatises.)

Loserth, J., Wiedertäufer in Steiermark (Mittheil. d. hist. Vereins f. Steiermark. Graz, 1894).

Loserth, J., Zur Gesch. d. Wiedertäufer in Mähren (Zeitschr. f. allgem. Gesch., 1884. Hft. 6).

Loserth, J., Zwei biographishen Skizzen aus der Zeit d. Wiedertäufer in Tirol. Innsbruck, 1895. (Contains a valuable account of Pilgram Marbeck.)

Luther, Martin, Works. (In many editions. His Briefe, ed. DeWette, are especially rich in notices of the Anti-pedobaptist movement.)

Mannhardt, W., Die Wehrfreiheit d. altpreussischen Mennoniten. Marienburg, 1863.

Mehrning, J., Der heilige Tauff Historie, 1647.

Menius, J., Der Widdertäuffer Lehre u. Geheimniss aus Heil. Schrift widderlegt. Wittemberg, 1530.

Menius, J., Vom Geist der Wiedertäufer, 1544.

Mennonitische Blätter (1855 onward).

Menno Simons, Works (Dutch, German, and English).

Merx, O., Thomas Münzer u. Heinrich Pfeiffer. Göttingen, 1889.

Meschovius, A., Historiæ Anabaptisticæ Libri Septem. Coloniae, 1617.

Meyer, C., Wiedertäufer in Schwaben (Zeitschr. f. Kirchengesch., Vol. XVII., p. 248, seq. A contemporary account of the Augsburg Anti-pedobaptist movement, edited from a Münich MS.).

Meyer, C., Zur Gesch. d. Wiedertäufer Oberschwaben (Zeitschr. d. hist. Vereins f. Schwaben u. Neuberg, Vol. I., 1874.

Merian, Topographia Bohemiæ, Moraviæ et Silesiæ. Frankfurt, 1650.

Michelis, A., Les Anabaptistes dans les Vosges. Paris, 1862.

Moded, H., Grondlich Bericht von de eerste Beghinsel der Wederdoopschen Secten. 1603.

Müller, W., Andreas Osiander. Elberfeld, 1870.

Müller, W., Lehrbuch d. Kirchengeschichte, Vol. III., ed. G. Kawerau. Freiburg, 1894 (excellent sections on the Anti-pedobaptist movement).

Mörikofer, J. C., Ulrich Zwingli. 2 vols. Leipzig, 1867-69.

Montet, E., Histoire littéraire des Vaudois du Piemont. Paris, 1885.

Mosheim, J. L. von, De Beghardis et Beguinabus Commentarius. Leipzig, 1790.

Mosheim, J. L. von, Institutiones Historiæ Christianæ Recentioris. Helmstadt, 1741.

Müller, E., Gesch. d. Bernischen Täufer. Frauenfeld, 1895.

Müller, J., Die deutschen Katachismen d. Böhmischen Brüder (Monumenta Germ. Pedagogica, Vol. IV.).

Müller, J. von, Gesch. d. Schweiz. Eidgenossenschaft, Vol. VII. Zürich, 1829.

Müller, J. P., Die Mennoniten in Ostfriesland. Emden, 1887.

Müller, K., Die Waldenses u. ihre einzelnen Gruppen bis zum Anfang d. XIV. Jahrh. 1886.

Newman, A. H., The Early Waldenses (Bapt. Quar. Rev., July, 1885).
Newman, A. H., The Moravian Baptists (Bapt. Quar. Rev., Jan., 1887).
Newman, A. H., The Peasants' War (Bapt. Quar. Rev., Jan., 1889).
Newman, A. H., Recent Researches concerning Mediæval Sects (Papers of the Am. Soc. of Ch. Hist., Vol. IV.).
Nicene and Post-Nicene fathers of the Christian church, ed. Schaff and Wace. New York, 1886 onward.
Nicoladoni, A., Joh. Bünderlin von Linz u. d. oberösterreichen Täufergemeinden in d. Jah. 1525-1531. Berlin, 1893.
Nippold, F., David Joris (Zeitschr. f. hist. Theol., 1863, 1864, and 1868).
Nippold, F., Heinrich Niclaes (Zeitschr. f. d. hist. Theol., Vol. XXXII.).
Nitsche, R., Gesch. d. Wiedertäufer in d. Schweiz zur Reformationszeit. Einseideln, 1885.

Ochs, P., Gesch. d. Stadt u. Landschaft Basel, Vols. V. and VI. Basel, 1821.
Odenbach, J., Ain Sendbrieff u. Rathschlag an verordnete Richter über den armen gefangenen zu Anzey, so man Wiederteuffer nennet. 1528.
Ottii, J. H., Annales Anabaptistici. Basel, 1672.

Palacky, F., Geschichte von Böhmen. 5 vols. Prag, 1836-68.
Palacky, F., Ueber d. Beziehungen und d. Verhältniss d. Waldenser zu den ehemaligen Secten in Böhmen. Prag, 1869.
Pantheon Anabaptisticum et Enthusiasticum, 1702.
Pearson, K., The Kingdom of God in Münster (Modern Review, January and April, 1884).
Pestalozzi, C., Leo Judæ. Elberfeld, 1860.
Philipps, Dirk, Enchiridion (Dutch and German).
Philipps [Filipsz], Obbe, Bekenntnisse. 1584.
Pistis Sophia, ed. Petermann. Berlin, 1851. (Copious extracts in English in King, The Gnostics and their Remains.)

Porta, R. de, Hist. Ref. Ecclesiarum Rhæticarum, Vol. I. 1772.
Preger, W., Beiträge zur Gesch. d. Waldesier im Mittelalter. München, 1877.
Preger, W., Das Verhältniss d. Taboriten u. Waldesier. München, 1887.
Preger, W., D. Tractat J. David von Augsburg über d. Waldesier. München, 1875.
Preger, W., Gesch. d. deutschen Mystik. Leipzig, 1874 onw.
Preger, W., Ueber d. Verfassung d. französischen Waldesier. München, 1890.
Process, wie es soll gehalten werden mit d. Wiedertäufern durch etliche Gelehrten, so zu Worms gersammelt gewesen. Worms, anno 1557, Phil. Melancthon, Joh. Brenz, etc. (Substance given in Menn. Blätter, 1893, No. 14, seq.).
Protcol, dat is de gantsche ghesprecx ghehonden tot Leeuwarden tusschen Ruardum Acronium . . . ende Peeter van Ceulen. 16 Aug.-17 Nov., 1596. Franeker, 1597.
Protocol, dath is, alle Verhandlinge d. Gesprecks tho Embden mit den Wedderdöpern, de sich Flaminge nömen. Embden, 1579.
Protocoll d. Religionsgesprächs mit den Wiedertäufern zu Frankenthal im Jah. 1571. Heidelberg, 1573.

Racovian Catechism (Polish, German, Latin, 1605 onwd. English edition with Hist. Introd. by T. Rees. London, 1818).
Ranke, L. von, Deutsche Gesch. im Zeitalter der Reformation. 6th ed. 6 vols. Leipzig, 1881.
Reiswitz u. Waldeck, Beiträge zur Kenntniss d. Mennonitengemeinden. Berlin, 1821-29.
Reitsma, S. J., Honderd Jaren uit de Geschiedenis der Hervorming en der Hervormde in Friesland. Leeuwarden, 1876.
Rembert, K., D. Wiedertäufer in Herzogthum Jülich. Münster, 1893.
Reuter, H., Gesch. d. religiösen Aufklärung im Mittelalter. 2 vols. Berlin, 1875-77.

Ritschl, A., Gesch. d. Pietismus, Vol. I. Bonn, 1880.

Rhegius, Urbanus, Ein Sendbrieff Hans Huthen etwa eines furnemen Vorsteers im Wiedertäufferorden. Augsburg, 1528.

Rhegius, Urbanus, Widderlegung der Munsterischen newen Valentinianer und Donatisten Bekentnus. Vorrhede Dr. M. Luthers. Wittemberg, 1535.

Rhegius, Urbanus, Zween wunderseltzam Sendbrieff zweyer Wiedertäuffer an ihre Secten gen Augsburg gesandt. Verantwortung aller Irrthum diser ob genannten Brief. Augsburg, 1528.

Rhesa, L., Historia Anabaptistarum et Sacramentariorum in Prussia. 3 Parts. 1834-38.

Reimann, V. M., Mennonis Simonis qualis fuerit vita vitaque actio exponatur. Jena, 1803.

Robinson, R., A History of Baptism. London, 1790.

Rogers, John, The Displaying of a Horrible Sect naming themselves the Family of Love. London, 1579.

Röhrich, G. W., Essai sur la vie, les ecrits et la doctrine de l'anabaptiste Jean Denk. Strassburg, 1853.

Röhrich, T. W., Die Gottesfreunde u. d. Winckeler am Oberrhein (Zeitschr. f. hist. Theol., 1840).

Röhrich, T. W., Gesch. d. Reform. im Elsass. 3 vols. Strassburg, 1840.

Röhrich, T. W., Mittheilungen zur Gesch. d. evang. Kirche im Elsass. 2 vols. Strassburg, 1855.

Röhrich, T. W., Zur Gesch. d. Strassburgischen Wiedertäufer (Zeitschr. f. d. hist. Theol., 1860).

Rommel, C. von, Gesch. Philipps d. Grossmüthigen, Landgr. v. Hessen. Giessen, 1830.

Roosen, B. E., Gesch. d. Mennonitengemeinde zu Hamburg u. Altona, Vol. I. Hamburg, 1886.

Roosen, B. K., Menno Simons. Leipzig, 1848.

Roth, F., Die Einführung d. Reform. in Nürnberg, 1517-28. Würtzburg, 1885.

Roth, F., Reformationsgeschichte Augsburgs, 1517-27. München, 1881.

Roth, F. W. E., Zur Gesch. d. Wiedertäufer am Mittelrhein (Menn. Blätter, No. 12, 1893).

Roth, F. W. E., Zur Gesch. d. Wiedertäufer zu Worms im XVI. Jahrh. (Menn. Blätter, No. 14, 1893).

Rothmann, Bern., Von Verborgenheit der Schrifft des Rickes Christi und von dem Tage des Herrn, durch die Gemeinde Christi zu Münster. Münster, 1535 (reprinted by Hochhut, Gotha, 1857).

Sandius, C. C., Bibliotheca Antitrinitariorum. Freistadii, 1684.

Schaff, P., The Oldest Church Manual, called The Teaching of the Twelve Apostles. New York, 1885.

Schaff, P., The Anabaptists in Switzerland (Bapt. Rev., July, 1889).

Schauenberg, L., Die Täuferbewegung in Grafschaft Oldenberg-Delmenhorst u. d. Herrschaft Jever zur Zeit d. Reform. Oldenberg, 1888.

Schelhorn, J. G., Balthasar Hubmaier (Acta Hist. Eccl., Vol. I., p. 100, seq. Ulm, 1738).

Schreiber, H., Balthasar Hubmeier (Taschenbuch f. Gesch. u. Alterth. Süddeutschlands, 1839).

Schreiber, H., Der Bundschuh zu Lehen u. d. arme Konrad zu Buhl. Freiburg, 1824.

Schreiber, H., Der deutsche Bauernkrieg. 3 vols. Freiburg, 1863-66.

Schmidt, C., Der Antheil d. Strassburger an die Reform. von Kurpfalz. Strassburg, 1856.

Schmidt, C., Die Secten zu Strassburg im mittelalter (Zeitschr. f. hist. Theol., 1840, Hft. 3).

Schmidt, C., Histoire et Doctrine de la Secte des Cathares ou Albigeois. 2 vols. Paris, 1849.

Schmidt, C., Joh. Tauler. Hamburg, 1841.

Schmidt, C., Nikolaus von Basel. Wien, 1866.

Schmidt, C., Nikolaus von Basels Bericht von d. Bekehrung Taulers. Strassburg, 1875.

Schwabe, L., Ueber Hans Denck (Zeitscr. f. Kirchengesch., Vol. XII., p. 452, seq., contains the text of a work attributed to Denck on Baptism, the Supper, Magistracy, Marriage, etc.).

Schyn, H., Historia Christianorum qui in Belgio Foederato Mennonitæ appelantur. 1723. (Also in Dutch, ed. Maatschoen. 2 vols. Amsterdam, 1743-44).

Seeck, O., Quellen u. Urkunden über die Anfänge d. Donatismus (Zeitscr. für Kirchengesch., Vol. X., p. 505, seq.).

Seidemann, J. K., Thomas Münzer. Dresden, 1842.

Seidemann, J. K., Zur Gesch. d. Bauernkriegs in Thüringen (Forsch. zur deutsch. Gesch., Vols. XI. and XIV.).

Sender, C., Historica Relatio de ortu et Progressu Haeres. 1654.

Sepp, C., Geschiedkund. Nasporingen. 3 parts. Leiden, 1872-75.

Sepp, C., Kerkhist. Studien. Leiden, 1885.

Servetus, M., Restitutio Christianismi. 1553.

Seyler, F., Anabaptista Larvatus. Basel, 1680.

Simler, J. J., Sammlung alter u. neuer Urkunden. Zürich, 1759-63.

Socinus, F., Opera, Vol. I.

Stähelin, R., Die ersten Martyrer d. evang. Glaubens in d. Schweiz. Heidelberg, 1883.

Stähelin, R., Huldreich Zwingli, Vol. I. Basel, 1895.

Starck, J. A., Gesch. d. Taufe u. Taufgesinnten. Leipzig, 1789.

Stern, A., Ueber die Zwölf Artikel der Bauern. Leipzig, 1868.

Strasser, G., Der schweizerische Anabaptismus zur Zeit d. Ref. (in Nippold's Berner Beiträgen zur Gesch. d. Schw. Ref.-Kirchen. Bern, 1884).

Strickler, J., Aktensammlung zur Schweizer Reformationsgesch. 5 vols. Zürich, 1878-84.

Strobel, G. T., Beiträge zur Literatur besonders des XVI. Jahrh. 1787.

Strobel, G. T., Leben, Schriften u. Lehren Thomas Münzers. Nürnberg. 1795.

Strype, Historical and Biographical Works. 27 vols. Oxford, 1822-28 (new edition).

Sturler, M. von, Urkunden d. Bernischen Kirchenreform. Bern, 1862.

Taylor, A., The Hist. of the English General Baptists. 2 vols. London, 1818.

Thesaurus Baumianus (a rich MS. collection of letters and other documents relating to the Reformation in Strassburg, etc. It is preserved in the Thomas archives of Strassburg).

Tollin, H., Das Lehrsystem Servets. 3 vols. Gutersloh, 1876-78.

Tollin, H., Servet un d. Oberländischen Reformatoren. Berlin, 1880.

Trechsel, F., Die Protest. Antitrinitarier vor F. Socinus. 2 vols. 1839-44.

Underhill, E. B., Historical Introduction to the Publications of the Hanserd Knollys Society. London, 1846-47.

Unger, Th., Ueber eine Wiedertäufer-Liederhandschrift des XVII. Jahrh. (Jahrb. d. Protestantismus, 1892. The hymns are published in several numbers of the review beginning with Heft I. The material was reproduced in part in Menn. Blätter, 1893, No. 1, seq.).

Usteri, J. M., Darstellung d. Tauflehre Zwinglis (Theol. St. u. Krit., 1882).

Usteri, J. M., Zwinglis Correspondenz mit den Berner Reformatoren über die Tauffrage (Theol. St. u. Krit., 1882).

Usteri, J. M., Zu Zwingli's Elenchus (Zeitschr. f. Kirchengesch., Vol. XI., p. 161, seq.).

Van der Smissen, H. A., Kurtzgefasste Gesch. u. Glaubenslehre d. altevangelischen Taufgesinnten oder Mennoniten. 1895.

Van Slee, J. C., De Rijnsburger Collegianten. Haarlem, 1895.

Veesenmeyer, Balthasar Hubmaier (Staudlin u. Vater's Kirchenhist. Archiv, 1826).

Vesenmayer, Beiträge zur Gesch. d. Literatur (on Langenmantel, etc.). Ulm, 1792.

Vogt, W., Vorgeschichte des Bauernkrieges. Halle, 1887.

Völter, D., Der Ursprung d. Donatisten. Freiberg, 1883.

Wachsmuth, W., Der deutsche Bauernkrieg zur Zeit d. Ref. Leipzig, 1834.

Wackernagel, P., Das deutsche Kirchenlied von d. ältesten Zeiten bis zu Anfang d. XVII. Jahrh. 3 vols. Leipzig, 1870.

Walch, J. G., Historia Pædobaptismi IV. priorum sæculorum. Jena, 1739.

Walch, W. F., Entwurf e. vollständigen Hist. d. Ketzereien. 1768.

Walker, W., A Hist. of the Congregational Churches in the U. S. New York, 1894.

Walker, W., The Creeds and Platforms of Congregationalism. New York, 1893.

Wall, W., History of Infant Baptism. London, 1705 (new edition Oxford, 1862).

Watt, Joach. von (Vadianus), Deutsche hist. Schriften, Vol. II. and III. St. Gall, 1877-79.

Weber, Gesch. d. akath. Kirchen und Secten v. Gr. Brit. 2 vols. Leipzig, 1845-53.

Weill, A., Histoire de la Guerre des Anabaptistes. Paris, 1874.

Weingarten, S. H., Die Revolutions-Kirchen Englands. Leipzig, 1868.

Whitsitt, W. H., A Question in Baptist History. Louisville, 1896.

Wider den newen Täufforden notwendige Warnung an alle Christglaubigen durch die Diener des Evang. zu Augsburg. Augsburg, 1527.

Wigandus, J., De Anabaptismo grassante adhuc in multis Germaniæ, Poloniæ, Prussiæ, Belgicæ et aliis quoque locis. Lipsiæ, 1582 (also German edition 1576).

Wilkins, Concilia magnæ Britanniæ. London, 1737.

Will, G. A., Beiträge zur Gesch. des Anabaptismus in Deutschland, 2d edition. Nürnberg, 1773. (Contains a reprint of a document issued by the Nürnberg authorities against the Antipedobaptists, and other important matter.)

Willis, R., Servetus and Calvin. London, 1877.

Winter, V. A., Gesch. d. baierischen Wiedertaufer im XVI. Jahrh. München, 1809.

Wolny, Die Wiedertäufer in Mähren (Archiv f.' Kunde österreich. Geschichtsquellen, 1850).

Wurstisen, Baseler Chronik. Basel, 1580.

Zezschwitz, G. von, Die Katechismen der Waldenser u. Böhmischen Brüder. Erlangen, 1863.

Zimmermann, W., Gesch. d. grossen Bauernkrieges, 2d ed. Stuttgart, 1856.

Zur Linden, F. O., Melchior Hofmann. Leipzig, 1885.

Zwingli, Opera. ed. Schüler u. Schulthess. 8 vols. Zürich, 1828-42.

INDEX

Aërius, a reformer, but not an Anti-pedobaptist, 20, *seq.*, 27.

Ainsworth ; an English Separatist, 373 ; against John Smyth, 382, 385.

Amon, Hans : an Anti-pedobaptist leader in Moravia, 229 ; death of, 230.

Anabaptism, "painted for those who could not read," 192.

"Ancient Records," spurious, 374, *seq.*

Anna, Countess, tolerance of, 301.

Anti-pedobaptists, wide diffusion of, 151.

Arnold of Brescia, possibly an Anti-pedobaptist, 35, *seq.*

Arnoldists, The, 38, *seq.*

Asceticism, pagan origin of, 12.

Askew, Anne, probably not an Anti-pedobaptist, 351.

Augsburg, Anti-pedobaptist movement in, *seq.*

Austerlitz : an important Anti-pedobaptist center, 223 ; schism in the community, 224, *seq.*

Austria : Anti-pedobaptist movement in, 205, *seq.* ; extent of the movement, 212.

Barrowe, Henry, an English martyr, 373.

Baptismal regeneration in the early church, 4, *seq.*

Basel: disputation on baptism in, 120 ; persecutes Anabaptists, 121.

Battenburg, Jan, a fanatical Dutch Anabaptist leader, 30.

Bernard of Clairvaux, as a heresy-hunter, 35, 36.

Bernard, Richard, against John Smyth, 382.

Berne, power and persistence of the Anti-pedobaptist movement in, 123,150.

Beza, Theodore, work of, in defense of the burning of heretics, published in the Netherlands (about 1601 or 1602), 319.

Bintgens' controversy, 316, *seq.*

Blaurer, Margaretta, a protector of Pilgram Marbeck, 249.

Blaurock, Georg : baptized by Grebel, 107 ; method of evangelizing and baptizing, 107, *seq.* ; defends his Anti-pedobaptism, 109 ; disputes with Zwingli, 110 ; sketch of, 131, *seq.* ; imprisoned at Zürich, 137 ; released, 144 ; re-arrested, scourged, and banished, 145, *seq.* ; in the Tyrol, 195 ; martyrdom of, 195.

Blawermel, Philip, a Moravian Anti-pedobaptist leader, 223.

Bohemia, Anti-pedobaptist movement in, 236, *seq.*

Bohemian Brethren : practised rebaptism and in part rejected infant baptism, 53, *seq.* ; abandoned rebaptism in 1534, 54.

Boucher, Joan, the martyr, may have been an Anti-pedobaptist, 354, *seq.*

Bouwens, Leonard, a Mennonite leader, 301, 304, *seq.*

Bozen : a Tyrolese Anti-pedobaptist center, 194 ; persecution in, 194.

Brandhuber, Wolfgang, an Austrian Anti-pedobaptist leader, 213.

Brixen : a Tyrolese Anti-pedobaptist center, 194 ; persecution in, 194 ; six hundred Anti-pedobaptists executed in, 202 ; weary of bloodshed, 202.

British church, the early, evangelical, but not Anti-pedobaptist, 22, *seq.*

Brötli, Hans : opposes infant baptism at Zollikon, 105 ; banished, 107 ; at Schaffhausen, 111, *seq.*

Browne, Robert : an English Separatist, 369, *seq.* ; indebtedness of to the Anti-pedobaptists, 370, *seq.* ; in Zeeland, 371, *seq.* ; returned to the Church of England and died in disrepute, 372 ; some followers of, became Anti-pedobaptists, 372.

INDEX

Bucer, Martin: Protestant pastor in Strasburg, 239, seq.; attitude of toward Anti-pedobaptists, 239, 240, 244, 247, 249, seq.; in England, 352.

Bünderlin, Joh.: accepts Anti-pedobaptist views, 217; rejects external ordinances, 218.

Calvinism: gains the ascendency in the Netherlands, 314, seq.; intolerance of, 318, seq.

Capito, Wolfgang, a Strasburg Protestant pastor: tolerant disposition of, 239, seq.; almost an Anti-pedobaptist, 240, 247.

Carlstadt, Andreas: influenced by the Zwickau prophets, 71; driven from Wittenberg, 73; at Orlamünde, 74; in Strasburg, 241, seq.

Castelberg, Andreas: an opponent of Zwingli, 101, seq.; rejects infant baptism, 105; banished, 107.

Catechism of Polish Anti-pedobaptists (1574), on baptism, 336, seq.

Cathari, 30.

Cellarius, Martin: influenced by the Zwickau prophets, 71, seq., 74; in Strasburg, 241; influence of, on Capito, 240, 247.

Chelcicky, Peter: evangelical views of, 50, seq.; almost an Anti-pedobaptist, 52.

Chiliasm: the corrupting element in the work of Storch, Münzer, and Pfeiffer, 85, seq.; of Hofmann, 257, 268, etc.; of Hut, 151; of Matthys, 284, seq.; in relation to the Münster Kingdom, 293.

Clementine Homilies and Recognitions, on baptism, 7, 8.

Clyfton, Richard, on John Smyth, 382, 385.

Collegiants, 321, seq., 387.

Cologne, Anti-pedobaptists in (1146), 35.

Communism: a course of persecution in Moravia, 229, seq.; description of the communistic organization of the Huterites, 234, seq.

Convention of Anti-pedobaptists in Augsburg, 170, seq.

Cooke, Robert: an English Anti-pedobaptist, 352; disputes with the court preachers of Edward VI., 353; accused of Pelagianism by Turner, 353.

Cranmer, Archbishop: influenced by foreign theologians to persecute Anti-pedobaptists, 352; an inquisitor, 354.

Cyprian, on baptism, 6, 7, seq.

Czechowitz, Martin, a Polish Anti-pedobaptist, 335.

Dachser, Jacob, an Anti-pedobaptist leader in Augsburg, 171.

Dakota, South, present abode of the Huterites, 233.

David of Augsburg, on the Waldenses, 46, seq.

Denck, Hans: in Augsburg, 160, seq.; in St. Gall, 163, seq.; his theological views, 164, seq.; driven from Augsburg, 167; return to Augsburg, 170; died at Basel, 172; in Strasburg, 242, seq.; at Zaubern, 243; at Landau, disputes with Baker, 243; at Worms, 243.

Doctrines and polity of the Moravian Anti-pedobaptists, compared with those of the old-evangelical parties, 235, seq.

Döllinger, erroneous view of, regarding Peter de Bruys and Henry of Lausanne, 34.

Donatists, not Baptists or Anti-pedobaptists, 18, seq.

Dubcansky, Joh., an evangelical Moravian nobleman, 175, 177.

Dutch Anabaptists: in England, 361; persecution of, 361, seq.; thirty seized in a suburb of London, 365; sufferings and confession of, 362, seq.

Dutch in England, 345, seq.

Eberle, H., Anabaptist worker at St. Gall, 116, seq.

Ebionitism, 26.

Echsel, W., an Anti-pedobaptist leader in Strasburg, 242.

Edward VI., of England: favored Protestantism, but persecuted Anti-pedobaptism, 351, seq.; excepted Anti-pedobaptists from the act of grace, 354.

Elizabeth, Queen, a persecutor of Anti-pedobaptists, 357, seq.

Emden, an Anti-pedobaptist center, 266.

England: Anti-pedobaptists in (1534 onward), 346, seq.; persecuting measures in, 346, 348, 350.

Enno, Count, a tolerant ruler, 266.

INDEX

Evervin, on mediæval Anti-pedobaptists in Cologne, 35, seq.

Eythorne, Baptist church at, its claims to antiquity, 355, seq.

Faber, Gellius, in controversy with Menno, 308.

Faber, J., seeks to convert Hubmaier, 186.

Falk, Jacob, executed at Zürich, 149.

Ferdinand, King, mandates of, against Anabaptism, 192, seq.

Foxe, John, against the burning of heretics, 365.

Freundberg, a Tyrolese Anti-pedobaptist center, 192.

Freistadt: an Austrian Anti-pedobaptist center, 218, seq.; Hut's labors in, 219.

Gabrielites, a Moravian Anti-pedobaptist party, 228.

Gerrits: Lubbert, Mennonite pastor in Amsterdam; negotiations of, with John Smyth and his followers, 389.

Gherlandi, Giulio: an Italian Anti-pedobaptist, who was converted to evangelical views in Moravia and returned to Italy to labor, 331, seq.; his confession and martyrdom, 333, seq.

Gillis of Aachen, a Mennonite leader, 304, seq.

Glaidt, Oswald: Hubmaier's colleague at Nikolsburg, 175, seq.; later labors of, 230.

Gnosticism, influence of, on Christian thought, 6, seq.

Göschel, Martin: an ex-bishop and Hubmaier's colleague at Nikolsburg, 175, seq.

Gonesius, Peter, a Polish anti-trinitarian Anti-pedobaptist, 335.

Grebel, Conrad; an associate of Zwingli, 90; opposes Zwingli, 101, seq.; resists infant baptism, 105, seq.; baptizes Blaurock and others, 107; in Schaffhausen, 112, seq.; at St. Gall, 116, seq.; sketch of, 129, seq.; imprisoned at Zürich, 137; released, 143, seq.; in Grüningen, 144.

Griesinger, Onophrius, a Tyrolese Anti-pedobaptist leader executed in 1538, 201.

Gross, Jacob: in Augsburg, 160, 170; in Strasburg, 242.

Grüningen: a stronghold of Anti-pedobaptism, 123; authorities of unable to suppress the movement, 136; continued growth of Anti-pedobaptism in, 144; immorality of clergy in, 144; refuses to execute Anti-pedobaptists, 147; compelled to yield, 149, seq.

Gufidaun, persecution of Anti-pedobaptists in, 193.

Haller, Berthold and Joh.: reformers at Berne, 91; disturbed about infant baptism, 123.

Hamsted, Hadrian, a defender of Anti-pedobaptists, 360, seq.

Helena von Freiberg, a Tyrolese Anti-pedobaptist, 190, 192.

Helwys, Thomas: an associate of John Smyth in introducing believers' baptism, 385; refused to follow Smyth in seeking union with the Mennonites, 388, seq.; denied the need of succession, 389; returned to England, 391; on liberty of conscience, 392.

Henry of Lausanne, an Anti-pedobaptist reformer, 32, seq.

Hermann, Hieronymus, sent forth from Steyer by Hut, 211.

Hesse, Anti-pedobaptist movement in, 273, seq.

Hetzer, Ludwig: an associate of Zwingli, 90; banished for Anti-pedobaptism, 107; in Augsburg, 160, seq.; in Strasburg, 242.

Hochrütiner, L.: banished from Zürich, 102; opposes infant baptism at St. Gall, 115.

Hofmann, Melchior: a native of Swabia, 254; at Wolmar, 254; at Dorpat, 254, seq.; endorsed by Luther, 255; banished, 256; in Sweden, 256, seq.; at Lübeck, 258; employed by Frederick I., of Denmark, 258; plundered and banished, 258, seq.; in East Friesland, 259; in Strasburg, 259, seq.; in the Netherlands, 261; imprisoned for life at Strasburg, 263; at Emden, 266; on baptism, 266, seq.; in Holland, 267, seq.; suspends the administration of baptism for two years, 268; on the will, 269; combats

INDEX

Lutheranism, 270; bewails his lack of followers in Germany, 270; on the incarnation, 271.

Hofmeister, Sebastian: rejects infant baptism, 112; driven by persecution to repudiate Anti-pedobaptism, 113, *seq.*

Hubmaier, Balthasar: in conference with Münzer, 82; at Zurich, disputation, 90; early career at Freiburg, Ingolstadt, and Regensburg, 91, *seq.*; a radical leader at Waldshut, 92, *seq.*; in Schaffhausen, 96, *seq.*; returns to Waldshut, 99; opposes OEcolampadius and Zwingli, 121, *seq.*; against infant baptism, 124, *seq.*; issues a challenge, 126; baptized by Reublin, 126; baptizes a multitude, 126; publishes on baptism, 128; leaves Waldshut, 138; takes refuge in Zurich, 139; his extradition demanded by Austria, 139; imprisoned and probab'y tortured, 139, *seq.*; partial recantation of, 141, *seq.*; allowed to depart, 143; in Augsburg, 160, 166; career in Moravia, 173, *seq.*; great literary activity of, 177, *seq.*; against Zwingli, 177, *seq.*; on the Supper, 178, *seq.*, and 180; on fasting in sacred seasons, 179; on the obligation of believers' baptism, 179; apology of, 179, *seq.*; on the will, 181; on the sword, 182, *seq.*; on baptism, 180, *seq.*; against community of goods, 183, *seq.*; controversy with Hut, 184, *seq.*; delivered to the Austrian authorities, 186; burned at the stake, 187.

Humiliati, The, 39.

Hut, Hans: a propagator of chiliastic views, 151; a leader in Augsburg, 167, *seq.*; his death, 168; at Steyer, 207, *seq.*; description of, 209; enthusiasm aroused by, 212; "The Seven Seals" of, 212; at Freistadt, 219.

Huter, Jacob: early career of, 194, *seq.*; goes to Moravia, 195; Tyrolese labors of, 197, *seq.*; tortured and burned, 200.

Idolatry, Christian, pagan origin of, 12, *seq.*

Infant baptism: rise of, 9, *seq.*; evils of, 28.

Italy: religious condition of, at the beginning of the Protestant Revolution, 323; influence of German and Swiss Protestants in, 323, *seq.*; antitrinitarian Anti-pedobaptist movement in, 325, *seq.*

Jesuits, The, promoters of persecution, 204.

Jewel, Bishop, on English Anti-pedobaptists, 359, *seq.*

John of Leyden, head of "the Kingdom of God" in Münster, 289, *seq.*

Johnson, Francis: an English Separatist, 373; pastor of a congregation in Amsterdam, 373; some followers of, became Anti-pedobaptists, 373.

Joris, David, a pantheistic Anti-pedobaptist leader, 301.

Jovinian, a reformer, but not an Anti-pedobaptist, 20, *seq.*, 27.

Julich-Cleve, evangelical movement in, 280.

Justin Martyr, on baptism, 4.

Käls, Hieronymus, an Anti-pedobaptist leader, executed at Vienna, 200.

Karapet, on Paulicians and Thondrakians, 25.

Kautz, Jacob: a mystical Anti-pedobaptist at Worms, 245; in Strasburg, 246, *seq.*; in Augsburg, 170.

Kent, Anti-pedobaptists in, 354, *seq.*

Kessler, Joh., an evangelical teacher at St. Gall, 115, *seq.*

Kitzbüchl: a Tyrolese Anti-pedobaptist center, 192; persecution in, 193, 194.

Klopriss, J.: an Anti-pedobaptist leader at Münster, 280, *seq.*; accepts the leadership of Matthys, 280.

Knipperdollinck, B., a Münster fanatic, 289, *seq.*

Knox, John: a confounder of Anabaptists, 356; polemical treatise of, against an Anabaptist, 357, *seq.*; justified the burning of heretics, 359.

Kodde, Van der, four brothers, who founded the Collegiants, 321.

Langecker, Hans, an Anti-pedobaptist martyr, 195.

Langenmantel, Eitelhans, an Anti-pedobaptist leader in Augsburg, 169, *seq.*

Lanzenstiel (or Seiler), Leonard: an Anti-pedobaptist minister, imprisoned

INDEX 411

at Moding, 200, seq.; a prominent leader in the Tyrol, 203; execution of, 203.

Lasco, John à: controversy of, with Menno, 362, seq.; befriended by Mennonites, 307, seq.; on Polish Anti-pedobaptists, 336; in England, 352.

Latimer, Bishop, a persecutor, 354.

Liberty of Conscience: Hubmaier on, 96, seq., advocated by an English Anti-pedobaptist in 1560, 357.

Lichtenstein, Leonard and Hans von, Hubmaier's patrons, 175, seq.

Linz, an Austrian Anti-pedobaptist center, 212, seq.

Lochmayer, Leonard, a Tyrolese Anti-pedobaptist minister, 203.

Lollards: not known to have been Anti-pedobaptists, 55, seq.; 340, seq.; persisted in England and Scotland till the sixteenth century, 340, seq.; evangelical position of, 343, seq.

Luther: radical character of his early teachings, 64, seq.; against the Zwickau prophets, 72, seq.

Mändl, Hans, an Anti-pedobaptist leader in the Tyrol, 203, seq

Manelfi, Pietro: an Italian Anti-pedobaptist, 126; his account of Tiziano's teachings, 326; his account of the Anti-pedobaptist convention at Venice, 327, seq.; an apostate and traitor, 328, 330.

Manz, Felix: an opponent of Zwingli, 101, seq.; rejects infant baptism, 105, seq.; disputes with Zwingli, 110; sketch of, 131, seq.; imprisoned at Zürich, 137; released, 143, seq.; in Grüningen, 144; re-arrested and executed by drowning, 145, seq.

Marbeck, Pilgram: an early Tyrolese Anti-pedobaptist, 189; in Strasburg, 249; disputation with Bucer, 249, seq.; banished, 250; later career and writings of, 251, seq.

Martyr, Peter, in England, 352.

Mary, Queen, a persecutor of Protestants, 356.

Matthys, Jan: a disciple of Hofmann and Trijpmaker, 271; character of, 284, seq.; assumes leadership of the Hofmannites, 285; proclaims the inauguration of the Kingdom of God in Munster, 288; chief prophet in Munster, 288, seq.; slain in battle, 289.

Maximilian II., a comparatively tolerant ruler, 204.

Meinardo, an Italian Protestant leader, 325.

Menno, Simons: early life of, 296, seq.; conversion of, 296, seq.; leader of the quiet Anti-pedobaptists, 299, seq.; teachings and controversies of, 300, seq.; at Cologne, 303, seq.; at Wismar, 304, seq.; at Wüstenfelde, 308; death of, 313.

Mennonites: prosperity of, 315, seq.; controversies and divisions among, 315, seq.

Micronius, M., in controversy with Menno, 308.

Millenarianism. (See Chiliasm.)

Montanists, not Baptists or Anti-pedobaptists, 15, seq.

Moravia: a land of promise for the persecuted, 150, 173; political and religious condition of, 173, seq.; first great persecution in, 228, seq.; second great persecution in, 230, seq.; "good time of the church" in, 231, seq.; misfortunes and decline of Anti-pedobaptists in, 232, seq.; Anti-pedobaptist movements in, after Hubmaier's departure, 222, seq.

Münster: suppression of evangelical life in, 277; Rothmann's activity in, 277, seq.; triumph of evangelicalism and social democracy, 279, seq.; Catholics driven from the city, 279; Anti-pedobaptism in, 280, seq.; Anti-pedobaptist confession, 282, seq.; Anabaptist kingdom in, 284, seq.; responsibility for the abominations of, 292, seq.

Münzer, Thomas: at Zwickau, 67, seq.; at Prague and Alstedt, 69, seq.; preaching against the princes, 77, seq.; at Mühlhausen, 79, seq.; at Nürnberg and at Waldshut, 80, seq.; at Frankenhausen, 83; not an Anabaptist, 86.

Murton, John, an associate of Helwys, 388, 389.

Mysteries, Eleusinian, Pythagorean, Orphic, Delphian, and Egyptian, 6.

Nespe, And. von, an Anti-pedobaptist leader in Silesia, 158.
Netherlands: religious condition of, at beginning of the Protestant revolution, 264; introduction of Lutheranism and Zwinglianism, 264, seq.; strife between Lutherans and Zwinglians, 264, seq.; Hofmann and Carlstadt in, 265, seq.
Nikolsburg, Hubmaier's Moravian home, 175, seq.
Novatians, not Baptist or Anti-pedobaptist, 17.

Ochino, Bernardo: possibly an Anti-pedobaptist, 335; in England, 352.
OEcolampadius, Joh.: a leader at Basel, 90; disputes with Blaurock on infant baptism, 120, seq.
Old-evangelical party, relation of, to the Anabaptist movement, 62, seq.

Paganism, corrupting influence of, 2.
Parkhurst, Bishop, lax in his dealings with Anabaptists, 360.
Particular Baptists, 393.
Passau Anonymous, The, on the Waldenses, 47.
Pastor of Hermes, The, on baptism, 4.
Paulicians, dualistic and iconoclastic, but not Anti-pedobaptist, 24, seq.
Paulus, Gregorius: a Polish antitrinitarian Anti-pedobaptist, 336; baptized by immersion, 336.
Payne, John, against English Anabaptists, 374.
Peasants' War: relation of Münzer to, 83, seq.; causes persecution of Anabaptists, 135.
Pelagianism charged against English Anti-pedobaptists, 353.
Persecution in Switzerland disperses Anabaptists and extends the movement, 135, seq.
Peter de Bruys, an Anti-pedobaptist reformer, 30, seq.
Peter of Cologne, a Mennonite leader, disputes with Acronius, 318, seq.
Pfeiffer, Heinrich, with Münzer at Mühlhausen, 79, seq.
Philip of Hesse: tolerance of, 273, seq.; warns Henry VIII. against the Anabaptists, 349.

Philippists, a Moravian Anti-pedobaptist party, 228.
Philips, Dirk, a Mennonite leader, 301, 304.
Philips, Obbe, a Mennonite leader, 301, 304, seq.
Peters, Jan, a martyr, 364, seq.
Pistis Sophia, on baptism, 7.
Poland: religious condition of, at the beginning of the Protestant revolution, 334; toleration in, 334; Anti-pedobaptist movement in, 335, seq.
Poor Men of Lombardy, 41, seq.
Poor Men of Lyons, 41, seq.
Portner, Jacob: chaplain at Steyer, 210; accepts Hut's views and becomes a missionary, 210; at Linz, 213; at Freistadt, 219.
Puritanism, in England, 368, seq.
Pythagorean theosophy, 26.

Racovian Catechism, on the person of Christ and on baptism, 337, seq.
Raidt, Balthasar, examines and reports on Melchior Rinck, 275.
Reck, Hans, an Anti-pedobaptist leader in Silesia, 158.
Regel, G., a friend of Denck and Hetzer, 160, 166.
Reimann, Henry, executed at Zürich, 149.
Renato, Camillo, an Italian Anti-pedobaptist leader, 325, seq.
Rattenberg, a Tyrolese Anti-pedobaptist center, 192.
Reublin, William: a reformer at Basel, 90; opposes infant baptism, 105, seq.; banished, 107; at Schaffhausen, 111, seq.; baptizes Hubmaier at Waldshut, 126; sketch of, 132, seq.; in Strasburg, 246; occasions a schism in the Austerlitz community, 224, seq.; withdraws to Auspitz, 226; maltreated by Wiedemann and Huter, 226; later career of, 226, seq.
Rhegius, Urbanus: urges the Augsburg authorities to persecute Anti-pedobaptists, 171.
Ridley, Bishop, a persecutor, 354.
Riedemann, Peter: chief pastor of the Huterites and author of an exposition of Anti-pedobaptist doctrine, 230.

Rinck, Melchior: a Hessian Anti-pedobaptist, 274, *seq.*; views of, 275, *seq.*; protected by Philip of Hesse, 275.
Robinson, John, a semi-Separatist, 383.
Roll, H.: a radical evangelical in Jülich-Cleve, 280; an Anti-pedobaptist in Münster, 280, *seq.*; carried away with the fanaticism of Matthys, 286.
Rothmann, carried away with the fanaticism of Matthys, 287.
Rhynsburgers, 321, *seq.*, 387.

Sacerdotalism: pagan origin of, 2; growth of, 10, *seq.*
Saga, Francesco Della: an Italian Anti-pedobaptist leader in Moravia, 331; letter to Italian brethren, 331, *seq.*; returns to Italy and suffers martyrdom, 333, *seq.*
Salminger, Sigismund: an Anti-pedobaptist leader in Augsburg, 171.
Salve Burce, on the Waldenses, 45.
Sattler, Michael: banished from Zürich, 137; in Strasburg, 243, *seq.*; author of the Schleitheim Confession, 244; executed at Rottenberg, 244.
Schärding, Gabriel: Anti-pedobaptist leader in Silesia, 157; pastor of large community of Silesian Anti-pedobaptists at Rossnitz in Moravia, 223.
Schaffhausen, Anti-pedobaptist movement in, 111, *seq.*
Schiemer, Leonard: an Austrian disciple of Hut, 211; suffered martyrdom in the Tyrol, 190.
Schlactscaef, H., an Anti-pedobaptist leader at Münster, 280, *seq.*
Schlaffer, Hans: an Austrian Anti-pedobaptist leader, 218, *seq.*; executed in the Tyrol, 192, 219.
Schmaus, Cuntz, an Austrian disciple of Hut, 212.
Schoferl, Georg: an Austrian Anti-pedobaptist leader, 219, *seq.*; theological teachings of, 220.
Schröder, Jan, an emissary of Matthys, 286.
Schützinger, Sigismund: Anti-pedobaptist leader, sent by Tyrolese brethren to Moravia, 226; pastor at Austerlitz, 227; excluded for non-communistic practices, 228.

Schwenckfeldt, Casper: conversion of, 154, *seq.*; opposes Lutheranism, 154, *seq.*; Anti-pedobaptist views of, 155, *seq.*; widespread influence of, in Silesia, 156; in Strasburg, 241, 246; controversy with Marbeck, 251, *seq.*
Sebastian von Freiburg, a friend of Denck, 166.
Silesia: religious condition of, 153; labors of Storch in, 153; Schwenckfeldt's activity in, 154, *seq.*; Gabriel Schärding's labors in, 156, *seq.*; Clemens Adler's activity in, 157, *seq.*; Andrew von Nespe's labors in, 158; Hans Reck's labors in, 158; expulsion of Anti-pedobaptists and Schwenckfeldtians from, 158.
Smyth, John: early life, 376; a Separatist at Gainsborough, 376, *seq.*; emigrated with his church to Amsterdam, 377; at variance with the older congregation, 379, *seq.*; introduced believers' baptism, 381, *seq.*; seeks union with the Mennonites, 388, *seq.*; on liberty of conscience, 392.
Socinian teachings, influence of, on the Mennonites, 320, *seq.*
Socinus, Faustus, on baptism, 339.
Socinus, Laelius, associated with Italian Anti-pedobaptists, 335; influence of, in Poland, 335.
Some, R., sought to prove that Separatists were essentially Anabaptists, 373.
Somers, Jacques de, his sympathetic account of the martyrdom of Pieters and Terwoort, 366, *seq.*
Speier, edict of, 151; enforced in the Tyrol, 194; influence of, in Strasburg, 248.
Spitalmaier, Ambrose: an Austrian Anti-pedobaptist leader, 213, *seq.*; theological views of, 214, *seq.*
Spitalmaier, Hans, Hubmaier's colleague at Nikolsburg, 175.
Staprade, H., an Anti-pedobaptist leader at Münster, 280, *seq.*
Sterzing, a Tyrolese Anti-pedobaptist center, 193, 194.
Steyer: a center of Old-evangelical life, 205, *seq.*; favorable to Lutheranism, 206; the Anti-pedobaptist movement in, 206, *seq.*; a council for judging Anabaptists, 210, *seq.*; executions, 211.

INDEX

St. Gall: Anti-pedobaptist movement in, 115, seq.; immersion practised in, 116.
Storch, Nicholas: at Zwickau, 68, seq.; at Hof, 75; in Strasburg, 241.
Strasburg: a center of Old-evangelical life, 238; toleration in, 238, seq.; Anti-pedobaptists in, 238, seq.; persecution of Anti-pedobaptists in, 244, seq.
Strasburg: Anti-pedobaptist convention in (1555), 309, seq.; another convention (1557), 311, seq.
Stumpf, Simon, an Anti-pedobaptist opponent of Zwingli, 101, seq.
Supper, the Lord's, perverted, 10.
Swabian League, persecutions of, 172.
Swiss Brethren, in Moravia, 230.
Switzerland, political, social, and religious condition of at beginning of Protestant revolution, 88, seq.

Taborites, Waldensian and Wycliffite element in, 49, seq.
Tasch, Peter, a Hessian Anti-pedobaptist in correspondence with his brethren in England, 349.
Teaching of the Twelve Apostles, The, on baptism, 5.
Tertullian, on baptism, 5, seq.
Terwoort, Hendrik, a martyr, 364, seq.
Thondrakians, ancient and mediæval, possibly Anti-pedobaptist, 25.
Tiziano, an Italian Anti-pedobaptist leader, 326.
Trent, Tyrolese Anti-pedobaptists driven into, 195.
Trijpmaker, Jan., a disciple of Hofmann, 268; executed, 268.
Turner, against Robert Cooke's Pelagianism and Anti-pedobaptism, 353.
Tyrol, The: Old-evangelical life in, 188; Lutheranism in, 188, seq.; Anti-pedobaptist movement in, 189, seq.; terrible persecutions in, 191, seq.

Uolimann, W., immersed by Grebel, 114, seq.; at St. Gall, 116, seq.

Vadianus, Joachim: evangelical leader at St. Gall, 115, seq.; publishes on baptism, 118.
Vigilantius, a reformer, but not an Anti-pedobaptist, 21, 27.
Vinne, D.: an Anti-pedobaptist leader at Münster, 280, seq.; accepts the leadership of Matthys, 280.
Vivetus, a Waldensian leader, 43.

Waldenses: origin, 40, seq.; doctrines, 42, seq.; polity, 45, seq.; more evangelical by, 1260, 43, seq.; wide diffusion of, 56, seq.; activity of, in Bible translation, 58, seq.
Waldshut, evangelical movement in, under Hubmaier, 92, seq.; fall of, 138.
Wiedemann, Jacob: against Hubmaier and Spitalmaier, 185; insists on community of goods, 222; leads a party from Nikolsburg to Austerlitz, 222, seq.
Whitgift, Archbishop, against Anabaptists, 362.
Wischenka, in S. Russia, Huterites in, 233.
Wolfgang, the cowherd, "a messenger of Anabaptism" in the Tyrol, 189.
Wolkenstein, Anton von, and his family: Tyrolese Anti-pedobaptists, 190; trial and recantation of, 199; his wife, reluctantly yielded, 199.
Works, meritoriousness of, 12.
Worms: Anti-pedobaptist movement in, 244, 245; Anti-pedobaptist convention at (about 1556), 312.
Wycliffe, not an Anti-pedobaptist, 55, seq.

Zaunring, Georg, an Anti-pedobaptist evangelist: executed in the Tyrol, 193; a Moravian Anti-pedobaptist leader, a supporter of Reublin, 225, seq.; excluded from fellowship, 227.
Zell, Matthew, Protestant pastor in Strasburg, liberality of, 239.
Zobel, Georg, a Bohemian Anti-pedobaptist physician, 237.
Zürich: radical movement in, 101, seq.; disputation on baptism in, 105, seq.; persecutes Anti-pedobaptism, 108, seq.; disputation with Grüningen Anti-pedobaptists, 136, seq.; statistics of Anti-pedobaptist organizations in, 145; discipline of clergy, 148, seq.; baptismal registers introduced, 149.
Zwickau prophets, 62, seq.
Zwingli, Ulrich: characterized, 89; reformatory work of, 89, seq.; defends infant baptism, 106; publishes against Anabaptism, 118.

www.ingramcontent.com/pod-product-compliance
Lightning Source LLC
Chambersburg PA
CBHW051735300426
44115CB00007B/570